Affirmative Action Policies and Judicial Review Worldwide

IUS GENTIUM

COMPARATIVE PERSPECTIVES ON LAW AND JUSTICE

VOLUME 47

More information about this series at http://www.springer.com/series/7888

George Gerapetritis

Affirmative Action Policies and Judicial Review Worldwide

Springer

George Gerapetritis
University of Athens
Athens
Greece

ISSN 1534-6781 ISSN 2214-9902 (electronic)
Ius Gentium: Comparative Perspectives on Law and Justice
ISBN 978-3-319-22394-0 ISBN 978-3-319-22395-7 (eBook)
DOI 10.1007/978-3-319-22395-7

Library of Congress Control Number: 2015945614

Springer Cham Heidelberg New York Dordrecht London

Printed on acid-free paper

Springer International Publishing AG Switzerland is part of Springer Science+Business Media
(www.springer.com)

The legal guarantees, important as they are from a technical standpoint, do not produce any vital difference in the human process. They simply describe and help to maintain the group process as it is actually proceeding.

Bentley, A.F. (1908). *The process of Government. A study of social pressures.* Chicago: The University of Chicago Press, p. 433.

Foreword

My first contact with George Gerapetritis was many years ago, when I supervised his doctoral thesis at Oxford, which was a comparative study of proportionality. He came highly recommended by friends and colleagues from Greece, and their expectation of him was fully borne out by his performance at Oxford over the following 3 years. He produced an insightful comparative analysis of proportionality, which was subsequently published in book form as *Proportionality in Administrative Law* (Sakkoulas 1997).

The doctoral thesis and subsequent book demonstrated his qualities as a lawyer and legal scholar. He was adept at analysis of primary legal materials, being equally at ease with case law and statutory material alike, able rapidly to discern salient similarities and differences. George was equally adept at standing back from the primary material and addressing the policy and normative issues that underpinned the subject of study.

These features of his scholarship inform this book on *Affirmative Action Policies and Judicial Review Worldwide.* It is a work of considerable scholarship and insight, which tackles an area on which there has been significant writing and in relation to which commentators hold strong views. George Gerapetritis steers the reader confidently through this complex area, making clear the distinctive views in existing scholarship, while at the same time expressing his own considered judgment of the relevant material, whether in the form of primary law or secondary comment.

The book is well-structured and the core substantive chapters follow a logical sequence that explicates the issues for the reader, whether the expert or the more generalist lawyer. The discussion begins with the moral question as to the correctness of affirmative action policies, which depends in large part on the meaning of equality. The argument traverses difficult terrain, engaging with debates as to formal and substantive conceptions of equality, while at the same time relating this discourse to ideas of democracy and justice.

He then turns to the second inquiry, as to whether affirmative action pursues a legitimate social goal, which is termed the sociological question. The focus is nonetheless primarily normative, not empirical, and entails identification of the purposes served by affirmative action policies, five such purposes being identified. They are remedial, in the sense of compensating for past disadvantage; cultural, viz enhancing diversity; societal, as manifested in the *social inclusion of vulnerable groups*; pedagogical, realised through establishment of group models; and economic, in that affirmative action can help to ensure that individuals are best able to fulfil their full economic potential.

The focus then shifts to the third part of the inquiry, what the author terms the policy question, where the spotlight falls on the implementation of affirmative action policies in many different countries. George Gerapetritis deserves great credit for marshalling such material from a diverse range of countries, rather than just examining the data from the countries whose law is already well known. This is more especially so, given that he draws interesting and insightful conclusions as to the variables, structural, institutional and constitutional that favour the development of such policies.

This naturally leads to what is termed the legal question, which concerns the ways in which different legal systems engage in constitutional review of affirmative action. He rightly notes that the standard of review is central to the legal dimension to affirmative action as policed by the courts, and so too is the way in which a court interprets the different elements of the proportionality test.

The analysis throughout is clear and succinct. The book is a valuable addition to the literature on affirmative action and will be read with interest by scholars engaged in such debates and also by public lawyers more generally, given the centrality and importance of the subject matter.

Paul Craig
Professor of English Law
St. John's College
Oxford, UK

Preface

While being in the USA for research in June 2003, the Supreme Court of the country delivered its long-awaited judgments concerning the constitutionality of the race-sensitive admissions policy of the University of Michigan Law School. This coincidence immediately motivated my interest, and I found myself becoming drawn to the study of affirmative action. Ever since, I have had the habit of collecting material about affirmative action in my academic trips worldwide. It happens that whenever I think of, or work on, affirmative action, the ancient Greek myth of chimera comes into my mind: a creature that breathes fire and has a lion's head, a goat's body and a snake's tail, symbolising something that exists only in the imagination and is not possible in reality. Affirmative action has many similarities with the chimera: it is composed of very diverse institutional parts and is usually perceived as targeting the impossible in a socially and financially structured society, namely substantive equality and equal representation for all.

This book has benefited from a great number of people, academic, judges, politicians and civilians, with whom I have discussed the topic in many countries. I thank them all anonymously. I want to take the opportunity to thank the German Marshal Foundation, the British Council and the State Scholarships Foundation of Greece for their assistance and finally my professors at Oxford, Edinburgh and Athens, and my students at the University of Athens, who have always been the most critical audience. Special thanks are given to Helen Xanthaki, professor of law and legislative studies at the Institute of Advanced Legal Studies of the University of London, and to Stylianos-Ioannis Koutnatzis, Lecturer at the University of Thrace and a genuine expert in the field, for having read a manuscript of the book and provided valuable comments. My thanks also to Ben Christman, Ph.D. candidate at Queen's University Belfast, for his valuable linguistic assistance. Finally,

I owe gratitude to Paul Craig, professor of English law at St. John's College, University of Oxford, whose writings have been a great influence for this book, and his personality has been—in affirmative action vocabulary—a genuine role model for me. The mistakes of the book obviously burden only me.

The book is dedicated to my family for their support and patience.

Law and jurisprudence are cited as in December 2014.

March 2015 George Gerapetritis

Contents

Chapter 1
Introduction

If one were to ask people of diverse social classes and cultural and academic backgrounds what the most valuable moral principle is, presumably the overwhelming majority would instantly respond "equality" or "liberty". Now, if one were to ask the same people what the major shortfall of liberal democracy is today, at least two thirds would instantly respond "equality". If, however, the aspiration to launch an equal society is such an undeniable value, why is it that the human community has so patently failed in that respect with major inequalities existing worldwide? Why have we not reached Martin Luther King's dream of a society where children—his children—would not be judged by the colour of their skin but by the quality of their character? If the natural state of human existence, under a "veil of ignorance" (in John Rawls' words), suggests that people are equal and this is acknowledged today as a minimum universal communitarian tradition, why is it that discrimination is so resilient? And, most importantly, why have the most sophisticated legal systems not reached a satisfactory level of lifting inherent social inequalities? Is it because the seemingly common desire towards equality is hypocritical or perhaps because there is no institutional or social tool to guarantee this result?

The gradual establishment of formal quality in the aftermath of the Enlightenment and the great revolutions of the 18th century was a remarkable historical milestone indeed. However, feudalism and the *Ancien Régime,* which awarded hereditary preferences on the basis of nobility and estate heritage, were evidently unsatisfactory. Formal equality presupposes that people inherently have the same starting point in their social, professional and political lives—a premise that is patently false in descriptive terms. Furthermore, society itself has been subject to great modifications since then: the ideal of the national state of the 19th century has declined and societies were unprepared to adapt. Easy transfer and communication of knowledge and ideas, as a result of industrial and technological revolution, have not significantly developed tolerance among people and mutual respect of difference. Instead, separating lines still prevail, with the most striking illustration set out by the theory of "clash of civilisations", developed and diffused by Samuel Huntington, arguing that on an international level cultural disputes would constitute the starting point of world crisis in the future (1993, 1997). Notwithstanding strong criticism (Senghaas 1998), the theory seems to be confirmed by the asymmetrical rise of religious fundamentalism and terrorism.

G. Gerapetritis, *Affirmative Action Policies and Judicial Review Worldwide*,
Ius Gentium: Comparative Perspectives on Law and Justice 47,
DOI 10.1007/978-3-319-22395-7_1

In light of the common desire to establish an equal society, but at the same time, the lack of fine tuning, a more proactive state intervention appears incumbent. Accordingly, affirmative action policies, i.e. award of privileges to designated groups as compensation for past discrimination or as a means to achieve proper diversity, became the most widespread institutional tool to exceed formal equality and seek a new version of true equality. Although this policy seemingly constitutes an abrupt subversion of the essence of equality by awarding privileges to groups having suffered discrimination in the past or being underrepresented on the basis of principally unacceptable criteria, it draws its legitimacy from the underlying rationale that one cannot place at the same starting point people who have been treated differently in the past, because in this way social divergences augment and social cohesion is endangered, or that a critical mass of minority representation is required to achieve an appropriate level of diversity.

1.1 Terminological Issues

Although affirmative action has a long tradition on both a national and an international level, there is not a universally accepted terminology. Usually, a two-word term applies: an adjective, "positive" or "affirmative", to imply that state activity is required to implement these plans, and a noun, "action" or "discretion". The choice on the latter is of both semantic and legal significance. In the US, albeit some critical voices, the widely accepted notion is that of action (*affirmative "action"*); whereas in Europe most authorities use the language of discretion (thus to a large extent in France *"discrimination" positive*, in the UK *positive "discrimination"* and in Germany *positive "Diskriminierung" or zulässige "Diskriminierung"*), and less so the language of action (thus in Greece *positive "action"*). In yet other cases mixed definitions apply using all the above terms, such as in the case of the Court of Justice of the European Union ("positive discrimination or positive action [affirmative action]")[1]; or, teleological terminology, such as reservations in India and standardisation in Sri Lanka (Sowell 2004: Chaps. 2 and 4 respectively). It is noteworthy that the first use of the term "affirmative action" in the US appearing in the *National Labor Relations Act 1935* had little to do with the doctrine as applied today. First use of the term implied the obligation of the employers to guarantee free vote of the employees for their professional unions. At any rate, terminology seems to evolve and mutate according to the context of the applications of the relevant measures, and differs in the literature according to the position of each scholar and the message they wish to convey. This is particularly true in the US due to the intense split of American society and of the relevant literature on the issue (Crosby 2004: 82–87; Gamson and Modigliani 1987). Thus, opponents to affirmative action use the semantically onerous term "preference", either as "racial preferences" (Cohen 2003)

[1]Opinion of Advocate General Jacobs of 15 May 1997 in Case C-409/95, *Hellmut Marschall v. Land Nordhein–Westfalen*, Rec. 1997, p. I-6363, para. 11.

or "group preferences" (Hollinger 1996: 97). At any rate, irrespective of personal predilection or normative assessment, the term "affirmative action" is comprehensible to every scholar and the majority of society, avoiding any confusion.

Irrespective of the above semantic differentiation, the most widely applied terms affirmative action and positive discrimination reflect the historical roots and the general predisposition vis-à-vis this policy in each country. The term affirmative *action* is quite neutral, thus minimising the risk of social anxiety as a result of the implementation of the measures. Given that affirmative action policies are socially sensitive, it is a legitimate cause for the legislator to ease social eagerness on the matter, especially on the part of the dominant social groups. On the contrary, the term *discrimination* by definition suggests that there is an afflicted party/group that might reasonably object to a measure affecting their vested interests. More importantly though, the choice of terminology may also have legal consequences. The language of "discrimination" seems to imply that the impugned measure constitutes an exception from equality, and is thereby viewed rather suspiciously, whereas "affirmative action" seems to suggest that the policy lies within the scope of equality and there must be favourable treatment towards it. Accordingly, positive discrimination creates a rebuttable presumption against the constitutionality of the measure, whereas affirmative action intimates a presumption to the opposite effect, with the correlating procedural consequences for the litigants in relation to the evidentiary process and the burden of proof.

On the level of legal terminology, the term positive discrimination seems to carry, in principle, greater typological clarity in comparison to affirmative action. Affirmative action in a more generic form is dissociated from equality, therefore also applicable in all instances where the entrenchment of a constitutional right entails the active intervention of the state, i.e. the *positive* obligation of the state, such as in the case of all social rights. On the other hand, one might reasonably object to "discrimination", in that it raises ethical questions, since it implicitly seems to uphold the existence of discriminatory situations within a society, albeit permissible ones. The argument is, nevertheless, of minor normative significance; all societies, in one way or another, encourage and embrace some differentiation criteria, and this is not only constitutionally acceptable but a condition of social sustainability.

In this book all the available technical terms "affirmative action" and "positive discrimination" will be used indifferently, depending on the applicable legal system. The former term has been used in the title and will be mostly used as a tribute to the historic origin of the policy and because it seems to be most recognisable around the world, albeit not necessarily in Europe.

1.2 Typology of Measures

There are various criteria that might be used to classify affirmative action measures. Based on their *legal source*, there are measures mandated by the constitution, a statute or international law; further, there are soft law measures (such as provisions included in political parties' statutes and labour or sports organisations' articles of association) or privately originated measures (such as those enforced within a workplace or an academic environment). Based on their *duration*, there are measures of definite or indefinite duration. Based on the *designated groups* to whom preferential treatment is awarded (hereinafter, collectively referred to as the "beneficiaries"), there are, among others, all-embracing measures (such as those securing minimum participation of both sexes in electoral processes), generic measures (such as those favouring all minorities) and sub-group measures (such as those favouring a specific minority). Based on the field of applicability, there are measures in the domain of higher education, public contracts, electoral process or measures of a horizontal effect.

An important last distinction is based on the *operative mechanics* of the measures, i.e. measures of direct or indirect effect. As eloquently put by Oppenheimer (1988, 1995), direct effect measures are those producing immediate end results for the benefiting groups; for instance, quotas, i.e. reservation of specific positions for members of a group. Indirect effect measures are those which do not exercise an automatic influence upon the end results. Direct effect measures are basically indifferent towards the actual process, thus aiming directly at producing specific *results*, which in this view is tantamount to substantive equality, whereas indirect effect measures are basically setting up a *procedure*, ignoring the outcome produced thereby, thus enhancing equality of opportunities as a means of achieving substantive equality.

There are two basic qualities in measures of indirect effect: they are causal and flexible. In relation to their causality, these measures aim at curing the causes of underrepresentation instead of providing relief at the end point. From this viewpoint, although quotas may seem more acute and vigorous, they are not equally radical since they do not cater for the roots of the pathology. Accordingly, measures of indirect effect, such as financial motives, special grants to individuals or NGOs promoting less-favoured groups, loans on a privileged basis, tailor-made programmes for preparation to enter labour or academia, subsidies to political parties on the basis of gender or race participation and social security benefits, might prove more effective in the long run than incremental quotas. In this way, measures of indirect effect are more flexible and open-ended than quotas since they can adjust to the particularities of each context in order to maximise the estimated results. This tailor-made approach is reflected in measures such as prohibition of multiple children per family in China (Article 25 of the 1982 Constitution) and the Aboriginal Fisheries Strategy in Canada, providing a communal fishing license to three aboriginal bands to fish for salmon in the mouth of the Fraser River for a period of 24 h prior to others and to sell their catch.[2]

Of course, characterising a measure as one of direct or indirect effect is not as simple as it may seem. Except for clear-cut reservations (rigid quotas), in which case the direct effect of the measure is indisputable, there is a significant grey zone

---

[2]2008 SCC 41.

where a typology is not readily apparent. For example, considering gender or race as a plus factor in a competitive setting produces a direct effect in that it adds to the candidate's score, it does not however immediately determine the outcome of the competition. The problem becomes all the more cloudy in measures which are in fact tantamount to quotas (quotas by effect). This parameter is particularly important when these disguised quotas are introduced in order to bypass the existing jurisprudential barriers. In the US, one year after the judgment pronouncing quotas on university admissions unconstitutional,[3] the defendant University of Texas revised its quota regulation so that all candidates who belong in the top 10 % of their respective high schools would be directly offered a place in the university. Given that high schools in the States were racially segregated to a great extent, the result of the new policy was that the vast majority of African American and Hispanic candidates were eventually admitted. Accordingly, there was undeniably a disguised race-based quota by effect. The US Supreme Court, as a general rule, controls the nature of the measure in order to identify if there is a case of an impermissible quota or quota by effect, by using the language of "set-asides"[4] or measures "insulating each category of applicants with certain desired qualifications from competition with all other applicants".[5] The same broadly happens also in European courts. In Germany the distinction is made between measures favouring women ("*Frauenförderungsmaßnahme*") and quotas ("*Quotenregelungen*"), whereas composite reading of judgments of the Court of Justice of the European Union and of the Opinions of Advocate Generals reveals a three-level typology: first, measures purporting to provide a better quality weaponry for entering the professional arena so as to secure equality of chances (e.g. reservation of seats in academic institutions); second, measures to soften the disadvantages of a certain professional group due to their social multi-tasking role (e.g. reservation of nursery places for women—and potentially men—at work); and, third, reservation of places within certain professions (e.g. quotas in public sector jobs).[6]

Discerning between measures of direct and indirect effect may also contribute significantly to the conceptual clarity of affirmative action. However, the most expedient linguistic approach would suggest that when the measure is of a direct effect, such as the imposition of rigid quotas or quotas by effect, it is more appropriate to use the terminology of "positive discrimination", whereas if the measure is of an indirect effect, thus encouraging participation of underrepresented groups without establishing quotas, the language of "positive/affirmative" action is more apposite. The above distinction indicates that quotas are by definition a mode of discrimination, since they award automatic end-result benefits, whereas measures

[3]*Hopwood v. Texas*, 78 F.3d 932, 945 (5th Cir. 1996).

[4]*Richmond v. Croson*, 488 US 469 (1989).

[5]*Regents of the University of California v. Bakke*, 438 US 265 (1978).

[6]Opinion of Advocate General Tesauro of 6 April 1995 in Case C-450/93, *Eckhard Kalanke v. Freie Hansestadt Bremen*, Rec. 1995, I-3051; Opinion of Advocate General Poiares Maduro of 29 June 2004 in Case C-319/03, *Serge Briheche v. Ministre de l'Intérieur, Ministre de l'Éducation nationale and Ministre de la Justice*, Rec. 2004, I-8807.

providing motives have a mere affirmative nature without immediate implications on social competition.

A special form of measures causally linked but antithetical to affirmative action is *reverse quotas*. Unlike typical affirmative action policies providing for a minimum threshold for the underrepresented group, reverse quotas set out maximum limits for the participation of particular groups. Thus, the groups falling in the ambit of the quotas are not the beneficiaries but rather the afflicted parties. An example of such reverse quotas is the provision that in order to secure maximum physical strength, women can join special armed forces up to a certain (normally low) percentage. It is also conceivable and also practiced to establish simultaneously a minimum and a maximum quota, e.g. participation of women in the armed forces at a set percentage. Other past examples of reverse quotas are the old rules to be found in elite US universities accepting Jewish or Asian students only up to a specific percentage of the total number of admitted students (Karabel 2005: 110–138; Dong 1995, respectively), or maximum quotas for minority or Roma pupils in public schools.[7] Of course, in this case there might, also, conceivably be room for reverse quotas by effect, i.e. by setting conditions that cannot be met by the majority of one sex, race or religion (physical strength, height etc.) or by designing entry tests akin to knowledge or experience of one sex, race or religion (history of an ethnicity, theological knowledge etc.).

1.3 Scope of Research

There are four major questions with regard to affirmative action policies. Are they ethically correct (*the moral question*)? Do they serve a legitimate social goal (*the sociological question*)? How are they applied and how successful are they (*the policy question*)? And, finally, what are the judicial vehicles to assess their constitutionality and what are the constitutional implications thereof (*the legal question*)? The above sequence is not haphazard. In the above chain of questions the answer to each ring presupposes as a premise a response to the immediately previous one. The eventual *legal question* depends upon a broadly utilitarian premise, namely that the design of such policy measures is able to produce generally positive, if not directly measurable, results towards actual equality. In turn, policy cannot be effectively designed unless there are very clear-cut objectives pursued; no policy irrespective of its conceptual soundness and its legal perfection can succeed, if its goals are not set in the first place. And this premise leads us to the fundamental question, what is the ethical standing of affirmative action policies? If they are not compatible with the prevailing community values, the endeavor is bound to fail either for lack of awareness or of regular compliance. The legal question might partly encompass the previous stages of moral, sociological and policy questions as

---

[7] *Meredith v. Jefferson County Board of Education*, 416 F3d 513 (6th. Cir. 2005).

part of the usual proportionality analysis, i.e. legitimacy of the pursued goal, effectiveness as an element of suitability etc.).

Although the responses to the above four questions might sometimes overlap, dealing with them separately allows the reader better to understand the background theory of affirmative action. Besides, their escalation reflects, to a certain extent, the historical development of affirmative action theory and practice, since it was first the literature, albeit not profoundly, that raised the question of the transformation of equality into a substantive principle, then, in sequence, voluntary social initiatives, executive practices, statutes and, ultimately, national constitutions and international covenants. The four questions are essentially reflected in Chaps. 2–5 of this book.

In the *second* chapter (the moral question), affirmative action is set in a broader conceptual background, as defined by other fundamental constitutional values, such as democracy (in a procedural or substantive conception), justice (on a distributive or attributive conception), meritocracy and the principle of equality itself. The inner relationship between affirmative action and equality is a key element for the better understanding and implementation of the former. If affirmative action is integrated, as an inexorable feature, into the rudiments of equality, it is incumbent on us to accept that the principle of equality has mutated and affirmative action needs to be taken into account when defining equality in the first place. If, on the contrary, there is no institutional transformation of equality, then affirmative action should be conceived and treated as any other exception from the principle. The dilemma is of great legal significance: if equality, as suggested in the present analysis, is still predominantly to be treated as a legal notion and affirmative action as an institutional vehicle, i.e. an exception from equality, the latter has only limited space for development as a permissible deviation from the constitutional structure of equality.

In the *third* chapter (the sociological question), my ambition is to detect the purposes in favour of which affirmative actions is introduced, namely the social benefits anticipated thereof. This is a rather complicated mental exercise, but at the same time a necessary prerequisite for the constitutional assessment of affirmative action policies. The significance of this exercise for constitutional review is twofold: only legitimate goals can justify deviations from fundamental rights (if affirmative action is to be seen as a departure from legal equality); and, second, even if the goal is deemed to be legitimate still the means employed must be in a state of fair proportion (basically, suitable and necessary) to the goal they aspire to promote. As reflected in the doctrine and jurisprudence of affirmative action, there are two basic and three auxiliary goals pursued by the policy. The two basic purposes are the *remedial* purpose (compensation for past discriminations), found in all legal systems applying the policy, and the *cultural* purpose (diversity as a means to further enhance unrepresented groups and improve the quality of the educational experience), which is mostly identified in the US. Auxiliary purposes are first, the *societal* purpose (aiming for social inclusion of vulnerable categories and social cohesion), the *pedagogical* purpose (aiming at establishing group models for the designated groups and raising confidence towards institutions) and the *economic* purpose (directed towards maximising/raising efficiency for individuals and an overall healthy economic environment).

In the *fourth* chapter (the policy question), descriptive and evaluative research outcomes stemming from the implementation of affirmative action plans worldwide are presented. Although the classification is based on territorial criteria, emphasis is placed upon the different structural mechanisms present in different jurisdictions and the historical grounds which explain, wholly or in part, the national attitude towards affirmative action policies. In that respect, readers will come across an extensive use of affirmative action policies by federal states, former colonial, social welfare and multi-ethnic states. Of course, it would be impossible to examine the said policies in all countries of the world. Thus, a number of countries have been selected from all continents, whereas in Europe research revolves mostly around EU and EU member states. A separate section is devoted to material and regional international conventions, the European Convention on Human Rights and the European Union Law. The evaluative part constitutes a comparative analysis of affirmative action policies worldwide. It includes an assessment of the variables favouring the launching of such policies, both structural (i.e. federal, former colonial, social welfare and multi-ethnic states) and material (i.e. institutional acknowledgment, constitution, statute, custom, and convention), the domains of application (education, politics, economy and labour) and designated groups (racial, ethnic or religious minorities, women). The chapter finally casts light upon the political identity of affirmative action, as a right/left, conservative/progressive tool, identifying but also probing beneath political agendas and statutes of political parties that might sometimes use the policy merely for political profit.

In the *fifth* chapter (the legal question), a breakdown of the constitutional review of the affirmative action plans based on the jurisprudence of national and international courts will take place, along with an assessment of how important affirmative action becomes for the human rights doctrine. In relation to the methodology of judicial review, three steps are identified. First, setting the standard of review with assurances relating to whether state authorities have mere discretion or a legal obligation to introduce such measures, whether it is basically addressed to the state thus being merely a policy or it introduces an enforceable right, the notion of equality stemming from the level of judicial review (equality of results or opportunities), the depth of judicial review (restrictive or broad interpretation), the evidence required and the threshold of burden of proof and the impact of judicial predilection in deciding such cases; second, identifying and assessing the goal pursued; and third, applying the proportionality test through the vehicles of suitability (appropriateness and fit) and necessity (less restrictive alternatives and temporal validity of action). The impact assessment of affirmative action upon the human rights doctrine focuses on whether the policy constitutes a "new" social right, in a broadly declining context because of the global financial crisis, and whether it eventually establishes "group" rights, contrary to the libertarian tradition of human rights protection and of the constitutional state.

References

Cohen, C. (2003). Why race preference is wrong and bad. In C. Cohen and J.P. Sterba. *Affirmative action and racial preference. A debate* (1-188). Oxford-New York: Oxford University Press.

Crosby, F.J. (2004), *Affirmative action is dead; long live affirmative action.* New Heaven-London: Yale University Press.

Dong, S. (1995). Too many Asians: The challenge of fighting discrimination against Asian-Americans and preserving affirmative action. *Stanford Law Review,* 47(5), 1027-1057.

Hollinger, D.A. (1996). Group preferences, cultural diversity and social democracy: notes towards a theory of affirmative action. *Representations,* (55), 31-40. Re-published in R. Post, and M. Rogin (Eds.), (1998). *Race and representation: Affirmative action* (97-111). New York: Zone Books.

Huntington, S.P. (1993). The Clash of Civilisations? *Foreign Affairs,* 72(3), 22-49.

Huntington, S.P. (1997). *The Clash of Civilisations and the Remaking of World Order.* New York: Touchstone

Gamson, W.A., and Modigliani, A. (1987). The changing culture of affirmative action. In R.D. Braungart (Ed.), *Research in Political Sociology vol. 3* (pp. 137-177). Greenwich: JAI Press.

Karabel, J. (2005). *The Chosen: The Hidden History of Admission and Exclusion at Harvard, Yale, and Princeton.* New York: Houghton Mifflin Harcourt.

Oppenheimer, D. (1988), Distinguishing Five Models of Affirmative Action. *Berkeley Women's Law Journal,* 4, 42-61.

Oppenheimer, D. (1995), Understanding Affirmative Action. *Hastings Constitutional Law Quarterly,* 23, 921-997

Sautman, B. (1999), Ethnic law and minority rights in China: Progress and constraints. *Law and Policy,* 21(3), 283-314.

Senghaas, D. (1998). *Zivilisierung wider Willen. Der Konflikt der Kulturen mit sich selbst.* Frankfurt am Main: Suhrkamp Verlag English edition: Senghaas, D. (2002). *The clash within civilisations: Coming to terms with cultural conflicts.* London-New York: Routledge Series in Global Political Economy.

Sowell, T. (2004), *Affirmative action around the world. An empirical study.* New Heaven-London: Yale University Press.

Chapter 2
The Moral Question: Interacting with Traditional Values

Affirmative action operates in a more or less established set of moral values, such as equality, human dignity and meritocracy, democracy, justice and political society. The extent to which the policy fits in the above values broadly determines its social recognition and legitimacy and its overall effectiveness. On the other hand, one cannot exclude the possibility that the institutional establishment of affirmative action may well exercise some influence on the way these values are generally perceived. This statement might be valid especially in the relationship between affirmative action and equality, given the close relationship between the two notions. The forthcoming chapter discusses this interaction as well as the procrustean endeavour to accommodate affirmative action with human dignity and meritocracy, the fine balance sought by the policy between majority ruling and minority entitlement, the fairness of the political identity of the policy. Obviously reasons of space preclude an in-depth analysis of these topics, each one of which could individually fill a free-standing thesis.

2.1 Revisiting or Abstaining from Equality?

Three issues need to be discussed in the context of the relationship between equality and affirmative action. The first question is where affirmative action stands between formal and substantive equality. It is presumed, albeit not always with the necessary conceptual clarity, that affirmative action constitutes a reflection of substantive equality. Even if this is convincingly substantiated, an issue which ought to be determined first is whether substantive equality is a more expedient/advantageous pursuit against formal equality so as to justify the enactment of affirmative action measures. The second question elaborates upon the influence potentially exercised by affirmative action on equality's basic features, namely similarity and difference. This question is again of primary significance, in that it presupposes a clear determination of where exactly equal treatment stands in order to accommodate the enactment of affirmative action measures. Using the conclusions drawn from the above themes, the third question probes into the heart of the matter. It examines the question of whether affirmative action lies intrinsically within the notion of

G. Gerapetritis, *Affirmative Action Policies and Judicial Review Worldwide*,
Ius Gentium: Comparative Perspectives on Law and Justice 47,
DOI 10.1007/978-3-319-22395-7_2

equality, or whether it is an external aspect of equality, in which case it should be treated mostly as an exception of this principle with all correlating consequences.

2.1.1 Formal and Substantive Equality

Equality cannot be viewed isolated from the interrelated principle of liberty. Liberty and equality are two concepts that have historically walked hand in hand along the road of the constitutional state. Seen from different angles in the course of time, the two principles have co-existed: freedom as a human *condition* and equality as a *means* for the effective enjoyment of human rights as a whole. The relationship between the two principles has passed through various phases in the course of history, varying from equal footing to domination of one upon the other; conjunction of the two principles aiming at justice according to Aristotle (E 10, 1134a 24–29); separate but equal existence in the Enlightenment and during the French revolution, whereby "men are born and remain free and equal in rights" as part of "natural, unalienable, and sacred rights" and "social distinctions may be founded only upon the general good (Article 1 of the 1789 Declaration of the Rights of Man in composite reading with its Preamble); the priority of freedom over equality after World War II; the contemporary composite reading and employment of the two as prerequisites for human dignity and justice in Rawlsian thought. Still, this synthesis is not easy. Bobbio (1994: 60–71, 1995), a major contemporary philosopher, historian and political scientist, suggests, with regards to the relationship between these two key notions that societies may consist of humans unequal in freedom or equal in lacking liberty. He argues that neither of the two great ideals can reach its ultimate purpose without the one restricting the other, given that the two have different idiosyncrasies; freedom constituting a personal goal, whereas equality a social good. In *Inda Sawhney v. Union of India*, the Supreme Court of India rendered an intriguing relevant obiter dictum:

> The formal equality advanced by Aristotle that equals should be treated equally and unequals unequally was as much result of social and economic conditions as the Rawls' theory of justice or the Dworkin's concepts of right of all to treatment as equals. Liberty and right to equality taken individually may appear to pull in different directions. But viewed as part of justice and fairness the two are the primary tenets of modern egalitarian society. The real difficulty is translating them into practical working.[1]

The typology and conceptual background of the equality principle go far beyond the scope of the present analysis. Suffice it to reiterate for the present discussion the classic distinction between formal and substantive equality (Pelerman 1971). The former version is based on objective mathematical criteria, in the sense that everyone should be treated equally before the law, both in rights and obligations.

---

[1](1992) Supp (3) SC 217, para. 678.

In the 18th and 19th century Europe, under the heritage of the Enlightenment and the pioneering legal thought of Immanuel Kant, formal equality was conceived as a necessary and adequate obstacle against arbitrary state action, a response to the police state which embodied the unlimited power of the state upon its subjects. Thus, in Germany's basic prior component Prussia, the restriction of state by the law and the constitution (*Rechtsstaat*) was the response to the police state (*Polizeistaat*). The essence of *Rechtsstaat* was gradually transferred to the other European states, adjusting to the peculiarities and the legal tradition of each of them. Accordingly, in France the *État de droit* placed emphasis on the legality principle, whereby there must be in any case a proper legal basis to justify any executive action. The constitutional inauguration of formal equality as prohibition of unequal treatment based on arbitrary factors, albeit taking the pre-legal world as it is, can be traced in the first revolutionary Constitution of 1791 in France:

> Neither nobility, nor peerage, nor hereditary distinctions, nor distinctions of orders, nor feudal regime, nor patrimonial courts, nor any titles, denominations, or prerogatives derived therefrom, nor any order of knighthood, nor any corporations or decorations requiring proofs of nobility or implying distinctions of birth, nor any superiority other than that of public functionaries in the performance of their duties any longer exists.

In spite of its fundamental antithesis with the *droit administratif*, this type of formal equality was also enhanced by British common law theory and its main authority Dicey (1885, Part II) as part of the Rule of Law, entailing that everyone, i.e. both the King and its subjects, ought to be subject to the same rules and the same jurisdiction. Under the basic premises developed by the above three major nations, the idea of the Rule of Law became commonplace in the modern world and a salient feature of constitutionalism (Silkenat et al. 2014; Schuppert and Koetter 2012–2013).

There are two kinds of formal equality: mathematical or proportional. The former has an absolute egalitarian quality, suggesting that every person should be treated in the same way before law, whereas the latter, conceptually rooted in Aristotle's philosophical thought,[2] suggests that equals should be treated equally. Mathematical equality is rigid in the sense that it is based primarily on countable quantitative indexes among people, which may be legally evaluated, whereas proportional equality is based on qualitative criteria. From this viewpoint, proportional equality transcends the boundaries of utilitarianism and establishes individualism as the basic feature in assessing *similarities* and *differences*. Mathematical equality does not tolerate deviations from absolutely equal conditions, whereas proportional equality entails different assessments, depending on the actual human qualities involved. Mathematical equality applies where individualism is not considered a relevant factor. In criminal law, for example, everyone should receive the same treatment; criminal sanctions must be blind towards gender or race. Also in political rights, the one human one vote maxim seems undeniable.

[2] *Politics*, volume III, chapter 12 and *Ethics Nicomachean*, line 1131a, b.

On the contrary, proportional equality applies *par excellence* to civil and social rights, where each person's individual standing may determine the scope of their rights (for example, members of minorities, homeless, people with disabilities); accordingly, different constitutional treatment is not only desirable but also mandatory (Ingram 2000: 14–17). To the extent that formal equality largely ignores social parameters, it might be considered to be *a priori* unfair, since it presupposes that everyone has the same possibilities to develop their skills and capacities. However, equality cannot properly operate where social relations broadly determine the starting point of each social actor.

Substantive equality embraces both equality of opportunities and equality of results. Equality of opportunities means that everyone should be given equal chances against all other social competitors in claiming state benefits. Equality of results means that everyone has the right to claim an equal share of state benefits. In this sense, equality of opportunities relates to the starting point of social struggles and particularly applies to everyone who starts from a disadvantaged position because of contextual (e.g. social class) or historical (e.g. past discrimination) grounds. The most elaborate contemporary theory of equality of opportunities, which is also akin to affirmative action conceptual background, has been sharpened by Rawls (1999: 57-92-49). This is based on the idea of democratic equality (as opposed to natural liberty and liberal equality) aiming at conferring all individuals with the same native talent and ambitions the same prospects of success in social competition by reducing the competitive advantages that favourable externalities confer on some individuals. The common thread of this theory with affirmative action is that they both aspire to reduce the adverse position of disadvantaged and vulnerable groups in gaining social benefits.

Conversely, equality of results relates to outcomes and connotes the idea that everyone, irrespective of its particular characteristics should be allocated equal portion of social goods and advocates parity in all deliberative organs and areas of social interaction. Affirmative action, thus, becomes a goal of statistical allocation of seats and benefits with a static character. Interestingly, parity was not amongst the claims of the 1960s civil rights movement in the US, but was developed as a feminist claim in Europe. In France, in the late 1990s, a strong movement claiming for *parité*, i.e. even allocation of political shares between males and females, was launched, which later expanded to other European countries (Fraisse 1995; Gaspard et al. 1992; Mossuz-Lavau 1998). The movement mainly operated as a pressure group in the direction of political changes in France, actually focusing on equal participation of men and women in institutional bodies, particularly in the Parliament: specifically, 50 % of each gender in each representative body. The contribution of the movement in the institutional acknowledgment of affirmative action in France was significant, although its claims have never been fully implemented. It is noteworthy, however, that the movement of *parité* was strongly criticised by affirmative action proponents on the grounds that it awarded great significance to biological and natural differences between the sexes (if each individual was thought of as sexed at birth, then sexual difference would no longer be relevant, instead of the actual social and institutional causes which have fed discrimination) (Wallach Scott 2005: 100–123). Irrespective of the potential problems from which this theory suffers within a liberal context, the main methodological problem is that parity trespasses conventional affirmative action policies, in that the latter is normally temporary whereas the former is permanent.

Equality of opportunities has a more subjective quality than equality of results, since in order to level the starting point for everyone it is a prerequisite that various particular impediments applying to different individuals and groups ought to be raised/overcome, whereas equality of results is characterised by a more objective quality, since the benchmark is the eventual share everyone gets. Obviously, equality of opportunities calls for a more elaborate institutional strategy addressing the roots that cause differences in the starting line, whereas equality of results merely sets the ratio that needs to apply in any particular field. Reasonably, equality of opportunity may take various forms (varying from a more formal/procedural to a more substantive version).

A necessary research disclaimer ought to be made in the first place: Neither the distinction between formal and substantive equality constitutes the only possible classification, nor is this classification free of typological inadequacies. Alternative terminology is also used in order to ease potential conflicts stemming thereof, a typical example being the use of the terms "real", "factual", "actual", "full" and "effective" equality. Both international treaties and national constitutions make explicit reference to such aspirations for equality. Examples of the former category are the Convention on the Elimination of all Forms of Discrimination against Women legitimising temporary special measures accelerating "de facto equality" between men and women (Article 4 para. 1) and the European Convention on Human Rights, which reaffirms in the Preamble of its Protocol 12 that the principle of non-discrimination does not prevent states from taking measures in order to promote "full and effective equality", provided that there is an objective and reasonable justification. Examples of the latter category are provided by the 1999 Swiss Constitution prescribing that legislation shall ensure "equality in law and in fact" between men and women (Article 8 para. 3), the 1976 Portuguese Constitution stating that one of the fundamental tasks of the state is to promote the well-being and quality of life of the people as well as "real equality" amongst the Portuguese (Article 9d); also, by the 1978 Spanish Constitution, which stipulates that it is the responsibility of the public authorities to promote conditions ensuring that the freedom and equality of individuals and of the groups to which they belong are "real and effective", to remove the obstacles preventing or hindering their full enjoyment and to facilitate the participation of all citizens in political, economic, cultural and social life (Article 9 para. 2).

Even when the text of the constitution seems to be neutral as to the version of equality it promotes, judicial interpretation has armed the relevant clauses with a more substantive quality. A vivid illustration is provided by the Federal Constitutional Court of Germany, which ruled that it was constitutionally acceptable for a measure to pursue the achievement of real equality, meaning equality between the sexes for the future, thus infusing the principle of equality with the logic of a future aspiration.[3] The sharpest distinction between formal and substantive equality was rendered in the Opinion of the Advocate General Tesauro in the Court of Justice of the European Union (then European Court of Justice), *Kalanke* case. He first considered that women do not merely merit the attainment of numerical—and hence only formal—equality, moreover at the cost of an incontestable violation of a fundamental value of every civilized society: equal rights and equal treatment for all. In his mind, formal–numerical equality is an objective which may salve some consciences but will remain illusory and devoid of all substance unless it goes together with measures which are genuinely destined to achieve equality: "Ultimately, what is necessary above all is a substantial change in the economic, social and cultural model which is the root of inequalities, a change which will certainly not be achieved by numbers and outdated dialectical battles which are now on the defensive".[4]

Obviously, the hereinabove legal systems do not use the pertinent terms in typological clarity in order to connote an alternative version of equality; what is suggested is a departure from an ostensibly strict version of formal equality. From this angle, it seems that real, full and effective equality all share a common root of substantive equality. Furthermore, the distinction seems to presuppose a common understanding that equality of opportunities can indeed be achieved in the same way as formal equality. However, opportunities can hardly be equal in a liberal society, since there are plenty of social, financial or political externalities, which hinder the actual equality of opportunities.

Affirmative action has produced a significant challenge to the traditional theory of equality. Even though the equality concept does not have an absolutely fixed content, it is still an inherent idea for the human mind, according to the Cartesian conceptual approach, which accompanies intellect. Although there have been various versions on equality, from Aristotle and Aquinas, to Locke, Marx and Mary Astell, the principle currently has a tangible content which is to a large extent common in the human mind: a society, which creates institutions and educates its citizens in ways that, today, have rendered factors such as skin colour or gender irrelevant considerations in any decision-making process, is a society which respects the principle of equality.

Affirmative action itself raises issues of clarity when entering into the formal/substantive equality distinction. Although this policy is generally considered a tool of substantive equality, even quotas do not guarantee the *actual expression* of the interests of the underrepresented groups. While, traditionally, we understand substantive equality as equal or proportional representation of different groups, reservations in collective bodies on the basis of race or gender do not secure more effective representation of the relevant groups. Thus, as Dworkin emphasizes (Dworkin 1987: 184), the request for democracy is curtailed to a mere process

[3]BVerfGE 57, 335 (1981) and BVerfGE 74, 163 (1987).

[4]Opinion of 6th April 1995 of Advocate General Tesauro in CJEU decision of 17th October 1995, case C-450/93, *Eckhard Kalanke v. Freie Hansestadt Bremen*, Rec. 1995, p. I-3051, para. 28.

request, as opposed to better quality of regulation for everyone, especially the vulnerable groups. Even if all groups are represented in a collective body, it is the actual decisions of this body that must reflect the interests of these bodies. Otherwise, participation becomes an illusion of inclusion that has no actual effect in the distribution of social benefits. This is why, eventually, affirmative action may be tantamount to substantive equality but constitutes in essence a form of preferential *formal* equality.

Even if, however, it is conceded that participation also reflects actual representation, and it is desirable to establish a proper ratio at all levels, serious practical problems emerge. In the *Kalanke* case before the Court of Justice of the European Union (then the European Court of Justice), evidence was submitted that the Bremen public authorities were composed 49 % of male and 51 % of female employees. However, the incremental scale of distribution of women was 75 % at low-level positions, 52 % at medium level, 50 % at the upper level and 30 % at principal positions.[5] Even so, one might reasonably think that employment balancing goes further than this. If at the top of the hierarchy there is only one person, full substantive equality would suggest a gender and time rotation in each occupation.

At any rate, affirmative action ought to be conceived as a neutral instrument of law and not as a means of establishing social balancing; otherwise it would result in mere political ideology (Slama 2004: 134–137). From this viewpoint, it is not useful and it might on occasions be misleading to apply the distinction between formal and substantive equality in the implementation of affirmative action policies. This is why other results-oriented typologies, such as symmetric/asymmetric equality (Bell and Waddington 2003) have been set forth.

2.1.2 *Similarity and Difference*

Establishing what is similar and different is a prerequisite for applying the standard of equality. The same is true for the conception and implementation of affirmative action. Similarity is essentially a *negative* prerequisite, since it imposes abstention from the use of unfair criteria, whereas difference is a *positive* prerequisite that individuals in different factual or legal situations ought to be treated differently. On occasions, difference explicitly becomes a relevant consideration in national Constitutions. For instance, the 1937 Irish Constitution allows the state to duly regard differences of capacity, physical and moral, and of social function in the exercise of its regulatory capacity (Article 40). The co-existence of similarity and difference is obvious in everyday life. Taxation laws in most jurisdictions provide that individuals are subject to different brackets on the basis of their overall income

[5] CJEU judgment of 17 October 1995 in Case C-450/93, *Eckhard Kalanke v. Freie Hansestadt Bremen,* Rec. 1995, p. I-3051.

or even the sources of their income; that individuals are treated in some respects differently than legal entities and that certain categories, such as entities not firmly established in national soil or entities bringing in foreign capital, are exempted from income taxation altogether. The most striking example of such permitted differentiation is, according to the late vice-president of the Conseil d'Etat Braibant (1999: 449–450), the total tax exemption for the poorest. Braibant considered these measures as different from genuine affirmative action, insofar as the former were deemed to be an expression of equality, whereas positive measures are deviations from the essence of the principle, therefore properly characterised as positive discrimination. However, this difference is not clear-cut, since no one is in a position to say what constitutes an *expression* as opposed to an *exception* of equality.

In the same manner that a legal system cannot tolerate a different treatment of similar situations, it can neither tolerate equal treatment in different circumstances. In the former case, if a rule awards a privilege to one category, such as a financial benefit to a group of employees, the exemption of a category of employees might be contrary to a constitutional clause regardless of whether it can be rectified through judicial intervention that will expand the privilege and restore equality. In the latter case, if a rule applies horizontally, irrespective of essential differences which are constitutionally protected, for example obligatory military service without proper consideration for conscientious objectors, it is equally unacceptable and will be quashed as violating constitutionally enshrined rights, including equality itself.

In all the above cases, the implementation of an Aristotelian concept of proportional equality would render the detection of the point where similar turns different to a critical prerequisite. This seems to be only fair since otherwise equality would just ignore relevant factors that set people or groups of people in a different position within a society, thus undermining the integrity of the ethical claim for equality. Gender in employment is a non-relevant factor, thus men and women ought to be treated equally, whereas in many countries gender is a relevant consideration in mandatory military service that might justify the exclusion of women altogether from this duty. Preferential treatment in favour of women in the former case is considered a positive measure, because it deviates from the basic perception of equality, whereas such treatment in the latter case is deemed to be an implementation of the equality principle in itself because some (mainly physical) aspects of the female gender differentiate women's factual and, in turn, legal position vis-à-vis mandatory army duty. Or, even within the same field, a different approach is required on occasions: in employment, women ought to have equal footing in terms of appointment or promotion or salary but need to be considered differently when it comes to maternity leave or child benefits. This inherent antinomy causes significant theoretical distress to the doctrine of affirmative action in the context of liberal democracy. On ethical grounds, Carl Cohen claims that affirmative action policies use criteria which ought not to be used; blacks and whites are equal in the same way that blond and brunette are equal, as Catholics and Jews are equal, as Americans of any origin are equal. He considers that irrespective of who the beneficiaries and the victims of such policies are, preference on grounds of race was and still is morally wrong and violates human equality as a basic premise

(Cohen 2003: 25). The argument is not conclusive. Affirmative action proponents would suggest at this point that indeed some of the justifications of the policy might in fact be based on recognition of dissimilarity of situation. Thus, the mere historical evidence of past discrimination in an apartheid or segregation regime would in that view justify the dissimilarity between members of the dominant and the oppressed groups.

Trying to liaise affirmative action with the determination of what is similar and what is different may raise significant ethical issues that might undermine the veracity of the theory. On policy grounds, with particular reference to the feminist movement, Joan Wallach Scott set out the argument that there is an impossible choice in feminist claims for wider female participation in decision-making insofar as they argue that in political rights gender plays no role and, at the same time, suggest the very idea of difference they seek to eliminate (Scott 1996). David Ingram also identifies a paradox in women's claim to have the sole right to decide on abortion, on the grounds that this decision affects their body, or to work from home as collateral to childcare, while they fervently argue on the need to decide on gender-neutral grounds. According to Ingram, the problem relates to the lack of a background affirmative action theory that might compellingly justify relevant claims without the need to seriously frustrate the cohesion of the argument (Ingram 2000: 9–34). This background theory ought to be multi-disciplinary and must be convincing both in terms of theory as well as its expediency in order to arm affirmative action with substantive coherence and legitimacy. All the above opposing arguments have a common core relating to the difficulty of affirmative action policies to be accommodated into a solid doctrine of similarity and difference as joint parameters of equality (Rawls 1999: 65–72).

The relativity of the criteria of equality and their space and time sensitivity makes it particularly difficult to establish a theory of equality that is devoid of a certain degree of fluidity and unpredictability. Trying to set out a solid background theory must necessarily be based in part on pragmatism and different prevailing ideologies in each state: women are in fact differently situated with respect to some questions such as the effects of an abortion on their bodies or their contribution to the military, and similarly situated with respect to others such as participation in the social/political debate about abortion or military service. The delineation problem becomes all the more important when a case is brought before a court of law. In such cases, jurisdictions with a tradition of a case-by-case common law decision-making, such as the Anglo-Saxon ones, are better equipped to treat the relevant conundrums, whereas jurisdictions with a more abstract, rule-based decision-making tradition, such as most of the European ones, are often found embarrassed. In the context of Article 14 of the European Convention on Human Rights prohibiting discrimination, the Strasbourg Court applies variable standards using a spectrum ranging from "*analogous situations*" to "*relevantly similar situations*".[6]

---

[6]ECHR Judgment of 22nd Octobert 1996, *Stubbings et als. v. UK* 23 (1997) EHRR 213, para. 71 and ECHR of 18th February 1991, *Fredin v. Sweden*, 13 (1991) EHRR 784, para. 60.

Proportionate equality, based on similarity and difference, constitutes a commonplace in the jurisprudence of national supreme courts as a means to preserve the integrity of formal equality. In the US a rule which emphasises similarity is deemed to use "gender/race neutral language", whereas a positive measure entailing preferential treatment is characterised as "gender/race specific language", with the exception of race-neutral wording effectively resulting in preferential treatment. The interrelation between affirmative action and a shift of the level of difference has also been illustrated by domestic case-law. The Spanish Constitutional Court has upheld positive measures to compensate for past discrimination on the grounds that preferential treatment is justified "because its goal is exactly to treat differently effectively different cases".[7] In the same line of argumentation, the Supreme Court of India ruled that once the principle, "in order to treat some persons equally, we must treat them differently" has been applied and advantaged and disadvantaged are made equal, any further benefit extended for promotion on the pre-existing inequality to be brought in the group would be treating equals unequally, since it would not be tantamount to eradicating the effects of past discrimination but rather perpetuating it.[8] By the same token, Advocate General Tesauro in his 1995 Opinion in *Kalanke* before the Court of Justice of the European Union conceded that any specific action in favour of a weak category conflicts with the principle of equality in the formal sense, therefore affirmative action needs primarily to address the question of whether it is nevertheless conceivable that, in clearly defined circumstances, provisions are permitted by law in order to achieve an objective corresponding to a social choice, which, in turn is calculated to cancel out the inequalities caused by past prejudice.[9]

At any rate, it seems incumbent to establish whether special treatment in the form of affirmative action is a *deviation* from equality, because those being treated are in fact situated similarly, or an *application* of equality because those being treated are in fact situated dissimilarly in the relevant way. The answer to this dilemma, which is handled below, is crucial to determine the legal ontology of affirmative action.

2.1.3 *Intrusion or Exception?*

In the equilibrium between similarity and difference, affirmative action intervenes in a rather violent way. This is so because by definition the policy makes use of criteria and of differentiation. A designated group is benefited by affirmative action policies because there is some identified difference, such as prior discrimination or underrepresentation, that justifies launching a corrective mechanism to set all

---

[7]Tribunal Constitucional nº 128/1987, judgment of 16th July 1987.

[8]*Inda Sawhney v. Union of India*, (1992) Supp (3) SC 217, paras. 405, 686.

[9]Opinion of Advocate General Tesauro of 6 April 1995 in Case C-450/93, *Eckhard Kalanke v. Freie Hansestadt Bremen*, Rec. 1995, p. I-3051, paras. 11, 16.

people or groups of people at a similar standpoint. The background idea is that affirmative action is applied for a temporary period of time as a means of substantive equality until formal equality is restored.

Here stands a set of major questions as to the morality and constitutionality of affirmative action policies: can a society, aiming at a noble cause, sustain similarity by building upon temporary, albeit of an initially indefinite duration, difference? If the answer to this question is in the affirmative, to what extent difference can be a relevant consideration without hurting equality and victimising the beneficiaries? In light of the above questions, two contradicting theories can be sustained: the *intrusion* and the *exception* theories.

The *intrusion* theory suggests that the acknowledgment of affirmative action policies has substantially changed the physiology of the principle of equality: equality cannot be seen deprived of the quality of affirmative action and, conversely, affirmative action permeates equality and provides a fresh understanding of the principle. There are three basic consequences of this fusion between equality and affirmative action. First, affirmative action does not operate as a transitional temporary tool in order to achieve formal equality but rather as a standing and constant feature of the principle. Second, the new standpoints of similarity and difference akin to affirmative action also apply to equality as a general principle and ought to be used in its legal interpretation. Third, affirmative action should not be treated suspiciously in the course of judicial review but a presumption of constitutionality of such measures must apply if a legitimate objective can be traced.

The *exception* argument suggests that affirmative action does not shape a new version of equality, nor does it give preference to any of the existing categories, but it merely constitutes an instrument, among others, towards achieving the constitutional goal of equality. Therefore, the institutional acknowledgment of affirmative action has only caused a low-level influence in the constitutional perception of the equality principle, since the means, regardless of how important it may be, cannot by itself alter the physiology of a constitutional principle. Seen from this angle, affirmative action is in fact inconsistent with the principle of equality, properly understood, but is nonetheless justified by some countervailing value or values, primarily justice and democracy in a substantive sense. Accordingly, affirmative action is perceived as a deviation from equality and, therefore, as an exception of this principle. In light of this doctrine, a judge will measure the constitutionality of an affirmative action policy not *within*, but *against* the principle of equality. Although affirmative action might change the spectrum of the permitted differentiation criteria by including underrepresentation and diversity, any such measure must survive a severe judicial review test. Consistent with a fundamental principle of legal interpretation in the constitutional state, deviations from any fundamental right should be interpreted restrictively, thus raising the standard of judicial review to a point where it would be difficult to ascertain the constitutionality of that deviation; the exception theory poses serious additional impediments to the survival of affirmative action policies under constitutional scrutiny.

Two arguments point in favour of the exception and against the inclusion theory: the temporary character and the incremental implementation of affirmative action policies. As regards the duration of the policy, unlike the argument raised on behalf of the inclusion theory, positive measures are in principle launched only for a limited, albeit not prescribed in advance, period, i.e. until conditions of actual equality have been restored. This is of course a utopia: differences constitute an omnipresent element in a liberal democratic context. If so, one might reasonably argue that affirmative action does acquire a permanent character leading to a standing social geometry. Still, all studied jurisdictions emphatically insist that affirmative action must be limited in time until the eradication of discrimination and the removal of the conditions which historically contributed to the actual differentiation of certain vulnerable categories have been achieved. If this state is achieved, there will be a *de facto* merger of formal and substantive equality, with the latter being merely obsolete. Thus, the desirable final destination of positive measures is indeed formal equality itself. Proponents of the intrusion theory claim that given the inherent inequalities present in any given society, the return to a state of formal equality is impossible, no matter what. Alice Yotopoulos-Marangopoulos discerns three stages on the road to equality: first inequality through the award of special privileges to individuals or groups; second, formal equality, i.e. equality before the law; and, third, effective equality through the preferential treatment for the eradication of disadvantages (Yotopoulos-Marangopoulos 1998: pp. 28–29). She abstains from declaring a fourth and final stage, where equality has been firmly established and positive measures are no longer justified by the constitutional order. The dilemma that presents itself when introducing affirmative action policies is whether we truly wish to have a transitional mechanism that will at some point fall into desuetude or a standing feature that will determine the competition between rival social groups. Even if actual equality of opportunities is recovered through affirmative action measures, equality of results may never be achieved. If this is due to persisting conditions that produce inequalities, affirmative action still has a role to perform; if not, affirmative action merely establishes social balancing. As regards the incremental implementation of affirmative action, in fact there has not, to my knowledge, been an all-embracing rule introducing positive measures in all fields and in favour of all disadvantaged groups, but merely incremental and sporadic insertion in certain fields, addressed to certain designated groups. The exception theory, which appears more coherent, morally neutral and sustainable, finds fertile territory in most of the countries that have implemented affirmative action policies.

2.2 Integrating Human Dignity and Meritocracy: A Procrustean Endeavour

In the context of the present analysis, human dignity and meritocracy are two principles with a strong conceptual and pragmatic connection, the latter being one of the prerequisites of the former. Both concepts have been raised to the level of international and domestic constitutional law. Human dignity has received a more widespread acknowledgment and culminated after World War II, whereas meritocracy is a much more contemporary constitutional value, although they both have their origins in the 18th century revolutions (Feldman 1999, 2000). There is still, however, a major difference between the two notions from a legal perspective: human value remains an uncompromising constitutional value not subject to any restrictions or concessions, whereas human dignity may well be subject to weighting in order properly to safeguard other civil rights. From this viewpoint, the axiomatic protection of human value does not occur at the same level in meritocracy.

Three major international law milestones make reference to human dignity and, partially, meritocracy. In the 1789 *Declaration of the Rights of Man and Citizen*, representation, equality and meritocracy formed part of an ensemble under the umbrella of the fundamental revolutionary perception of the general will (*volonté générale*):

> The Law is the expression of the general will. All citizens have the right to take part, personally or through their representatives, in its making. It must be the same for all, whether it protects or punishes. All citizens, being equal in its eyes, shall be equally eligible to all high offices, public positions and employments, according to their ability, and without other distinction than that of their virtues and talents [*sans autre distinction que celle de leurs vertus et de leurs talents*] (Article 6).

The 1948 UN *Universal Declaration of Human Rights* links human dignity with all the fundamental premises of the constitutional state, i.e. liberty, justice and equality: in the opening statement of the Preamble, it is noted that "the recognition of inherent dignity and of the equal and inalienable rights of all members of the human family is the foundation of freedom, justice and peace in the world" whereas the peoples of the United Nations further reaffirmed "faith in fundamental human rights, in the dignity and worth of the human person and in the equal rights of men and women and have determined to promote social progress and better standards of life in larger freedom". Finally, the *Charter of Fundamental Rights* of the EU, part of the Union's primary law as of 2009, firmly declares in its Preamble that human dignity is its foundation (alongside freedom, equality and solidarity as indivisible and universal values), whereas in Article 1 it is stipulated that "human dignity is inviolable" and "must be respected and protected".

Further, most domestic Constitutions acknowledge human dignity as an inviolable right and a foundation of democracy. Indicatively, according to the case-law of the Federal Constitutional Court, Article 1 of the 1949 German Constitution renders human dignity as a superior constitutional value[10]; the 1947 Italian Constitution is rather innovative and relates dignity to equality and the social state by preserving "equal social dignity" (Article 2), but also uses dignity as a basic restriction (along with the common good, safety and liberty to private economic activity) (Article 41). The common thread of all legal systems in relation to human dignity is the Kantian philosophy that humans are not to be used as instruments, but as ends in themselves.

---

[10]BVerfGE 45, 187 (1977).

On the other hand, meritocracy is, today, of utmost importance due to diffuse social and financial competition. Competition becomes all the more important as a consequence of the gradual exhaustion of natural resources and the development of technology, which might lead to limited demand for non-expert personnel. This decrease reasonably raises the intensity of competition not only amongst individuals but also amongst groups. In a state of social risk, people carrying the same characteristics tend to gather together in order to be better placed in competitive struggles and achieve better bargaining positions through collective claims. Furthermore, competition takes place in a context of free market economy which pays little attention to social claims, including labour, in a way that meritocracy appears as a defense mechanism against arbitrariness or greed of the financial actors. In this respect, affirmative action opponents argue that the aim of statistical balance results in downgrading of personal merit, since selection is made on grounds that should in principle play no role whatsoever in any admission or promotion process since they are not even remotely related to personal value. This serious diminishment of meritocracy might also produce secondary adverse effects: The first potential effect has to do with the subversion of the *legitimate expectations* upon which any organised society is more or less established. Although everyone gathers qualifications and skills in order to become competitive and claim a greater part of the allocation of social benefits, their foreseeable pay-off might be dismissed as collateral of an affirmative action policy. However, in such a case the motivation for better achievements in expert fields—a basic instrument of progress—is curtailed, since no guarantee of success is produced thereof. Of course, expectations might be raised in either way: if, conversely, affirmative action policies are in place long enough, it would be illegitimate to expect not to be affected by it. The second effect has to do with the loss of the *causal link* between claim and competition, since grounds not related to the contested post become decisive. In a sense, as Marinoff (2000) argues, affirmative action sets *de facto* biological quotas whereby the skin chromosomes and the sex genes become selection criteria, albeit altogether non-relevant.

Accordingly, merit is not seen as the sole outcome of personal effort or capacity but becomes a contextual quality, i.e. according to the opportunities everyone was presumed to have had. As a result, individuals with the same potential will only accidentally release this potential, given that social and other variables, such as class, gender or race will impact upon the eventual outcome. In essence, what affirmative action theory suggests is that the presence of merit should not be checked at the end point, when a person's ability has been fully expressed, which is eventually the result of non-relevant factors, but at the starting point; merit is not what has developed but what would have developed if externalities did not exercise influence. In that respect, in order to assess one's merit you should place them in a value-free environment, a Rawlsian *veil of ignorance* so as to be fair and equitable.

Understanding perceptions of the relationship between affirmative action and meritocracy is very significant. In their survey Reyna et al. (2005) demonstrated that disagreement on the expediency of said policy lies with different perceptions of meritocracy, i.e. "*merit-upholding v. merit-violating manifestations*". In fact, there are various arguments for combining affirmative action and meritocracy. The first argument to that effect is *conceptual* and connected to the inherent relativity of meritocracy itself. Indeed, meritocracy can be understood in various ways. On the one hand, meritocracy by individual assessment aims to reward personal value. In this way, the candidates' qualifications should be assessed objectively and impartially against each other's and the candidate of the higher quality should be chosen. On the other hand, meritocracy by effect sets the benchmark to the actual effectiveness of the selection outcome. Accordingly, the evaluation should not occur on the basis of the applicants' qualifications but in relation to the optimisation of effectiveness. It follows that a candidate who enjoys more qualifications than any other competitor should not necessarily be recruited since they may not produce optimum results when set in place. This might not be solely due to the particular skillset required for the contested post, but also because the selected candidate will normally be required to operate in a group environment, whereby social or labour cohesion is essential to productivity. Accordingly, selection of a woman over a man to occupy a position in a collective body, even if the latter is formally better qualified, might improve the overall composition though diversity and fuller representation, consequently also improving the intellectual product of that body. Evidently, affirmative action better fits the concept of meritocracy by effect, provided that even candidates from the beneficiary group must hold at least the minimum qualifications required for the respective post. However, a potential criticism might challenge this point by suggesting that meritocracy by effect does not properly qualify as meritocracy but rather as a distinct notion of overall effectiveness.

The second argument is *procedural* and concerns the quality of the means to determine merit. According to this, there is no plausible means to objectively assess personal value. Thus, every competitive procedure, no matter how well-structured, merely constitutes a formal assessment on mainstream assets established in a society (Sturm and Guinier 2001: 6–24). In this way, the candidates who succeed come from groups already positioned towards the top of the social structure, due to the continuous lack of discrimination against them, while, on the other hand, they are more familiar with prevailing values and structures of society. In other words, it was this previous discrimination itself that prevented the members of the vulnerable groups from acquiring this value—knowledge, skills etc. As Justice Burger put it in the 1971 US Supreme Court case *Griggs v. Duke Power Co.*,[11] in relation to the inherent defaults of any accreditation system, the facts of the case before the Court demonstrated the inadequacy of broad and general testing devices, as well as the infirmity of using diplomas or degrees as fixed measures of capability: "History is filled with examples of men and women who rendered highly effective performance without the conventional badges of accomplishment in terms of certificates, diplomas, or degrees. Diplomas and tests are useful servants, but Congress has mandated the common sense proposition that they are not to become masters of

[11]401 US 424 (1971).

reality". The Court unanimously found that the defendant company's employment requirements did not pertain to the applicants' ability to perform the job, and was therefore unintentionally discriminatory in effect against black candidates.

The third argument is *pragmatistic*. Regardless of the potential constitutional acknowledgment of meritocracy, every legal system accepts, either explicitly or tacitly, deviations from formal meritocracy in favour of individuals or groups on the basis of their sensibilities and/or past experiences. For example, preferential treatment might be provided for expatriates, persons with disabilities, single parents, persons whose parent has died in public service or young university applicants when it comes to admissions to universities of which their parents are alumni. In the context of this last *sui generis* inherited right, Justice Thomas deconstructed the idea that merit reigned in Michigan University admissions in 2003 US Supreme Court judgment *Grutter v. Bollinger*. In his mind, meritocracy ignores the fact that the university admission process was poisoned by numerous exceptions to merit, such as legacy preferences for children of alumni.[12]

It is true that affirmative action is hardly compatible with formal meritocracy; it is however equally true that meritocracy can be seen from various angles. Cavanagh (2002: esp. 33–48, 79–80), after conceding that merit is deemed to be the starting point of any selection process, without however being properly determined, suggests two very illustrative case-studies to discern the various types of meritocracy: a beauty contest and an athletic competition. The former is based on formal criteria of merit, insofar as the contestants have nothing to do but project their image; if the most beautiful competitor does not win, there has been an evaluation error and the competition has, therefore, failed. The latter is not about which competitor is generally more competent but who managed to perform better in the actual context of the particular race. This suggestion does not imply that the inferior athlete who managed to win in the particular race has automatically qualified as the best athlete overall. Between the two versions of meritocracy, which broadly correspond to *formal* and *substantive* meritocracy, the author supports the latter on the grounds that it is reasonable and not unethical that someone is chosen not on the basis of objective qualifications but on the basis of their ability to perform better under the particularities of a concrete contest.

Besides, according to the original idea of John Locke on property, there is nothing that a person can achieve, apart from what they make with their own two hands that belongs only to them. Wealth is social because people do live in organised societies and natural environments that allow the production of such wealth:

> Though the earth, and all inferior creatures, be common to all men, yet every man has a property in his own person: this no body has any right to but himself. The labour of his body, and the work of his hands, we may say, are properly his. Whatsoever then he removes out of the state that nature hath provided, and left it in, he hath mixed his labour with, and joined to it something that is his own, and thereby makes it his property. It being

[12]*Grutter v. Bollinger*, 539 US 306, 368 (2003).

by him removed from the common state nature hath placed it in, it hath by this labour something annexed to it, that excludes the common right of other men: for this labour being the unquestionable property of the labourer, no man but he can have a right to what that is once joined to, at least where there is enough, and as good, left in common for others" (Locke 1690: Chap. 5, Sect. 27).

In more contemporary language both John Rawls and Ronald Dworkin, especially the latter by setting the standard of personal responsibility in the distribution of social resources (Dworkin 2002: 11, 2002: 65), seem to agree in that as a matter of political morality no one should be attributed benefits as a result of natural talent rather than hard work, thus merit should not amount to a legitimate claim to receive a greater portion of common benefits without evidence of work upon this talent. This form of structural meritocracy is in broad terms the most convincing justification for the ostensible departure of affirmative action from the idea that merit should prevail at all times. Overall, either as part of a more elaborate version of meritocracy or as a legitimate departure from meritocracy, which is a value subject to qualification, affirmative action seems to fit properly in the concept.

2.3 Democracy: Between Majority Ruling and Minority Entitlement

The relation between affirmative action and democracy cannot of course be isolated from the wider context of the fundamental relation between equality and democracy. This inexorable link, on the grounds of representation, which goes back to Aristotelian philosophical thought (Aristotle, *Politics*, esp. D1291b), finds its first historical reflection in classical Athens, tightly bound to the reality of the Athenian city-state where all citizens equally participated in government, while the 10 *races* equally represented one of them running the executive in rotation. In the field of human rights, it has been the basic argument for the abolishment of discrimination regimes, such as the apartheid in South Africa or slavery and segregation in the US.[13] Democracy requires that equality is guaranteed as a political and civil right, since any shortfall of democracy ultimately hurts the equality of the citizens. This view is based on a political process theory of legitimacy, which does not guarantee optimum results of the deliberative processes in favour of the public interest. This is why Plato presents Socrates in his *Apology*, a dialogue with his prosecutor Melitos while standing trial for not recognising the state gods and for introducing novel deities, to consider the representative assimilation of the city with its citizens not as a blessing but mostly as a pathology (Plato, 24d10–25c4).

In some constitutions, equality is explicitly or by reference upgraded to an essential requirement of democracy. The 1976 Portuguese Constitution stipulates that direct and active participation in politics is a key element in the consolidation of

[13]*Brown v. Board of Education*, 347 US 483 (1954).

the democratic system and the law shall promote equality in the exercise of civic and political rights (Article 109), whereas both the Spanish and the French Constitutions place the equality clause not in their respective chapters on Rights but rather in their chapters on Fundamental Provisions and Sovereignty (Article 9 para. 2 under *título preliminar* and Article 3 *de la souveraineté* respectively).

The relationship between democracy and equality varies from one constitutional system to another, on the basis of three variables: the constitutional choice on the specific format of *democracy*, the constitutional choice on the version of *equality* adopted and the level of *tolerance* acknowledged for non-majority individuals (Phillips 1993). In essence, democracy varies according to the political theory embraced. Political theory thus provides the umbrella which accommodates not only the selected version of democracy, but also the concept of justice and morality and the level of protection of constitutional rights which constitute the basic feature of limited government. As Craig (1990: 5) notices:

> Particular conceptions of democracy diverge not only in relation to the nature of the participatory right to be afforded to citizens. Proponents of these differing conceptions disagree also about the nature of rights, distributive justice, and the extent to which the state should be able to advance morally valid ideas. This disagreement may, for example, manifest itself in the recognition of distinctive rights, or in radically distinctive interpretations accorded to the same right. In this sense any discussion of democracy shades into, and becomes part of, a broader political theory….

As regards the format of democracy, using Ronald Dworkin's terminology, there is the *dependent* conception of democracy which suggests that the best form of democracy is whatever form is most likely to produce the substantive decisions and results that treat all members of the community with equal concern, thus prompting the state to intervene in the distribution of political shares (Dworkin 1987: 186). This is contrasted to the *detached* conception of democracy, whereby the state is indifferent in the distribution of political shares and merely caters to guaranteeing equal political rights (Dworkin 1987: 184). Formal political equality, based on the latter concept of dependent democracy, is process-oriented and mostly based on a pattern of democratic self-regulation so as to allow free expression of public will and prevent manipulation under the disguise of democracy. It is exactly this type of democracy that has led, in the view of some scholars, to the decline of the representative system by allowing disproportionate influence from minorities upon the dominant political views (Dahl 2006: 77–99). What affirmative action in fact suggests is a system of proportional democracy, whereby the electoral process should lead to an absolutely accurate mirroring of society on the representative body. Since this form of democracy cannot be achieved if the electorate is free to decide at its own will, since the majority will tend to dominate political process, the state must set rules proportionately favouring those who would not otherwise be represented or would be represented in disproportionately low figures, mainly due to past discrimination (Ely 1980: 135–180).

Affirmative action policies affect democracy in two respects. First, they promote the model of pluralistic or even multicultural democracy, which is a value *per se* (Taylor 1994). Multicultural democracy constitutes a more advanced form of democracy than mere pluralistic democracy since, according to Appiah (1998: 37), it promotes wider levels of participation and tolerance. Second, they shape the model of representative democracy. Affirmative action aspires to provide a more "legitimate" amalgamation within representative authorities by reserving seats or favouring underrepresented groups (normally due to past discrimination); it is acceptable, if not desirable, so as to eventually overcome utilitarianism, associated with the thought of John Stuart Mill and the subordination of individual or group interests to the general interest (Mill 1960). The claim for wider participation becomes all the more important when it comes to state organs which do not enjoy direct legitimacy through popular elections, which is often the case for the judiciary. UK Supreme Court Justice Hale (2001) has accused the British judiciary of low legitimacy because it is composed—although the situation seems to be changing in the last two decades, as substantiated by Bindman and Monaghan (2014)—to a great extent of a certain stereotypical persona, i.e. white male, upper-class, having studied at high profile academic environments. In any case, it is acutely important that leaders of any branch of government or society enjoy essential legitimacy through wider representation and equality of opportunities.

A variety of concerns might be raised on the relationship between democracy and affirmative action. On a *theoretical* level, the counter-argument to raising legitimacy through widening of representation, especially in electoral processes, is that it represents an aberration of the electoral mandate. The electoral quotas rationale, especially if they refer to the reservation of posts, is based on the presumption that group members vote according to their own group interests. If this is upgraded into a genuine political criterion, then members of parliament elected through quotas certainly carry an additional political burden in the form of a sub-mandate. Accordingly, different levels of political legitimacy and electoral mandate emerge whereby general public interest might concede to minority group interest. US Supreme Court Justice O'Connor illustratively put it in 1993 judgment *Shaw v. Reno*, concerning the delineation of electoral districts in order to set up Afro-American majority districts. In her view, the message that such districting sends to elected representatives was pernicious: when a district was obviously created solely to effectuate the perceived common interests of one racial group, elected officials were more likely to believe that their primary obligation was to represent only the members of that group, rather than their constituency as a whole. This was according to Justice O'Connor "altogether antithetical to our system of representative democracy".[14]

On a *practical* level, the argument that wider representation provides a better quality of decisions cannot be empirically substantiated, either at the level of general interest or at the level of the interests of the sub-category involved. What is established is a rather symmetrical, "quantitative", thus superficial, democracy, devoid of guilt for past discrimination, whereas at the same time there might still well exist actual discrimination in diverse forms. One might reasonably argue, as

[14]*Shaw v. Reno*, 509 US 630, 648 (1993).

Sturm and Guinier do (2001: 3, 31–34), that affirmative action is better placed in intermediate social institutions outside the Parliament, such as education or employment, where equal opportunity in access exactly constitute a "*democratic imperative*" for substantive, not merely symbolic, participation of groups having suffered discrimination.

On a *dogmatic* level, upholding affirmative action as a form of strengthening political legitimacy seems to be incoherent, if not hypocritical. Affirmative action political quotas reflect the idea that minority group interests should be adequately represented. In essence this model suggests that there must be symmetry in democratic representation so that majority rule does not override minority interests. This form of proportional democracy is based on an over-representation of minority groups. At the same time, however, a great number of legal systems worldwide oppress minority groups by establishing a majority electoral system (which in most versions favours large political parties at the expense of minor parties) or by setting electoral thresholds that ought to be achieved at a national level in order to be represented to the Parliament. This, however, constitutes a clear paradox. An electoral system aiming at proportional democracy ought to be coherent in all the applied standards. Therefore, one cannot without being vulnerable to hypocrisy allegations accept affirmative action policies and, at the same time, embrace a majoritarian electoral system, because the underlying principles of the two are essentially pointing at the opposite direction.

On a strictly *constitutional* level, one should not overlook that electoral quotas concern fundamental components of the democratic regime, i.e. the right to elect and be elected, uninhibited functioning of political parties, sovereignty, equality and universality of suffrage. The existence of electoral quotas in favour of under-represented groups affects all the above rights and principles. The rights to elect and be elected as well as the freedom of political parties are hampered if the quotas require the lists of electoral candidates to reflect minimum participation of candidates from the designated groups. The above, plus sovereignty, equality and universality of suffrage, are also curtailed if the quotas refer to the composition of a collective body, in which case a candidate with more votes than a competitor (who belongs to one of the designated groups) might be excluded in order for the prescribed ratio to be satisfied resulting in a subversion of the peoples' will as reflected in the elections (Roberts and Stratton 1995).

The response of the proponents of affirmative action is based on the inherent inadequacies of contemporary democracy and legitimacy, especially after the explosion of the late 2000s economic crisis. Popular participation is reduced to voting once every 4 or 5 years with a corresponding inertia in between elections; political oppositions to governments do not have significant minority rights so as to exert a genuine threat or at least be able to articulate a composite counter-argument; political chiefs of the executive have accumulated extensive powers and exercise authority often ignoring even members of their own government; political parties have lost their genuine role of guaranteeing political participation and have been reduced to fundraising mechanisms for their candidates. In that, one might reasonably argue, as Plato suggested, that there are some features inherent in democracy that undermine the well-being of society (Lovatt 2015: 31–44). These essential flaws of national representative democracies have been transferred to supra-national organisations, such as the European Union, where the democratic deficit has dominated the political process irrespective of amendments to reinforce the political role of the representative organs of the Union (Weiler et al. 1995). The portrayed profound crisis of representative democracy calls for a progressive version of multicultural democracy through positive state measures to ensure participation of underrepresented groups, so as to secure effective expression of interest of suppressed groups in a broadly majoritarian environment.

The most modern and challenging discussion on the relationship between democracy and affirmative action was taken up by the US Supreme Court in 2014. *Schuette v. Coalition to Defend Affirmative Action*,[15] upheld the constitutionality of the Michigan initiative to ban affirmative action altogether, through a constitutional amendment by referendum, prohibiting the use of race-based preferences as part of the admissions process for state universities. According to this ruling, the issue in question was not how to address or prevent injury caused on account of race but whether voters may determine whether a policy of race-based preferences should be continued. In the majority opinion, the US constitutional system seems to embrace the right of citizens to speak, debate and learn and then, as a matter of political will, to act through a lawful electoral process, provided there is no hurt or injury inflicted on racial minorities due to encouragement or mandate coming from legislation or other state action, which was not found to be the case in Michigan. Three members of the Court (Chief Justice Roberts and Justices Kennedy and Alito) based their judgment on the argument for democracy. Two members (Justices Scalia and Thomas) predictably thought that racial preferences were prohibited by the Constitution. Finally, Justice Breyer (generally considered one of the liberal members of the Court), agreed that the amendment was consistent with the Equal Protection Clause, but for different reasons, i.e. that the Constitution permitted, but did not require, the use of the kind of race-conscious programmes barred by the Michigan Constitution and that the particular case involved an amendment that took decision-making authority away from unelected actors and placed it in the hands of the voters, thus it did not involve a diminution of the minority's ability to participate in the political process.

Justice Anthony Kennedy, writing the plurality opinion, extensively used arguments from democracy and anti-paternalistic discourse on the grounds that it is demeaning to the democratic process to presume that the voters are not capable of deciding an issue of this sensitivity on decent and rational grounds. In his mind the process of public discourse and political debate should not be foreclosed even if there is a risk that during a public campaign there will be those, on both sides, who seek to use racial division and discord to their own political advantage, since an informed public can, and must, rise above this and the idea of democracy can, and must, mature. The judge relied heavily on the issues of citizens' duty to engage in a

[15] 572 US, Case No. 12-682 (2014).

rational civic discourse and the effectiveness of the First Amendment that might considerably be hampered if a political question of great significance, such as the implementation or prohibition of affirmative action plans, lied beyond debate and, eventually, public determination. On the other hand, Justice Sotomayor, joined by two other justices, in a very emotional 58-page opinion, dissented and responded to the majority by emphasising a reverse view of democracy, i.e. the need to respect minority rights against majority domination and the rather political argument that there is still a historical debt towards those who suffered inequalities in the past. The *rights* argument suggested that the Equal Protection Clause, properly understood, constitutes such a restriction upon majority on the ground that the Constitution guarantees meaningful and equal access to the political process; thus, the majority may not win by stacking it against minority groups permanently, forcing the minority alone to surmount unique obstacles in pursuit of its goals that cannot reasonably be accomplished through race-neutral measures. In light of the above, it appears evident that the question before the Court, especially in the eyes of the dissenting judges, was not about who may resolve the debate over the use of race in higher education admissions, i.e. the judge or the people, but about how the debate over the use of race-sensitive admissions policies may be resolved in constitutionally permissible ways. Justice Sotomayor's historical argument suggested that the US has long denied many of its citizens the right to meaningfully and equally participate in its political life and there remains a call that must be addressed with candor given that the political-process doctrine is best understood against the backdrop of this history.

Overall, affirmative action in the process of representation enhances a proportional as opposed to a procedural version of representative democracy. By establishing quotas for the participation of underrepresented gender or races in politics, pluralistic democracy is reinforced to the extent that the statistical sample of representatives mirrors the composition of the electorate. What lies in the essence of affirmative action policies is that any deliberative body must be composed of members that will reflect *pro rata* the electorate in all aspects, i.e. gender, race, class, religion or any other variable that is thought to be critical for self-determination in order to represent the identity of a given society. However, the task is practically impossible because even if one manages to draw an algorithm that would place all of the critical variables on an equal footing, the eventual implementation of the algorithm would undoubtedly curtail any pure democratic process, since it would eventually result more or less in a selection of people which would only serve to satisfy this necessary multi-criteria formula.

Apart from practical hindrances in achieving proportional democracy in the above form, this task is also conceptually vulnerable because it is based on a mathematical calculation that does not incorporate any criteria related to human nature. For, democracy, at least contemporary representative democracy, is founded upon the principle that political rights do not differ and political privileges are unacceptable. This is where, presumably, the most significant achievement of political society lies: democracy is and ought to be faceless. Unlike civil rights which are in principle relevant to each individual and reject the idea of majoritarianism, representative democracy operates in absolute equality. Therefore, civil rights may more easily acquire a substantive dimension, as opposed to political rights which have been seen in a more procedural manner—as a mathematical determinant. In the case of civil rights, the rule of law provides adequate support for positive measures in favour of vulnerable categories, whereas in the case of political rights the uncompromising principle of popular sovereignty opposes any such action.

It is doubtful whether the aim of pluralistic democracy can *per se* legitimise a deviation from political equality. First, pluralism is inherent in political rights, since everyone enjoys the same level of participation in political life. Second, pluralism in a substantive sense is not guaranteed through mere participation of members of particular groups in elected bodies, but foremost through policies advancing the interests and releasing the potential of these groups. At any rate, rigid quotas in electoral processes have been used to advance a more proportional version of democracy, but clearly abstain from the idea of a process-oriented democracy, which albeit its inadequacies, has secured equal participation for everyone.

2.4 Justice: The Diverse Views of Fairness

It appears that there is an inherent element of justice in affirmative action policies in that it aims at restoring previous injustices. According to the classic saying of Martin Luther King in his 1964 book *Why We Can't Wait* (1963: 147):

> Whenever this issue of compensatory or preferential treatment for the Negro is raised, some of our friends recoil in horror. The Negro should be granted equality, they agree, but should ask for nothing more. On the surface, this appears reasonable, but it is not realistic. For it is obvious that if a man enters the starting line of a race 300 years after another man, the first would have to perform some incredible feat in order to catch up.

It was exactly this saying that inspired President Lyndon Johnson's June 4, 1965, Commencement Address at Howard University to enhance affirmative action (Stohr 2004: 62; Lewis 2004: 17) by arguing on the basis of the need for fair competition of all social actors:

> You do not wipe away the scars of centuries by saying: 'now, you are free to go where you want, do as you desire, and choose the leaders you please.' You do not take a man who for years has been hobbled by chains, liberate him, bring him to the starting line of a race, saying, "you are free to compete with all the others", and still justly believe you have been completely fair…. This is the next and more profound stage of the battle for civil rights. We seek not just freedom but opportunity - not just legal equity but human ability - not just equality as a right and a theory, but equality as a fact and as a result.

In contemporary phrasing, Sterba (2003: 232–233) cites the example of runners in a race who for a time had been forced to compete at a disadvantage with the other runners by having weights tied to their legs; when later they were allowed to compete against those other runners after having the weights removed, they ought first to receive some special assistance to adjust for an appropriate period of time so that the results of the race will turn out to be fair. In employment relations, systematic selection of men for high level workplace positions has enriched them with a significant actual and psychological advantage, while at the same time a false perception that men do better at work than women is established among employers. In this context, establishing strict formal equality is merely tantamount to the perpetuation of male dominance.

Of course, discussing affirmative action in relation to justice to a large extent exceeds the classic discussion on the relation between justice and equality in general, derived from the Aristotelian notion that a condition is considered fair insofar as it respects or establishes a state of equality (*Ethics Nicomachea* E 130 a, b). It seems that there is an inherent contradiction in the perception of affirmative action: depending on the version of justice one endorses and the relevant value of its intrinsic components in relation to the distribution of social goods within society, the same measures might be simultaneously characterised either as just or unjust. Aristotle himself thought of justice as either distributive or corrective: the former relates to the division of shares in social benefits and obligations; the latter relates to correction of injustice through institutional means.

Although a number of theories of justice have been advanced since Aristotle's, a common thread connects them all with equality. John Rawls, who suggested the most structured and articulate contemporary theory on justice, considers that the minimum denominator needed for any institution to be considered fair is to avoid/preclude arbitrary discrimination among persons over the distribution of primary social goods and for the relevant rules to draw/strike a proper balance between competitive claims for societal advantages. The great philosopher of law adds to the Aristotelian two-fold justice an analytical account of procedural justice, i.e. fairness based on the procedures set to achieve such eventuality. In his theory, procedural justice can be *perfect* if allocation of goods is based on a procedure securing fair outcomes and an independent criterion defined separately from and prior to the implementation of the procedure, which is to be followed to assess these outcomes; while considered *imperfect* if there is no procedure to secure fair outcomes but rather an objective and independent criterion to assess outcomes and *pure* if there is no objective and independent criterion for what constitutes a fair outcome other than the procedure itself which as such ensures the fair result (Rawls 1999: 73–77, 2001: 39–79). Procedural justice conceptually corresponds to formal equality, with emphasis given on equal treatment of persons, while distributive justice is closer to the logic of substantive equality in that it entails positive state intervention in the distribution of social benefits.

In distributive justice what is critical is not the actual procedure of distribution but predominantly the *ratio* of the allocated shares. Rawls places distributive justice in the context of the traditional social contract theory set out by Thomas Hobbes, John Locke, and Jean-Jacques Rousseau and further suggests that the ideal original position is one under a veil of ignorance, preventing knowledge of any specific characteristic of social actors. In such a context two principles of distributive justice would apply. First and foremost, the *equal liberty principle* justifying a claim of equal basic political rights and liberties that would be the same for all and the *difference principle* allowing social and economic inequalities provided that they have been produced through fair equality of opportunity and aiming to the maximum benefit of the least advantaged members of society in order to preserve the sustainable maintenance of all social goods and the participation of all citizens in public official posts (Rawls 1999: 52–56).

On the other hand, Ronald Dworkin, in his classical writings, sets two theoretical viewpoints that link distributive justice and equality: the *equality of welfare* and the *equality of resources*. Under the former premise, people are equals if the distribution of social wealth makes them equal in welfare; under the latter premise people are equals if their resources are equal (Dworkin 1981a, b). Based on his preference towards equality of resources, Dworkin was a great proponent of affirmative action thinking that this policy fits with his theories of justice and equality (Dworkin 1998a, b). Both Rawls and Dworkin go beyond egalitarianism in that they both uphold benefits in favour of those who face disadvantages in society; they do not altogether enhance the egalitarian dogma that equality entails equal shares irrespective of the conditions within which these distributions operate, and suggests/produces optimum happiness for the widest spectrum of individuals in society. By the same token, Bobbio (1995) suggests the distinction between retributive justice ("*giustizia retributive*"), which connotes the idea of equality in a state of human, especially financial, interdependence and attributive justice ("*giustizia attributive*").

The general aphorism against procedural justice is that it is so formalistic that it ends up essentially undermining the idea of justice itself. However, no one can ignore that procedure contains its own objective worth, which is naturally related to the system of values upon which the concept of justice is based, and strongly depends on the fundamental rudiments of each legal system. In continental Europe the idea of natural justice connotes elements of justice as fairness in a substantive sense. By way of contrast, in English law, the historical *terminus technicus* of natural justice, now broadly absorbed by the duty to act fairly, set out the procedural rules of unbiased justice (*nemo iudex in causa sua*) and of fair hearing for both litigants (*audi alteram partem*). The value of procedural justice lies with its generality and objectivity that transcend time, thus largely guaranteeing a formally fair judgment.

Affirmative action can hardly be integrated into the idea of procedural justice. This is so because affirmative action is by definition incremental, in that it does not entail a generic *in abstracto* procedure for all subjects of law, but sets particular standards for different social groups; and temporary in that it applies until equality is restored. Of course, not *all* groups which have sustained such treatment are restored and not *all* individuals within the designated groups who have suffered discrimination in the past are compensated. Therefore the political branches of government essentially participate in a way that cannot be objective and they do not operate in a state of ignorance as the Rawlsian theory would suggest—quite the contrary, they must operate in a state of full awareness of the differing conditions already developed within society. On the other hand, one could reasonably argue that affirmative action also fails to introduce an independent criterion defined separately from and prior to the procedure which ought to be used as a benchmark to assess these outcomes, a necessary component for perfect procedural equality according to Rawls. This criterion could be restoration or substantive equality, both of which, however, suffer from a certain degree of circularity: they produce at the same time the conceptual foundation for the enactment of the policy and the actual criterion of eventual success without any particular justification for these goals so that the result (i.e. the statistical balance) also provides the justification of the policy (the need to have a social or political or financial symmetry). In a sense, although it might be questionable on other grounds, only the criterion of parity could be at the same time justified and measurable.

Affirmative action seems to be better accommodated within the concepts of distributive justice in its corrective sense. According to Sen (1995: 307, 328), distributive justice requires allocating adequate resources to those with limitations so that they can achieve essential abilities, thus creating "basic capability equality". Accordingly, the shares to be distributed due to positive measures are not equal, but instead differ according to a socially oriented *political* choice. If this mode of justice is employed, the debate then turns to the issue of the moral justification of employing varying standards for the allocation of social benefits. However, as the moral justification retreats, the more the issues of over—and under-inclusiveness come to light. By the same token, justification for affirmative action is provided by the relevant theory of 'justice as recognition', most notably illustrated by Fraser (1997: esp. 11–40) in the context of feminism, suggesting that justice, alongside the more traditional views of justice as requiring certain patterns of distribution and fair procedures, also requires the elimination of humiliation or disrespect for certain cultures or minorities so that they can properly exercise fair procedures and enjoy a fair distribution of goods.

At any rate, affirmative action supporters raise the legitimate claim that this policy is altogether compatible with any version of justice to the extent that it aims to establish macro-justice, which is *per se* a goal of great value, therefore accepting micro-injustices as collateral damages of minor importance that society ought to pay in order to achieve true justice (Clayton and Tangri 1989). However, the ethical cogency of the above consideration may be questioned. A state intervention may be fair or unfair, based on the prevailing idea of justice, but cannot be dependent on the equilibrium of macro-justice v. micro-injustice. This relativity of justice ignores that persons ought to be at the centre of consideration and cannot be manipulated as a mere means to achieve a presumably higher social goal. Accordingly, it would be equally unacceptable to reject a merited person in order to select someone less worthy, as much as to select a privileged member from disadvantaged groups. To the extent that any affirmative action by definition operates against people characterised as privileged and cannot fully discern those in true need amongst the advantaged groups, justice cannot be satisfied. Therefore, justice cannot be served by measures favouring or disfavouring groups, but only on a case-by-case basis through individualised justice and tailor-made regulatory measures. Nonetheless, the demand for a narrowly tailored approach, which has been a commonplace in the

US Supreme Court case law,[16] has been strongly criticized by the prominent American constitutional lawyer Tribe (1979); accordingly, a tailor-made approach is not expedient because from the point of view of attribution of justice there cannot be different treatment of basically the same constitutional phenomenon, i.e. individualised justice, which necessarily suffers from subjectivity and fluidity. This argument based on the quality of normativity of regulation was in essence used in the minority opinion in the 2003 Michigan University affirmative action judgment *Gratz v. Bollinger* of the US Supreme Court in 2003, where Justice Ginsburg concluded that among constitutionally permissible options, those that candidly disclose their consideration of race seem preferable to those that conceal it, albeit achieving similar numbers through "winks, nods, and disguises".[17]

The idea that collateral damages are permissible when it comes to the implementation of affirmative action plans raises further ethical concerns. One cannot ignore that to the extent that members of the historically privileged class continue to benefit from membership of that class, affirmative action might operate as a corrective for their unfair benefit, by accepting collective and objective responsibility for past injustices on the part of individuals merely because they belong to a class or group that have benefited in the past; in so doing, however, the law seems somehow to reflect theological perceptions of collective sin and guilt. This rationale appears equally problematic in case of diversity-based affirmative action measures that can be theoretically unrelated with such perceptions. In this case, justice actually operates as rehabilitative relief burdened by individuals, who are not in principle personally to blame for the past. For instance, in this line of reasoning, Daniel Maguire, an eminent analyst of theological ethics, suggests that for consistency reasons even a lawful and just individual, who has committed no offence and largely respects the rudiments of natural law, owes to justice merely because of his/her nature as a social being, to the extent that he/she effectively failed to act or omit what was proper. Accordingly, he asserts that any American pleading their innocence of a social offence, such as past discrimination, is a liar (cited with critique by Urofsky 1997: 27). Obviously, the more one probes beneath the outer shell of law and seeks an ethical justification, there is no end to collective or individual burdening. It was exactly that version of justice as rehabilitative relief that led, in Cohen's words (2003: 17–20), to the establishment of "racial proportionality" in the US, which nevertheless goes contrary to the idea of justice as value. If justice required proportional representation, the same argument should sustain the premise that European nations based on a single race or religion should be able to exclude insignificant minorities from decision-making or university admissions. The principle that proportionality needs to be preserved as a justice value should lead to the conclusion that a representative balance should be guaranteed irrespective of whether it refers to dominant or disadvantaged social groups. This is not, however, the rationale of affirmative action, seeking compensation for past

---

[16] *Infra*, 5.2.3.1.2.

[17] *Gratz v. Bollinger*, 539 US 244, 305 (2003).

discrimination and encouragement of discredited groups. No one would suggest that in order to achieve justice through racial proportionality, the US national basketball team should reflect the racial ratio nationwide.

The truth is that justice, even in its substantive perception, the same as equality, is presented in different versions that may or may not accommodate affirmative action. Trying to resolve a dispute or regulate social relationships is a multi-dimensional experiment that cannot be fully curbed or rationalised. This is especially true of the difficult co-existence of justice and equality which necessarily calls for the implementation of a value theory. Should babies be put in incubators (of which there is limited availability) on the basis of their weight and, accordingly, their chance of survival, or on the basis of their ranking in a priority list, or as part of a random selection once an incubator becomes available (Brock 1995)? Clearly, cost-effectiveness and ethical issues are inexorably connected to justice and equality.

References

Appiah, K.A. (1998). The limits of pluralism. In A.M. Melzer, J. Weinberger and M. R. Zinman (Eds.), *Multiculturalism and American Democracy* 37-54. Lawrence: University Press of Kansas.

Bell, M. and Waddington, L. (2003). Reflecting on inequalities in European equality law. *European Law Review,* 28(3), 349-369.

Bindman, Sir G. and Monaghan K. (2014), *Judicial Diversity. Accelerating change.* Resource document. http://www.matrixlaw.co.uk/uploads/other/06_11_2014_12_11_31_06.11.14.pdf. Accessed 31 Dec 2014.

Bobbio, N. (1994). *Destra e Sinistra: ragioni e significati di una distinzione politica.* Rome: Donzelli. English edition: Bobbio, N. (1997). *Left and Right: The Significance of a Political Distinction* (trans: Cameron, A.). Cambridge: Polity Press, Chicago: The University of Chicago Press.

Bobbio N. (1995), *Eguaglianza e libertà.* Torino: Einaudi Contemporanea.

Braibant, G. (1999). Réflexions sur le principe d'égalité. *European Review of Public Law,* 11(2), 443-454.

Brock, D. (1995). Justice and the A.D.A. *[Americans with Disabilities Act]*: Does prioritizing and rationing health care discriminate against the disabled?. *Social Philosophy and Policy,* 12(2), 159-184.

Cavanagh, M. (2002). *Against equality of opportunity.* Oxford: Clarendon Press.

Clayton, S.D., and Tangri, S.S. (1989). The justice of affirmative action. In F.A. Blanchard and F.J. Crosby (Eds.). *Affirmative action in perspective* (177-192). New York: Springer Verlag.

Cohen, C. (2003). Why race preference is wrong and bad. In C. Cohen and J.P. Sterba. *Affirmative action and racial preference. A debate* (1-188). Oxford-New York: Oxford University Press.

Craig, P.P. (1990). *Public law and democracy in the United Kingdom and the United States of America.* Oxford: Clarendon Press.

Dahl, R.A. (2006). *On political equality.* New Heaven-London: Yale University Press.

Dicey A.V. (1885), *Introduction to the study of the Law of the Constitution.* 10th ed., 1959, London: Palgrave Macmillan.

Dworkin, R. (1981a). What is equality? Part I: Equality of welfare. *Philosophy and Public Affairs,* 10(3), 185-246. Reprinted in R. Dworkin, *Sovereign virtue*: *The theory and practice of equality* (pp. 11-64). 2002, Cambridge MA: Harvard University Press.

Dworkin R. (1981b), What is equality? Part 2: Equality of resources. *Philosophy and Public Affairs,* 10(4), 283-345. Reprinted in R. Dworkin, *Sovereign virtue*: *The theory and practice of equality* (pp. 65-119). 2002, Cambridge MA: Harvard.

Dworkin R. (1987). What is equality? Part 4: Political equality. *University of San Francisco Law Review,* 23(1), 1. Reprinted in R. Dworkin (2002), *Sovereign virtue*: *The theory and practice of equality* (pp.184-210). Cambridge MA: Harvard University Press.

Dworkin, R (1998a), Affirming Affirmative Action, Review of The Shape of the River: Long-Term Consequences of Considering Race in College and University Admissions by William G. Bowen and Derek Bok. *The New York Review of Books*, 22 October. Reprinted: Affirmative Action: Does it Work?. In R. Dworkin, *Sovereign virtue*: *The theory and practice of equality* (pp. 386–408). 2002, Cambridge MA: Harvard.

Dworkin, R (1998b), Is Affirmative Action Doomed? *The New York Review of Books*, 5 November. Reprinted: Affirmative Action: Is it Fair? In R. Dworkin, *Sovereign virtue*: *The theory and practice of equality* (pp. 409-452). 2002, Cambridge MA: Harvard.

Ely, J.H. (1980). *Democracy and Distrust: A Theory of Judicial Review.* Cambridge MA: Harvard University Press.

Feldman, D. (1999). Human dignity as a legal value. Part I. *Public Law,* 682-702.

Feldman, D. (2000). Human dignity as a legal value. Part II. *Public Law,* 61-76.

Fraser, N. (1997). *Justice Interruptus: Critical Reflections on the "Postsocialist" Condition.* New York – London: Routledge.

Fraisse G. (1995), *Muse de la raison. La démocratie exclusive et la différence des sexes.* Paris: Gallimard.

Gaspard, F., Servan-Schreiber, C., and Gall, Le A. (1992). *Au pouvoir citoyennes!: Liberté, égalité, parité.* Paris: Seuil.

Hale B. Rt. Hon. Dame (2001). Equality and the Judiciary: We want more women judges. *Public Law.* 489-504.

Ingram, D. (2000). *Group rights: reconciling equality and difference.* Lawrence: University Press of Kansas.

Lewis, E. (2004), Why history remains a factor in the search for racial equality. In P. Gurin, J.S. Lehman and E. Lewis (Eds.), *Defending diversity: Affirmative action at the University of Michigan* (pp 17-60). Ann Arbor: University of Michigan Press

Locke, J. (1690), *Second Treatise of Government.* C. B. Macpherson (Ed.), 1980, Cambridge MA: Hackett Pub Co.

Lovatt, S.C. (2015), *The democratic deficit.* Seattle WA: CreateSpace Independent Publishing Platform.

Marinoff, L. (2000). Equal opportunity versus employment equity. *Sexuality and Culture,* 4, 23-44.

Mill, J.S. (1960), *Utilitarianism, liberty, representative government.* London-New York: Everyman Edition.

Mossuz-Lavau, J. (1998). *Femmes/Hommes pour la parité.* Paris: Presses de Sciences Po.

Pelerman, Ch. (1971). *Egalité et valeurs.* Bruxelles: Bruyant L'Egalité I, Travaux du Centre de Philosophie du Droit de l'Université Libre de Bruxelles.

Phillips, A. (1993), *Democracy and difference.* London: Polity Press.

Rawls, J, (1999). *Theory of Justice.* Revised ed., Boston MA: Belknap Press, Harvard University Press.

Rawls, J., and Kelly E. (2001). *Justice as fairness: A restatement.* Cambridge MA: Belknap Press, Harvard University Press.

Reyna, C., Tucker, A., Korfmacher, W., and Henry P.J. (2005). Searching for common ground between supporters and opponents of affirmative action. *Political Psycology,* 26(5), 667-682.

Roberts, P.C. and Stratton, L.M. (1995). *The new color line: How quotas and privilege destroy democracy.* Washington DC: Regnery.

Schuppert, F. and Koetter, M. (Eds.), (2012-2013). Understandings of the Rule of Law in various Legal Orders of the World. http://wikis.fu-berlin.de/display/SBprojectrol/Home. Accessed 31 Dec 2014.

Scott, J.W. (1996). *Only paradoxes to offer. French feminists and the rights of man.* Boston: Harvard University Press.

Sen, A. (1995). Equality of What?. In S.L. Darwall (Ed.). *Equal Freedom: Selected Tanner Lectures on Human Values* (307-330). Ann Arbor: University of Michigan Press.

Silkenat, J.R., Hickey J.E.Jr., Barenboim, P.D. (Eds.), (2014), *The Legal Doctrines of the Rule of Law and the Legal State (Rechtsstaat).* Heidelberg-New York, Dordrecht, London: Springer, Series: Ius Gentium: Comparative Perspectives on Law and Justice, Vol. 38.

Slama, A.G. (2004) Contre la discrimination positive. La liberté insupportable. *Pouvoirs – Revue Française d'Études Constitutionnelles et Politiques (Discrimination Positive),* 111, 133-143.

Stohr, G. (2004). *A black and white case: How affirmative action survived its greatest legal challenge.* Princeton: Bloomberg Press.

Sturm, S., and Guinier, L. (2001).The future of affirmative action. In S. Sturm, and L. Guinier (Eds.). *Who's qualified?* (3-36) Boston: Beacon Press.

Taylor, Ch. (Ed.) 1994. *Multiculturalism: Examining the Politics of Recognition.* Princeton: Princeton University Press.

Tribe, L.H. (1979). Perspectives on Bakke; Equal protection, procedural fairness, or structural justice. *Harvard Law Review,* 92, 864-877.

Urofsky, M.I. (1997). *Affirmative action on trial: Sex discrimination in Johnson v. Santa Clara.* Lawrence: University Press of Kansas.

Wallach Scott J. (2005), *Parité!: Sexual Equality and the Crisis of French Universalism.* Chicago: University of Chicago Press.

Weiler, J., Haltern, U., and Mayer F. (1995). *European Democracy and its Critique. Five Uneasy Pieces.* Florence: European University Institute, Robert Schuman Centre Working Papers 11/95.

Yotopoulos-Marangopoulos, A. (1998), *Affirmative Action. Towards effective gender equality.* Athens–Brussels: Ant. N. Sakkoulas Publishers- Établissements Émile Bruylant.

Chapter 3
The Sociological Question: Goals and Legitimacy

The purposes of affirmative action cannot be totally isolated from its morality/ethics. Nevertheless, the goal broadly refers to the intention of the state authority enacting an affirmative action plan, thus being essentially subjective in nature, whereas the ethics of the policy is measured against the prevailing notions of morality, thus it is not necessarily tantamount to the actual purpose of the enacting authority. Having said that, it appears as an exercise of major doctrinal and legal significance to identify the purpose of an affirmative action plan: first, a coherent doctrinal background based on a solid goal theory is necessary so as to legitimise this policy and enhance regular acceptance and compliance. According to Hollinger (1996: 97–98), it is exactly this failure of affirmative action theory to come up with a solid doctrine of acceptable objectives that prohibits the policy from being widely acknowledged and implemented. This is particularly true in the case of the US, where the Supreme Court has overruled compensation for past discrimination as a permissible rationale for racial affirmative action in higher education, which in turn further blurred the conceptual clarity of the policy. Second, in order to assess the constitutionality of a particular positive measure there is the conceptual precondition that it pursues a legitimate aim. If this is so, the judiciary must further evaluate the particular side-effects of the measure in question (mostly adverse consequences for the fundamental rights involved) against the scope and quality of the goal pursued. This legal approach may take place either in a more pragmatic way, through the application of the reasonableness/rational basis test, or through a more doctrinal approach, i.e. the proportionality test.[1] Thus, the relative value of the goals pursued by each legal system when introducing an affirmative action plan not only provides the substantive legitimacy of the state intervention but also constitutes the legal foundation for the technical/legal evaluation of the measure.

There are two basic and three auxiliary *rationales* justifying the enactment of affirmative action measures, the distinction based on the extent and regularity that each goal appears in the literature and the jurisprudence worldwide. The basic purposes are *remedial*, i.e. compensation for past discriminations and *cultural*, i.e.

[1]*Infra*, 5.1.3.

G. Gerapetritis, *Affirmative Action Policies and Judicial Review Worldwide*,
Ius Gentium: Comparative Perspectives on Law and Justice 47,
DOI 10.1007/978-3-319-22395-7_3

diversity. The former has been the initial driving force behind the introduction of such measures and still applies as their basic teleological justification on a world-wide level, whereas the latter tends to become the most up-to-date term for seeking substantive equality. Three auxiliary purposes are also conceivable and have on occasion been used by courts: the *societal* purpose which relates to the perception of each society in relation to the role of marginal or minority groups; the *pedagogical* purpose which highlights the role-model function of the policy and the *economic* purpose which indicates the balanced growth aspired by the policy.

3.1 The Remedial Purpose: Compensation for Past Discrimination

The most easily conceivable social task of affirmative action policies is to compensate groups that have suffered discrimination in the past. It sounds reasonable, fair and morally acceptable that society should bridge the inequality of opportunities that has occurred due to the unequal distribution of social benefits and the historically disadvantageous position of certain societal actors. Thus, women, racial minorities, religious groups etc. ought to gain some advantage in the fields of education, economy and political participation. The remedial purpose has historically been the driving force for the enactment of affirmative action policies. This is so because of an evident ontological persuasiveness that it operates in a corrective manner for injustices that undeniably took place in the past. The idea seems relevant to a theological approach to the distribution of social resources and is largely based on the idea of collective guilt that a society bears towards individuals belonging to groups that have been treated unfavourably in the past.

Moving the affirmative action debate from the individual to the group raises issues with respect to the policy's doctrinal coherence. The idea of group compensation for past discrimination logically presupposes that all groups ought to be granted, in aggregate, the same value throughout time. This premise suggests that the current status of a suppressed group is still disadvantageous because of past discrimination. In this line of argumentation, there is wide literature justifying the remedial purpose of affirmative action. Crosby (2004: 42–46) and Ridgeway (1991: 70) highlight the structural imbalances as correlating to sexism or racism. Galanter (1986: 77) speaks of the "*cumulative structural character of inequality*" in India that trespasses time exactly because it cannot be radically erased; and Brest (1987: 281) stresses that the actual justification of affirmative action's remedial purpose is the "*perpetual racial underclass*" of African-Americans. In judicial words, the most illustrative reflection of the compensatory rationale of affirmative action was furnished by Justice Sotomayor in her dissenting opinion in 2014 US Supreme Court case *Schuette v. Coalition to Defend Affirmative Action*, by stating that although the Nation's "long and lamentable record of stymieing the right of racial minorities to participate in the political process might not have been discriminatory in purpose, minority members do possess a right to participate meaningfully and equally in the political process".[2] One may, of course, validly challenge the historical validity of the above statement, in that discrimination in the US was largely purposeful.

Preliminary factors that need to be addressed in the context of compensation for past discrimination concern the identification of cause, time and place of past discrimination. In relation to the *cause* of underrepresentation of a group, there must be strong evidence that is due to discrimination and is not related to the group's desire to remain outside social competition. This is of course an extremely difficult exercise because it refers to collective psychology. Only in very exceptional cases where there has been institutional differentiation, such as, in general terms, under slavery, apartheid, segregation regimes or deprivation of the political rights of women, could group discrimination be claimed altogether and undeniably. In relation to *time*, it is clear that discrimination must have been systemic (not incidental) and must have occurred for a relatively long time in order to justify the moral claim for restoration. This evidence is not always easy to retrieve because by definition it refers to the past and constitutes a largely subjective approach entailing a review of the overall environment where underrepresentation occurred. In relation to the *place* of past discrimination the question is where it should have occurred in order to justify *ex post* group compensation. There are two approaches to the issue: the first suggests that there must be evidence of global institutional and/or social discrimination; according to the second it suffices that discrimination is proven within a specific sub-community (i.e. a local region, a specific workplace environment, a particular academic institution). The former version seems to be the prevailing one when remedial purposes are recognised as legitimate, although the latter version has on occasion been invoked by the courts as well. Thus, in *Hopwood v. Texas*,[3] the US Court of Appeals held that Texas Law School could not act to alleviate the effect on its applicant pool of past discrimination in elementary, secondary and undergraduate education, since the effects of such discrimination were too difficult to measure and the Law School was not responsible for those effects in any event (see footnote 1 in Chap. 1).

The remedial purpose has a number of conceptual and practical issues to put up against. Conceptual issues relate to ethical questions: "who compensates?" and "who is the beneficiary of compensation?" Practical issues relate to empirical evidence as to how successful this retroactive compensation is for beneficiaries and for society as a whole.

3.1.1 Who Compensates? Social Policy and State Outsourcing

Affirmative action is a policy intended to redistribute power. Independently of whether such measures apply in labour, academia or political representation, they

[2] 572 US, Case No. 12–682 (2014).
[3] 84 F.3d 720 (5th Cir 1996).

converge on one major target: subverting historical divergences by (institutionally) redrafting the balance amongst normally competing social groups. If this is the essence of affirmative action, it is merely one form of state social policy. What makes the difference between a typical social policy plan and affirmative action is that the former aims *directly* at redistributing social resources whereas the latter does the same thing but only *indirectly.* Implementation of social policy entails cost for the state budget, mainly drawn from taxation, whereas affirmative action may or may not entail pecuniary cost. Certain categories of affirmative action are directly linked to state budgetary issues, e.g. party financing depending on the number of women in parties' candidate lists. However, all affirmative action plans do have indirect burdens, albeit not necessarily in a monetary form. A racial affirmative action for preferential university admissions means that a *specific* non-benefiting person ends up not being admitted, despite his/her better record. The cost for the discarded individual is indeed significant: apart from the immediate, mostly psychological, damage there is a potential future loss in professional life. This cost is not borne by the state, not even by a class of people. It burdens specific individuals. It is not of course uncommon from the point of view of social psychology to encounter the phenomenon of collective responsibility, especially in highly entitative groups, such as families, in the sense that members are seen as sharing responsibility for other members' misbehavior or wrongdoings. As the well-known sociologist Frederick Lynch, one of the greatest opponents of affirmative action, has substantiated in a series of books and papers (Lynch 1991, 2001; Lynch and Beer 1990), affirmative action programmes do produce individual adverse effect, since there are particular persons whose lives are severely impacted, whereas society as a whole suffers a backlash. Cohen (2003: 27) crudely put the same argument "The wrong people benefit, the wrong people pay the price of that benefit". And, usually, as Hook suggests, the harmed individual is not amongst the privileged persons of his/her class who would ordinarily have the resources to access academia since they might have had the chance to have better high school education, better access to out-of-school knowledge, and better opportunities to gain additional qualifications (Hook 1995). What follows is that affirmative action is in fact a form of social policy, which, unlike other social policies, burdens altogether or disproportionately certain individuals on the basis of their group membership as opposed to all individuals in proportion to their relative power to contribute to public finances, in a sense an outsourcing of state obligations with respect to the social state (Anderson 2004: 280–281). The question as to who pays for social preferences is of acute significance not only in terms of ethics but also from a legal perspective, posing, according to Chopper (1987: 255, 268–270), overwhelming constitutional complications. For those burdened by the policy, the reverse angle of compensation for past *group discrimination* seems to apply: a form of punishment for past group favouritism. If it is conceded that affirmative action is essentially remedial in nature (which by definition presupposes past harm and differentiates it from traditional social policies), affirmative action, by setting a form of objective liability, arguably contravenes the long-standing Roman maxim that no one is considered as causing harm, unless they do what they have no right to do ("*nemo damnum facit, nisi qui id fecit quod facere jus non habet*").

Interestingly, the burden of preferential treatment may also be incurred by non-dominant social groups, such as minorities or women. The case-law of national courts, especially in the US, has assessed adverse impact upon particular social groups when examining the constitutionality of such measures. In *United Jewish Organizations of Williamsburgh, Inc. v. Carey* (1976),[4] where several districts in New York were restructured to create districts with a minimum non-white majority of 65 %, reapportionment resulted in a Hasidic Jewish community splitting in two. Despite opposing arguments from the adversely affected group, the Court found in favour of the reapportionment plan. Further, in the 1979 US Supreme Court judgment *Personnel Administrator of Massachusetts v. Feeney*, the plaintiff, a woman who had scored highly on state civil service examinations was passed over for employment opportunities in favour of male candidates with lower scores, due to legislation imposing veteran preference for civil service positions. In a 7–2 decision, the Court held that the law was enacted to serve legitimate and worthy purposes and not to discriminate on the basis of sex, irrespective of the small number of potential female candidates who might eventually be eligible for its benefits. In delivering the opinion of the Court, Justice Stewart noted that "discriminatory purpose" implied more than intent as volition or intent as awareness of consequences; it implied that the decision maker selected or reaffirmed a particular course of action at least in part "because of," not merely "in spite of," its adverse effects upon an identifiable group: "When the totality of legislative actions establishing and extending the Massachusetts veterans' preference are considered, the law remains what it purports to be: a preference for veterans of either sex over nonveterans of either sex, not for men over women".[5] Although, it is not unquestionable that the said measure qualified as affirmative action for remedial purpose, it illustrates the causal link between the preference awarded and the burdened individuals.

There is a two-fold response to the conceptual and pragmatic deficiencies of compensation for past discrimination in relation to those burdened by the policy. The first response negates that there are actually victims of affirmative action policies, or at least more so in relation to conventional social policies. This approach places emphasis on affirmative action mostly as a preventive mechanism. Relevantly, the Canadian Supreme Court in *CN v. Canada (Canadian Human Rights Commission)* in 1986,[6] held that an employment quota programme was designed to break a continuing cycle of systemic discrimination and not to compensate past victims or even to provide new opportunities for specific individuals who have been unfairly refused jobs or promotion in the past. Rather, it was an attempt to ensure that future applicants and workers from the designated group will not face the same insidious barriers that blocked others before them. In this respect, as the Court itself ruled, in

[4]430 US 144 (1976).

[5]442 US 256, 258 (1979).

[6](1987) 1 S.C.R. 1114.

any employment equity programme, there is no prevention without some form of remedy. Although it found that the dominant purpose of such programmes has always been to improve the situation of the target group in the future, it upheld the necessity to look to the past patterns of discrimination and destroy them.

The second response upholds the burden imposed by affirmative action but essentially considers it a fair price to pay for past injustices. In Fredman's syllogism (2002: 128–129), it is reasonable that when the state intervenes in a corrective way by awarding benefits based on unjust treatment against certain social groups, those who have, even by association, profited from past injustice as members of the dominant group, bear the consequences. Given that social policies have winners and losers and the state must seek alternatives to compensate for past injustices, it seems on balance that the consequences for the non-preferred individuals are less onerous than the consequences assumed by the members of groups that suffered past discrimination. Irrespective of the fact that the presumed harm for non-preferred individuals will vary significantly in relation to each particular measure, individual harm might in essence be a statistical one in the light of a risk analysis approach: the non-preferred individual has a slightly lower likelihood of receiving the benefit in question, such as admission to a prestigious university, than members of designated groups would have without the affirmative action plan. From this viewpoint, while the harm of not receiving the benefit might be substantial in the ways suggested by affirmative action opponents, the harm actually caused by said policy usually does not equate to denial of the benefit; thus the risk of not receiving the benefit typically is increased only marginally by affirmative action programmes.

3.1.2 Who Is Compensated? Actual and Presumed Victims of Discrimination

Affirmative action aspires to compensate individuals belonging to groups that have suffered discrimination and social undervaluation of their merit in the past by using improper criteria. In that respect one might challenge affirmative action on the basis that it lacks a distinctive approach upon the issue of societal damage and merely constitutes a confession of state failure to identify those in true need. Indeed, discrimination is suffered not by groups *per se* but rather by members of a group (most probably the majority in the case of subordinate groups). Affirmative action arguably departs from the basic doctrine in torts that compensation is owed only when the harmed individuals would have been in a better position had the discriminatory practice not occurred.[7]

[7]The argument should of course be used cautiously and not stressed to produce outrageously sophistic results that essentially undermine its conceptual articulation. Thus, Morris (1984) discards racial affirmative action in the US claiming that most of the Afro-American beneficiaries

The technical issue of defining the designated groups presents significant difficulties. Given that there is no automatic, or even easy, answer, as to which groups should fall within the benevolent umbrella of affirmative action, it is difficult to launch a fair and rational awarding system. What races should be considered as having suffered discrimination and what is the priority amongst the various groups that might benefit from the relevant measures? These are only a few of the questions indicating the inclusion problem. This is why even strong proponents of affirmative action, such as Skrentny (2002), admit that this constitutes the hardest task of the policy. Edley (1996), advisor to President Clinton's One America Initiative and chairman of his 1998 Affirmative Action Review, member of the US Commission on Civil Rights and later Dean of the University of California Berkeley School of Law, himself conceded the inadequacies in terms of the determination of the affirmative action beneficiaries and thought that this exercise constitutes the most threatening feature for the eventual success of any such project.

The basic relevant question raised is why should there be a group remedy in the first place. Compensation functions merely as a means to liberate the human value that has been suffocated due to past discrimination. This is why it is suggested that affirmative action can only operate as a means to elevate the status of oppressed groups by releasing their true capacity and not to establish an appropriate social balance. Affirmative action policies, however, might operate as an out-of-date break-even process between competing social groups and does not necessarily result in fair awards, precisely because of its non-individualistic methodology. As Nickel (1974) puts it, the only thing which is common in the person who suffered discrimination in the past and the one eventually compensated at present is that they both belong to the same race, religion or gender. In other words, this balancing process may statistically provide satisfaction to members of designated groups but, technically, not to all members of these groups and, most probably, not to those who actually suffered discrimination in the past. In this line of argumentation, Gutman argues (1998: 343–345) that gender affirmative action policies in the US have accomplished their purpose exactly because they set women free to become competitive and prove their undeniable skills, whereas race affirmative action policies in the same country have failed because minorities are still far from having released their inherent potential.

In legal terms, the question of whether compensation for past discrimination ought to be given is an issue of the strength of the causal link between act or omission and damage. As Sterba notes (2003: 258), both proponents and opponents of affirmative action agree that damage should be restored. Its proponents claim that damage transcends the period within which discrimination took place and, depending on the source and extent of discriminatory practices, produces lingering

---

(Footnote 7 continued)

would not have been born if their ancestors had not been transferred to America because of slavery, in the absence of which even those who would have arrived would have been in the same starting position as any other immigrant.

effects for a further period of time. Its opponents insist that a remedy should only be awarded on the basis of conclusive evidence of true damage. There are two stages in this process of delineating the affirmative action beneficiaries. First, the policy criteria should be set out, e.g. race, sex, religion; and, second, there must be a process of inclusion of groups into the settled criteria. The former decision is mostly a policy one based on historical assumptions about past discrimination. Given the wide differences between different members of a group, one might convincingly argue that instead of using a more or less arbitrary criterion, such as gender or race, a more objective and secure yardstick, such as class or financial capacity, should apply. This way, institutional encouragement could be given to individuals in true need in a more Marxist approach (Kahlenberg 1997). Essentially, the proposition suggests that affirmative action policies should be inserted into the broader social policies, thus being disassociated from past discrimination, in the form of class-based and race-neutral measures. Otherwise, any generic affirmative action plan constitutes an over-simplistic approach to a rather complicated social phenomenon.

Clearly, racial affirmative action provides more drafting difficulties compared to other types. Cohen (2003: 172) wonders how much 'blood' of a given race is enough to justify one's claim of inclusion: "Is 'one drop' enough? If the absurd 'one drop' rule were applied to 'Caucasians', we might agree that since the drops of white blood are very widely spread, we are all whites". The situation becomes even murkier in states where due to the historical mixing of races through the centuries, it is not an easy task to determine who is eventually qualified to be a benefiting category. Thus, in Brazil, a basic argument against launching positive discrimination measures was that racial boundaries are not as rigid as in the US and, therefore, it is impossible to know who is "black". As Sales Augusto dos Santos noted (2006: 30), the difficulty in determining who is black, in a very racially mixed society like Brazil, renders the policy ineffective.

Following the above line of argumentation/reasoning, it seems that affirmative action policies are systemically more akin than other general rules to the pathologies of over-inclusiveness (thus benefiting individuals not in true need) and under-inclusiveness (thus not benefiting individuals in true need). Over-inclusiveness can occur because some beneficiaries have not suffered direct past discrimination and might not need any benevolent treatment, but will nevertheless benefit merely because of their group membership. In a random survey conducted in the US, it emerged that two-thirds of non-white entrepreneurs, who benefited from sub-contracting subsidies for minority-owned enterprises, had a net income over one million dollars each (Sowell 2004: 120). The renowned American sociologist Wilson (1987: 109–124), assessing race, employment and education from 1950s onwards concluded that that there is a very large number of members of the designated groups who take advantage of preferential treatment in higher paid jobs or university admissions but are not, at least financially, in true need; whereas people from hyper-segregated ghettos, who would actually deserve to be included due to their social condition and prior discrimination would not normally have the resources or even the awareness to do so; the eventual result being widening of social discrepancies within the minority groups themselves. In the same line of argument, Terry Anderson argues (2004: 280–281), that privileged university admission for minorities only makes sense when applying in less popular institutions, since such a policy in *Ivy League* universities, where the fees are exorbitant, would merely benefit financially powerful minority members that would perhaps have a chance to be admitted to the university anyway. Of course, the argument based on under-inclusiveness underestimates secondary effects caused by systematic discrimination policies, in that members of the victimised groups may have not suffered direct and evident harm, but past group exclusion from opportunities or the isolation from social fusion most likely have produced adverse effects in their standing vis-à-vis social competition. In this way, the circle of victims from discrimination is broadened so as to essentially be tantamount to group membership.

There is a crucial ambiguity in the phrase "suffer discrimination". It might mean to be victimized by some direct act of intentional discrimination: for example, the minority applicant who is denied a job because of her race. Or it might mean to be victimized by the lingering, indirect effects of historical policies of discrimination: the minority applicant who is denied the job because her substandard education in *de facto* segregated urban public schools prevented her from acquiring the necessary skills. For affirmative action proponents, this is a crucial distinction.

Of course, over-inclusiveness may also occur as a matter of political manipulation in order for a party or candidate to become more appealing to the political base. As La Noue and Sullivan recall (2001: 73), Cuban Americans in the Nixon era and Indians in the '90s in Ohio were added to the designated groups because in the former case exiles from the Castro regime were overwhelmingly Republican, where in the latter case they were mostly donors to the electoral campaign of the Governor. The authors, challenging the necessary over-inclusiveness of any affirmative action programme and, especially, those designed in the US in relation to education and public procurement, wonder why American Indians, Native Americans, Eskimos and Aleuts are considered for purposes of implementation of the policy as separate groups, whereas members from as many as twenty-five Asian countries with very diverse characteristics, such as religion, tradition, language, compose a single category under the title "Asian-Americans". Obviously, the wider the grouping for the purposes of affirmative action, the more dangerous it becomes for the policy to become over-inclusive because of the lower level of individual treatment.

Sowell (2004: 48–49), a prominent comparativist and opponent of affirmative action finds disproportionate over-inclusiveness as a commonplace fallacy in India, where racial affirmative action has been introduced for over a century, albeit with limited success in treating racial discrepancies and with collateral rise of maximum resentments and hostility toward them in the part of others. The author argues that need for supplementary contributions from members of the designated beneficiary groups themselves, in order to make preferences and quotas effective have gone disproportionately to those individuals and subgroups who are already most fortunate rather than those most in need. In substantiating this assertion, he cites two major case-law authorities in India in the 90's that tried to rationalise the design of affirmative action policies, whereby the Supreme Court of the land struck down a State statute declaring that there should be no "creamy layer", i.e. members of nobility, among those granted preferences and, reversely, upheld the exclusion of more fortunate individuals and groups from quotas for socially and educationally disadvantaged classes (Sowell 2004: 49). Furthermore, due to the continuous enlargement of designated groups, almost three-quarters of the population of India are members of officially preferred groups; "[w]hile the remaining minority are generally members of higher castes, that ascribed status does not automatically translate into economic privilege" (Sowell 2004: 47).

There are, of course, more striking examples of undeserved benefits through affirmative action plans. Thus, a very wide list of beneficiaries exists in Pakistan, in relation to preferential university admissions, including children of "sportsmen", a category which includes those who have served in the military, civil servants, doctors, attorneys and university employees (Kennedy 1986: 79). These affirmative action plans do not render prior discrimination as a condition to become beneficiary, but on quite the contrary they provide benefits to privileged classes in the country, arguable as a class reward for services to the country. The evident result stemming thereof is the maintenance of social hierarchy and the curtailment of the opportunity for members of suppressed groups to effectively participate in social competition.

Under-inclusiveness can occur when individuals who had been the victims of social inequality are excluded from the catalogue of eligible beneficiaries whilst carrying the burden of the policy. In light of the actual equality of opportunities and without prejudicing other correlating goals of affirmative action policies, it is questionable why a female from a politically powerful family should qualify for reserved seats in parliament due to an affirmative action plan over a male candidate with no social, political or financial means. At the end of the day, the price to be paid for affirmative action is not left to dominating groups as a whole, but rather to particular members of such groups. A group remedy necessarily suffers from a certain degree of improper classification.

A clear illustration of the false machinery of affirmative action is provided if one examines the implementation of such measures in the US. In the '60s, such plans only benefited blacks who were the most sizeable minority community in the country. Massive immigration from Asia and Latin America in the late '60s (following the introduction of *Immigration Reform Act 1965* about 20 million legal immigrants came to the US) produced a steady but radical change in the orientation of the measures: the contrast has been made ever since not between whites and blacks, but between whites and others (Hollinger 1996: 106; Schrag 1995: 41). Today, in the US there are over 20 race (unique or joint) classifications in the official census.[8] According to the 2010 census, outside the dominant white

[8]European American, African American, Asian American, Native Americans or Alaska Native, Native Hawaiian or other Pacific Islander, Some other race, Two or more races, Non-Hispanic White or European American, Non-Hispanic Black or African American, Non-Hispanic Asian, Non-Hispanic American Indian or Alaska Native, Non-Hispanic Native Hawaiian or other Pacific Islander, Non-Hispanic some other race, Non-Hispanic two or more races, White or European

population (72.4 %), the largest non-white community is that of Hispanic or Latinos (16.3 %), that have surpassed the numbers of the black community (12.6 %), whereas Asian-Americans constitute 4.8 % and American Indian and Alaska Natives have been reduced to less than 1 %.[9] According to US Census Bureau population projections, non-Hispanic whites will no longer be the majority of the population in 2042[10]; between the 2000 and 2010 censuses, there was a remarkable 43 % increase of Hispanic or Latinos.

The result of this evolution has been that blacks, who were originally the only beneficiaries of affirmative action, must now compete with other minority groups in order to gain such benefits. In this way, an affirmative action race has developed not only among individuals, but also among minority groups. Given that a very significant portion of the population determines themselves as multi-race, a racial and sometimes aggressive clash amongst groups is very likely, especially when massive affirmative action plans have resulted in strong competition among the beneficiaries (Brest and Oshige 1995). The debate, which is eventually a matter of politics and may end up as an issue of dominance of the various pressure groups, may take either direction: affirmative action in the US is denounced either because it is not restricted to Afro-Americans (Steinberg 1995), or because of the exact opposite—it does not embrace Asian-Americans (Choy 2005). In fact, one of the most powerful NGOs in the field is *Chinese for Affirmative Action*, founded in 1969 to promote equal opportunity for Chinese Americans. The organisation has been involved in a variety of cases affecting the Chinese American community, most predominantly in the 1974 case *Lau v. Nichols*,[11] which resulted in setting bilingual education provisions for Chinese- and Spanish-speaking public school students in San Francisco where the organisation is located.

The political debate can become even more explosive when other potential beneficiaries of affirmative action, such as women, who have an obvious legitimate interest to participate in the discussion so as to claim a larger portion of the benefits awarded, enter the struggle. Statistics in this debate provide impressive feedback. While in the 1970s two-thirds of the actual beneficiaries of affirmative action plans in the US were Afro-Americans, this ratio has been significantly reduced (below 50 %) in less than 25 years (Zelnick 1996: 300). And all the above is true, when the group that received the least benefits is the one that has also suffered the most violent exclusion: Native Americans. Although they have been given a status of partial self-administration through reservations, the results of the policy have been

---

(Footnote 8 continued)

American Hispanic, Black or African American Hispanic, American Indian or Alaska Native Hispanic, Asian Hispanic, Native Hawaiian or other Pacific Islander Hispanic, Some other race Hispanic, Two or more races Hispanic.

[9]http://www.census.gov/prod/cen2010/briefs/c2010br-02.pdf (last accessed 31.12.2014).

[10]US Census Bureau an older and more diverse nation by midcentury, 14 August 2008.

[11]414 US 563 (1974).

particularly adverse due to the sometimes counterproductive nature of the benefits awarded to them, e.g. casino licenses (Pevar 2012: 81–108, 185–220, 275–290).

The confusion emanating from the lack of coherent delineation is also apparent in judicial decisions. In the well-cited US case *Hopwood v. State of Texas*,[12] it was admitted that the language used in the admission policy "for the sake of simplicity and readability" was that of "Caucasians" including whites and other non-benefiting races, as opposed to "minorities", i.e. blacks and Latinos. Of course, the issue of competing interests when it comes to award of privileges transcends affirmative action plans and touches upon all social policies. Thus, in Australia, the High Court in *Gerhardy v. Brown*[13] was called to decide on the validity of Section 19 of the South Australian Act, providing that a person, other than a Pitjantjatjara may not enter upon Pitjantjatjara land except with the permission of the corporate body representing the Pitjantjatjara people. The defendant, an Aborigine but not a Pitjantjatjara, entered upon the land without such permission and was prosecuted. The case essentially came down to the way beneficiaries of special measures ought to be designated and the Court eventually found that legislative exclusion of persons from designated land on any grounds, including race, was tantamount to unacceptable discrimination.

In Canada, in the early 1990s, country natives (*First Nations* tribes) approached the Ontario government for the right to control reserve-based gaming activities, the profits from which were to be used to strengthen tribe economic, cultural, and social development. As a result, Ontario and representatives from Ontario's First Nations entered into a process of negotiation with the goal of partnering to develop the province's first reserve-based commercial casino-indeed, an analogous process with what happened in the US. It was agreed that proceeds from the casino ("First Nations Fund") were to be distributed only to Ontario First Nations communities registered as tribes under the Indian Act, a 1951 Canadian statute concerning registered Indians, their tribes and the system of Indian reserves. Non-status communities sought a declaration that Ontario's refusal to include them in the casino project was unconstitutional and that they should be allowed to participate in the distribution negotiations. The Canadian Federal Supreme Court held the measure to be constitutional in *Lovelace v. Ontario* in 2000.[14] Its rationale was broadly contextual and purposive. The Court granted that the petitioners had been subjected to differential treatment since the province confirmed that they were excluded from a share in the First Nations Fund and any related negotiation process. The question remained as to whether the differential treatment was justified. In this respect, the Court elaborated upon four contextual factors: (i) pre-existing disadvantage, stereotyping, prejudice, or vulnerability; (ii) the correspondence, or lack thereof, between the ground(s) on which the claim is based and the actual need, capacity, or circumstances of the claimant or others; (iii) the ameliorative purpose or effects of

[12]84 F.3d 720 (5th Cir 1996), note 4.

[13](1985) 57 ALR 472.

[14]2000 SCC 37. Also see *Ardoch Algonquin First Nation v. Ontario* (2000) SCC 37.

the impugned law, programme or activity upon a more disadvantaged person or group in society; and (iv) the nature and scope of the interest affected by the impugned government activity. The Court concluded that the First Nations Fund did not conflict with the general equality clause because, although the appellants had established pre-existing disadvantage, stereotyping and vulnerability, first, they failed to establish that the First Nations Fund functioned by device of stereotype, second, the appellants failed to prove the correspondence between their actual needs, capacities and circumstances vis-à-vis the programme; and, third, irrespective of the appellants' unfavourable conditions the programme was targeted at ameliorating a specific disadvantaged group. This precedent was confirmed in *Alberta (Aboriginal Affairs and Northern Development) v. Cunningham*,[15] where the Métis community and the government entered into negotiations centered on establishing settlement lands for their communities, extending self-government and ensuring the protection and enhancement of their culture and identity, as distinct from Indians. The *Metis Settlements Act* enacted in the aftermath of the negotiations was challenged by formal members of a Métis community, who had opted to register as Indians in order to obtain medical benefits, thus loosing Métis entitlements. The Court upheld the statute on the basis that it was a selectively ameliorative programme, thus promoting substantive equality, even though excluded groups might have suffered equivalent discrimination as the designated groups. In both cases cited above, the Supreme Court refused to enter into a discussion as to the relevant ontological and historical situation of potential affirmative action beneficiaries, thus altogether rejecting the argument of under-inclusiveness.

In India, an illustrative case of legal and political failure to build a rational system of preferential treatment is provided by the 22/2012 judgment of the High Court of India in *R. Krishnaiah v. Union of India.* The facts concern two sub-quota policies of 4.5 % in favour of a particular category of a "specific socially and educationally backward class of citizens belonging to minorities", namely Muslims, Christians, Sikhs, Buddhists, and Zoroastrians, for admission in some central educational institutions out of a 27 % reservation for the general category of "other backward classes". The Court found that there was no evidence to demonstrate that persons belonging to the designated religious groups were more backward than any other category of backward classes or that they need any preferential treatment as compared to other backward classes, therefore there was a case of impermissible discrimination on religious grounds. The Court further probed into the question of whether the cluster of groups (Muslims, Christians, Sikhs, Buddhists and Zoroastrians) was homogeneous or not and ruled that the Government had failed to justify that the classification of these religious minorities as a homogeneous group or as *more* backward classes deserved special treatment. Accordingly, the Court set aside the sub-quota of 4.5 % as violating the non-discrimination clause. The divergent approaches of Canada and India in this respect lie presumably with the actual numbers of races in their respective territories. In Canada, because of

[15]2011 SCC 37.

the limited number of minorities the issue of delineation of affirmative action beneficiaries is not as acute as in the case of India with the exorbitant number of races competing among each other in the social arena.

In Europe, delimiting the ambit of beneficiaries is not normally as acute a concern, given that gender is the dominant criterion of granting privileges. The most astonishing case-study of drafting a catalogue of beneficiaries is found in Flemish legislation in Belgium. The Decree of 8 May 2002 on equitable participation in the employment market concerning professional orientation, vocational training, career counselling and the action of intermediaries on the labour market,[16] allowed for positive measures for labour integration of target groups (*groupes cibles*). Originally, there was a horizontal non-group inclusion of vulnerable individuals into the target list embodying individuals whose level of employment, defined as the percentage of the active population of vulnerable individuals who effectively work, were under the average level of employment of the overall population. This includes non-EU citizens, people with disabilities, workers above 45 years of age, individuals who had not completed their secondary education, or persons belonging to the underrepresented sex in a particular professional field.[17]

An additional problem is posed if one takes into account that even amongst the benefiting groups there are invariably conflicting interests. Women or blacks are by definition such sizeable and non-homogeneous groups that there is no point in trying to establish a common core legitimate interest. A vivid illustration to that effect is provided by the facts of the US Supreme Court case *Geduldig v. Aiello*.[18] California had a disability insurance system for private employees temporarily barred from working due to an injury or illness not covered by workmen's compensation, under which employees must contribute 1 % of their salary to an Unemployment Compensation Disability Fund. Certain disabilities attributable to pregnancy were not compensable, whereas according to the programme's policy the exclusion applied only to normal pregnancies. Four women who had suffered employment disability because of pregnancies, only one of which was normal, challenged the pregnancy exclusion. A three-judge District Court, albeit acknowledging that coverage of disabilities resulting from normal pregnancies would entail substantial additional expense, upheld the petitioners' contention that the exclusion violated the Equal Protection Clause on the grounds that increased cost could be accommodated through adjustments in the rate of employee contribution, the maximum benefits payable and the other variables affecting the solvency of the programme. In contrast, the Supreme Court upheld the constitutionality of the

[16]*Decreet houdende evenredige participatie op de arbeidsmarkt*, *Moniteur belge*, 26 July 2002, p. 33262.

[17]Art. 2 para. 2 of the Regulation of 30th January 2004 of the Flemish Government concerning the execution of the Decree of 8 May 2002 (*Besluit van de Vlaamse regering tot uitvoering van het decreet van 8 mei 2002 houdende evenredige participatie op de arbeidsmarkt wat betreft de beroepskeuzevoorlichting, beroepsopleiding, loopbaanbegeleiding en arbeidsbemiddeling*), *Moniteur belge*, 4 March 2004, p. 12050.

[18]417 US 484 (1974).

exclusion by indicating that the decision not to insure the risk of disability resulting from normal pregnancy did not constitute an invidious discrimination and that there was no evidence that it discriminated against any definable group or class in terms of the aggregate risk protection derived from the programme. The Court considered that the sole contention was the asserted under-inclusiveness of the programme's coverage, but the State was not obligated by the Equal Protection Clause to sacrifice the self-supporting nature of the programme by reducing the benefits payable for covered disabilities or by increasing the maximum employee contribution rate just to provide protection against another risk of disability, such as normal pregnancy. Although it is questionable whether the challenged scheme could properly be qualified as an affirmative action plan or merely a social benefit, the argument stands and is reflected in the design of the former plans that in this case the Court operated in favour of the majority of women (who would carry the burden of increased contributions), rather than enlarging the beneficiaries of a benevolent preferential regime for a smaller percentage of women (those delivering normally and suffering employment disability thereof).

3.1.3 How Useful Is the Policy for Beneficiaries? Stigma and Stereotyping

Stigma and stereotyping constitute a commonplace in affirmative action literature and apply equally to the remedial as well as the cultural rationale; however, in the former rationale the phenomenon is more relevant because the idea of compensation might more easily convey unfounded questions of group inferiority. Although stigma and stereotyping have interrelated sociological roots of prejudice and are often used indiscriminately, they are not identical. Stigma refers to social infamy, disgrace, or reproach attributed to people or groups either because of idiosyncratic characteristics they are presumed to carry or because of externalities associated with them. Stereotyping suggests that a certain category of people have the same characteristics which are normally considered negative. Normally stigma follows stereotyping, although the opposite direction is not to be excluded.

Affirmative action enthusiasts often invoke that the policy contributes to the elimination of social stigma by softening a *de facto* relationship of social submission and by strengthening the self-esteem of underrepresented groups (Yotopoulos-Marangopoulos 1998: 36–37). Accordingly, institutional acknowledgement of prior discrimination eases social biases and contributes to the elimination of actual or potential stereotype threats, especially in social environments where performance is a key factor, such as in academia or labour (Aronson et al. 1998). Further, it is reasonably suggested that when stereotypes result from social inequality, they typically persist under even seemingly neutral procedures of admissions or hiring, therefore the goal of equal treatment and decrease of stereotypes calls for some affirmative action, albeit some level of (unavoidable) perpetuation of stigma (Krishnamurthy and Edlin 2014). Empirical data show a benevolent impact of the fusion between members of dominant and affirmative action designated groups from the point of view of social psychology, when a critical mass of the latter is represented so as to prevent isolation and frustration (Truax et al. 1998).

Nonetheless, although an affirmative action plan generally improves participation statistics, it might result in secondary discrimination as a result of the coexistence of people with diverse standards of entry within the same environment. Consequently, it is not only the stereotypical stigma relating to undeserved entry, but also a generic stigma in relation to the (inherent) inability of the beneficiaries to be successful in a state of free social competition. Even when success by a woman or a member of a minority has been the outcome of hard work and is fully deserved, as psychologists Perloff and Bryant (2000) suggest, the stigma of preference will remain and haunt their academic or professional career. According to Van Alstyne, any governmental measure that lowers the criteria for a certain group constitutes a confession that the benefit would not otherwise be awarded to them and, therefore the message to society is that there are different levels of ability in each group (Van Alstyne 1979: 787). Consequently, failure to join the community on grounds of merit in a free social competition context is not due to external social circumstances, but mostly because of individual incompetence or inertness. If this is true, affirmative action policies do not only maintain stereotypes, but augment and diffuse them, through the institutional projection of reduced competence of certain social categories (Gutek 1982; Beer 1992; Loury 2001).

Given that most of the criteria for the designated groups, such as race or gender, are in principle inherent and immutable, there is a danger of perpetuating the stigma involved. If members of a group share the same idiosyncratic characteristics, which constitute an implicit precondition of affirmative action, any stereotype will have a domino effect on the totality of group membership. The result is: (a) those benefiting from affirmative action continue to suffer from (or start feeling) an institutionally originated inferiority syndrome, and (b) those not falling in the affirmative action categories continue to have (or start having) a strong bias against those benefiting. Even the strongest proponent of cultural diversity Will Kymlicka concedes that special entitlements for minority groups may well convey the message that these groups are outbid or outvoted on matters crucial to their survival as a cultural community. He suggests that equality of historically disadvantaged minority groups will only occur when, instead of subsidising their choices, special measures are set in place to correct a disadvantage that they have before anyone makes their choices. Thus, he refuses the practical utility of institutional compensation for past injustices insofar as it undermines membership in the broader social community (Kymlicka 1989: 182–205).

The issue of the psychological effect of affirmative action has sometimes been part of judicial reasoning. Although one might reasonably argue that stigma cannot operate as a relevant consideration of constitutional interpretation, because that way any benefit of a social character, such as those awarded to senior citizens or handicapped, would be legally vulnerable, still the argument is not deprived of normative value (Sunstein 1998: 320). Indeed, there has been a very extensive discussion on a judicial level before the US Supreme Court about the psychological side-effects of affirmative action. In the 1954 decision *Brown v. Board of Education*, the Court used stigmas as support for its holding that mandatory racial segregation in public schools is unconstitutional. Chief Justice Warren, famous for his liberal pro-rights predilection, made a very strong statement on the issue, to the effect that separating children in grade and high schools "from others of similar age and qualifications solely because of their race generates a feeling of inferiority as to their status in the community that may affect their hearts and minds in a way unlikely ever to be undone".[19]

In the landmark 1978 decision *Regents of the University of California v. Bakke*[20] the problem was whether affirmative action requirements for university admissions had any adverse effects upon the new students. It was suggested by members of the Court that the contested plan did not simply advance less qualified applicants but rather compensated applicants who were fully qualified to study for the educational disadvantages reasonably produced by state-fostered discrimination. The fact that, once admitted, these students should satisfy the same degree of requirements as regularly admitted students and their performance was evaluated by the same standards by which regularly admitted students were judged led those Justices to conclude that there was no reasonable basis for the Court to conclude that affirmative action students would be stigmatised as inferior. In this way *Bakke* introduced the, rather foggy in practice, distinction between "benign" and "invidious" racial preferences. In contrast, Justice Brennan's concurring opinion subtly noticed that both race and gender-based classifications have been inexcusably utilised to stereotype and stigmatise politically powerless segments of society. In his view, given that the line between honest and thoughtful appraisal of the effects of past discrimination and paternalistic stereotyping is not so clear and that a statute based on the latter is patently capable of stigmatising vulnerable groups, affirmative action policies create the same hazard of stigma, since they may promote separatism and reinforce the views of those who believe that members of minorities are inherently incapable of succeeding on their own.

This jurisprudence was essentially confirmed in the *Michigan Cases* where the majority of the Court took the view that academic diversity (not compensation for prior discrimination) serves to mitigate stereotypes because a mixed environment reasonably leads to better understanding amongst the students.[21] In contrast, it was stated in *Richmond v. Croson* (1989) that "classifications based on race carry a danger of stigmatic harm" and "unless they are strictly reserved for remedial settings, they may in fact promote notions of racial inferiority and lead to a politics of racial hostility".[22] Justice Antonin Scalia in his majority opinion in *Schuette v. Coalition to Defend Affirmative Action* (2014) made a most impressive in-depth

---

[19]*Brown v. Board of Education*, 347 US 483, 494 (1954).

[20]*Regents of the University of California v. Bakke*, 438 US 265, 357–358 (1978).

[21]*Gratz v. Bollinger*, 539 US 244 (2003) and *Grutter v. Bollinger*, 539 US 306 (2003).

[22]*Richmond v. Croson*, 488 US 469, 493 (1989).

analysis of potential psychological effects of affirmative action. He first reiterated Supreme Court's dicta against impermissible racial stereotypes that members of the same racial group, regardless of their age, education, economic status, or the community in which they live, think alike, share the same political interests, and will prefer the same candidates at the polls. He then went on to suggest that government action that classifies individuals on the basis of race is inherently suspect and carries the danger of perpetuating the very racial divisions the polity seeks to transcend and the Court should necessarily embark in "inquiries and categories dependent upon demeaning stereotypes, classifications of questionable constitutionality on their own terms".[23]

The European courts do not seem to be engaged in relevant considerations, probably because they might be considered to fall outside strict judicial deductive reasoning, as European judicial tradition suggests. In case 103/1983 the Spanish Constitutional Court ruled that Article 160.2 of the General Law on Social Security (*Ley General de la Seguridad Social*), which meant that the award of a pension to (male) widowers was dependent upon proof that they were unable to work (a clause not effective for female widows) on grounds of sex discrimination, speaking of "perpetuation of traditional biases between men and women" because of the implementation of positive measures.[24] Further, Advocate General Tesauro in his Opinion in *Kalanke* (1995), intimated these fears (interestingly, in a mere footnote) without, however, taking any strong position, by stating that there was in fact a tendency to assert that preferential treatment in favour of certain groups would end up increasing the feeling of inferiority vis-à-vis the majority, thus "triggering a definitive marginalisation of those in whose favour it is done within rigid social cages".[25]

The relationship between affirmative action and the creation or perpetuation of stereotypes can also be seen from the opposite point of view. In certain instances, reverse quotas were launched in order to prevent domination from a certain group which seems most probable to occupy the majority of the available positions. That was the case with the *Ivy League* Universities' admission policies in the US concerning Jews. The fact that only a small number of Jews were allowed to be admitted to these institutions as a result of a conscious reverse quota admission policy created a very strong social perception for Jews, therefore considered as persons of very high intelligence and potential. Although this image initially applied only to those admitted in these universities, there was a domino effect so that gradually a high intelligence profile was attributed to Jews collectively as a race (Cohen 2003: 125).

Surveys cannot provide safe evidence when it comes to stereotyping and stigma, given that the issue in question usually reflects unrevealed opinions. In relation to racial affirmative action, it seems that members of minorities are divided, whereas non-beneficiaries are normally in favour of affirmative action policies. This attitude

[23]572 US, Case No. 12–682 (2014).

[24]Tribunal Constitucional nº 103/1983, judgment of 22nd November 1983.

[25]Opinion of Advocate General Tesauro of 6 April 1995 in Case C-450/93, *Eckhard Kalanke v. Freie Hansestadt Bremen*, Rec. 1995, p. I-3051, para. 8, fn. 9.

is explicable if one considers three factors: first, due to wide ignorance about the policy, the results of surveys are significantly divergent depending on the actual question, e.g. if people are asked whether they are in favour of "affirmative action" and/or "positive discrimination"; people have a positive predilection towards the former and a negative towards the latter (Bell et al. 2000: 792). Second, the fear of potential or presumed adverse psychological effects upon members of the benefiting groups is present (Niemann and Dovidio 2005). Third, the feeling of guilt of the historically dominating groups for discrimination in the past at least verbally also plays a role (Steele 1998); it was not ancient history when in a survey in 1962, only 42 % of white people in the US responded that they should have equal chances to get a job as African-Americans (Anderson 2004: 275).

In relation to gender affirmative action, men are overwhelmingly favourable, clearly assuming that their dominant position in the field of employment is not endangered and intimating a strong cultural view of the position of women in society. Smith (2001: 194) gives an apt explanation in stating that modern reforms have sometimes been supported by men in part for reasons that have implicitly expressed and reinforced traditional notions of gender. Thus, male citizens sometimes seem to be endorsing these measures in the same spirit that leads them to send flowers on Mother's Day or sweets on Valentine's Day, whereas at the same time they remain essentially the same in all the areas most important to men's psyches and to the traditional gender division of labour. Despite supporting affirmative action however, white men seem to cast stigma upon the actual beneficiaries of the measures (Heilman et al. 1992; Heilman et al. 1996; Heilman et al. 1998). According to affirmative action enthusiasts, this is to be attributed to subconscious sexism and racism (Crosby 2004: 175–216).

On the other hand, despite some decline in enthusiasm, women still seem to maintain faith in this policy. In the International Women's Rights Action Watch report over the January 1997 meeting on affirmative action policies, Bond (1997) illustrated the frustration deriving from the implementation of the policy but also the hope invested in it. In her view, although successful affirmative action programmes may draw resentment and anger-backlash from those who perceive themselves to be losing opportunities because of group-based preferences and goals, this should not be allowed to stop the affirmative action efforts that remain a primary hope for elimination of discrimination in the foreseeable future as an essential instrument for achieving equality in fact. However, in Germany feminist organisations have opposed the launching of quotas in favour of women in political representation on the grounds of the unfavourable message conveyed on the status of women (Lemke 2001: 137), whereas in other parts of the world there are cases of "redesignation", following the terminology used by Sowell (2004: 8–13), i.e. disclaimers relating to eligibility as beneficiaries of affirmative action policies, either individually or *en bloc* by groups.

At any rate, the results of official surveys ought to be treated with caution, since they might be outcomes of a result-oriented survey strategy and in any case they cannot possibly cover elements relating to sociology or psychology but merely statistics. Two seemingly paradoxical elements show up in this respect, relating to incoherent responses and reverse approval.

In relation to the *incoherent responses* paradox, although there is very wide consensus on the actual aim of achieving substantive equality, public opinion seems to become divided the more the particular issue of affirmative action comes up: they are acceptable from a philosophical standpoint but not as an effective means of the redistribution of social benefits. There are two methodological explanations to this paradox and a likely substantive one. The methodological explanations are either that people do not exactly know what affirmative action stands for in practice or that people do not consider affirmative action as part of substantive equality policy. It seems that only directly involved parties possess sufficient knowledge of the policy since the vast majority of people merely have a vague idea of its desired results. Confusion or lack of awareness on the issue is also created by the incredibly extensive and contradictory political, philosophical and legal literature on the issue, which nevertheless does not extensively disseminate information on the actual policies addressed to underrepresented groups. Thus, in spite of the wide publicity of the relevant Supreme Court judgments in the US, people are not equipped with basic knowledge to effectively elaborate upon the issue. In light of this misapprehension, it is self-evident that statistical data may suffer from significant inaccuracies naturally impacting the conclusions that can be drawn thereof. The substantive explanation of the paradox lies with the -admittedly difficult to prove-assumption that people cannot overcome an inherent conservatism that keeps them from accepting the need for specific state measures benefiting those who have suffered discrimination in the past. Of course, an opposite assumption is also conceivable in the sense of an inherent reluctance to express disagreement with affirmative action policies in order to avoid false perceptions of association with discrimination ideas.

In relation to the *reverse approval* paradox, it appears that benefiting groups seem to be overall more skeptical than the majority of people who seem to be, in principle more positive, especially when it comes to policies favouring women as the underrepresented sex. A possible explanation to the second paradox is that members of the benefiting groups are seriously in fear of secondary discrimination, especially the stigma attached thereof, whereas members of the conceding groups do not seem to generally consider affirmative action plans as a serious threat to their long-standing dominance; this is particularly true of the attitude of men towards affirmative action plans favouring women in the employment arena.

3.1.4 Does the Policy Fulfil Its Potential? Restoring or Perpetuating Inequality

In the field of gender equality, the annual Global Gender Gap of the 2013 World Economic Forum Report,[26] assessing gender gaps in 136 countries on the basis of

[26]http://www3.weforum.org/docs/WEF_GenderGap_Report_2013.pdf (last accessed 31.12.2014).

economic participation and opportunity, educational attainment, health and survival and political empowerment shows that divergences between genders are very resilient, irrespective of the institutional tools used to achieve a proper equilibrium. The 2013 index features Nordic countries prominently, i.e. Iceland on top of equality standards for the fifth consecutive year, followed by Finland, Norway and Sweden, whereas Denmark ranks 8th, followed by other northern and central European states (Ireland 6th, Switzerland 9th, Belgium 11th, Netherlands 13th, Germany 14th, UK 18th, Austria 19th). From the northern American countries Canada ranks 20th, US 23rd; from Latin America Nicaragua ranks 10th, Cuba 15th, Ecuador 25th, Argentina 34th, whereas Brazil ranks 62nd; from African countries Lesotho ranks 16th, South Africa 17th, whereas Nigeria ranks 106th; from Asian countries the Philippines ranks 5th, whereas China ranks 69th, India ranks 101st and Malaysia 102nd; from the oceanic countries New Zealand ranks 7th and Australia 24th.

In the field of racial equality, the 2010 Migrant Integration Policy Index,[27] examining the *ex post* treatment provided for victims of discrimination in 37 countries, nevertheless with a very limited sample of countries outside the west, features Canada and the US on the top followed by Sweden, UK and Portugal. Overall in terms of inclusion policies, Nordic countries feature on the top (Sweden 1st, Finland 4th, Norway 7th), whereas Canada ranks 3rd and the US 9th.

According to the 2013 World Value Survey,[28] a global network of social scientists studying changing values and their impact on social and political life by measuring social attitudes of people in different countries, indicated that the countries with the highest proportion of intolerant people (i.e. people in a given country claiming that they do not want neighbors from other races as a matter of principle) were Jordan and India followed by Egypt, Saudi Arabia, Iran, Vietnam, Indonesia, South Korea. At the bottom of the list are United States, Canada, Brazil, Argentina, Colombia, Guatemala, Britain, Sweden, Norway, Latvia, Australia and New Zealand.

The results stemming from the above surveys are mixed. The clear result is that countries which extensively apply quotas, like India, Malaysia and Nigeria, do not always manage to achieve either better representation for underrepresented groups or an adequate level of social inclusion. It rather seems that a better record in substantive gender and race equality is observed by countries which neither extensively use affirmative action nor have constitutional provisions to that effect, but enjoy a very high overall level of social welfare, e.g. the Scandinavian countries. This result makes absolute sense. Affirmative action is merely a tool to achieve better results in formal representation; it does not guarantee a substantive improvement of the position of disadvantaged groups, nor does it operate effectively unless the broader context is favourable to the implementation of social

---

[27] http://www.mipex.eu/countries (last accessed 31.12.2014).

[28] http://www.worldvaluessurvey.org/wvs.jsp (last accessed 31.12.2014).

policies. From this viewpoint, rigid quotas might prove less effective than measures which are not as drastic but target the actual causes of discrimination encountered in each state.

The majority of measures enacted worldwide takes the form of quotas which, notwithstanding their strong façade, do not always produce their expected outcomes. Rigid end-quotas are *prima facie* the most suitable to achieve better representation ratios for women and minorities in light of the compensatory ratio of affirmative action. However, even rigid quotas (a) do not as such redress the causes that triggered the underrepresentation pathology, (b) compensate merely a very small percentage of members of groups having suffered discrimination in the past and (c) do not compensate for individuals who have *actually* suffered discrimination in the past. From this angle, rigid quotas may provide immediate but merely ephemeral results. Positive measures of an indirect effect, such as special educational programmes, are more suitable in principle but do not guarantee admission, appointment or promotion for women or minority candidates.

The example of the low presence of women in hierarchically higher workplace positions is rather illustrative: less than 15 % of Fortune 500 executive officer positions were held by women between 2009 and 2013, with a rather non-significant 1 % increase in between these years.[29] This actual inequality may be due to obvious or less obvious reasons. The obvious reasons could include: (a) limited labour availability of women (e.g. for overtime requested by the employer) due to the concurrent family obligations they assume which make them unattractive for such promotions; (b) social distrust for women's effectiveness with regard to positions of high responsibility; (c) manifest or latent employer preference for men, due to their reduced requirement of parental benefits. Less obvious reasons may include: (d) less spare time available for women, in order to further their skills and expert knowledge; and (e) the existence of work hierarchy and ethics structured around male standards. In light of the above, two sets of affirmative action plans could be launched: The first set would aim at radically diminishing statistical inequality, irrespective of its causes; such measures, mainly quotas, would be simpler to design and implement since they entail no further inquiry besides the observation of statistical imbalance itself. The second set would be aimed at the causes of underrepresentation by setting policies to treat each problem at its roots: (a) part-time, flexible and remote employment for women; (b) programmes of equal opportunity for access to employment, as well as the diffusion of information, wide enforcement mechanisms of labour laws and penalties for potential violations; (c) state coverage for the whole or most of the cost of parental benefits in order to ease the employers' discontent for having to subsidise workplace equality-oriented social policies; (d) establishment of a wide and effective network of public nurseries for children and infants, with longer opening hours; (e) launching in-work (within the working hours) and remote training sessions with the relevant cost paid by the

[29]http://www.catalyst.org/knowledge/statistical-overview-women-workplace (last accessed 31.12.2014).

state; (f) the redesign of the entire employment pyramid so as to equally accommodate the skills and availability of both sexes and meet the needs set by employees; and finally (g) the merging of employment posts where women are adequately represented in the posts where they are underrepresented. Evidently, the first set of conventional affirmative action policies would be impractical and ineffective. A radical policy, on the other hand, would suggest an overturn of the structures that have generated the dominance of a certain gender or race, structures which are quite resilient in time, as opposed to temporary measures establishing statistical but fragile balances.

In light of the above thoughts, it becomes apparent that the proportionality test assessing the constitutionality of an affirmative action plan, more precisely the suitability sub-test presupposes the identification and a good understanding of the real causes of underrepresentation of particular groups. A measure can only be suitable to achieve the envisaged purpose if it comes up against the true causes of underrepresentation. This is probably why in most legal systems there is a general distrust towards quotas or quotas by effect and a preference towards measures of indirect effect.

3.2 The Cultural Purpose: Diversity

In a broader context, diversity is a worldwide pursuit stemming from tolerance and multiculturalism. For some, cultural diversity is merely a legitimate goal; for others, such as Ingram (2000: 252–257), it is not an existentialist or philosophical issue but mostly one of social continuation, since it is incumbent for civilisations to absorb other cultures in order to adapt and survive.

The most composite theory on multiculturalism, linked with the perception of diversity and affirmative action, has been developed by Will Kymlicka, with reference to Canadian aboriginals. Kymlicka (1989, 1995) argues that orthodox liberalism has failed to accommodate the universal call for protection of group rights due to its inherent link to individualism (Raz 1994: 170; Fatouros 2001: 217; Bowen et al. 1998; Orfield and Kurlaender 2001). Diversity of the social structure has been gradually rising due to the interconnection of modern societies attributable to comfortable transportation and telecommunications, in conjunction with immigrant mobility around the world. In Kymlicka's view, to preserve this cultural diversity of both national minorities in multination states and of ethnic groups in multi-ethnic states, the necessary co-existence of many ethnicities requires a different approach of diversity and tolerance, ranging from addressing the psychological attitude of each individual towards other people and societal groups, to that of the institutions. He stresses the example of Canada where government policy and programmes on immigration, land claims, self-government, language and customs provide an initial response to the changing composition of society.

In the context of affirmative action theory, especially in the US, "diversity" constitutes a technical term implying the legitimate interest in ensuring that, in every segment of human interaction, whether social, political or academic, a critical mass of group representation should exist so that the societal body can become richer and more representative. In this way, members of the underrepresented groups should not be afraid that, when expressing their opinions, they might become victims of stereotypical treatment and left isolated, as that would certainly jeopardise their future uninterrupted social interaction.[30]

Although diversity is closely linked to the formal concept of multiculturalism, in legal terms it also embraces the active expression of differentiation through participation. In this meaning, diversity is also expressed in national constitutions, such as the 1996 Constitution of the Republic of South Africa, which aspires to bury, once and for all, the country's disgraceful apartheid past by declaring in its Preamble that "South Africa belongs to all who live in it, united in our diversity". In this process-oriented view, diversity produces directly or indirectly beneficial results for all participants in the social struggle. Thus, members of the benefiting groups draw direct earnings from their participation in the schemes (Card and Krueger 2005); members of the non-benefiting groups have indirect positive results because of their exposure to various non-familiar incentives that raise their social awareness and enrich their cultural background; and, finally, society as a whole collectively benefits from the creation of a productive environment of human variety, within which every different group contributes according to their own experience and knowledge. Arguing in favour of diversity as an affirmative action goal Brown (1998: 333, 337) suggests that since we are all full of prejudice that we cannot eliminate, because it is more or less subconscious, we should pursue knowledge in a way that a variety of different prejudices are struggling in order to create a balanced environment of a "diversity" of rival theories: "pluralism for the sake of epistemology".

It is particularly interesting to see the different historical backgrounds to the demand for diversity. In the US, diversity reflects the anxiety to develop a homogeneous society through the establishment of actual equality. The fact that diversity is mostly related to race is easily explicable given the discrimination institutionally imposed upon minorities. Race in the US has been the axis around which the effort to establish a national identity revolves. Further, diversity in the US context was rather a fallback position against the background of increasing concerns raised against purely remedial approaches. On the other hand, although in Europe race has not traditionally been a point of acute dispute, due to the rise and dominance of the idea of the national state, the co-existence of various nations in the European Union renders diversity a defense mechanism to maintain a level of national identity. Therefore, it is not a surprise that, by way of contrast to the US where diversity is a notion shaped by case-law, in the EU the Treaty establishing the European Community made direct reference to this notion stipulating that "the Community shall contribute to the flowering of the cultures of the Member States while respecting their national and regional diversity and at the same time bringing

---

[30]*Grutter v. Bollinger*, 539 US 306 (2003).

the common cultural heritage to the fore" (Article 167 of the Treaty on the functioning of the EU, ex-Article 151 para. 1 of the Treaty of the European Communities). Thus, diversity in Europe reflects the antithesis inherent in a free market transnational union: while each nation struggles to maintain its national identity (not an easy task in a very powerful supra-national community that naturally tends to expand its fields of competence), at the same time societies must become more tolerant towards outside intrusions; otherwise, free movement becomes impossible.

The different views of diversity from the two sides of the Atlantic become apparent in the very field where affirmative action has been mostly applicable in the US, namely higher education. The Treaty on European Union stipulated in Article 126 para. 1 that "the Community shall contribute to the development of quality education by encouraging cooperation between Member States and, if necessary, by supporting and supplementing their action, while fully respecting the responsibility of the Member States for the content of teaching and the organisation of education systems and their cultural and linguistic diversity" (later Article 165 para. 1 of the Treaty on the Functioning of the European Union). The recognition of the auxiliary competence of the Union in the particular area,[31] in conjunction with the explicit recognition of the particularities of each Member State rendered education a *de jure* field of state regulation. However, secondary union law, particularly *Directive 2005/36*,[32] treated the issue of the harmonisation of academic legislation by placing emphasis not upon the state's sovereign competence but mostly upon the guarantee of freedom of the establishment of institutions and the academic qualifications stemming thereof, a component clearly linked to the fundamental Union freedoms. This reflects the conflicting rationales in the division of competence in the EU: although there are clearly areas akin to state sovereignty, there are hardly any areas that are entirely devoid of any economic interest. The situation becomes even more complex given the movement of Europe towards a political union, an ambition far beyond its original post-war concept. However, the European Union still seems to be haunted by the original intent of its framers as an economically-oriented community, whereby basic free market liberties ought to be respected almost at any cost. Thus, in the most important judgment on academic diversity *Valentina Neri v. European School of Economics*,[33] the Court of Justice of the European Union essentially held that the community right of establishment supersedes education as a matter of public interest and, accordingly, cultural diversity does not constitute a goal of such importance that it supersedes fundamental community rights. It is apparent that diversity operated in the US as a cohesion mechanism aiming at

[31]Somewhat reinforced through Title II, Article 9 of the Treaty on the Functioning of the European Union providing that "in defining and implementing its policies and actions, the Union shall take into account requirements linked to the promotion of [...] a high level of education and training".

[32]EE L 255 of 30th September 2005, p. 22. This Directive replaced Directive 89/48EE L 19 of 24th January 1989, p. 16.

[33]CJEU Judgment of 13th November 2003, Case C-153/02, *Valentina Neri v. European School of Economics (ESE Insight World Education System Ltd)*, Rec. 2003, I-13555.

melting identities into a single national pot, whereas in Europe it has served the conflicting ideals of national identity and tolerance, although the gradual expansion of EU competences until recently seemed to limit the scope for diversity. In the context of affirmative action, diversity operates in the US also as a surrogate to remedial measures, while in Europe it does not constitute a distinct rationale for affirmative action but is mostly embedded in separation of powers and fundamental rights controversies.[34]

A last word needs to be said on this issue. There are certain fields of human interaction that call for further diversity—particularly where a difference of perceptions is naturally desired, such as in education or dissemination of information. This is why in such fields, in the US, the remedial purpose is in total decline, whereas the cultural purpose advances significantly. In education, originally the opinion of Justice Powell in Supreme Court *Bakke* and later the Michigan admission policies decisions described diversity as an added value to the academic process, whereas in broadcasting the Court stated as early as 1945 that minority ownership policies serve an important governmental objective—not because they provide a remedy for victims of demonstrable discrimination in the media, but rather because this field ought to be regulated in light of the rights of the viewing and listening audience and that the widest possible dissemination of information from diverse and antagonistic sources is essential to public welfare.[35]

The diversity doctrine is to some extent founded upon two premises: the *anthropological* premise entails that all members of a group, mostly an underrepresented one, carry the same idiosyncratic features that they will contribute to the body they participate in; the *sociological* premise presumes, in turn, that the mere participation of different groups within a body will by itself make it diverse.

3.2.1 The Anthropological Premise: Do All Group Members Carry the Same Identity?

Entitativity and similarity of group membership constitute salient features of sociology and social psychology that go far beyond the purpose of the present analysis. The former studies the degree and mode by which groups are perceived as having the nature of an entity, whereas the latter addresses the issue of the arguably common characteristics of the members of any specific group in goals, beliefs and behaviour. An element of similarity exists by definition in order to trigger entitativity (e.g. race, religion, ethnicity, family liaison, sports club), but groups may in fact share no further characteristics (Crump et al. 2009). However, according to the prevailing literature, the basic perception of a group lies with the common core

[34]Further case law references to US and EU case law, *infra*, 4.1.1 and 4.2.1 respectively.

[35]*Associated Press v. United States*, 326 US 1, 20 1945; *Metro Broadcasting, Inc. v. Federal Communications Commission* 497 US 547, 549 (1990).

similarity that broadly relates to a prototype composition (Campbell 1958; Haslam et al. 1994). Limited similarity, nevertheless, might connote that society at large assumes that common features are held by the group, even if these features do not largely exist. Both entitativity and similarity are necessary components of a debate on stereotyping since this pathology is produced exactly on the basis of common properties of membership and the social perception on the constitution and cohesion of a group.

If diversity does indeed constitute a compelling public interest, then this naturally intimates the underlying idea that these individuals have a single common characteristic and, potentially, share some basic characteristics peculiar to their group. On the other hand, the critical mass prerequisite, especially as applied in the US Supreme Court case-law concerning university admissions, suggests that different views within the designated groups do exist and proper institutional care is taken to allow for the expression of any diverging views. However, the idea that cultural difference follows race or sex is a notion that is rather vulnerable, if not dangerous, since it is exactly this grouping that constitutes, according to Ingram (2000: 42–43), the core of racism or sexism. Although long-term suppression may indeed bring people of a group together, it does not necessarily imply that the group is homogeneous in its constituent elements. The premise is clearly unfounded and goes against the very essence of the perception that affirmative action aspires to eliminate. According to the famous jurist and Posner (1974: 12), the use of a racial characteristic to establish a presumption that the individual also possesses other, and socially relevant, characteristics, exemplifies, encourages, and legitimises the mode of thought and behavior that underlies most prejudice and bigotry in modern US.

The patently false perception of a group's consolidated opinion is even more evident in two different circumstances (albeit circumstances which are linked to the essence of democracy): in political representation and in radio/television licensing. In the former case, clearly the interests within the same gender or race by definition vary significantly. This was a ground upon which the US Supreme Court discarded a reapportionment plan to establish minority-ruled electoral districts, by explicitly stating in *Miller v. Johnson* (1995)[36] that while redistricting usually implicates a political calculation in which various interests compete for recognition, it does not follow that individuals of the same race share a single political interest. In the latter case, the entrepreneurial nature of broadcasting has diluted the potential added value of having preferential treatment for minority-controlled channels. In *Metro Broadcasting, Inc. v. Federal Communications Commission* (1995),[37] Justice Brennan, writing the majority opinion, tried to establish a fine balance so as to afford support to the constitutionality of the Federal Communications Commission's preferential policies for minorities. He rejected the argument that expanded minority ownership and broadcaster diversity rest on impermissible stereotyping on the grounds that: (a) it is not assumed that in every case minority ownership and

[36] 515 US 900 (1995).

[37] 497 US 547.

management will lead to more minority-oriented programming or to the expression of a discrete 'minority viewpoint' on the airwaves given that members of a particular minority group do not necessarily share some cohesive, collective viewpoint; and (b) not all programming that appeals to minority audiences can be labeled "minority programming" or programming that might be described as "minority" may not appeal to non-minorities. Although, in this view, admittedly there was no iron-clad guarantee that each minority owner will contribute to diversity, Justice Brennan thought reasonable that a broadcasting industry with representative minority participation would produce more variation and diversity than one whose ownership is drawn from a single racially and ethnically homogeneous group, thus resulting "in the aggregate, … in greater broadcast diversity".

3.2.2 The Sociological Premise: Does Participation Promote Group Interests?

The idea that participation of different groups within a body will by itself make it diverse renders diversity a rather formalistic goal. Accordingly, it is mostly conceived as a means to formally bring together various bodies and not as a substantive principle requiring true expression of the various social groups. By assimilating the goal with the means, the doctrine becomes rather circular in its argumentation: instead of the goal legitimising the means, the inverse is accepted. To achieve genuine diversity, it is necessary that the members of groups participating in a body, irrespective of how proportionate this representation is, contribute their own experience and social understanding. In other words, the essence of diversity is not accomplished if affirmative action beneficiaries do not themselves carry the typical characteristics of their respective groups. However, the idea that the more women in party politics or more minority members in public procurement would result in better substantive representation for them is based on a logical leap. It is very often the case, that individual beneficiaries of affirmative action plans are either unrepresentative of their group or, after their accession to a collective body, they adapt their behaviour so as to melt within the *esprit de corps* in order to avoid the accusation that their success was not merited.

Unlike Europe, where the affirmative action emphasis is placed upon gender representation and women do seem to apply gender solidarity criteria in their decision-making (Maier and Klausen 2001: 11–12), in the US and elsewhere where race is the main criterion of preference, evidence shows that on many occasions affirmative action beneficiaries do not render race conscious decisions. Justice Clarence Thomas of the US Supreme Court (second black judge to be appointed in the history of the Court after Justice Thurgood Marshall) constitutes the most vivid illustration in this respect. After having graduated from Yale Law School as an affirmative action entry, he was appointed to the Court by President Bush and became the most active opponent of this policy. It was exactly his views on the matter that led to a fierce split of the Congress when called to give its consent for his appointment (Dworkin 1991). Justice Thomas in 2003 *Grutter v. Bollinger* effectively tried to demolish the concept of diversity as a compelling public interest by using rather questionable language to assimilate it with "aesthetics" and "racial balancing" rather than substance and real equality respectively. In his view, diversity is more a fashionable catchphrase than a useful term in that the Law School wanted to have a certain appearance "from the shape of the desks and tables in its classrooms to the colour of the students sitting at them". He claimed that a distinction between unique educational benefits based on racial aesthetics and race for its own sake was purely sophistic, given that classroom aesthetics yields educational benefits, racially discriminatory admissions policies are required to achieve the right racial mix, and therefore the policies are required to achieve the educational benefits. And all that by improving "marginally the education it offers without sacrificing too much of its exclusivity and elite status".[38]

From this viewpoint, the goal of essential diversity would be better served if a member of the dominant group, supporting minority rights, was selected instead of a member of the minority group who would, nevertheless, be unfavourable against his/her own race or sex. As Circuit Judge Jerry Smith put it in *Hopwood v. State of Texas*, to believe that a person's race controls his point of view is exactly to stereotype him. The judge went on to make a virtual comparison of the possible *in concreto* effects of the affirmative action minority selection. In that case, Hopwood, a Caucasian applicant omitted in order for the less qualified affirmative action minority members to enter the University of Texas, was at the time of litigation thirty-two years old, the wife of a member of the Armed Forces stationed in San Antonio and raising a severely handicapped child whose presence in academia, according to the Judge, would bring a different perspective to the law school; thus, the school "might consider this an advantage to her in the application process, or it could decide that her family situation would be too much of a burden on her academic performance".[39]

In other words, if the main target of an affirmative action policy is to allow preferences for individuals who due to their group identity have failed to follow the patterns of evolution of civil society in terms of education or employment, the scheme is inherently deficient. In societies where wide class or racial inequalities exist, the actual beneficiaries of affirmative action policies will be those who have decided to be detached from their fellow community members and follow an individual path which melts into the dominant social trends. Those left behind, either as a matter of conscience/principle or as a matter of limited awareness, will remain outside the selection process for preferential treatment, ultimately irrespective of race/gender/minority status (Nnoli 1996: 235–236, with reference to Nigeria).

This point clearly illustrates the inherent deficiencies of institutional instruments that purport to establish substantive equality: they are all formal, for they

[38] 539 US 306, 354–356 (2003).

[39] 84 F.3d 720 (5th Cir 1996), fn. 4.

presuppose segmentation of society and, within this segmentation, certain generic criteria of distinction are selected which do not actually secure the expression of differentiation. As Cohen (2003, 37–40) put it, diversity is merely a "euphemism" to promote an easier acceptance of affirmative action since, irrespective of the application of the policy, the big universities normally admit incoming students with the same (rather elitist) characteristics irrespective of their race. Consistent with this, the call for diversity can easily be bypassed either because it is profitable nominally to use the members of the underrepresented groups or because it is genuinely difficult to find such members. This has been the case in the US with the mandatory sub-contracting of public procurement contracts to minority ownership companies or in Europe with the mandatory female representation in political parties' candidate lists. In either case, the affirmative action does not fulfil its essential profoundly cultural purpose, but becomes a mere façade resulting in a purely superficial equilibrium with negative long-term consequences.

All in all, diversity in the context of affirmative action carries specific characteristics that distance the concept from its original sociological roots. In that sense, diversity is a quality *per se*, following that it ought to apply in every field of human interaction as an ethical component. In the context of affirmative action however, not all fields of activity incorporate the call for diversity with equal intensity; it is most prominent in those fields where there is an expectation for reciprocal gain for both the beneficiaries of an affirmative action policy and the institution as a whole as well as, in turn, of all those participating in it. The latter gain is particularly evident when cultural disparity between members is desirable because it improves either the *process* itself, such as in higher education, where cultural interaction is part of its pedagogical function, or the *outcome* of the process, such as trial by jury, which by definition aspires to infuse judicial decision-making with the representative public sentiment. In the latter case, the civil right to receive a fair trial conflicts with the political right to participate with a view to ensuring a proper balance so as to guarantee that the defendant is treated fairly and objectively. Thus, diversity in this field goes further than simply securing impartiality, which relates to the members of the deciding body individually and requires a fair representation in collective terms. Jury diversity becomes all the more important if one considers that, unlike judges, jurors do not have a command of the law (which is of course considered a positive aspect of the trial by jury system) and do not enjoy extensive functional and organic independence that would allow them to reach a decision deprived of any physical or psychological pressure. In any case, it is self-evident that any form of jury selection, including random selection, may conceivably produce a composition with either positive or negative predisposition to the class, race or gender of a defendant. Even in the US legal system, where the parties in the litigation do have a say in the jury selection by discarding a certain number of members at their discretion, which has created a whole industry in the field, still the pattern is not deprived of the systemic asymmetries that may produce biased jury compositions.

Irrespective of whether diversity operates as process or result-oriented, the crucial question remains concerning the transposition of a strongly theoretical concept to reality. In other words, what is the level of critical mass or representation required in order to satisfy the diversity test and, conversely, what is the threshold beyond which diversity conflicts with other constitutional values and, especially, equality itself. These limits are certainly unclear; they may conceivably fluctuate from mere participation, to critical mass or proportionate (to the overall or field population) representation. With the reservations already set out in this section, when diversity relates to the process, a *critical mass* that would allow free expression without the fear of isolation and with a view that class views are heard effectively seems reasonable and sufficient. On the other hand, when diversity is result-oriented proportionate representation seems appropriate.

3.3 The Societal Purpose: Social Inclusion and Cohesion

Affirmative action's societal objective suggests that the policy operates towards inclusion into the social thread of disadvantaged groups and altogether contributes to social cohesion. It is distinct from the cultural purpose of diversity in that it embraces a much broader aspiration for the society as a whole, whereas diversity basically aims to improve the experience within the particular environment it applies (e.g. academic). The societal rationale has been used in a variety of forms outside Europe and America, mostly in Nigeria, India and Malaysia as an—eventually unsuccessful—means to bring together the very heterogeneous racial and ethnic mix (Sowell 2004: 177–178; Government of Malaysia 1996: 69). In the domain of European Union, the broader issue of non-discrimination on the basis of gender has gradually become a key feature of the social policy agenda to safeguard and promote social inclusion (Stratigaki 2012, 169–186).

The societal goal, in principle, supersedes both the remedial and the cultural rationale. In relation to the former, the societal purpose is wider since even a rich black man or a successful female employee or politician can still be the victim of bias due to their race or gender respectively. In relation to the latter, the societal purpose goes further insofar as, by definition, inclusion and cohesion are not tantamount to participation; therefore, unlike diversity, they are not bound to particular fields of human interaction, such as education, attribution of justice or political participation. Prejudice and the stereotypes resulting thereof, may be detected more strongly in some human activities than in others, but the wide-ranging horizontal domino effects that they generate, call for corresponding horizontal positive state intervention.

From this viewpoint, affirmative action policies seem to fit with the contemporary theory of "inclusive institutions", as opposed to "extractive institutions", introduced by Acemoglu and Robinson (2012), MIT and Harvard Professors respectively. Their theory, which attributes great emphasis on the role of institutions in the well-functioning, economic growth and prosperity of societies worldwide, suggests that institutions can be either inclusive in political terms (i.e. encouraging pluralism through large-scale participation at every level, allocating state resources more evenly, and establishing the rule of law and constitutional constraints upon the executive and the legislature) and/or in economic terms (i.e. access to education and opportunities for everyone, guarantee of property rights, sufficient regulation of the free market to secure quality provision of services and lower entry barriers for new businesses). On the contrary, extractive political institutions tend to result in the accumulation of political power in the hands of oligarchies without operation of proper checks and balances, while extractive economic institutions consist of regulations which set high barriers to entry for those outside the existing market structure and cultivate serious divergences in equality of opportunities. Affirmative action, especially in the light of its goal towards social inclusion, doctrinally approaches the inclusive institution since by definition it tends to favour wider access to fundamental services (mostly higher education), participation and representation. Thus, affirmative action policies aiming at social inclusion eventually result in inclusive institutions for social cohesion.

The societal purpose may apply directly in favour of vulnerable social groups, such as families with many children, handicapped individuals, low-income persons or families, without necessarily any evidence of past discrimination or even underrepresentation. From this viewpoint, social inclusion and tolerance may prove to be a wider state aim or even a condition of survival, particularly in multi-racial countries. Thus affirmative action based on societal purposes may conceivably go beyond the boundaries of equality or even beyond a human rights doctrine altogether, a doctrine which has constituted its natural *locus* of constitutional acknowledgment, and become a stand-alone, genuine constitutional mandate towards state policy in order to deepen and strengthen democracy.

A variation of the societal goal of affirmative action is also traced in the "social emergency" theory. As a fallback position, after having altogether rejected the role of affirmative action as a means of compensation for past discrimination, Justice Antonin Scalia of the US Supreme Court expressed the view that a compelling public interest is to be found solely in cases of social emergencies. In *Richmond v. Croson*,[40] the appellant city adopted a Minority Business Utilisation Plan requiring prime contractors which had been awarded city construction contracts, to subcontract at least 30 % of the dollar amount of each contract to one or more minority business enterprises, which the plan defined as to include a business from anywhere in the country, at least 51 % of which is owned and controlled by black, Spanish-speaking, Oriental, Indian, Eskimo, or Aleut citizens. Although the Plan declared that it was "remedial" in nature, it was adopted after a public hearing during which no direct evidence was presented that the city had exerted discrimination on the basis of race in awarding contracts or that its prime contractors had discriminated against minority subcontractors. In a 6–3 decision, the Supreme Court upheld the Court of Appeal's ruling deciding that the city's plan violated both elements of the applicable strict scrutiny test; in particular, it was not justified by a compelling governmental interest, since the record revealed no prior discrimination by the city itself in awarding contracts, and the 30 % set-aside was not narrowly

[40] 488 US 469 (1989).

tailored to accomplish a remedial purpose. Concurring with the majority and building upon prior judicial dicta[41] and doctrinal theses (Bickel 1975), Justice Scalia took the view that the difficulty of overcoming the effects of past discrimination is as nothing compared with the difficulty of eradicating from the society the source of those effects, thus a solution to the first problem that aggravates the second is no solution at all. In the light of this presumption, he acknowledges that only a social emergency rising to the level of imminent danger to life and limb (for example, a prison race riot calling for temporary segregation of inmates) could justify an exception to the "colourblind" Constitution.

This "social emergency" theory, as conceived by Justice Scalia would, however, mostly justify discriminatory practices rather than allow for institutional affirmative action, although Scalia would most probably respond that no distinction is possible between the two. Anyhow, this theory has not enjoyed a diffuse effect across the Court's case-law both in principle, as to the question of whether only a social emergency might justify affirmative action policies, and in practice, since no authority has ever invoked such exceptional circumstances to substantiate such a policy. Obviously if such a theory was to be widely acknowledged it would result in a very significant shrinking of the potential spectrum of the policy with only very few marginal cases being suitable for such action.

The societal objectives of affirmative action are not altogether devoid of serious concerns. Obviously, the level of counter-argumentation varies significantly on the basis of whether equality of opportunities or equality of outcomes is the aspired end. This is so because the latter is in essence self-legitimised, since it is mostly goal-oriented and its success can be quantified, therefore ignoring potential side effects for non-beneficiaries and for society as a whole. By way of contrast, equality of opportunities could lead to the introduction of a great variety of affirmative action measures; its assessment is, in principle, qualitative and basically constitutes a variation of a cost-benefit analysis among multiple variables both individual and collective. At any rate, when it comes to positive state intervention or measures deeply intruding into the essence of human interaction, such as in the distribution of social goods, the evaluation entails a multidisciplinary and complex approach. In this light, there are, basically, two objections in relation to the expediency of affirmative action vis-à-vis societal purposes: state paternalism and social division.

3.3.1 State Intervention in Society. Paternalism and Self-corrective Function

Affirmative action by definition tends to regulate social relations by setting a starting or end point for members of social groups. From this viewpoint, affirmative

[41] *Lee, Commissioner of Corrections in Alabama v. Washington* 390 US 333 (1968); *Plessy v. Ferguson* 163 US 537 (1896).

action, first, constitutes a policy that presupposes the existence of an entrenched irrational bias vis-à-vis social competition based on merit, thus the state must intervene to set (in fact *reset*) the basic rules of human interaction. Second, while setting these rules, the state classifies people into groups, irrespective of their desire to be part of them, especially when it comes to vulnerable groups, contrary to liberal societies' claim for human self-determination and autonomy. Even when opt-out mechanisms exist, entitativity seems to stem as a matter of institutional imposition that connotes a specific message of social grouping.

A liberal theory critique of affirmative action would suggest that the policy ignores society's self-corrective mechanisms, including democracy itself, which allow people to live together in a state of basic freedom. The more interventionist the state becomes, the more concessions to liberty may emerge. At a first level, the institutional establishment of benefiting categories is *de lege* tantamount to unnecessary and detrimental paternalism. According to this liberal view, state intervention should be limited to guaranteeing a state of liberty to overcome deficiencies on the state of nature, and society should be generally left to self-regulate based on the relative power of social actors: the balance of social powers in each era merely constitutes, therefore, a natural social pendulum that need not be externally interrupted. Only neutral, or close to neutral, state institutions should exert influence over society causing the least possible adverse effects to the natural coexistence within the community. In this architecture, the role of the state is simply to set up and passively maintain the conditions within which all groups of the social thread may develop, without preventing anyone and reversely, without giving priority to anyone. Thus, it suffices that the state abstains from interference with traditional civil liberties, without employing positive action in order to set standards imposing social or political balance.

Accordingly, no quotas in favour of women are allowed in candidate lists, since political parties, which by definition wish to render their political "product" attractive, will necessarily include an appropriate number of women on their lists because not only have the latter proven their worldwide political success but also because they constitute at least half of the electorate. In this view, if a political party cannot comprehend the added value of including women in party lists, it is society itself that will intervene in a self-regulating manner, initially punishing this electoral policy and then encouraging parties to include a larger number of female candidates. Or, if a woman cannot understand her interests in voting a candidate of the same gender, it is not the role of the state to impose such a perception. As Offe (2001: 50) points out, the underlying claim is that female voters are blinded (by traditions, culture, irrational preferences) to their 'true' interests and, hence, they must be encouraged and educated to come to a better understanding of their interests, and giving them a representational 'head start' is a way to do so.

Respectively, no quota is required in favour of racial minorities for university entry, since eventually an equilibrium will be reached as the market will assess the relative competence of any university graduate, irrespective of their classification as affirmative action beneficiaries or not. Although a university degree represents standard academic qualifications, its relative worth is determined also according to secondary variables (such as grading), which broadly determines its appeal to the market. At a second level, problems are also caused by the forced categorisation of individuals into groups. Even when someone belonging to the designated groups, e.g. a minority applicant for university admission has a chance to waive his/her privilege, mere identification with a *benefited* social group might produce secondary discrimination even against individuals who explicitly wish to dissociate themselves from the potential beneficiaries as a matter of personal choice. Justice Clarence Thomas agreed on this point in his concurring opinion in 1995 *Adarand Constructors v. Pena*, when stating that from a constitutional law point of view it was irrelevant whether racial classifications are drawn by those who wish to oppress a race or by those who have a sincere desire to help those thought to be disadvantaged, in that paternalism that appears to lie at the heart of set-aside programmes in public works sub-contracting was "at war with the principle of inherent equality that underlies and infuses our Constitution".[42]

In view of the liberal theory, this is, nevertheless, a major systemic fault: people are deprived of their fundamental right of self-determination and autonomy. In a sense, it is equally unethical and unconstitutional to directly discriminate against an individual because of his race, sex or religion and to prohibit someone from the free choice to abstain from any social classification and to *enforce* social and, in turn, institutional assimilation. Reversely, even when people are left free to declare their race and/or origin, the mere existence of affirmative action policies seems to exercise a significant influence upon them. In 1960s in the official US census, those self-classified as Native Americans at the age of 15–19 were 50,000; in the 1980 those self-classified as Native Americans at the age of 35–39 were 80,000. Given that, naturally, immigration could not have been the cause, the logically impossible 60 % increase was at least partly due to the implementation, in the meantime, of affirmative action policies especially for this racial minority (Sowell 2004: 8–9), without ignoring other factors, such as more extensive census coverage, improved literacy of Native Americans and improved attitudes towards completing censuses.

Nonetheless, the argument based on paternalism has certain deficiencies based mostly on grounds stemming from humanities and economic literature. At first, it largely trusts the ability of societies to be self-corrective without the state's regulatory intervention and overlooks the perplex relationship between law and society and the pedagogical role of the former in shaping a rational and balanced community: it is exactly by legal coercion that discrimination regimes have been usually perpetuated through slavery, apartheid, segregation and limited voting rights. Since regulation itself carries a significant portion of blame for the establishment and perpetuation of inequalities within societies, in a way it seems appropriate, reasonable and ethical for regulation to intervene to restore what has been created (at least partly) because of it. From this viewpoint, deregulation at a certain point in time with its existing social balance, would essentially be tantamount to an institutionally mandated perpetuation of this balance in non-institutional ways. As Dahl

[42]515 US 200 (1995).

(1983: 42–43) explains, organised pluralism is a stabilising force that is highly conservative towards innovative structural change since each of the major organised forces in a country prevents the others from making changes that might seriously damage its interests, therefore the desired equilibrium is not achieved.

On the other hand, if underrepresentation is caused predominantly by gradual social dominance, the situation might become more complex. In most cases, one cannot really discern between the above two situations; the source of discrimination is an amalgamation of the two, since as a matter of historical sequence and irrespective of the level of state intervention, social relationships by definition are not developed in a state of equality. There are far too many externalities where coercion is used by dominant social actors against parties, whose individual or collective bargaining power is very weak. This is particularly true for example in employment relationships, where in principle there is one powerful and decisive party, i.e. the employer, and a party in need, i.e. the employee, so that a lack of regulation is tantamount to the award of *de facto* dominant power to the former. This happens because the employer does not always decide on the basis of merit (which by definition will secure better production efficiency) but also applies other non-merit related considerations. Thus, the employer may prefer a less capable man to a more capable woman, thinking of an actual or potential pregnancy, or a less capable white person to a more capable black person to avoid potential stereotyping on the part of the clientele. For this reason, total self-regulation is neither possible nor suitable.

The paternalist argument seems to borrow the theoretical foundation of market competition and falsely transplant it into social relationships. Apart from the obvious precondition that competition requires a sufficient level of external monitoring and intervention so as to, actually, operate freely, the market economy is not an end in itself, but caters to the interests of one body, the consumers, in favour of which it operates. Conversely, social relationships are developed within society and aim to serving its members and not any third party. Furthermore, the emphasis on social self-correction clearly underestimates the human rights doctrine whereby restrictions are set in place exactly to diminish the potential imposition of the majority. After all, a response of a liberal critique would emphasise that eventually affirmative action is indeed embodied in society's self-corrective mechanisms when, for instance, race-sensitive admissions policy comes not as a result of state coercion, but rather because of the relevant determination reached by the university bodies because of the compelling arguments associated with diversity and improvement of the academic experience.

3.3.2 Grouping Society: Promoting Actual Inclusion or Further Division?

The argument that institutional encouragement for disadvantaged groups produces social inclusion and cohesion is not self-evident. An affirmative action skeptic would suggest exactly the opposite: because of the acute effects of these measures on peoples' lives, instead of social peace (which is eventually the basic end of *any* institutional tool), they may produce social anxiety and division.

Anxiety might originate both on a personal and group level. On a personal level, an understandable discomfort could be caused on afflicted individuals, e.g. persons who were rejected because of quotas: affirmative action "engender*[s]* attitudes of superiority or, alternatively, provoke*[s]* resentment among those who believe that they have been wronged by the government's use of race" (Justice Clarence Thomas in *Adarand Constructors v. Pena*, 1995).[43] In 2006, there were very extensive riots in New Delhi, Kolkata and Mumbai and more than 100 medical students went on a hunger strike in Delhi's All India Institute of Medical Sciences when the Government announced that a Bill would be introduced to the national Parliament raising the university admission reserved quotas from 22.5 to 49.5 % of overall admissions (Gaur 2007: 109).

As for the benefited groups not all members welcome the effects of such policies. It is worth noting that even activists from such groups are, at times, against affirmative action; some of them choose to opt out from respective benefits where possible. The reason is that affirmative action may turn out to be a lose-lose situation for qualified candidates. If they succeed, they will be accompanied by the stigma of privileged success, even if this was well deserved. If they fail, the stigma will turn to incompetence; failing as a regular candidate causes more or less pain but may not be an unsurprising outcome; failing as a privileged candidate connotes the idea of total worthlessness.

On a group level, three different cases with differing levels of intensity can be discerned. The first and obvious case is the non-benefited groups. The second case is subdivisions of the benefiting groups. If the criterion to award privilege is, for instance, race, separate minorities might—reasonably or unreasonably—argue that they should be treated more favourably due to the level of past discrimination. This might be the case in multicultural societies, where affirmative action normally applies negatively, thus merely excluding the historically dominant race. This is the case in the US with policies favouring all "non-Caucasian", including Afro-Americans, Hispanics, Native Americans and immigrants from central and eastern Asia etc. Obviously, the more all-embracing the affirmative action criterion is, the less room for preference remains with each designated group. This is why the strategy of "affirmative action within affirmative action" has been developed in order to render the system more just and expedient in relation to all potential beneficiaries. The third case is the accumulation of affirmative action policies. When multiple such policies apply, there might be tension amongst the respective designated groups in relation to the manner and hierarchy of the respective favourable measures, such as, for instance, if affirmative action exists at the same time in favour of women and in favour of minorities in the field of political representation. In such a case, it is necessary to establish a rational allocation of benefits, which may raise conflicts amongst the various beneficiaries.

---

[43] 515 US 200 (1995).

From this utilitarian viewpoint, one might reasonably suggest that affirmative action is a strongly debatable policy, since it might operate both as a means to reduce divisions but also as a way of unacceptably triggering social anxiety. This conundrum was obvious in the US Supreme Court case *Lee, Commissioner of Corrections in Alabama v. Washington*, concerning the permanent racial segregation of all prison inmates so as to reduce the possibility of racial conflict.[44] The Court upheld a decree of a three-judge District Court declaring that certain Alabama statutes violated the Fourteenth Amendment to the extent that they required segregation of races in prisons and jails and established a schedule for the desegregation of these institutions. In so doing, the majority declared that state or local prison authorities had the right, acting in good faith and in particularised circumstances, to take into account racial tensions in maintaining security, discipline, and good order in prisons and jails, without impairing however the constitutional prohibition of racial discrimination.

Although affirmative action policies cannot by definition be equated to any inhumane state of segregation, the dilemma is obvious. It might be expedient to segregate races in order to secure tranquility at the cost of sacrificing self-evident social homogeneity through racial diffusion. However, one may ask whether the compelling public interest of safety overrides the (equally) compelling interest not to use means of segregation? By the same token, with respect to affirmative action, Cohen (2003: 164) has a categorical opinion that ethnic preferences presuppose some generally understood sorting of the community into ethnic categories, necessary for the award of advantages to this group or to that one. In that opinion, each person must be identifiable—by others and by himself- as a member of one ethnic group or another since, without identifiable memberships, preferences make no sense. However, "what obliges individuals to identify themselves by group divides the groups, builds barriers between them".

Given all the above considerations, it does not come as a surprise that affirmative action does not always produce social cohesion. Even in the US, with a relatively long tradition in applying affirmative action, the use of the race criterion has not resulted in a desirable osmosis amongst American citizens. Thus, the "ethno-racial pentagon" (Hollinger 1995), founded on immutable external human attributes, mostly one's colour, still haunts American society: white (Caucasian), black (Afro-Americans), brown (Hispanics), red (Native Americans), yellow (Asians). Justice Stevens in his dissent in the US Supreme Court judgment in *Fullilove v. Klutznick*, made a relevant historical comment. In his opinion history teaches us that the costs associated with a sovereign's grant of exclusive privileges often encompass more than the high prices and shoddy workmanship that are familiar handmaidens of monopoly; they engender animosity and discontent, as well: "The economic consequences of using noble birth as a basis for classification in 18th-century France, though disastrous, were nothing as compared with the terror

[44]390 US 333 (1968) (per curiam).

that was engendered in the name of "egalité" and "fraternité". Grants of privilege on the basis of characteristics acquired at birth are far from an unmixed blessing".[45]

Finally, nothing can prevent authoritarian regimes from using affirmative action policies as a tool of favouritism of one or some ethnic groups over another or others, which according to Sowell (2004: 110) was the case in post-colonial Nigeria, that eventually resulted in a fierce civil war. In his opinion, group polarisation which preceded and produced the preferences and quotas has been deadly in its effects, both in peace and in war, and under both civilian and military governments.

The truth is that affirmative action, either because of genuine political will or a sincere sense of guilt, might become a very powerful tool in the hands of the politicians for the redistribution of social power. In this way however, as Steele (1990: 119) comments, instead of a compensation vehicle affirmative action potentially becomes a source of corruption through which selective inclusions and exclusions may be triggered.

3.4 The Pedagogical Purpose: Group Models and Confidence to Institutions

The pedagogical objectives of affirmative action policies are self-evident. Neither past discrimination nor underrepresentation is necessary to uphold their constitutionality. There are three separate affirmative action pedagogic goals relating to its social aspirations: the role model, the professional goals and raising confidence vis-à-vis state and social institutions.

The *role model* goal mirrors the terminology of social sciences. In an affirmative action context it means that underrepresented groups must have a critical mass of role models of the same group to look up to, in order to increase self-esteem and be able to set high aims. This is particularly the case in employment, where a minority or female employees should be able to come across members of their own race or gender respectively occupying high-level professional positions; and also academia, where students of these groups can receive substantive encouragement when interacting with academic or administrative staff of their race or gender. The pedagogical goal of affirmative action is by nature dissociated from past discrimination and only relates to balanced representation. The role-model rationale was explicitly rejected by the US Supreme Court in *Wygant v. Jackson Board of Education* (1986). Although both the District Court at first instance and the Court of Appeals had found that a racial preference was permissible under the Equal Protection Clause as an attempt to remedy societal discrimination by providing role models for minority schoolchildren and upheld the constitutionality of the layoff provision for members of the dominant social group to achieve an appropriate racial balance, the Supreme Court reversed these decisions. The Court held that societal discrimination

[45] *Fullilove v. Klutznick*, 448 US 448, 553 (1980).

alone was insufficient to justify a racial classification and that there must have been convincing evidence of prior discrimination by the governmental unit involved before allowing limited use of racial classifications to remedy such discrimination. According to the judgment, the invoked role model theory would, on the one hand, allow discriminatory hiring and layoff practices long past the point required by any legitimate remedial purpose and, on the other hand, it did not bear any relationship to the harm caused by prior discriminatory hiring practices: "Societal discrimination, without more, is too amorphous a basis for finding race-conscious state action and for imposing a racially classified remedy".[46]

The role model rationale has been treated favourably by part of the American literature in the field (Chung 2000). Within the US Supreme Court's case-law, the argument has essentially been subsumed under the broader rubric of diversity in the sense that it allows broader representation.[47] However, there is a principal difference between the two. Diversity operates in a two-fold way: with reference to the designated groups it operates sociologically by preventing isolation (or the fear of isolation) and allowing for a better performance; with reference to the overall environment, especially academic, it allows interaction of a variety of cultures and opinions, which is arguably a benefit in any process of acquiring knowledge. The role model rationale operates in a single way towards members of the designated groups by raising self-esteem and favouring the setting of high aims. A common prerequisite of the two rationales is the need for a critical mass of the underrepresented groups as a fertile ground for better results.

The *professional* goal relates to the quality of "group services", i.e. services provided by professionals to members of the same group. The idea, basically developed in the context of university admissions, emphasises human predilection (which applies *a fortiori* in the case of underrepresented or discriminated groups) towards seeking services from members of the same group, thinking that they will enjoy better treatment and more substantial understanding, and vice versa that affirmative action beneficiaries feel a professional moral responsibility to assist members of their own group (since it was exactly this classification that facilitated their preferential treatment). If this premise is true, the use of quotas in favour of all racial minorities for university entries, whereby they will receive academic and professional qualifications, makes sense since the state must always see for the provision of the best possible service to any segment of society. This theory, however, is based on a largely humanistic premise that is not by definition accurate within the social struggle and, eventually, produces outcomes which the policy of affirmative action, especially the diversity goal, fundamentally aims to discourage, i.e. the solidification of social groups through a self-originated segregation. Self-motivated philanthropy and voluntarism, elements of American society of which it is particularly proud, do not have such a general application so as to be raised from individual predilection to standard group ethics. From this viewpoint, the

---

[46]*Wygant v. Jackson Board of Education*, 476 US 267, 268 (1986).

[47]*Grutter v. Bollinger*, 539 US 306, 332–333 (2003).

theory of provision of services on a group basis seems to be contrary to the essence of affirmative action and is not, at any rate, confirmed by empirical evidence.

The *increase of confidence* goal vis-à-vis state and social institutions entails that all members of a community, especially those in a disadvantaged position ought to believe that they will all be equally welcomed and receive proper treatment and opportunity to earn qualifications irrespective of the gender, race or religion. This is a prerequisite of a progressive and open society that makes the best out of its citizens and a condition of community welfare. As put in 2003 US Supreme Court judgment *Grutter v. Bollinger*, all members of the heterogeneous society in the US must have confidence in the openness and integrity of the educational institutions that provide this training, thus access to legal education (and, in turn, to the legal profession) must be inclusive of talented and qualified individuals of every race and ethnicity, so that all members might participate in the educational institutions that provide the training and education necessary to succeed in the country.[48]

Although the confidence argument supposedly argues in favour of affirmative action in order to enhance the educational outcome for all involved parties as well as the institution as a whole, it eventually becomes rather over-simplistic. Universities, like any other academic institution, are places of knowledge, value and merit. Accordingly, concession on these mainstays in order to project an aesthetically proper image that might positively appeal to certain classes is by definition problematic. Koutnatzis (2002) convincingly argues that affirmative action in university admissions hampers the presumption of trust that they ought to cultivate within society.

3.5 The Economic Purpose: Balanced Growth

Affirmative action policies essentially constitute the continuation of the economic reform in the US emanating from the crash of 1929 and the correlating recession in the 1930s. It reflects the social and political claim for balanced growth as a necessary condition for economic sustainability that was incorporated in the 100-day New Deal programme of President Roosevelt, a benevolent positive measures package for employees and farmers to treat the obvious default of the deregulated liberal economy. In spite of very extensive popular backing of the measures, the US Supreme Court systematically found unconstitutionalities between 1932 and 1936 by interpreting financial clauses of the Constitution and the competences of the Congress in a formalistic and inflexible manner. It is of course questionable whether such economic subsidies can properly be considered as affirmative action measures in a conventional way of thinking, which mostly entails positive measures on the basis of gender, race and religion. Irrespective of background differences, there is a

[48] *Grutter v. Bollinger*, 539 US 306, 332–333 (2003).

common core in that both affirmative action and purely economic measures tend on occasions to ease market economy imbalances and enrich the liberal state with elements of distributive justice.

The historical link between affirmative action and balanced economic growth might be of greater significance in the institutional evolution of the European Union, given that this supranational legal order is essentially governed by market considerations and historically overlooks, if not ignores, concessions to the four fundamental free Union freedoms for the benefit of broader social goals. It is, therefore, easily explicable that the antithetical nature of the human-centred goals of affirmative action (remedial, cultural, societal and pedagogical) as pitted against the economic goals was stressed in the 2004 Opinion of Advocate General Maduro in Judgment *Briheche* before the Court of Justice of the European Union. He argued that there are two main reasons to justify compensatory measures. First, as a means for improving the prospects of victims of discrimination to the point where they would have been without any such discrimination; and, second, and most relevant to the economic purpose of affirmative action, as the only effective means to generate the right incentives for the underrepresented groups to invest in human capital (breaking the cycle of discrimination) and to address market failures (social monopolies and information costs) that, by reinforcing current societal discrimination, actually prevent the best persons from being chosen.[49] All in all, the argument supporting the economic goals of affirmative action is twofold, based on the micro and macro-economic effects produced thereof.

3.5.1 Micro-economic Effects: Efficiency and Human Potential

The micro-economic argument presumes that affirmative action raises the level of productivity within a specific market pool in two ways: by maximising motives and optimising the composition of the labour force. The former proposition is linked to the assumption that motivation through affirmative action activates members of benefited groups, which, knowing that they have an actual chance to develop their abilities and skills, shall invest more resources in achieving their aims and possibly set their ambition standards at a higher level. In this way, the working capacity is broadened since otherwise inactive working forces become part of the production machinery. Of course, the mathematical logic of the argument is not deprived of objections relating to the human reaction caused by the policy. From the point of view of the members of designated groups, motivation might produce adverse psychological effects, in the sense that these individuals will refrain from

[49] Opinion of Advocate General Poiares Maduro of 29 June 2004 in Case C-319/03, *Serge Briheche v. Ministre de l'Intérieur, Ministre de l'Éducation nationale and Ministre de la Justice*, Rec. 2004, p. I-8807, para. 49, fn. 3.

developing their full potential by themselves, knowing that they will receive an institutional boost that will anyhow place them in a better professional position. From the point of view of the members of non-benefited groups, affirmative action might operate as counter-motivation to the extent that their effort will not be reflected in the eventual outcome of their professional achievements since they will have to bridge the gap institutionally separating them from affirmative action competitors.

The above considerations also reduce the conclusiveness of the second assumption on micro-economic positive effects, namely that diverse composition raises production capacity, thus optimising the composition of the labour force. According to Advocate General Tesauro in his 1995 Opinion in *Kalanke*, "another accusation levelled against preferential treatment in favour of disadvantaged groups is that it lowers the rate of efficiency of the system by jeopardizing the social commitment to the best".[50] However, if the yardstick for working efficiency is merely the results produced thereof, this proposition should apply in principle at any level, not only the affirmative action policies. Thus, *any* composition of a body ensuring a better result would be legitimate and tolerable provided that it maximizes the eventual outcomes. Accordingly, bodies where special attributes apply, e.g. physical strength in security or armed forces should exclude females or should be composed of men of a certain race that carry physically strong characteristics. By the same token professionally vulnerable categories, such as handicapped persons or single parents or pregnant women should be totally excluded, thus creating a working environment of potentially high performance. The argument applies *a fortiori* in services related to public order and security, as Gottfredson (1994) indicates.

In any case, it should be stressed that in a fierce capitalistic environment, overall efficiency improvement is not tantamount to a respective improvement of the position of each member of the production machinery. However, the most striking argument against the utilitarian use of affirmative action is utility itself. The best working mixture might indeed be produced by a diverse composition, if the members of the body are willing to work jointly to produce optimum results. This is not at all self-evident. A diverse composition may conceivably produce a sharp division between those selected through a procedure based on merit and those selected merely to optimise body composition. This division might raise tensions and rivalries that will, in turn, be detrimental for the overall efficiency of the collective body. From this angle, one might reasonably argue that diverse composition is a potential but uncertain condition for optimum collective results. In this scenario, there will be an overall lowering of the level of performance in order for all members of the body to be able to contribute.

The case of university admissions of minority students, in case they are less-equipped, is illustrative in this respect: the universities will either be forced to

[50]Opinion of Advocate General Tesauro of 6 April 1995 in Case C-450/93, *Eckhard Kalanke v. Freie Hansestadt Bremen*, Rec. 1995, p. I-3051, para. 8, fn. 9.

somehow reduce the scale and quality of the education provided, so that all students may attend and be examined, or the affirmative action entries will be failing to follow the full syllabus and eventually fail to conclude their studies. In either case the system might fail to achieve the affirmative action aim pursued. Either beneficiaries will fail their studies or non-beneficiaries will fail to achieve their full educational potential. In either case, the progression of research and science will be held back. This equation is of course not undeniable: (a) even affirmative action beneficiaries, albeit not the best applicants, must still have the minimum requirements needed to adequately follow the curriculum; (b) affirmative action at the entry level does not altogether abolish competition but merely transfers the field of competition to actual practice (e.g. studies, work); (c) affirmative action beneficiaries still carry the moral burden of proving that they are worthy of the position they acquired and therefore are more likely to be equally or more resilient than the average student and rise to the required standards of study, contributing to both personal and overall improvement and (d) eventually, it is for the free market to assess everyone irrespective of whether they have benefited from affirmative action plans or not. And, after all, the commitment of higher education institutions to affirmative action policies, especially in the US, seems to contradict the above reservations in practice, since it would be unreasonable for them to sustain a policy that undermined their very purpose, i.e. academic excellence.

3.5.2 Macro-economic Effects: Competition, Stability and Growth

The macro-economic argument suggests that a primary purpose of affirmative action must be the establishment of a fair competition system so as to remedy the unfair results of formal equality by releasing all productive powers and making them truly competitive. The assumption is that formal equality actually perpetuates the existing status, since privileged groups are better equipped to further advance their competitive advantage, whereas disadvantaged groups cannot reasonably combat the prevailing class without affirmative action. Affirmative action in this respect restores true equal opportunity and secures equal competitive power for the future by bridging the gap caused by historical discrimination; what in the US is characterised by the advocates of affirmative action as "*leveling the playing field*".

The relationship between affirmative action and fair competition exceeds the field of economy and expands to all forms of social competition where competitive balance is required. From this viewpoint, affirmative action seems to be very akin to the American tradition and very unfamiliar to EU mainstays. In the latter system non-discrimination *ex nunc* and absence of any social variables, along with transparency are deemed to be the key point to securing fair competition. If concessions are recognised to the above scheme of formal equality, the compact legal construction of the economically-oriented EU freedoms would start to disintegrate.

Anyhow, there is not adequate empirical evidence to measure affirmative action policies, where applied, vis-à-vis the goal of balanced economic growth. This is predominantly so because economic growth depends on a wide variety of parameters and is very time and context-sensitive in a way that does not allow for the financial indicators to be assessed in isolation.

Such macro-economic view of affirmative action policies can be traced to the provision for set-asides in public works sub-contracting for minority-owned enterprises. According to Robinson (1998), the measures contributed not only to the well-being of the benefited enterprises, but also to market competition altogether through the establishment of a new circle of powerful business actors and to the minorities through the launching of new employment positions that were to a great extent occupied by members of the corresponding minorities. Even in this field, however, as in any other area where affirmative action was implemented, there were strong opposing voices. Speaking before the US Senate, Senator Orrin Hatch stressed the argument that affirmative action has a serious cost for the economy, including, apart from direct costs, the shrinking of competition, ineffectiveness due to unmerited appointments and disappointment on the part of worthy employees (Leonard 1984).

Still, the prevailing US competition orientation remains that of indirectly strengthening the market by broadly leveling the power of competing actors. The way basketball teams participating in the National Basketball Association league make new recruits provides an example of this dynamic in action. Generally speaking, the teams select players for the new season in a bottom-up fashion, i.e. according to their position in the previous year's league. Given that the objectively worst performing teams have the opportunity to be first to select the best players from a worldwide pool, who from that point onwards can only play for that particular team in the US, in conjunction with the budget ceiling for acquiring new players, horizontally applicable to all teams, every year there is a relative redistribution of power among teams, keeping the athletic "product" provided always challenging and appealing. Such a system would be largely inconceivable in Europe, both economically and legally, insofar as the athletic power of each team is broadly determined by the investment it makes. Given that investment improves quality, whereas financial prizes and income from advertising correspond to the quality of the team, the gap between top and mediocre European teams is always widening, despite some recent efforts to counteract this development.

As Dworkin (1981) argues actual equality and a market economy are not fundamentally incompatible. To the extent that the latter is a means to determine prices and provision of services, it should be the foundation of any realistic equality theory. Of course, the tension between the two deepens and the relevant debate becomes all the more important at the time of financial crisis where diverse, equally supportable economic concepts claim to treat the adverse effects of recession. In political economic terms there is, on the one hand, the *stability* priority, founded upon traditional liberal approaches and orthodox economics based on the prevalence of monetarism, seeking financial discipline through, mainly, severe austerity measures without any concessions towards wider social state aims, particularly for those countries with immense deficit and sovereign loans, and dogmatically opposing inflation. On the other hand, there is the *growth* priority, an effectuation of social liberalism reshaped in a new social economic policy narrative, emphasising the partial redistribution of wealth, both among and within states, arguing in favour of the easing of strict measures of financial discipline, of longer adaptation periods for endangered states and of solutions at an EU level, such as the Eurobonds and standing against forced austerity in depressed economies (Gerapetritis 2014: 107–110). In the time of this acute policy dilemma, affirmative action as embedded in a social policy agenda provides a social indicator in a liberal economy and, eventually, a liberal democracy. It becomes a key policy to reverse the ever-expanding prevalence of economy over politics and the shift from political liberalism to mere economic liberalism, a phenomenon well-depicted in Ferguson's (2009: 342–343) assumption that in capitalism wealth mutates in a way that democracy may eliminate growth and a financial crisis may undermine democracy: "Financial history is a roller-coaster ride of ups and downs, bubbles and busts, manias and panics, shocks and crushes… so much about the future lies in the realm of uncertainty, as opposed to calculable risk". Of course, one should not overlook Poulatzas' classical theory (1975), focusing upon the concept of "authoritarian statism", according to which there is a general trend of capitalist states moving towards authoritarianism through coercive measures and state surveillance to safeguard the prevailing notion of the free economy. Affirmative action can become part of this strategy.

References

Acemoglu, D., and Robinson, J. (2012). *Why Nations Fail: The Origins of Power, Prosperity and Poverty*. New York: Crown Business.

Anderson, T.H. (2004). *Pursuit of fairness: A history of affirmative action.* Oxford-New York: Oxford University Press.

Aronson, J., Quinn, D.M., and Spencer, S.J. (1998). In J.K. Swim and Ch. Stangor (Eds.), *Prejudice: The Target's Perspective* (85-105). New York: Academic Press.

Augusto dos Santos, S. (2006). Who is black in Brazil? A timely or a false question in Brazilian race relations in the era of affirmative action? *Latin American Perspectives*, 33(4), 30-48.

Beer, W.R. (1992). Affirmative action: Social policy as shibboleth. In P. Suedfeld and P.E. Tetlock (Eds.), *Psychology and social policy* (137-147). New York: Hemisphere Publishing Corp.

Bell, M.P., Harrison, D.A. and McLaughlin, M.E. (2000). Forming, changing and acting on attitude toward affirmative action programs in employment: A theory-driven approach. *Journal of Applied Psycology*, 85(5), 784-798.

Bickel. A.M. (1975). *The Morality of Consent*. New Heaven-London: Yale University Press.

Bond, J. (1997). Achieving the rights result: affirmative action and Article 4 of the Women's Convention. Resource Document. International Women's Rights Action Watch. http://www1.umn.edu/humanrts/iwraw/achieving_rights1997.html#contents. Accessed 31 Dec 2014.

Bowen, W., Bok, D., and Loury, G.C (1998). *The shape of the river: Long-term consequences of considering race in college and university admissions*. Princeton: Princeton University Press.

Brest, P. (1987). Affirmative action and the Constitution: Three theories. *Iowa Law Review*, 72, 281-285.

Brest, P., and Oshige, M. (1995). Affirmative Action for whom? *Stanford Law Review*, 47(5), 855-900.

Brown, J.P. (1998). Affirmative action and epistemology. In R. Post and M. Rogin (Eds.), *Race and representation: Affirmative action* (pp. 333-338). New York: Zone Books.
Campell, D.T. (1958). Common fate, similarity, and other indices of the status of aggregates of persons of social entities. *Behavioral Sciences,* 14-25.
Card, D., and Krueger, A.B. (2005). Would the elimination of affirmative action affect highly qualified minority applicants? Evidence from California and Texas. *Industrial and Labor Relations Review,* 58(3), 416-434.
Chopper, J.H. (1987). Continued uncertainty as to the constitutionality of remedial racial classifications: Identifying the pieces of the puzzle. *Iowa Law Review,* 72, 255-274.
Choy, V. (2005). Perpetuating the exclusion of Asian Americans from the affirmative action debate: An oversight of the diversity rationale in Grutter v. Bollinger. *University of California Davis Law Review,* 38(2), 545-571.
Chung, K.-S. (2000). Role models and arguments of affirmative action. The American Economic Review, 90(3), 640-648.
Cohen, C. (2003). Why race preference is wrong and bad. In C. Cohen and J.P. Sterba. *Affirmative action and racial preference. A debate* (1-188). Oxford-New York: Oxford University Press.
Crosby, F.J. (2004), *Affirmative action is dead; long live affirmative action.* New Heaven-London: Yale University Press.
Crump, S.A., Hamilton, D.L., Sherman S.J., Lickel, B., and Thakkar, V. (2009). Group entitativity and similarity: Their differing patterns in perceptions of groups. *European Journal of Social Psychology*, 40, 1212-1240. doi: 10.1002/ejsp.716.
Dahl, R.A. (1983). *Dilemmas of pluralist democracy. Autonomy vs. control.* New Heaven: Yale University Press.
Dworkin R. (1981), What is equality? Part 2: Equality of resources. *Philosophy and Public Affairs,* 10(4), 283-345. Reprinted in R. Dworkin, *Sovereign virtue*: *The theory and practice of equality* (pp. 65-119). 2002, Cambridge MA: Harvard.
Dworkin, R. (1991). Justice for Clarence Thomas. *New York Review of Books, 38(18)* 7th November. Reprinted: The Thomas nomination. In R. Dworkin (1997), *Freedom's Law. The moral reading of the American Constitution* (pp. 306-320). Oxford: Oxford University Press.
Edley, Ch. (1996). *Not all black and white: Affirmative action, race and American values.* New York: Hill and Wang.
Fatouros, A. (2001). Cultural diversity and human rights. In M. Vassiliou and H.J. Psomiades, *Human rights in the 21st century* (pp. 217-223). Athens-Komotini: Human Rights Defense Centre, Ant. N. Sakkoulas Publishers.
Ferguson, N. (2009). *The Ascent of Money: A Financial History of the World.* New York: Penguin.
Fredman, S. (2002). *Discrimination law.* Oxford-New York: Oxford University Press Clarendon Law Series.
Galanter, M. (1986). The "compensatory discrimination" theme in the Indian commitment to human rights. *India International Centre Quarterly,* 13(3A), 77-94.
Gaur, M. (2007). *Indian Affairs. Annual 2007.* Delhi: Kalpaz Publications.
Gerapetritis, G. (2014). Europe's new deal: a new version of an expiring deal. *European Journal of Law and Economics,* 38, 91–115. doi 10.1007/s10657-013-9422-z.
Gottfredson, L.S. (1994). The science and politics of race-norming. *American Psychologist,* 49(11), 955-963.
Government of Malaysia (1996). Seventh Malaysia Plan 1996-2000. Resource document. Kuala Lumbur: Percetakan Nasional Malaysia Berhad
Gutek, B. (1982). *Sex role stereotyping and affirmative action policy.* Los Angeles: University of California Institute of Industrial Relations.
Gutman, A. (1998). How affirmative action can (and cannot) work well. In R. Post and M. Rogin (Eds.). *Race and representation: Affirmative action* (341-346). New York: Zone Books.
Haslam, N. (1994). Categories of social relationship. *Cognition,* 53, 59-90.
Heilman, M.E., Block, C.J. and Lucas, J.A. (1992). Presumed incompetent? Stigmatisation and affirmative action efforts. *Journal of Applied Psycology,* 77(4), 536-544.

Heilman, M.E., Block, C.J., and Stathatos, P. (1998). The Affirmative Action stigma of incompetence: Effects of performance information ambiguity. *Academy of Management Journal,* 40, 603-625.

Heilman, M.E., McCullough, W.F., and Gilbert, D. (1996). The other side of Affirmative Action: Reaction of nonbeneficiaries to sex-based preferential selection. *Journal of Applied Psychology,* 81(4), 346-357.

Hollinger, D.A. (1995). *Post-ethnic America: Beyond Multi-culturalism.* New York: Basic Books.

Hollinger, D.A. (1996). Group preferences, cultural diversity and social democracy: notes towards a theory of affirmative action. *Representations*, (55), 31-40. Re-published in R. Post, and M. Rogin (Eds.), (1998). *Race and representation: Affirmative action* (97-111). New York: Zone Books.

Hook, S. (1995), Reverse discrimination. In S. Kahn (Ed.). *The affirmative action debate.* New York-London: Routledge.

Ingram, D. (2000). *Group rights: reconciling equality and difference.* Lawrence: University Press of Kansas.

Kahlenberg, R. (1997). *The remedy: class, race and affirmative action.* New York: Basic Books.

Kennedy, Ch.H. (1986). Policies of redistributional preference in Pakistan. In N. Nevitte and Ch. H. Kennedy (Eds.). *Ethnic preference and public policy in developing states* (63-93). Boulder CO.: Lynne Rienner Publishers Inc.

Koutnatzis, S-I.G. (2002). Affirmative action in education: The trust and honesty perspective. *Texas Forum on Civil Liberties & Civil Rights*, 7(2), 187-286.

Krishnamurthy, P., and Edlin, A. (2014). Affirmative Action and stereotypes in higher education. http://scholarship.law.berkeley.edu/cgi/viewcontent.cgi?article=1013&context=law_econ. Accessed 31 Dec 2014.

Kymlicka, W. (1989). *Liberalism, Community and Culture.* Oxford: Clarendon Press.

Kymlicka, W. (1995). *Multicultural citizenship. A liberal theory of minority rights.* Oxford: Oxford Clarendon Press.

La Noue, G., and Sullivan J. (2001). Deconstructing affirmative action categories. In J. Skrentny (Ed.). *lines: affirmative action, immigration, and civil rights options for America* (71-86). Chicago: University of Chicago Press.

Lemke, C. (2001). Changing the rules of the game: The role of law and the effects of party reforms on gender parity in Germany. In C.S. Maier and J. Klausen (Eds.). *Has liberalism failed women? Assuring equal representation in Europe and the United States* (123-139). New York: Palgrave.

Leonard, J. (1984). Anti-discrimination or reverse discrimination: The impact of changing demographics, Title VII, and affirmative action or productivity. *Journal of Human Resources,* 19(2), 145-174.

Loury, G. (2001), *The anatomy of racial inequality.* Cambridge MA: Harvard University Press.

Lynch, F.R. (1991). *Invisible victims: white males and the crisis of affirmative action.* New York: Praeger.

Lynch, F.R. (2001). *The Diversity machine: the drive to change the "white male workplace".* 2nd ed., New Jersey: Transaction Publishers.

Lynch, F.R., and Beer, W.R. (1990). You ain't the right color, pal: White resentment of affirmative action. *Policy Review,* 51, 64-67.

Maier, C.S., and Klausen, J. (2001). Introduction. In C.S. Maier and J. Klausen (Eds.). Has liberalism failed women? Assuring equal representation in Europe and the United States (3-17). New York: Palgrave.

Migrant Integration Policy Index (2010). Country Results. Resource Document. http://www.mipex.eu/countries. Accessed 31 Dec 2014.

Morris, C. (1984). Existential limits to the rectification of past wrongs. *American Philosophical Quarterly*, 21 (2), 175-182.

Nickel, J. (1974). Should reparations be to individuals or to groups? *Analysis,* 34(5), 154-160.

Niemann, F., and Dovidio J.F. (2005). Affirmative action and job satisfaction: Understanding underlying processes. *Journal of Social Issues*, 61(3) 507–523.

Nnoli, O. (1996). Ethnic and regional balancing in Nigerian Federalism. In J. Isawa Elaigwu and R.A. Akindele, (Eds.), *Foundations of Nigerian Federalism: 1960-1995*. Foundation of Nigerian Federalism Series 3. Abuja: Institute of Governance and Social Research.

Offe, C. (2001). The politics of parity: Can legal intervention neutralize the gender divide? In J. Klausen and C.S. Maier (Eds.), *Has liberalism failed women? Assuring equal representation in Europe and the United States* (pp. 39-54). New York: Palgrave.

Orfield, G., and Kurlaender, M. (Eds.), (2001). *Diversity challenged: Evidence on the impact of affirmative action*. Cambridge MA: Harvard Education Pub. Group.

Perloff, R., and Bryant, F.B. (2000). Identifying and measuring diversity's playoffs: Light at τhe end of the Affirmative Action tunnel. *Psychology, Public Policy, and Law*, 6(1), 101-111 (2000). doi: 10.1037/1076-8971.6.1.101.

Pevar, S. (2012). *The Rights of Indians and Tribes*. 4th ed., Oxford: Oxford University Press.

Posner, R.A. (1974). The DeFunis case and the constitutionality of preferential treatment of racial minorities, *The Supreme Court Review*, The University of Chicago Press, 1-32.

Poulatzas, N. (1975), *Clashes in Contemporary Capitalism*. London: New Left Books.

Raz, J. (1994). Multiculturalism: A liberal perspective. In J. Raz, *Ethics in the public domain, essays in the morality of law and politics* (pp. 155-176). Oxford: Clarendon Press.

Ridgeway, C. (1991). The social construction of status value: Gender and other nominal characteristics. *Social Forces*, 70, 367-386.

Robinson, A.A. (1998). The business of affirmative action. In G.E. Curry (Ed.), *The affirmative action debate*. Cambridge MA: Perseus.

Schrag, P. (1995). So you want to be color-blind: alternative principles for affirmative action. *The American Prospect*, June, 38-43.

Skrentny, J.D. (2002). Inventing race. *Public Interest*, 146, 97-113.

Smith, R.M. (2001). The distinctive barriers to gender equality. In J. Klausen and C.S. Maier (Eds.), *Has liberalism failed women? Assuring equal representation in Europe and the United States* (pp. 185-199). New York: Palgrave.

Sowell, T. (2004). *Affirmative action around the world. An empirical study*. New Heaven-London: Yale University Press.

Steele, S. (1990), *The content of our character: A new vision of race in America*. New York: Harper Perennial.

Steele, S. (1998). *A dream deferred: The second betrayal of Black freedom in America*. New York: Harper Collins.

Steinberg, S. (1995). *Turning back: The retreat from racial justice in American thought and policy*. Boston: Beacon Press.

Sterba, J.P (2003). Defending affirmative action. Defending preferences. In C. Cohen and J. P. Sterba (Eds.). *Affirmative action and racial preference. A debate* (pp. 258-275). Oxford-New York: Oxford University Press.

Stratigaki, M. (2012). Gendering the Social Policy Agenda. Anti-discrimination, social inclusion and social protection. In G. Abels and J.M. Mushaben, *Gendering the European Union: New Approaches to Old Democratic Deficit* (169-186). London:Palgrave Macmillan.

Sunstein, C.R. (1998). Casuistry. In R. Post and M. Rogin (Eds.). *Race and representation: Affirmative action* (309-332). New York: Zone Books.

Truax, K., Cordova, D.I., Wood, A., Wright, E., and Crosby, F. (1998). Undermined? Affirmative action from the targets' point of view. In J.K. Swim and Ch. Stangor (Eds.), *Prejudice: The Target's Perspective* (172-185). New York: Academic Press.

Van Alstyne, W.W. (1979). Rites of passage: Race, the Supreme Court and the Constitution. William & Mary Law School Research Paper, *University of Chicago Law Review* No. 09-200, 46(4), 775-810.

Wilson, W.J. (1987). *The Truly Disadvantaged: The Inner City, the Underclass, and Public Policy*. Chicago, University of Chicago Press.

World Economic Forum (2013). The Global Gender Gap Report. Resource Document. http://www3.weforum.org/docs/WEF_GenderGap_Report_2013.pdf. Accessed 31 Dec 2014.

World Value Survey (2013). Resource Document. http://www.worldvaluessurvey.org/wvs.jsp. Accessed 31 Dec 2014.

Yotopoulos-Marangopoulos, A. (1998). *Affirmative Action. Towards effective gender equality.* Athens–Brussels: Ant. N. Sakkoulas Publishers - Établissements Émile Bruylant.

Zelnick, B.H. (1996). *Backfire: A reporter's look at affirmative action.* Washington DC: Regnery Publishing.

Chapter 4
The Policy Question: Diverse Worldwide Practices

Affirmative action policies have been applied in many, geographically dispersed and culturally diverse countries of the world in all continents, such as India, Australia, New Zealand, Canada, Brazil, China, South Africa and Nigeria and European countries. In an analogous way, the same is true at the level of international law. Affirmative actions are less evident in regional international conventions for the protection of human rights, such as the European Convention on Human Rights, and more intense in sectorial covenants under the auspices of large scale international organisations, such as the United Nations. For the purposes of the present comparative approach, the institutional landscape of affirmative action in a wide spectrum of countries around the world is presented hereinafter on the basis of their diverse historical, geographical and legal characteristics and the level of implementation of affirmative action policies. Although space precludes a very wide analysis, there has been an effort to identify all the key elements that allow the identification of comparative syntheses and antitheses that follow.

4.1 America

Three legal orders have been selected for this comparative presentation: The US arguably constitutes the birthplace of affirmative action and in any case this is where the most extensive relevant legislation and case-law originates; Canada is a multicultural state with a mature social welfare system; and Brazil is the largest and most influential state of Latin America. While there is a long affirmative action history and debate in the US, in the last few decades the use of quotas, mostly in gender and less so in race, seems to be rapidly expanding in Latin America (Araujo and Garcia 2006).

G. Gerapetritis, *Affirmative Action Policies and Judicial Review Worldwide*,
Ius Gentium: Comparative Perspectives on Law and Justice 47,
DOI 10.1007/978-3-319-22395-7_4

4.1.1 The US

The US experience on affirmative action is particularly useful in many respects. It is mostly the American literature which has to a large extent revealed the constitutional penumbras related to affirmative action policies. It is interesting that in other countries there is often a false, or at least inaccurate, perception of implementation of affirmative action in the US. The US is commonly considered to be the country in which the policy was born. Although one can substantially challenge this argument by reference to earlier measures of a positive nature around the world, it is beyond any doubt that the issue has first been approached in a systematic way in this country and, therefore, the applied terminology usually goes back to these roots.

Sugrue (2001) approaches affirmative action in the US from a historical perspective and stresses that it was the product of the convergence of five major currents in post-New Deal liberalism: a racially divided rights consciousness; a highly influential moralistic current of racial liberalism during the 40s; the increasingly militant civil rights activism targeting employment discrimination, particularly in declining major northern cities; the liberal faith that government should be the agent of moral reform, especially by detached bureaucrats; and the deep rooted white resistance to anti-discrimination efforts that threatened their racial privileges. One might add in this in-depth analysis a rising collective guilt amongst the white community for past discrimination against minorities and especially Afro-Americans as well as the institutional role performed by the Supreme Court which has been, as in other socially sensitive policies, a true barometer reflecting social trends and evolution (Bickel 1962; Ely 1980). It is true, however, that the New Deal era stood for a significant shift in the US in the perception of equality from a rather formal economy-oriented principle to a more social one, cognisant of vulnerable groups' value (White 2000: 167–197; Kushman 1998). From another point of the literature, Rubio (2001), in the most analytical approach of the doctrine to date, breaks US history of affirmative action into seven periods. First, the white dominance over the citizenship debate in the course of the formation of the new state (1619–1861); second, the first affirmative approach over the Civil War (1861–1877); third, the period of absolute marginalisation of the black community through segregation and the evolution of the overall Caucasian typology (1877–1933); fourth, the intrusion of black labour in the New Deal package (1933–1945); fifth, the social division and the steady rise of "black awareness" towards the claim for positive state intervention (1945–1955); sixth, the rise and fall of the civil rights movement (1955–1993); and, seventh, the affirmative action boom and the rise of "white awareness" towards the idea of compensation for past discrimination (1993–2000). Most probably, had his account been published later, Rubio would have extended the last period until 2003 to include the Michigan Cases judgments of the Supreme Court which marked the starting point for the step-by-step withdrawal of the affirmative action rhetoric.

Unlike the French Revolution, fueled by the spiritual current of the Enlightenment, suggesting formal equality as a means to overcome the *ancien régime* and curb the unlimited powers of the monarchy, in the US revolution only sought the nation's independence without much regard for the issue of equality of the people. The new state had to wait for about a century, until the end of the Civil War, in order to constitutionally embrace equality through the enactment in 1868 of the Fourteenth Amendment and the Equal Protection Clause and abolish the most brutal violation of equality and human dignity, slavery. Still, in spite of the explicit recognition of equality and the formal abolition of slavery, in reality the constitutional declaration was a façade. Until the mid-1950s racial discrimination was imposed through segregation, meaning that certain places of human interaction were isolated from racial mixing. Accordingly, in most southern and central states, there were either distinct installations of public services (e.g. schools, hospitals) or distinct areas within the same installations (e.g. sanitary places, restaurants, leisure places and mass transportation means). In both cases the treatment of racial minorities was disgraceful: schools for whites were of much higher quality in relation to infrastructure and the personnel employed, while in the buses the front seats were reserved only for whites; blacks were not allowed to use these seats even if they were vacant.

Prior to the 20th century evolution, the Supreme Court performed a rather counterproductive role. It declared in the *Civil Rights Cases*[1] in 1883, that the *Civil Rights Act 1875*, permitting access for blacks to hotels, restaurants, trains, theatres and other premises, unconstitutional on the grounds that the delegation of the Fourteenth Amendment to Congress did not allow for positive federal intervention to combat existing discriminations. A basic argument used by Justice Bradley to declare the incompatibility of the legislation with the Constitution was that entrepreneurs could not be deprived of their right to select their own clients on the grounds of non-discrimination, since this clause was not applicable in the sphere of private relations. This decision paved the way for widespread racial discrimination and segregation within private enterprises.

In 1896, the Supreme Court with a large 8-1 majority further explicitly authorised segregation by public entities or as enforced by law in *Plessy v. Ferguson*[2] by establishing the doctrine of "*separate but equal*", which haunted social cohesion in the US for more than half a century. According to this doctrine, equality did not necessarily suggest that all racial groups were the same but their differences were allowed to be reflected in almost every aspect of social interaction so it would be permissible to isolate them by designating separate places for each one. Thus, the Court held that a Louisiana statute providing for distinct train wagons for blacks and whites was in conformity with the Federal Constitution. The majority argument can be summarised in Justice Henry Brown's words that the object of the Fourteenth Amendment might have been to enforce the absolute equality of the two races before the law, but in the nature of things, it could not have been intended to abolish distinctions based upon colour, or to enforce social, as distinguished from

---

[1]*Civil Rights Cases,* 109 US 3 (1883).

[2]163 US 537 (1896).

political, equality, or a commingling of the two races upon terms unsatisfactory to either. History, nevertheless, redeemed the solitary statement of dissenting Justice John Marshall Harlan of a "*color-blind Constitution*" that neither knows nor tolerates the existence of classes among citizens. The "colour-blindness" doctrine might be used as an argument against affirmative action, in the sense that no deviation from equal protection clause through racial data and profiling or classifications and distinctions based upon race can be tolerated by the constitutional order.

During World War II, a new perspective of privileged treatment for whites was added to the discussion, mainly against Asian-Americans, especially of Japanese origin. The well-known *Korematsu case*,[3] legitimised the institutional isolation of these individuals but left an indication of future change in judicial attitude by establishing the rule that any restriction of the racial equality principle was automatically considered a "*suspect classification*", which essentially introduced a much higher judicial threshold in these cases, namely the strict scrutiny test; indeed, *Korematsu* remains until today one of the very few cases where this exacting standard has been successfully met by the government. The case concerned the constitutionality of Executive Order 9066. The applicant was convicted for evading internment imposed on May 9, 1942, two days after the US Navy tanker *Neosho* had been attacked by Japanese dive-bombers, drifting with 123 men on board. In a 6-3 decision, the Court upheld the government's arguments on the grounds that the need to protect against espionage outweighed individual rights, including the rights of Americans of Japanese descent. Although this strongly controversial decision has not been explicitly overturned, Korematsu's conviction was in fact overturned on November 10, 1983, after Korematsu challenged the earlier decision by filing for a writ of *coram nobis* (an order by an appeals court to a lower court to consider facts not on the trial record which might have changed the outcome of the lower court case if known at the time of trial) on the grounds that in the original case, the government had knowingly submitted false information of material impact.

Explicit recognition of racial equality came in 1954 with the *Brown v. Board of Education* decision of the Supreme Court.[4] The Court ruled that racial segregation in the field of education was contrary to the Fourteenth Amendment to the extent that it was "*inherently unequal*" for minorities in that "separate" could never be "equal", thus explicitly overruling *Plessy v. Ferguson*. The almost metaphysical declaration of this "self-evident" equality, which was supported by arguments drawn from the mentality of the American people and culture, did not have an immediate effect. Restoration of full racial equality should according to the judgment occur "*with all deliberate speed*". Through this *obiter* comment, the Court tried to absorb the estimated social and state impact, which indeed followed (Stohr 2004: 59–62). States supporting segregation suffered from wide riots known as

[3] *Korematsu v. United States,* 323 US 214 (1944).

[4] 347 US 483 (1954). In fact there are 6 decisions that have been, nevertheless, treated in unity by the literature.

"*massive resistance*". In traditionally segregated Arkansas, the Governor, wishing to express his opposition to the Supreme Court ruling, came into conflict with the federal police when he tried to prohibit black pupils from entering schools reserved for whites. Although *Brown* technically applied only in the context of public education, its result was quickly extended by the Supreme Court (typically without explanation) and by lower courts to other contexts. This landmark decision, in conjunction with the civil rights movement at the time, strengthened the demand for the elimination of all forms of racial discrimination.

The symbolic peak of the civil rights movement came with the march to the capital city and the seminal "*I have a dream*" speech of Martin Luther King Jr., on August 28th 1963, pleading for work and freedom: "And so even though we face the difficulties of today and tomorrow, I still have a dream. It is a dream deeply rooted in the American dream" (Carson et al. 2002: 75). Of course, the social pressure for wide civil rights recognition found fertile ground amidst ample economic growth and the prevailing political ideology of that era. Essentially, the policy of incorporating racial minorities in the industry in a broader sense—education, labour market, entrepreneurial activities—was part of a larger scale scheme to improve an already thriving economy. This is why social tensions that were bound to occur with the introduction of measures in favour of the black community were partially absorbed.

Although some aspects of positive state intervention in favour of underrepresented races were intimated in an Executive Order during World War II, through which President Roosevelt allowed African Americans better access to the labour market in the field of defense and mandated that public contractors abstain from any discriminatory practices,[5] the actual implementation of the policy began in the 1960s (Skrentny 1996: 193–211). Indeed, two months after his inauguration in 1961, President Kennedy issued an Executive Order to introduce the *Committee on Equal Employment Opportunity*.[6] This Order used the language of *affirmative action* for the first time as a means to prevent racial discrimination on the grounds of race, beliefs, colour or national origin. In the same line of policy, President Kennedy also focused on the issue of equality between men and women through the enactment of *Equal Pay Act 1963* that prohibited different pay for equal work. A more solid policy was, however, introduced through the Executive Orders of President Johnson that obliged public contractors to take affirmative action measures in hiring blacks and women.[7] A further boost was given when President Nixon introduced the "*Philadelphia Plan*", a financial project aimed at producing a fairer and more balanced racial representation in the construction market in the long run.[8]

[5]Executive Order 8802 of 25th June 1941. The same Order launched the significant *Fair Employment Practices Committee.*

[6]Executive Order 10925 of 6th March 1961.

[7]Executive Order 11246 of 24th September 1965 and amending Executive Order 11375 of 13th October 1967.

[8]Office of Federal Office Compliance (OFCC) Revised Order No. 4.

Two more state interventions configured the affirmative action environment at the time. The *Civil Rights Act 1964*, extended for the first time explicitly in Title VII the ambit of application of the Fourteenth Amendment by prohibiting any discrimination on grounds of race, colour, sex or national origin, thus extending the Amendment's scope in private industry (Swain 2001: 319). This statute provided also for the establishment of the *Permanent Equal Opportunity Commission*, still in existence today, which guarantees the proper implementation of the relevant legislation and the restoration of equality, where necessary. There was not, however, a clear positive stance towards affirmative action; members of Congress seemed to adopt conflicting views on the issue, some arguing that, in light of the statute, no racial quotas could be acceptable in the labour market[9] and others suggesting that it remained at the discretion of the executive to launch such measures.[10] On the latter view, a vivid illustration is provided by Senator MacGregor's speech, where he explicitly stated that when drafting the bill issues of preferential treatment or quotas were largely excluded because the problems raised by these controversial questions were more properly handled at a governmental level and by communities and individuals themselves.

New legislation for the protection of civil rights was set in place in 1972 and 1991, which also used neutral language in relation to affirmative action. In fact, in the process of voting on the 1972 statute, an amendment was proposed to the effect that affirmative action would be altogether prohibited; but the amendment was not upheld in Congress (Sterba 2003: 193–194).

The judicial reaction to the *Civil Rights Act 1964* and the Executive Orders in favour of affirmative action was positive. Thus, in *Green v. County School Board of New Kent County* in 1968,[11] the Supreme Court set out a legal obligation of the Education Boards to immediately take expedient measures to promote actual equality. Indeed, the measures should be such, as to allow immediate results. In this respect, the policy of racial dispersion to avoid purely same-race schools was not only tolerated but also considered as expedient in the pursuit of substantive equality. The response of academia to the mandates of the Court was positive. This was especially true in the case of state or private universities that were obliged to adopt racial affirmative action plans in the process of admitting new students in order to secure state financing. Overall, in the 1960s, the reading of the Fourteenth Amendment changed in order to enhance affirmative action. Until then, this constitutional clause had been constantly invoked by opponents of affirmative action on the grounds that the Amendment's formal interpretation was being breached.

---

[9]See Senator Humphrey, 110 Cong. Rec. 11848 (1964) and relevant comments by Senator Williams, 110 Cong. Rec. 8921 (1964).

[10]110 Cong. Rec. 15893 (1964). Also see speeches of Senator Dirksen (110 Cong. Rec. 12819, 1964), Senator Clark (110 Cong. Rec. 13079-13080, 1964) and Senator Lindsay (110 Cong. Rec. 15876, 1964), most of which are cited in the very well documented *United Steelworkers of America v. Weber,* 443 US 193 (1979).

[11]391 US 430 (1968).

The Supreme Court not only consolidated the *Brown* case-law by upholding the legitimate aim to achieve substantive equality,[12] but on occasion did not hesitate to demand the introduction of such measures by the state.[13] The first path breaking judicial authority on affirmative action came in 1978 with the milestone decision in *Regents of the University of California v. Bakke*.[14] The petitioner, whose application for admission to the University of California had been rejected, requested the annulment of the affirmative action policy in favour of the minority candidates in university entry, a policy which reserved 16 positions for every 100 applications. The system established a direct quota in favour of minority candidates and the Court would have to decide whether this academic practice was compatible with the Fourteenth Amendment, which, according to the petitioner, did not allow deviations from racial equality, but also with ordinary legislation, which provided that educational institutions receiving state funds in the US were not permitted to use race as a criterion for admissions. The Court first found that the purpose of racial diversity in an academic environment serves a compelling public interest—namely the first prong of the strict scrutiny test, given that the Constitution did not introduce "*absolute color-blindness*". However, with a narrow 5-4 majority, the Court eventually held that the admissions policy of the University of California reserving places for minority candidates contravened the equality principle because it did not entail the assessment of non-minority candidates for all university entries, but merely for the remaining entries outside the reserved ones and was not, therefore, narrowly tailored to serve the admittedly compelling interest of diversity—that is, it failed to meet strict scrutiny's second prong. Although the *Bakke* outcome was clearly against positive discrimination quotas, the rationale was ambiguous and became an object of extended analysis. Confusion was caused mostly because of the separate concurring opinions rendered by the individual majority justices. Paradoxically, the view considered as authority in *Bakke* was that of Justice Powell, with whose reasoning all the remaining eight justices disagreed. It was, in essence, the swing vote which bound subsequent case law; a great number of essays have been written in the US with the sole purpose of identifying the actual meaning of this opinion.

Bakke case-law exercised significant influence on the contested matter and encouraged affirmative action policies both in the private and public spheres. The following year the Court issued the *United Steelworkers of America v. Weber* decision,[15] perhaps the most affirmative action-friendly decision of the Court ever. In this case, the Court dealt with the legality and constitutionality of an affirmative action plan introduced voluntarily by a company in collaboration with a labour syndicate. The plan set up an education programme for specialised technicians, access to which would be obligatorily provided to a body of employees at least half

---

[12] *Loving v. Virginia,* 388 US 1 (1967).

[13] *Green v. County School Board of New Kent County,* 391 US 430 (1968).

[14] 438 US 265 (1978).

[15] 443 US 193 (1979).

of which were African-Americans. A white applicant who was refused access to the programme due to the quota mainly argued that Title VII of the 1964 Civil Rights Act, entailing no categorisation on grounds of race, had been violated. Although both the first instance and appeal decisions decided against the legality of the measure, the majority of the Court gave prevalence to the systematic and historical interpretation of the relevant legislation and held that compensation for discrimination against oppressed labour groups in the past justified the right of the private sector to voluntarily assume affirmative action. Once the Court resolved the principal issue, it provided—although not very strictly—the limits within which such action might be introduced. First, the measures should not prejudice the benefits of white employees more than necessary and, secondly, the action must be temporary. Given that the impugned measure did not entail the dismissal of white employees so as to recruit African-Americans, it was found to serve the legitimate purpose of eradicating racial imbalance and not to introduce or sustain an unacceptable racial proportion and was thus found lawful. Interestingly, in this case, the applicable standard of scrutiny was considerably more lenient vis-à-vis previously and subsequently applied strict scrutiny test.

In the 1980s, the Supreme Court set out its case-law in the field of affirmative action in the award of public contracts. Conversely to inferior court judgments which exhibited a negative attitude towards racial privileges in the awarding of public contracts, in 1980, the Court in *Fullilove v. Klutznick*[16] dealt with the programmes established by Congress to assist companies controlled by representatives of racial minorities. The impugned programme obliged public sector contractors to reserve part of the public work, amounting to 10% of the total object of the project ("*set asides*") for companies controlled by absolute majority of their capital by minority members. The Court upheld the constitutionality of the measure, on the grounds that the legislator had several historical and statistical indications to conclude that there was discrimination against those minorities in the past, in order to substantiate the claim for compensation. However, there was no follow-up of the favourable case-law for affirmative action in public contracts. In the *City of Richmond v. Croson* decision in 1989, the Supreme Court ruled by 6-3 majority that a state law obliging municipality contractors to subcontract 30 % of the work to minority ownership companies was unconstitutional. The majority of the Court found no amount of past damage caused to underrepresented groups could justify a 30 % quota. The different approach in *Richmond* can be attributed to the significant difference of the quota threshold (10 % against 30 %), to the variation in the composition of the Court between 1980 and 1989 and to the legal level of the impugned measure (federal and state respectively). The case sharply divided academia and society. In a rather unusual move, 30 professors of constitutional law of the top law schools in the US submitted a written statement against the rationale of the decision, including "*guidelines*" addressed to the judiciary and the

[16]448 US 448 (1980).

administration on the way they should manage issues regarding affirmative action (Joint Statement 1989: 1711–1716).

Eventually, despite the introduction of the new Civil Rights Act in 1991, *Adarand Constructors Inc. v. Pena* marked a jurisprudential retreat.[17] The Supreme Court decided to tighten its control upon such affirmative action by applying strict scrutiny in any case of deviation from formal equality, either by federal or state authority, so that eventually no measure could possibly survive the test. According to a statutory clause, most federal agency contracts ought to contain a subcontractor compensation clause, which gave a prime contractor a financial incentive to hire subcontractors certified as small businesses controlled by socially and economically disadvantaged individuals, and required the contractor to presume that such individuals include minorities or any other individuals found to be disadvantaged. It was in fact unclear to which extent the law explicitly distinguished on the basis of race rather than covering in general socially and economically disadvantaged individuals. The programme, unlike relevant statutory predecessors, did not establish any numerical set asides. A petitioner, who was rejected although admittedly having presented the lowest bid on the subcontract because it was not a certified business, filed suit against respondent federal officials claiming that the race-based presumptions used in subcontractor compensation clauses violated the Equal Protection Clause. Although the District Court granted the respondents a summary judgment and the Court of Appeals affirmed this, the Supreme Court vacated and remanded to the lower courts for further consideration.

In the relevant field of licensing, in between *Croson* and *Adarand* the Supreme Court rendered another very favourable decision for racial affirmative action in 1990. *In Metro Broadcasting, Inc. v. Federal Communications Commission,*[18] the Court assessed the constitutionality of two minority preference policies adopted by the Federal Communications Commission in the context of the Communications Act of 1934 aiming at promoting the diversification of radio-television programming, i.e. on the one hand the award of an enhancement for minority ownership and participation in management, which is weighed together with all other relevant factors in comparing mutually exclusive applications for licenses for new radio or television broadcast stations and, on the other hand, the "distress sale" policy which allowed a radio or television broadcaster whose qualifications to hold a license have come into question to transfer that license before the Commission resolved the case, provided the transferee is a minority enterprise that meets certain requirements. The Court in its 6-3 judgment held that the Commission's policies did not violate equal protection, since they bear the *imprimatur* of long-standing congressional support and direction and were substantially related to the achievement of the important governmental objective of broadcast diversity. In that respect, *Metro Broadcasting* applied merely intermediate rather than strict scrutiny standard of judicial review. The upholding rationale might be broken down in five propositions: (a) minority

[17] 515 US 200 (1995).

[18] 497 US 547 (1990).

ownership programmes had been specifically mandated by Congress, (b) minority ownership policies serve an important governmental objective, i.e. broadcast diversity, (c) minority ownership policies are substantially related to the fulfilment of the Government's interest in broadcasting through the deference of the range of programming available and diverse programming, (d) the judgment that there is a link between expanded minority ownership and broadcast diversity does not rest on impermissible stereotyping and (e) the minority ownership policies are in other relevant respects substantially related to the goal of promoting broadcast diversity, mostly the examination of (less restrictive) alternatives and assessment of surveys in the field.

During the same period, the Supreme Court set its case-law on gender-related affirmative action in *Johnson v. Transportation Agency.*[19] The case regarded the constitutionality of an affirmative action policy in the recruitment and promotion of women employees, applied voluntarily by an employer in the field of road works maintenance, in order to achieve an annual, statistically measurable improvement of the men-women ratio towards the goal of reflecting the gender ratios in the regional employment market. The company's policy was challenged before the Court on grounds of equality by a male employee, who although having the same qualifications as a female colleague, was passed over for promotion. The Court, after praising the non-governmental initiatives, set out the following prerequisites in order to uphold the constitutionality of such a measure: Firstly, the plan must apply in "*traditionally segregated workplaces*" so as to promote gender equilibrium. Secondly, the particular workplace must show "*conspicuous/manifest imbalance*" in the participation of men and women in relation to the total numbers of the local specialised human resources of the area, which need not necessarily be due to the particular employer who introduced the affirmative action. Thirdly, the affirmative action should not "*unnecessarily trammel*" the rights of male employees or establish the absolute prohibition of their promotion; the action should constitute "*minimal intrusion on the legitimate expectations*" of non-benefited employees. Fourthly, the measure ought to be of a temporary character and not introducing permanent ratios with regard to the gender of the company's employees. Based on the above prerequisites and with a 6-3 majority, the Court upheld the measure involving the use of gender as a parameter for the promotion of employees. The argument set forth by the majority was that this particular policy was based on a milder, more flexible, plan for the personalised approach of all recruitment and promotion cases, to achieve the reasonable pursuit of balancing genders in the workplace, where the dominance of men often occurred. To reach this conclusion, the majority emphasised that the measure neither constituted nor was tantamount to an unacceptable quota, nor was it exclusively relying on numerical data. In this way the case-law prohibition of the establishment of quotas was also expanded to gender affirmative action. *Johnson* caused major and diverse reactions from bodies,

[19] 480 US 616 (1987).

organisations and the press, thus this chapter is also considered open for future adjustments.

In the 1990s the major domain of constitutional review of affirmative action was political participation. As early as 1976 in *United Jewish Organizations of Williamsburgh, Inc. v. Carey*,[20] the Supreme Court had found that a reapportionment plan, which according to Section 5 of the Voting Rights Act ought to be submitted to the US attorney general or the District Court of the District of Columbia for approval, was valid under the Constitution, since the use of numerical quotas to establish a certain number of black majority districts did not violate the Fourteenth nor the Fifteenth Amendment since there was no evidence of "fencing out" of the white population in the county from electoral participation and did not result in underrepresentation of whites relative to their percentage in the overall population. In this initial case the Supreme Court had concluded that a state could use apportionment plans to attempt to prevent racial minorities from being repeatedly outvoted. In contrast, seventeen years later, in *Shaw v. Reno* (1993),[21] the Supreme Court reflected on the constitutionality of a reconfiguration plan of electoral districts in the State of North Carolina, aiming at creating an artificial geographic unit inhabited mostly by African Americans. This plan, in alignment with a federal Department of Justice guidance, aimed to ensure elementary representation for African Americans, which would otherwise be endangered because of the majoritarian nature of the electoral system. However, in order to create under these prerequisites, the new electoral district, a geographic oddity 160 miles long was created, where in some cases the width was several miles and in others only as wide as the central motorway, so as to obviously exclude voters on both sides. The reapportionment plan was based on the *Voting Rights Act* 1965, which explicitly provided that racial issues should be taken into consideration as well. The Court held that although the race criterion may be taken into consideration in the relevant planning, it could not constitute the basic pursuit of the districts' planning. According to this, while it is not prohibited for an electoral district to be imbalanced in geographical terms, it could not have a "*bizarre shape*". Thus, the Court applied the strict scrutiny standards and required the administration to prove that a compelling public interest was served and that the measure was tailor-made and necessary. In the absence of such evidence, the Court concluded that the plan unconstitutionally used race as a basic criterion.

The Supreme Court later reiterated the *Shaw v. Reno* ruling, always however with a narrow and thus fragile majority. The most emphatic confirmation came in the *Miller v. Johnson* decision of 1995,[22] which ruled that the drawing of electoral districts by reference to their population in terms of race was no different to racial segregation. In the facts of this case, in order to treat the evident difficulty in the state of Georgia, which had a 27 % black population but only one out of 10

---

[20]430 US 144 (1976).

[21]509 US 630, 648 (1993).

[22]515 US 900 (1995).

congressional districts being of black majority, the state Assembly established an additional majority-black district, called a "geographic monstrosity" because it extended 6784.2 square miles from Atlanta to the Atlantic Ocean merging metropolitan black neighbourhoods together with the poor black populace of coastal areas 260 miles away. The appellants, voters in the new eleventh district, challenged the drafting on the grounds that it was a racial gerrymandering in violation of the Equal Protection Clause. The District Court agreed, holding that evidence of the State legislature's purpose, as well as the District's irregular borders, showed that race was the overriding and predominant force in the districting determination. The court assumed that compliance with the *Voting Rights Act* would be a compelling interest, but found that the plan was not narrowly tailored to meet that. The Supreme Court affirmed that decision, holding with a narrow 5-4 majority the reapportionment plan to be unconstitutional for violating the Equal Protection Clause.

Affirmative action in university admissions came to the forefront again in the 2000s. In general, the *Bakke* case-law remained the main authority until 2003. Finally, after 25 years of case-law ambivalence, in June 2003, the Supreme Court revisited its doctrine on affirmative action in cases concerning the admission policy of the University of Michigan and rendered two long belated decisions, known as the *Michigan Cases*. Although the cases had different outcomes, their composite reading is necessary to trace what is acceptable according to the jurisprudence and what is not. In fact, two different affirmative action plans introduced by the University of Michigan at different times in order to facilitate admission to the University for minority candidates were challenged. In *Gratz v. Bollinger*,[23] a "strict" admission policy was challenged, according to which a number of variables had to be taken into account for deciding admission to the undergraduate college (these included high school grades, entry test results, quality of graduating high school, curriculum vitae, the geography of the origins of applications, the relations of candidates with university alumni, leadership capacity and race). For candidates falling within each of the criteria, the University added a bonus of 20 points out of a total possible maximum of 150 points. This practice essentially meant that all average candidates of the benefiting categories would be admitted since 100 points would normally suffice in order for a candidate to be admitted. The "flexible" admission policy, which was challenged in *Grutter v. Bollinger*,[24] concerned admission to the Law School, a graduate professional school which suggested that candidates should be admitted on the basis of an evaluation of their academic qualifications in conjunction with a flexible assessment of their talents, experience and potential, as revealed through their dossier (especially their statement of why they wished to pursue their studies), their recommendation letters, a statement on what they perceived their contribution could be, their undergraduate grades, their entry test results, as well as a series of "*soft variables*" such as the enthusiasm of those providing recommendations, the quality of their undergraduate school and the

[23]*Gratz v. Bollinger*, 539 US 244 (2003).

[24]*Grutter v. Bollinger*, 539 US 306 (2003).

difficulty of graduating, thus entailing race as a plus factor. Throughout the period when the two admission policies applied, the University considered African-Americans, Hispanics and Native Americans as "underrepresented" races.

When legal proceedings were initiated in 1997 white individuals filed applications with the Michigan federal court against the rejection of their applications to the University. The University did not admit the candidates although admittedly one of them was deemed "*well qualified*" and the other "*within the qualified range*". On the grounds of the Fourteenth Amendment and the legislation implementing this clause,[25] the applicants claimed compensation for damages, recognition that their rights to non-discrimination had been violated, and the issuance of injunctions requiring the University to abstain from future discriminatory practices and to offer the applicants a university place that would allow them to be transferred from other universities in which they had already enrolled.

In *Gratz v. Bollinger* the Supreme Court found in favour of the applicant and struck down the strict admission policy. The six judges' majority opinion, written by Chief Justice Rehnquist, applied the strict scrutiny test and accepted that securing diversity within an academic environment constituted a compelling public interest and therefore "*some*" measures could be taken in favour of this goal. However, the Court held that the particular policy was not "*narrowly tailored*" to achieve the legitimate aim of diversity. Building upon Justice Powell's swing vote in *Bakke*, the Court held that although it is permissible for a university to adopt an admissions policy that takes into account the national or racial origin of a candidate as "*a 'plus' factor*", this policy should not prevent an individualised assessment of the candidate's qualifications, i.e. their capacity to contribute to the academic environment. Accordingly, while the Court accepted that assessment of each candidate might entail administrative difficulties (an argument invoked by the university during the judicial proceedings), it rejected the system of automatic addition of admission points for minority candidates. Thus, the Court essentially declared that race might be one of the considerations of the admission policy but could not go as far as to set up a "*racial point-system*" that would violate the Constitution and the law. In contrast, in *Grutter v. Bollinger*, the Court upheld the constitutionality of the flexible admission policy with a narrow 5-4 majority by emphasising that the policy in question did not award direct benefits to candidates but merely set out the criteria of assessment, thus allowing for an overall evaluation of all candidates. The Court found that the flexible admission policy was not drafted in generic terms but was narrowly tailored for a limited period of time to serve the compelling public interest of diversity in academia. Careful analysis of the two decisions reveals a paradox. Although the whole argumentation revolves around the constitutionality of affirmative action, which is a term fully consolidated in both literature and case-law, this expression does not appear *eo nomine* in the majority opinions. This is presumably due to an effort of the justices to prevent any domino effect of the

[25]Especially Title VI of *Civil Rights Act 1964*.

decisions and to avoid any positive connotations towards the policy that might upset the conservative Supreme Court justices.

The Michigan University decisions received a very enthusiastic welcome by both supporters and opponents of affirmative action. This paradox clearly reflects the desire of the Supreme Court to find a proper balance for the sustainability of this policy. Thus, it declared that racial affirmative action, narrowly tailored to serve the compelling public interest of diversity, was constitutional as a means of encouraging minority participation, but rejected measures entailing not only quotas or reserved seats but also automatic preferences or measures of equivalent effect. However, the precise nature of this distinction remains unclear. This is because, on the one hand, there is still a range of unacceptable measures which, nevertheless, do not entail rigid or *de facto* rigid quotas and, on the other hand, because there can be no clear-cut definition of what constitutes a (direct or indirect) quota. In a sense the Court specified only what measures are considered clearly unconstitutional and left the issue of the constitutionality of the remaining measures to be decided on an *ad hoc* basis. Justice Scalia in his dissenting opinion predicted that these decisions would not put an end to social anxiety and judicial dispute due to the adverse reading of the equality clause and the fluidity of the criteria employed. In his view, unlike a clear constitutional holding that racial preferences in state educational institutions were impermissible, or even a clear anticonstitutional holding that racial preferences in state educational institutions were permissible the *Grutter-Gratz* was bound to prolong the controversy and the litigation in the sense that some future lawsuits would focus on whether the discriminatory scheme in question contains enough evaluation of the applicant "as an individual," and sufficiently avoids "separate admissions tracks", whereas others would focus on whether a university has gone beyond the bounds of a "good faith effort" and had so zealously pursued its (mystical in the exact scope) "critical mass" requirement as to make it an unconstitutional *de facto* quota system, rather than merely "a permissible goal". Justice Scalia's categorical conclusion was that the Constitution proscribed government discrimination on the basis of race, and state-provided education was no exception.[26]

In the meantime, in June 2007, the Supreme Court decided the case *Parents Involved in Community Schools v. Seattle School District*[27] relating to affirmative action in high schools. The judgment constitutes a typical example of how the interpretation of the constitutional equality principle has been developed over time in the US, from the age of discrimination and racial segregation, to that of equality of opportunities and the renaissance of formal equality. Here, the respondent school districts had voluntarily adopted high school student assignment plans that relied on race (white or non-white) to determine which schools certain children may attend (the petitioners contended that allocating children to different public schools based solely on their race violated the Fourteenth Amendment), with a quota of minority

[26]*Grutter v. Bollinger* 539 US 306, 348 (2003).

[27]551 US 701 (2007).

students in high schools, ranging from 15 to 50 %. The questions raised were particularly acute and, to some extent, novel, i.e. whether diversity constituted a compelling public interest for racial allocation in public high schools, whether the racial allocation project was tailor-made and whether the reverse quota of a maximum 50 % of minority students in public high schools was in conformity with the Constitution. All state courts found that the school districts had asserted a compelling interest in maintaining racially diverse schools, and that their plan was, in all relevant respects, narrowly tailored to serve that interest. However, the Supreme Court reversed the lower courts' judgments in a 5-4 decision, holding that the policy was not narrowly tailored to serve the compelling state interest; in fact, Chief Justice Roberts' opinion for the Court suggested the lack of a compelling state interest altogether that would justify the assignment of school seats on the basis of race. Thus, the Supreme Court reshaped the *Green v. County School Board of New Kent County* case law[28] and took a step back towards formal equality.

Much sooner than anyone would expect, the jurisprudence in the US appears to leave the relatively friendly attitude towards affirmative action as a means of substantive equality. In fact, there were several signs to this effect in previous case-law as well (e.g. *Adarand* and *Croson*), while also the Michigan cases were rather a retreat vis-à-vis *Bakke* case law, so as one might reasonably argue that the predominant approach in recent years would seem to be continuity rather than jurisprudential shift. The argument of *Parents Involved* that a classification of blacks and "others" cannot be accepted for a good cause, namely to build an educational environment that is racially balanced and not ghettoised, marked a new era of negative judicial attitudes against the use of race as a criterion in favour of oppressed racial groups, a result partly of the new judicial entries at the Supreme Court after the appointment of two new, naturally conservative, justices by President George W. Bush, i.e. Justice Samuel Alito and, less so, Chief Justice John Roberts (since his predecessor Chief Justice Rehnquist had also been quite conservative). The two new justices, aligning with three of the other members of the Court, created a new bloc with a clear predilection towards formal equality, which is jurisprudentially unfavourable to the affirmative action doctrine in the US.

Two years later, in June 2009, the Supreme Court handed out its *Ricci v. DeStefano* judgement.[29] The applicants, city firefighters, claimed race discrimination due to the state of New Haven's decision to disregard written promotion tests because of a disparate impact on minorities caused by the fact that none of the black candidates had managed to score highly enough to be considered for the positions and that there was therefore a risk of lawsuits by the rejected minority candidates on the basis of the disparate impact argument. The Court held with a 5-4 majority that the New Haven decision to ignore the test results violated Title VII of the *Civil Rights Act 1964*. In the light of the applicable for racial discrimination in general

[28] 391 US 430 (1968).

[29] 557 US 557 (2009).

strict scrutiny test and suspect classification presumption, the state failed to produce evidence to uphold the constitutionality of the measure.

In June 2013, the US Supreme Court rendered a further affirmative action decision in *Abigail Noel Fisher v. University of Texas*.[30] The case concerned an affirmative action plan of the public University of Texas in favour of racial minorities. The Court's holding was awaited with great interest and anticipation in the US with the hope or fear (depending on one's attitude towards affirmative policies) that the 2003 Michigan University case-law would be revisited. The Supreme Court in a 7-1 decision eventually remanded to the Fifth Circuit, which had found in favour of the University of Texas' affirmative action plan. It found that the appellate decision was incorrect because it failed to effectively exercise the demanding burden of strict scrutiny required in any case where there appears to be a deviation from the colour-blindness principle required by the Equal Protection Clause.

Following the announcement of *Fisher*, once again, both parties claimed victory. The plaintiff herself said that she was "grateful to the justices for moving the nation closer to the day when a student's race isn't used at all in college admissions",[31] whereas civil rights groups emphasised that there was no concession from precedent, namely that states have a compelling interest in achieving student diversity provided that the measures taken are tailor-made to the needs of each institution and provide no direct advantage. It seems though that the Court in *Fisher* did not take a favourable stance towards affirmative action. In light of this, the reiteration of precedent with a hint of a conservative turn was not altogether unexpected, given also the passage of time since the Michigan cases that explicitly referred to the limited duration of affirmative action policies. In the meantime, the Fifth Circuit of the Court of Appeals later re-endorsed the University of Texas' use of racial preferences in undergraduate admissions decisions and the Supreme Court has been asked to intervene again after Fisher filed a new case on February 10th 2015 arguing violation of the ruling of the Supreme Court on the interpretation of the Equal Protection Clause.

In the meantime, in the 2000s and 2010s, very significant state legislative votes and state ballots took place in relation to banning affirmative action policies at the state level. In *Nebraska*, a ballot measure was passed by voters in 2008 to eliminate affirmative action programmes at state colleges and universities, political subdivision or government institution (Initiative 424, 2008).[32] In *Arizona*, a state legislature (as opposed to citizens' initiative) put in 2010 the question on the ballot to prohibit the state from granting preferential treatment to or discriminating against any individual or group on the basis of race, sex, colour, ethnicity or national origin

---

[30]570 US (2013), S. Ct. 2411.

[31]*The New York Times*, June 24, 2013, http://www.nytimes.com/2013/06/25/us/affirmative-action-decision.html?_r=0 (last accessed 31.12.2014).

[32]https://web.archive.org/web/20081107110152/http://www.nebraskacri.org/ballotlanguage.html (last accessed 31.12.2014).

in public employment, education and contracting (Proposition 107, 2010),[33] eventually approved. In *Washington*, after a citizen initiative to the legislature in 1998 (Initiative 200, 1998),[34] the state legislature passed a law in 2000, by which policies of an affirmative action nature were excluded. In *Oklahoma*, voters approved legislative referendum in 2012 prohibiting the state from granting preferential treatment to or discriminating against any individual or group on the basis of race, colour, sex, ethnicity or national origin in the operation of public employment, public education or public contracting (State Question 759, 2012).[35] In *New Hampshire*, a statute was passed in 2011, applying to state agencies, universities, community colleges and the post-secondary education commission, which prohibited preferential treatment or discrimination in recruiting, hiring, promotion or admission based on race, sex, national origin, religion or sexual orientation (House Bill 0623, 2011).[36] In *California*, the most populated state in the US, following the result of a statewide vote, a provision was included in the state Constitution in 1996 (Proposition 209, 1996, Civil Rights Initiative), by which the adoption of positive actions in favour of minorities for the admittance to local universities was prohibited. In 2014, Senate Constitutional Amendment No. 5 passed in the State Assembly,[37] essentially to abolish the prohibiting provision and allow recruitment and selection programmes giving preferential treatment in public education to individuals and groups on the basis of race, sex, colour, ethnicity or national origin; however, it was withdrawn from consideration in the Senate. On the contrary, in *Colorado* in 2008, an amendment (Amendment 46, 2008)[38] that would have prohibited any discrimination or preferential treatment by the State in public employment, public education and public contracting was narrowly defeated by public voting, thus making it the first and only US State to reject an anti-affirmative action ballot initiative. In *Michigan*, three years after *Grutter* and *Gratz,* in November 2006 the majority of the people approved a ballot initiative (Michigan Civil Rights Initiative), introducing an amendment to the State Constitution to the effect that any affirmative action awarding privileges to groups or individuals on the grounds of race, sex, colour or national origin in the fields of labour, education or public procurement should be prohibited. This prohibition entered into force on December 22, 2006, as Section 26 of Article I of the Michigan Constitution, entailing that "the state [*including any city, county, any public college,*

[33]http://apps.azsos.gov/election/2010/info/PubPamphlet/english/Prop107.htm (last accessed 31.12.2014).

[34]https://wei.sos.wa.gov/agency/osos/en/press_and_research/PreviousElections/documents/voters%27pamphlets/1998%20wa%20st.pdf (last accessed 31.12.2014).

[35]https://www.sos.ok.gov/documents/questions/759.pdf?7,12 (last accessed 31.12.2014).

[36]http://www.gencourt.state.nh.us/legislation/2011/HB0623.html (last accessed 31.12.2014).

[37]http://leginfo.ca.gov/pub/13-14/bill/sen/sb_0001-0050/sca_5_bill_20121203_introduced.pdf (last accessed 31.12.2014).

[38]http://www.colorado.gov/cs/Satellite%3Fblobcol%3Durldata%26blobheader%3Dapplication%252Fpdf%26blobkey%3Did%26blobtable%3DMungoBlobs%26blobwhere%3D1231572736266%26ssbinary%3Dtrue (last accessed 31.12.2014).

university, or community college, school district, or other political subdivision or governmental instrumentality of or within the State] shall not discriminate against, or grant preferential treatment to, any individual or group on the basis of race, sex, colour, ethnicity, or national origin in the operation of public employment, public education, or public contracting".[39]

The Michigan Constitution amendment was challenged before the Federal courts by a great number of NGOs and individuals. In fact, the day after the proposition passed, an *ad hoc* "Coalition to Defend Affirmative Action, Integration and Immigration Rights and Fight for Equality by Any Means Necessary" was established and its first collective move was to sue the Governor and the Regents and Boards of Trustees of three state universities in district court arguing that the proposition as it related to public education violated the Equal Protection Clause. The Court of Appeals decided in December 2006, that there was no violation of the Federal Constitution and rejected the application.[40] The plaintiffs then appealed to the Supreme Court for interim relief—their appeal was rejected in January 2007 in the opinion of Justice Stevens.[41] In March 21, 2008, Judge David M. Lawson of the District Court for the Eastern District of Michigan finally dismissed the case.[42] About a month later, the Michigan Attorney General and Eric Russell, an applicant to the University of Michigan Law School, filed separate motions to intervene as defendants, which were granted. The district court granted a summary judgment in favour of them. In 2012, the Court of Appeals for the Sixth Circuit in a divided judgment affirmed that decision by holding the proposed amendment unconstitutional vis-à-vis the Equal Protection Clause. In essence, it was ruled that although it was constitutional not to use affirmative action policies, prohibiting it altogether via a state constitutional amendment violated the minorities' rights to fully participate in the creation of legislation, thus enabling the majority to manipulate the channels of change and impeding change on issues of importance to minority citizens. The constitutionality of the Michigan Civil Rights Initiative was eventually decided by the Supreme Court in April 2014 in *Schuette v. Coalition to Defend Affirmative Action.*[43] The Court ruled by a 6-2 vote that Michigan voters had a right to ban affirmative action in their state via a ballot initiative which amended the state's Constitution, on the basis that voters may determine whether a policy of race-based preferences should be continued or not. In the aftermath of *Schuette,* opponents of affirmative action policies seem to have gained a significant jurisprudential precedent to move towards further narrowing the substantive reading of the Equal Protection Clause, in spite of the fact that the decision was taken mostly with a view to the political process theory and the substantive

[39]Proposal 06-2 paras. 2 and 3, 3.696.701 registered voters voted. See the official results in http://miboecfr.nictusa.com/election/results/06GEN/90000002.html and the official ballot in http://www.michigan.gov/documents/Statewide_Bal_Prop_Status_145801_7.pdf (last accessed 31.12.2014).

[40]*Coalition to Defend Affirmative Action et al v. Jennifer Granholm, Governor of Michigan*, Application no 06-2640 (6th Cir 2006).

[41]Application no 06A678.

[42]Case nr 06-15024.

[43]572 US, Case No. 12-682 (2014).

meaning of democracy, whereas clear-cut equality arguments were auxiliary. By dispelling the view that affirmative action was constitutionally required, albeit constitutionally permissible provided that the *Gratz* and *Grutter* requirements were met, the Supreme Court abstained from a clear constitutional upgrade of affirmative action.

The above, necessarily schematic, analysis in relation to the implementation of affirmative action policies in the US, needs to be supplemented by some evidence on social awareness of these policies. The signals from legislative and private initiatives, public opinion polls and NGOs' activities have been mixed, when, at the same time, a number of States have altogether banned consideration of race in admissions to their public colleges and in public contracting. On the other hand, private companies and institutions (especially in the education sector) very often voluntarily initiate affirmative action, as part of their social responsibility policy. Not surprisingly, 30 major US companies submitted amicus briefs in favour of the University of Michigan in *Grutter* and *Gratz* before the Supreme Court, as a means to safeguard the constitutionality of their own entry or employment policies; whereas, apart from the Obama administration, 57 of the Fortune 100 companies and large numbers of public and private colleges supported the University of Texas' plan in the course of the *Fisher* case. This "industrialisation" of affirmative action from all sides of the debate has reasonably altered the means through which the policy is promoted. An entire industry now revolves around affirmative action in the US: pressure groups of benefiting or potentially benefiting groups or sub-groups (e.g. African American women), professional "civil rights leaders", i.e. managers specialising in promoting the rights of groups or sub-groups, "affirmative action personnel" within public entities, enterprises and institutions who are entrusted with the task to supervise and implement such policies, and are staffed mainly by people who have themselves benefited from affirmative action plans. Furthermore, a significant number of NGOs are engaged in the promotion of their respective views on affirmative action, especially by launching research programmes, lobbying, fund-raising and the open and active sponsoring of litigants in most of the relevant landmark judgments. Amongst the most powerful such organisations are the pro-affirmative action American Association for Access, Equity and Diversity[44] and the opposing Center of Individual Rights.[45] Not unreasonably, the headquarters of the two NGOs are found in Washington DC. Undeniably, affirmative action divides American society, as one can easily perceive through the front pages of the press just before and immediately after *Grutter/Gratz*, *Fisher* and *Schuette* decisions and the corresponding massive demonstrations outside the Supreme Court and throughout the capital in the course of this trial.

In summary, although it is *par excellence* an issue of US interest, there is a tendency, mainly on the part of the literature and public perception overseas, to overestimate its significance in the US legal system: Anderson (2004: 284) speaks of an "American dilemma"; Fredrickson (1998: 340) thinks of this policy as an

[44]http://www.affirmativeaction.org/.

[45]http://www.cir-usa.org/.

expression of the liberal or progressive conception of the American dream; Hollinger (1998: 108) envisages affirmative action theory as part of a vision for the US, Eastland (1996: 193) claims that the policy touches the heart of the nation itself; and Lipset (1996: 139), in more skeptical thinking, suggests that affirmative action constitutes an effort to maintain or change some of the basic values of the nation. The truth is, however, that only a limited and clearly delineated use of affirmative action plans has been initiated by federal or state authorities. More often than not, relevant legislation either entrenches the general principle of equality (in the same way the federal Constitution does), in which case a formal reading would result in the rejection of affirmative action, or only applies such measures in compartmentalised domains of public life, explicitly preventing spill-over effects. Even in the latter case, however, the measures do not introduce inflexible quotas but merely provide for plus factors on the part of underrepresented groups, thereby enhancing the equality of chances as opposed to the equality of results. A survey held by the US Congress in 1995 revealed that among 200 affirmative action plans introduced until then, there was not a single one that set out an explicit quota system but rather they included general measures of encouraging participation (Dale 1995).

Further, the US Supreme Court upholds affirmative action measures of indirect effect, whereas it discards rigid quotas or *de facto* quotas. The Court assesses measures using race as a criterion of differentiation on the basis of a thorough *ad hoc* standard of judicial review, i.e. strict scrutiny, of an arguably rather pragmatic nature (Sullivan 1993; Scalia 1989), which implies a test as to whether the impugned measure is narrowly tailored to achieving a compelling public interest. In the case of racial affirmative action, the Court departs from the general presumption of constitutionality[46] and from the conventional judicial self-restraint of American judges in the application of the Equal Protection Clause[47] through the vehicle of strict scrutiny as a result of a suspect classification.

It seems that the constitutional boundaries of affirmative action plans have not been firmly established yet. The sharp division of the Supreme Court in the 2003 *Grutter* and *Gratz*, its readiness to render a complimentary ruling on the issue 10 years later in *Fisher* and the continuous change in its composition suggest jurisprudential fluidity. The lengthy literature following all relevant decisions has maintained the issue's high position on the social and political agenda.

4.1.2 Canada

Section 15(2) of the 1982 Canadian Charter of Rights and Freedoms, which forms part of the Canadian Constitution, provides a general equality clause, stating that

[46]*Hazelwood School Dist. v. United States,* 433 US 299, 307–308 (1977) and *Teamsters v. United States*, 431 US 324, 339 (1977); the argument was nevertheless interpreted narrowly in *Richmond v. Croson,* 488 US 469 (1989).

[47]See indicatively, *Williamson v. Lee Optical Co.*, 348 US 483, 488–489 (1955).

"every individual is equal before and under the law and has the right to the equal protection and equal benefit of the law without discrimination and, in particular, without discrimination based on race, national or ethnic origin, colour, religion, sex, age or mental or physical disability".[48] Further, under the title "affirmative action programmes", the Charter adds that the general equality clause "does not preclude any law, programme or activity that has as its object the amelioration of conditions of disadvantaged individuals or groups including those that are disadvantaged because of race, national or ethnic origin, colour, religion, sex, age or mental or physical disability".[49] In light of the latter provision, affirmative action plans have been launched in Canada—especially with reference to natives, First Nations citizens, in various areas of public life, including university admissions (Busby 2006). These policies have, nevertheless, been accused on grounds of efficiency, not necessarily on constitutional grounds, of providing little assistance to the benefiting groups, because there remains an overwhelming emphasis on traditional quantitative criteria (basically tests scores e.g. UGPA and LSAT), thereby requiring minimum scores irrespective of the applicants' origins, whereas non-numerical criteria such as work experience, community service or membership in an underrepresented group would only be considered once test scores reached very high levels or in "borderline" cases (Tong and Pue 1999: 850–853).

The most analytical approach on affirmative action, and perhaps the most illustrative case-study worldwide, is to be found in the Quebec Charter of Human Rights and Freedoms which was passed by the National Assembly of Quebec on 27 June 1975 and became effective a year later. The Charter includes Part III (composed of 7 articles) exclusively on the implementation of the policy (Articles 86–92). It sets, amongst others, the object of the policy, i.e. "to remedy the situation of persons belonging to groups discriminated against in employment, or in the sector of education or of health services and other services generally available to the public" and provides guidance for the authorities, mostly the judiciary, that an affirmative action programme is deemed non-discriminatory if it is established in conformity with the procedure of the Charter for launching concrete affirmative action plans on the basis of race, colour, gender or ethnic origin. Accordingly, except for cases in which affirmative action measures are imposed by order of a tribunal, the established Human Rights and Youth Rights Commission (*Commission des droits de la personne et des droits de la jeunesse*) (Article 57), after investigation confirms the existence of a situation involving discrimination, may propose the implementation of an affirmative action programme within such time as it sees fit and has the authority to then approve it. Where its proposal has not been followed by the political branches of government, the Commission may apply to a tribunal and, on proof of the existence of a discrimination situation, obtain, an order to devise and implement a programme within the time fixed by the tribunal. The programme thus devised is filed with the tribunal which may, in accordance

---

[48]Article 15 para. 1.

[49]Article 15 para. 2.

with the Charter, make any appropriate amendments. The Commission also supervises the administration of the affirmative action programmes and may make investigations and require reports. Where the Commission becomes aware that an affirmative action programme has not been implemented within the prescribed time or is not being complied with, it may, in the case of a programme it has approved, withdraw its approval or, if it had proposed implementation of the programme, apply to a tribunal. A programme may be modified, postponed or cancelled if new facts warrant it. If the Commission and the person required or having consented to implement the affirmative action programme agrees on its modification, postponement or cancellation, the agreement shall be evidenced in writing. Failing agreement, either party may request the tribunal to which the Commission has applied, to decide whether the new facts warrant the modification, postponement or cancellation of the programme.

The leading judicial authority in the equality clause is *Law v. Canada* of 1999.[50] This decision of the Canadian Supreme Court requires that the determination of a discrimination claim shall be based on three broad inquiries: (1) whether the law, programme or activity imposes differential treatment between the claimant and others; (2) whether this differential treatment is based on race, colour, gender or ethnic origin or analogous grounds; and (3) whether the impugned law, programme or activity has a purpose or effect that is substantively discriminatory. Each of these inquiries proceeds on the basis of a comparative analysis which takes into consideration the surrounding context of the claim and the circumstances of the claimant. Two further authorities establish the ameliorative dimension of Section 15. In 1989, the Supreme Court in *Andrews v. Law Society of British Columbia*[51] declared that the state must cater to the amelioration of the position of those who have suffered disadvantage by exclusion while preventing the attribution of stereotypical characteristics to individuals. Further, in 1997 *Eaton v. Brant County Board of Education*,[52] the Court found that a decision by an Administrative Board and Tribunal to place a child in a special education classroom did not violate the amelioration mandate since the measure did not impose on the child a burden or disadvantage.

The particular relationship between the general equality clause and the affirmative action clause, co-existing in the same article, was determined in the 2008 Federal Supreme Court case *R. v. Kapp.*[53] In this decision the Court found the Aboriginal Fisheries Strategy allowing for a privileged, prior to regular, period of 24 h for Aborigines to fish for salmon compatible with the federal Constitution, reversing the appellate decision to the opposite effect. The appellants, who were all commercial fishers, mainly non-aboriginal, excluded from the fishery during this 24-h period, took to the water in protest and were charged with fishing at a

[50](1999) 1 SCR 497.

[51](1989) 1 SCR 143.

[52](1997) 1 SCR 241.

[53]2008 SCC 41.

prohibited time. During the judicial proceedings, the state set forth various objectives for the programme, such as negotiating/furthering solutions to aboriginal fishing rights claims, providing economic opportunities for native tribes and supporting their progress towards self-sufficiency. The Court found, first, that the means chosen to achieve these purposes were rationally related to serving them and, accordingly, the state had established a credible ameliorative purpose for the programme (which was a statutory requirement); and, second, that the programme targeted a disadvantaged group identified in terms of income, education and a host of other characteristics, while discrimination continuing until the trial. Before *R. v. Kapp,* the Supreme Court had also taken a favourable stance towards affirmative action in *Lovelace v. Ontario,*[54] *Athabasca Tribal Council v. Amoco*[55] and *Canadian National Railway Company v. Canada (Canadian Human Rights Commission).*[56] In this last decision, Action Travail des Femmes alleged that the Canadian National Railway Company was guilty of discriminatory hiring and promotion practices, by denying employment opportunities to women in certain unskilled blue-collar positions. The *ad hoc* Human Rights Tribunal found in favour of the plaintiff and concluded that it was essential to impose upon the defendant a special temporary order requiring a 13 % national average increase of the percentage of female employees and, until that goal was achieved, to hire at least one woman for every four relevant posts. The Federal Court of Appeal reversed this on the grounds of excess of power on the part of the Tribunal, which was restricted to merely prescribing measures for the purpose of preventing the future recurrence of discriminatory practices which had been found to exist, and not to remedy the consequences of past discrimination, although one might reasonably argue that the distinction between the two is not as clear-cut as it might seem. Eventually, the Supreme Court, after identifying systematic denial of women's equal employment opportunities, upheld the constitutionality of the Tribunal's order by declaring its statutory power to impose upon an employer an "employment equity programme" to address the problem of "systemic discrimination" in the hiring and promotion of a disadvantaged group.

Overall, Canada provides an adequate institutional basis for large-scale affirmative action policies. However, when challenged before a court of law, these policies will be subject to very thorough scrutiny so as to justify/meet/comply with the two-fold constitutional requirement that it awards benefits to truly disadvantaged, compared to the rest of society, individuals and that it effectively ameliorates their position. In so doing, the Canadian courts will take into consideration plentiful statistical and other contextual data, which is not very common in US jurisprudence, and to some extent will substitute their own judgment for that of the legislature or the

---

[54]*Lovelace v. Ontario* 2000 SCC 37.

[55](1986) 1 SCR 699.

[56](1987) 1 SCR 1114.

executive. Consistent with the explicit constitutional acknowledgment, the general tendency seems to be towards upholding, in principle, affirmative action, without prejudice to a protected core of equality *per se* (Clancy 2004). In Christopher Totten's assessment, Canada's constitutional pre-commitment towards affirmative action, at least at the federal level, as compared to the European Union and Germany, reflects a degree of consensus, which may reflect either a strong belief on the expediency of the policy or a faith that the Constitution entails the enactment of such measures (Totten 2003: 50–51).

Nevertheless, affirmative action in Canada seems to be oriented mostly towards race as opposed to gender. The "politics of displacement", as Bacchi (1996: 57–78) suggests, caused by the historical division between English and French speakers in Canada, has led to the introduction of new identity categories, thus fusing employment equity for four targeted groups jointly, i.e. visible minorities, Aboriginals, disabled and women, without a specific tailor-made plan for adopting positive actions in favour of the underrepresented sex.

4.1.3 Brazil

Brazil is a very interesting case in the field of affirmative action. The most populated nation of South America, inhabited by a great number of races, albeit slavery having been abolished only in 1888, it is in a sense more homogeneous than other American states, because the Portuguese colonists were not established in the country, but mostly used it as a stopover to extract national wealth for the metropolitan state. In the 19th and 20th centuries, in light of further immigration from Europe and Asia, Brazil launched a series of institutional tools to promote racial integration and mixing (Telles 2004). Part of the integration policy, concerned affirmative action plans introducing minority quotas in the field of higher education, largely following the US model (Telles and Paixao 2013). This was a rather unexpected development given that there was no prior experience of such measures and Brazilian society was not accustomed to similar positive state actions. In fact, there was a complete subversion of the political paradigm from a long-lasting and very persistent policy of "racial democracy" entailing equal treatment as a means of integration, i.e. a more passive attitude of the state merely to safeguard non-discrimination, to one of positive action to provide racial equilibrium (Da Silva Martins et al. 2004). The policy change was largely motivated, if not attributed, to the findings of the 3rd World Conference against Racism held in Durban in 2001, in which Brazil had very extensive levels of participation and representation. Interestingly, and similarly to South Africa, the benefiting groups constitute the majority of the population but they are widely underrepresented in most domains of public life. Further, in Brazil, electoral lists of political parties for both Houses and States parliaments must contain 30–70 % of candidates from each gender. If the gender ceiling is trespassed by 150 % of total seats per constituency, candidates of the over-represented sex are removed from office.[57]

The very activist Supreme Federal Court of Brazil has rendered two authoritative decisions on the matter. Both decisions upheld the constitutionality of affirmative action by indicating that such positive measures fulfil the State's responsibility to achieve diversity and compensate for past discrimination, and are proportionate, temporary and reasonable. The first case concerned racial quotas in student admissions at the University of Brasilia for a period of 10 years for specific underrepresented groups, i.e. reservation of 20 % of places for Afro-Brazilian students and a small portion for indigenous members of ethnic groups, who inhabited the country prior to the European invasion around 1500.[58] Paradoxically, the application against the University of Brasilia's Regulations was filed by the Democratic Party (Democratas Party, DEM), on grounds of a breach of the Constitution stipulating the establishment of a free, fair and united society and the eradication of social marginalisation and inequality, of the principles of human dignity and equality, the elimination of racism and provisions for universal access to education (Article 3). The Court unanimously found in favour of the University policy. The second case upheld the constitutionality of statute 11.096/2005 providing combined race-based and socio-economical scholarship quotas for private higher education in favour of low-income vulnerable groups (i.e. Afro-descendants, indigenous persons and persons with disabilities), entitled the "ProUni - University for All Program".[59] The petitioner, National Confederation of Educational Institutions (Confenen), claimed unconstitutionality of the statute by alleging violations, inter alia, of the equality principle[60]; of the separation of powers due to the awarding to the Chief Executives of authority to make use of positive discrimination in the absence of a compelling public interest[61]; of university autonomy[62]; of the freedom of enterprise[63]. In upholding the statute with a majority vote of 7-1, the Court emphasised the significance of positive discrimination quotas as a means to achieve social integration (Francis and Tannuri-Pianto 2013).

In the above two cases, the rationale of the Supreme Federal Court might have been influenced by political considerations. Justice Joaquim Barbosa, black himself with an exceptionally strong personality, later Chief Justice and selected by Time magazine as one of the 100 most influential people in the world, argued that one cannot neglect the fact that world history does not provide a single case of a nation rising from a regional nation to a political and economic power, respectable in the international arena, by domestically maintaining a policy of exclusion regarding a

[57]Article 10 para. 3 of Law 9504/30.09.1997.

[58]ADPF 186/2012.

[59]ADI 3330/2012.

[60]Article 135 of the Constitution.

[61]Article 62 in conjunction with Article 2 of the Constitution.

[62]Article 207 of the Constitution.

[63]Article 107 of the Constitution.

significant part of its population. In the same line of argumentation, then Chief Justice Ayres Britto categorically declared that this was the way to build a nation. Irrespective of their potential political motivations, these judgments render Brazil as the friendliest legal system in the Americas towards affirmative action, even in its most intrusive form, namely racial quotas entailing positive discrimination. In this way, Brazil has indeed gone further than the US prototype (Skidmore 2003).

4.2 Europe

The literature on positive discrimination in Europe is not as extensive as it is in America. From a legal point of view, the issue seems to have started to attract academic attention only in the late '90s following major decisions issued by the then European Court of Justice. Broadly speaking, the debate on positive discrimination in Europe seems to be to a great extent subsumed in the broader discussion on equality and non-discrimination, thus lacking specific reference work.[64] This sub-section begins with the developments at the level of European Union law, followed by a description of the legal situation in a selection of EU Member States.

4.2.1 European Union Law

The non-discrimination principle has had a significant status within EU law as a rudimentary condition needed to guarantee the basic community freedoms. In fact, although equality may present a social perspective in the sense that it broadly determines a model of social interaction, its concrete aspects, such as equal access to markets, equality of labour conditions and equal pay, also have economic implications and therefore clearly fall within the scope of EU law. Unsurprisingly there is a very large volume of judgments by the EU courts relating to the implementation of the non-discrimination principle[65] and an equally extensive

[64]The most elaborate research database in the field is that of the European Network of Legal Experts in the Non-Discrimination Field (http://www.non-discrimination.net), which periodically publishes national reports on equality status, from which significant information has been drawn in the following analysis.

[65]CJEU Judgment of 11th January 2000, Case C-285/98, *Tanja Kreil v. Germany* Rec. 2000, p. I-69, para. 18; CJEU Judgment of 19th March 2002, Case C-476/99, *Lommers v. Minister van Landbouw, Natuurbeheer en Visserij,* Rec. 2002, p. I-2891, para. 25; CJEU Judgment of 30th September 2004, Case C-319/03, *Serge Briheche v. Ministre de l'Intérieur et als.,* Rec. 2004, p. 8807, para. 18; CJEU Judgment of 15th June 1978, Case 149/77, *Gabrielle Defrenne v. Société anonyme belge de navigation aérienne Sabena,* Rec. 1978, p. 1365. The Court has made use of the European Social Charter to ground the non-discrimination principle in labour relations in its 1978 judgment, *Gabrielle Defrenne v. Société anonyme belge de navigation aérienne Sabena* (CJEU

academic literature which analyses this body of case-law (Bribosia 1999; Martin 2006; Schiek and Chege 2009).

From an institutional point of view, the recognition of positive action followed a different evolutionary path: it was first acknowledged at the level of secondary law and then became part of the revised treaties. In relation to non-discrimination on grounds of sex, the first measure of secondary Community law was Council *Directive 76/207* of 9th February 1976, on the implementation of the equal treatment principle for men and women regarding access to employment, vocational training and promotion, and working conditions, applying both to public and private labour relations. According to Article 2 para. 4 of the Directive, its implementation "shall be without prejudice to measures to promote equal opportunity for men and women, in particular by removing existing inequalities which affect women's opportunities". *Directive 76/207* was later amended by *Directive 2002/73* of the European Parliament and of the Council of 23rd September 2002,[66] which in relation to the application of affirmative action makes reference to the Treaty of Amsterdam, which had entered into force in the meantime (Recital 15 of the Preamble). The new Directive also indicated that the prohibition of discrimination should be without prejudice to the maintenance or adoption of measures intended to prevent or compensate for disadvantages suffered by a group of persons of one sex, including the establishment of organisations of persons of one sex where their main object is the promotion of the special needs of those persons and the promotion of equality between women and men (Recital 15 of the Preamble). *Directive 76/207*, as amended, has been historically the basic institutional tool for gender-based positive action requirements in employment in the European Community context.

Meanwhile, affirmative action considerations in favour of women at work can be traced to the process of drafting strategies for equality policies, irrespective of their legal nature/binding force. Thus, the European Council, in its 1994 resolution regarding the fair participation of women in a strategy of financial development oriented towards reinforcing employment, has stressed the need to improve working time, promote high levels of women's qualifications and encourage independent professional activity and female entrepreneurship.[67] Underrepresentation of women in the Community decision-making was examined as part of the democratic deficit through the 1992 Athens Declaration, which resulted in the Commission taking active steps to combat this pathology and develop strategies for wider participation of women in cooperation with the network "Women in Decision-Making", while underrepresentation of women in high ranking positions was considered a serious default of community obligations (Hubert 2001: 152–154).

(Footnote 65 continued)

Judgment of 15th June 1978, Case 149/77, Rec. 1978, p. 1365) considered to be the milestone for the upgrade of equality to a fundamental community principle.

[66]OJ L 269 of 5th October 2002, p. 15.

[67]OJ C 368, 23rd December 1994, p. 3.

The most explicit reference to positive measures was made in two Council Recommendations. Through *Recommendation 84/635* of 13th December 1984 the Council recommended that Member States adopt a positive action policy designed to eliminate existing inequalities affecting women in working life and to promote a better balance between the sexes in employment, comprising appropriate general and specific measures, within the framework of national policies and practices. The purposes of those measures should be to eliminate or counteract the severe impacts of existing attitudes, behaviour and structures based on the idea of a traditional division of societal roles between men and women, on women in employment or seeking employment, and to encourage the participation of women in various occupations in those sectors of working life where they are at present underrepresented, particularly in "the sectors of the future", and at higher levels of responsibility in order to achieve better use of all available human resources. The Recommendation also provides for mechanisms for controlling the implementation of such measures and the gathering of all relevant information.

In addition, through *Recommendation 96/694*, of 2nd December 1996 on the balanced participation of women and men in the decision-making process,[68] the Council recommended that the Member States: (a) adopt a comprehensive, integrated strategy designed to promote the balanced participation of women and men in the decision-making process and develop or introduce the appropriate measures to achieve this; (b) raise social awareness at all levels in relation to equal participation and towards the abolition of stereotypes; (c) promote or improve the collection and publication of relevant data; and (d) promote balanced participation by women and men at all levels of administration.

Explicit reference to positive measures is made in the secondary EU law in the early 2000s. In the field of racial equality, Council *Directive 2000/43* of 29th June 2000,[69] applying to the public and private sectors in relation to the conditions of access to employment, to self-employment and to occupation, including selection criteria and recruitment conditions, promotion, access to all types and to all levels of vocational guidance and training provides that with a view to ensuring full equality in practice, the principle of equal treatment does not prevent any Member State from maintaining or adopting specific measures to prevent or compensate for disadvantages linked to racial or ethnic origin (Article 5). In the field of non-discrimination on grounds of religion or belief, disability, age or sexual orientation, Council *Directive 2000/78* of 27 November 2000,[70] provided that the principle of equal treatment shall not prevent any Member State from maintaining or adopting specific measures in employment and occupation to prevent or compensate for disadvantages linked to grounds (Article 7 para. 1). Finally in the field of gender equality, Council *Directive 2004/113* of 13 December 2004,[71] provided

[68]OJ L 319 of 10th December 1996, p. 11.

[69]OJ L 180 of 19th July 2000, p. 22.

[70]OJ L 303 of 2nd December 2000, p. 16.

[71]OJ L 373 of 21st December 2004, p. 37.

that the principle of equal treatment shall not prevent any Member State from maintaining or adopting specific measures to prevent or compensate for disadvantages linked to sex in the access to and supply of goods and services. The above set of Directives is of particular importance for the implementation of positive measures. For, they are the only institutional vehicle that applies horizontally in the whole of Europe in their respective areas of application after having been incorporated into domestic legal orders.

At the level of primary law, positive action was initially acknowledged through the *Social Policy Agreement* signed by 11 of the EC Member States in December 1991 annexed to the Social Policy Protocol and eventually incorporated into the Social Chapter of the EC Treaty through the Treaty of Amsterdam. The Agreement confirmed that the equal pay principle does not prevent Member States from introducing measures awarding benefits to women to prevent or compensate for disadvantages in their professional careers.[72] The *Treaty of Amsterdam* upgraded affirmative action through the introduction of a new para. 4 in Article 141 (formerly 119) according to which Member States "may maintain or adopt measures providing for specific advantages in order to make it easier for the underrepresented sex to pursue a vocational activity or to prevent or compensate for disadvantages in professional careers".[73] The Treaty of Amsterdam generally adopted the concept of substantive equality by providing in its general principles that the Community shall pursue equality between men and women and the prevention of discrimination (Article 2). The upgrade of social rights and, in turn, of the social aspect of equality was facilitated by the politics of the relevant time. At the Maastricht summit in December 1991, the United Kingdom rejected the proposal on the future direction of social policy in the new European Union and refused to be bound by the Agreement on Social Policy. Accordingly, the Social Policy Protocol to the Treaty of Maastricht embodied a compromise in the form of an "opt-out" for the UK, thus creating a two-track EU social policy. In contrast, in May 1997, the newly elected labour UK government decided to terminate the "opt-out" and, therefore, by the Treaty of Amsterdam, the Social Policy Protocol was deleted and the Agreement on Social Policy was incorporated into a revised 'Social Chapter' of the EC Treaty (Rubery et al. 1999: 54).

Two particular aspects of the Treaty of Amsterdam provision are note-worthy. First, there is no mention of the beneficiaries of the positive measures but merely a reference to the "underrepresented sex". Accordingly, even men could be the beneficiaries of positive action provided that they are underrepresented within a particular labour environment; it seems, anyway, that no other criterion apart from sex, such as race or religion, can be an acceptable ground for the application of the clause. Second, the goals pursued by a positive measure are clearly set out and delineated, namely assistance to pursue a vocational activity, the prevention of disadvantages and compensation for disadvantages in professional careers. Strictly

[72]OJ C 321 E of 29th December 2006, p. 110.

[73]OJ C 321 E of 29 December 2006, p. 110.

speaking however, only help in pursuing a profession or compensation for past discrimination is causally linked to the implementation of a positive action plan. Due to the inherent fluidity of the criterion, "prevention" cannot be a strictly legal *ratio* able to justify the introduction of a measure in favour of substantive equality.

Finally, equality constituted a special seven-article chapter (III) of the *Charter of Fundamental Rights* drafted in the first Convention and approved at the Nice Summit that became part of the Treaty establishing a Constitution for Europe (Braibant 2001; Carlier and Schutter 2002; Eeckhout 2002). In spite of the rejection of the Constitutional Treaty following negative referenda in France and the Netherlands in May and June 2005 respectively, the abandonment of partially complete ratification procedures by Finland, Germany and Slovakia and the indefinite postponement of consideration in seven other Member States, the Charter became part of primary law through the entry into force of the *Lisbon Treaty* on December 1st, 2009, upgraded through an amendment of Article 6 para. 1 of the *Treaty on the European Union*.[74] Through the Treaty of Amsterdam and the incorporation of the Charter, affirmative action received two-fold primary legal recognition, both as a principle and a policy.

First, affirmative action as a *principle* is guaranteed in Article 43 of the Charter of Fundamental Rights (Article II-112 para. 2), according to which the principle of equality shall not prevent the maintenance or adoption of measures providing for specific advantages in favour of the underrepresented sex. The legal nature of Article 43 of the Charter on the ability to assume affirmative action does not reach the point of being properly characterised as a right, but merely constitutes a principle (Article 52 para. 5 of the Charter). From this viewpoint, the Charter's equality provision has a mixed character: with regard to providing equality of men and women in all sectors, it introduces a fully enforceable right, whereas in relation to retaining or establishing measures in favour of the underrepresented sex it merely acknowledges a principle that ought to be taken into account when drafting policies or conducting legal interpretation. Unlike fully-fledged rights, principles cannot be directly invoked by European citizens but are mostly addressed to the Union authorities and the Member States, when they act in the field of EU law. Accordingly, it is within the discretion of these bodies to turn the principle into actual policies; only on this condition does the principle produce immediate effects for the individuals involved. The Charter explicitly provides that principles cannot have a spill-over interpretative effect in all areas of Union activity, but merely casts light upon specific rules when enacted. This shortfall in the effectiveness of the Charter can be explained in light of the political considerations accompanying any effort to institutionally reinforce the European Union, i.e. the fear that full acknowledgment of social rights at a Union level will result in a corresponding

---

[74]Pursuant to Protocol 30 on the Application of the Charter of Fundamental Rights to Poland and the UK, national and EU courts do not have the ability to find that national provisions of the two countries are inconsistent with the rights and freedoms of the Charter, and these rights and freedoms only apply to said Member States insofar as they are recognised by domestic law.

enlargement of its competences in fields strictly reserved for state sovereignty, and place an additional financial burden upon the Member States to meet the costly requirements of an extensive social state.

Second, affirmative action as a *policy* is established in the section concerning the policies and functioning of the Union by Article II-83 of the Charter, of Fundamental Rights, according to which secondary EU legislation shall establish measures to ensure the application of the principle of equal opportunity and equal treatment of women and men in matters of employment and occupation, including the principle of equal pay for equal work or work of equal value. Article II-83 is exercised "with the terms and within the limits" of Article III-214 para. 4, which stipulates that the Charter reaffirms the EU's adherence to positive action with a view to ensuring full equality in practice between women and men in working life—included in the same line within the Treaty of Amsterdam. Institutional recognition of affirmative action as a policy should not be overrated. It is exclusively reserved for professional activities of men and women ("issues of employment at work" for Union authorities, or "professional life" for Member-States). Therefore, it does not have the essence of an individual-oriented right but mostly reflects the orientation and delimitation of the Union's competences. This is why the provision makes a clear-cut distinction as to the origin of the positive measures. If the measure is introduced by a Union authority, then not only equal treatment (entailing formal equality) but also equal opportunity (entailing substantive equality) need to be preserved; whereas policies introduced by Member States may maintain or adopt measures providing for specific advantages in favour of the underrepresented sex. As a result, the Member States *may* choose to launch such measures or not, whereas the Union authorities *must* embrace policies to establish substantive equality measures. Thus, the Charter seems to provide adequate institutional grounds for the enactment of affirmative action EU policies in favour of the underrepresented sex in employment, but not in any other fields arguably falling outside the Union scope or in favour of other underrepresented groups, for example on the grounds of race or religion.

On the level of secondary EU law, in November 2012 the European Commission adopted the proposal of EU Justice Commissioner Viviane Reding for a Directive that would regulate a women's quota in management boards of European listed companies in all 27 countries of the European Union ("Proposal for a Directive of the European Parliament and of the Council on improving the gender balance among non-executive directors of companies listed on stock exchanges and related measures").[75] In November 2013, the European Parliament enhanced the Directive through a Resolution pursuant to ordinary legislative procedure.[76] Among the proposed amendments by the Parliament, the most relevant is an addition of a recital (7c) reading as follows:

---

[75]COM(2012) 614 final of 14 November 2012.

[76]COM(2012) 614 – C7-0382/2012 – 2012/0299 (COD).

> The attainment of gender equality in society as a whole entails the establishment of equal academic and professional rights for men and women, and of shared family, childcare and household responsibilities. The fact that women are typically responsible for the large majority of family and household chores may hinder their advancement to top professional positions. Active participation and involvement of men in family responsibilities is crucial for the attainment of a work-life balance and for the creation of equal career opportunities for both men and women. Attention should be paid to tackling gender stereotyping, inflexible and outdated employment policies and inadequate parental leave provisions. Provisions should be in place for women and men to combine family and work life should they so wish. Member States should be encouraged to ensure the implementation of welfare elements such as fair parental leave allowances for both women and men, extensive provision for childcare and opportunities for shared parental leave.

Accordingly, as of 2020, 5000 large listed companies (i.e. excluding those with less than 250 employees, or less than 50 million euros in turnover, or an annual balance sheet of less than 43 million euros) would have to fill two of five board positions with women. As far as non-executive directors are concerned, the overall goal is to achieve a minimum representation of 40 % of the underrepresented sex by 2020 for companies in the private sector and by 2018 for state-owned companies. The Directive is a temporary measure envisaged to cease being in effect by 2028. Companies are also required to annually provide information on gender representation on their boards and to ensure a transparent recruitment process. Companies not meeting the objectives of the Directive will be called to provide justification for their failure, whereas Member States would themselves decide effective, proportionate and dissuasive sanctions for the violating companies (Selanec and Senden 2011–2012). The Commission, thus, used the Norwegian prototype, which has been indeed diffused in the national legislation of many countries around Europe. Accordingly, binding quotas are provided in France for 40 % to be reached by 2017, in Italy for 33.3 % by 2015 and in Belgium for 33.3 % by 2019. Non-binding quota goals are set in the Netherlands for 30 % and in Spain for 40 %. The proposal has encountered, however, hindrances in its way to become binding through the ordinary EU legislative procedure. In November 2013, the proposal passed through the first reading in the European Parliament but a year later, in December 2014, the Council discussed the proposal but "was not able to reach a general approach" because of substantive and subsidiarity concern raised by Member States.[77]

As regards the EU jurisprudence on the issue, even before the explicit recognition of positive action, there were judicial voices arguing in favour of this policy as part of the overall structure of equality.[78] In *Commission v. France*, the Court of Justice of the European Union placed emphasis upon the goal of equality of opportunity as the prevailing notion of equality.[79] However, the landmark case-law

[77]Press Release 16803/1/14 REV1 of 11th December 2014, http://www.consilium.europa.eu/uedocs/cms_data/docs/pressdata/en/lsa/146172.pdf (last accessed 31.12.2014).

[78]Opinion of Advocate General Darmon of 27 June 1984 in Case 184/83, *Ulrich Hofmann v. Barmer Ersatzkasse*, Rec. 1984, p. 3047, para. 9.

[79]CJEU Judgment of 25 October 1988, Case C-312/86, *Commission v. France*, Rec. 1988, p. 6315.

on affirmative action was beyond any doubt shaped during the years 1995–1997 with the two major *Kalanke* and *Marschall* decisions. Over these years the Court assumed responsibility for assessing affirmative action plans against *Directive 76/207*, following the general tendency in many domestic legal systems to employ measures to approach substantive equality, although such measures were rather unknown within the EU legal system.

In *Kalanke*, the Court held that a measure aiming at facilitating women's access to male dominated employment areas was in principle compatible with EU law, provided that the law does not establish a direct and unreserved priority to women.[80] Accordingly, the Court of Justice of the European Union upheld affirmative action measures of an indirect effect, by essentially rejecting rigid quotas on the grounds that they produce discrimination on another level. The case was brought before the Court after a preliminary reference sent by the German Federal Court of Employment Disputes (*Bundesarbeitsgericht*) with regard to the interpretation of Article 2 paragraphs 1 and 4 of *Directive 76/207*. In particular, the Bremen law on the equal treatment of men and women in public services provided that in the recruitment, development and salary status of public employees, women who have equal qualifications as male candidates, must be given priority of consideration in the sections in which they are underrepresented. The referring court held that the controversial legislation was compatible both with the German Basic Law and the Constitution of the Bremen Land and submitted a preliminary request regarding the compatibility of the controversial affirmative action measure against the said Directive.

The first premise in the Court's deductive reasoning was that a national rule which automatically provides priority of one sex over the other is tantamount to discrimination, thus generally upholding the mainstays of formal equality. The Court found though that a legitimate exception to this rule was affirmative action policy stemming from Article 2 para. 4 of *Directive 76/207* as an expression of equal opportunity. The rule-exception scheme raised two methodological consequences. First, according to general principles of interpretation, any permissible deviation from an EU right ought to be interpreted narrowly. Second, equality of chances constituted the furthest limit of the formal equality rule within EU law, which, therefore, did not embrace more acute versions of substantive equality such as rigid quotas, characterised by the Court as "representation equality". Nonetheless, careful deconstruction of the *Kalanke* rationale demonstrates partial inconsistency. The court's unconditional premise that a system aiming at establishing equal representation between men and women at all levels of a professional environment was contrary to EU law, could be logically explained to lead to an unconditional rejection of the challenged positive discrimination measure. However, at the end of its *ratio decidendi* the Court placed particular emphasis upon the "automatic" preference awarded by the impugned law to members of one

[80]CJEU Judgment of 17 October 1995, Case C-450/93, *Eckhard Kalanke v. Freie Hansestadt Bremen*, Rec. 1995, p. I-3051.

sex. Thus, the critical issue was the *ipso facto* preference and the corresponding lack of other criteria for relative weighing and evaluation. In this respect, the Court deviated from Advocate General Tesauro's opinion, which suggested that no positive discrimination measure operating at the end results could be tolerated by EU law since it would be definitely disproportionate in relation to the aim pursued by directly conferring the results on women.[81]

In light of the above, the scheme providing for the unreserved priority of women against men of the same qualifications for access to public service was considered as violating EU law. This judgment provoked huge criticism mainly on the grounds that it failed to tackle/respond to the call for more substantive equality (Moore 1996; Klinck 1997; Peters 1996; Fredman 1996; Szyszczak 1996). Pager (2003) further argues that the Court overstepped its jurisdiction and should have left the issue to the national courts as a matter of "judicial subsidiarity". These reactions raised the awareness of the European Commission which issued a Communication addressed to the Council and the Parliament essentially delineating the *ratio decidendi* of the Court by "clarifying its interpretation of the judgment". Interestingly, the Communication cited an indicative list of measures that might be acceptable and suggested an amendment to *Directive 76/207* in order for the *Kalanke* ruling to be overcome. According to the Commission:

> The only form of positive action condemned by the Court is the rigid quota system under which there is no possibility of taking particular individual circumstances into account. It [*the Commission*] believes that there are many forms of positive action which are not affected by the judgment in question, and that Member States and employers may avail themselves of a wide range of positive measures such as State subsidies granted to employers who recruit women in sectors where they are underrepresented, positive training-oriented action, vocational guidance, child care and flexible quotas.[82]

A few months later, in light of the *Kalanke* case-law the Commission issued a proposal for a Council Directive, amending *Directive 76/207*, to the effect that measures to promote equal opportunity for men and women, in particular by removing existing inequalities which affect the opportunities of the underrepresented sex, such as giving preference as regards access to employment or promotion, are tolerated, provided that they do not preclude the assessment of the particular circumstances of an individual case.[83] The proposal was rejected by the European Parliament in the course of the consultation procedure as inadequate. The Parliament asked the Commission "to submit a proposal for a directive based on the Treaty of Amsterdam and on recognition of the collective nature of positive action measures, which contains mandatory legal instructions to take positive action wherever necessary in order to achieve equal treatment and opportunities for men

[81]Opinion of Advocate General Tesauro of 6 April 1995 in Case C-450/93, *Eckhard Kalanke v. Freie Hansestadt Bremen*, Rec. 1995, p. I-3051, para. 24.

[82]COM 96/88 of 27th March 1996.

[83]COM 96/93, EE C 179 of 22nd June 1996, p. 8.

and women and to remedy the underrepresentation of women at all levels of decision-making".[84]

Two years after *Kalanke*, the Court of Justice of the European Union had the opportunity to revisit its positive action doctrine in *Marschall*. The pressure with respect to this case was immense not only because of the delicate issue involved but also because of the participation of a significant number of Member States and of the Commission itself, which intervened in favour of upholding the compatibility of the affirmative action measure in question. The facts of the case were identical to *Kalanke* with the only variation being that the crucial statute provided a 'saving clause' to counterbalance its general prioritisation of women over men. Accordingly, the Law on Civil Servants of the German Land Nordrhein-Westfalen provided that where, in the sector of the authority responsible for promotion, there were fewer women than men in a particular higher level employment post, women were to be given priority for promotion in the event of equal suitability, competence and professional performance, "unless reasons specific to an individual [male] candidate tilt the balance in his favour". This saving clause constituted the ground for upholding the statute. According to the judgment, unlike the rules at issue in *Kalanke*, a national rule which contained a saving clause did not exceed permissible limits if, in each individual case, it provided for male candidates who were equally qualified as the female candidates a guarantee that the candidatures would be the subject of an objective assessment which would take account of all criteria specific to the individual candidates.[85]

Of course, for reasons of credibility and sustainability of its case-law the Court could not expressly concede that its very recent *Kalanke* judgment was wrong and in need of being revisited. On the other hand, the Court ought to balance the reactions caused because of its precedent, as well as the constantly widening trend of claiming women's rights during the critical period between the two decisions. This is why the Court tried to build an interpretative bridge between its two decisions by maintaining two basic premises that survived in both *Kalanke* and *Marschall*. First principle: the aim sought by affirmative action cannot be equal results, but only starting point of equality to claim a professional position. Second principle: no affirmative action measure awarding automatic prevalence can *in globo* claim EU legality. Nonetheless, the deviation of the Court from its prior case-law might be explicable in light of the context of the case but does not enjoy a sound rationale. In *Kalanke*, the Court demanded criteria for the objective evaluation of candidates and in *Marschall* it was satisfied with the saving clause in question. However, the need to have criteria is a demand relating to the decision-making process and is logically prior to the eventual result of an evaluation.

---

[84]COM 96/93, EE C 175 of 21st June 1999, p. 67. The force of the suggested amendment expired on 9th January 2004.

[85]CJEU Judgment of 11th November 1997, Case C-409/95, *Hellmut Marschall v. Land Nordhein-Westfalen,* Rec. 1997, p. I-6363, paras. 24, 33.

In order to achieve its conclusion, the Court deviated from the *Kalanke* precedent, as well as two judicial opinions to the contrary. On the one hand, the referring German Court, applying the *Kalanke* standards, found that positive discrimination quotas are not, in principle, permissible, whereas the saving clause did not effectively prevent discrimination against men. In light of the recent *Kalanke* judgment, the German Court might well had abstained from referring a preliminary question based on the *acte claire* doctrine which allows domestic courts to decide cases of an EU interest if there is an EU ruling determining the legal issues in question. On the other hand, the Court went contrary to the view expressed by Advocate General Danton that the Court should abide by *Kalanke* and overturned the impugned measure on three grounds. First, an escape clause cannot change the scope and the binding effect of a discriminatory rule. Second, the escape clause was vague and fluid, thus violating the principles of legitimate expectations and consistency of law. Third, in order for a discriminatory rule to become compatible with EU law on the grounds of including an escape clause, the escape clause itself must be in line with EU law. However, according to the Advocate General's view, the escape clause triggers secondary discrimination due to the criteria it used: if an unconditional rule in favour of women on ground of their gender is unacceptable, the rule allowing prevalence of women due to their gender or of men due to undefined criteria (e.g. the defendant State alleged antiquity and social grounds) in implementation of the escape clause should *a fortiori* be considered unacceptable; thus, this clause necessarily presupposed some criteria in favour of men that would be nonetheless discriminatory.[86] In any case, the Court classified in a negative way the relevant permissible criteria by ruling that only equality at the starting point and not equality of end-results was permissible and, therefore, no rigid quota system could be acceptable. Anyhow, the Court clearly adopted a more substantive view of equality in *Marschall* that left an open window for future case law adaptations (Cabral 1998; Barnard and Hervey 1998).

Later decisions of the Court, such as in *Badeck*,[87] essentially confirmed the *Marschall* jurisprudence. In *Abrahamsson and Anderson,* the Court held that a selection procedure can include some priority clauses in favour of women as long as their implementation is transparent and any arbitrary assessment is prohibited.[88] By the same token, the European Free Trade Association (EFTA) Court in decision *Surveillance Authority v. Norway,* rejected a measure according to which permanent or temporary academic posts were reserved for women on the grounds that there was no flexibility in the 1978 Norwegian Gender Equality Act, which

[86]Opinion of Advocate General Jacobs of 15 May 1997 in Case C-409/95, *Hellmut Marschall v. Land Nordhein–Westfalen,* Rec. 1997, p. I-6363, paras. 8, 34-36.

[87]CJEU Judgment of 28 March 2000, Case C-158/97, *Georg Badeck et als,* Rec. 2000, p. I-1875.

[88]CJEU Judgment of 6 July 2000, Case C-407/98, *Katarina Abrahamsson and Leif Anderson v. Elisabet Fogelqvist,* Rec. 2000, p. I-5539.

automatically excluded men from these very posts allowing the different treatment that promotes gender equality, thus violating Article 3 para. 1 of *Directive 76/207*.[89]

Further case law not directly assessing affirmative action programmes but mostly differential treatment between men and women based on traditional assumptions about stereotypical allocation of roles between men and women were issued by the Court in the 2000s. In *Griesmar*, it held that the stipulation of the French civil and military pension's retirement scheme excluding men from a service credit for children, even in a case where a man could prove that he had the care of his children, was contrary to EU law.[90] In the same way, it was decided in *Briheche* that provisions reserving for widows who had not remarried the benefit of the exemption from the age-limit for obtaining access to public sector employment was contrary to EU law because it treated differently men who were in the same factual situation with women of the same status.[91] In *Lommers* the Court upheld a Dutch measure according to which there were places in nurseries reserved only for children of female officials, save in cases of emergency to be decided by the employer, on the grounds that there were no employment position reservations but merely the establishment of better working conditions for working mothers. The measure was deemed suitable to advance equality of opportunity in the sense that it prevented women from resignation due to a potential inability to accommodate both professional and family tasks.[92] Finally, in *Commission v. Greece*, the Court held that different pension ages based on gender and length of service violated the principle of equal treatment, since they were not of a nature to offset the actual disadvantages present in women's careers.[93]

Irrespective of some antithetical jurisprudence on the matter, the composite reading of the Court of Justice of the European Union's case-law suggests that equality of chances is the prevailing version of equality, whereas quotas and other measures of direct effect are not acceptable. The Court sustains this proposition not only on the grounds that positive discrimination quotas render sex as an essential qualification for entry into employment but also because it essentially entails a political choice as to the employment structures not related to the nature of work. All other positive measures are compatible with EU law provided that they ensure an objective and individualised judgment and respect the principle of proportionality. This is particularly true when the affirmative action measure operates at the level of professional education, as opposed to the entry into employment.

---

[89]EFTA Court Decision of 24 January 2003, Case E-1/02, *EFTA Surveillance Authority v. Norway*, EFTA Court Report 2003, p. 1.

[90]CJEU Judgment of 29 November 2001, Case C-366/99, *Joseph Griesmar and Ministre de l'Économie, des Finances et de l'Industrie, Ministre de la Fonction publique, de la Réforme de l'État et de la Décentralisation*, Rec. 2001, p. I-9413.

[91]CJEU Judgment of 30th September 2004, Case C-319/03, *Serge Briheche v. Ministre de l'Intérieur et als.*, Rec. 2004, p. 8807.

[92]CJEU Judgment of 19th March 2002, Case C-476/99, *Lommers v. Minister van Landbouw, Natuurbeheer en Visserij*, Rec. 2002, p. I-2891.

[93]CJEU Judgment of 26 March 2009, Case C-559/07, *Commission v. Greece*, 2009 I-47.

The above rationale resulted in upholding the exceptional nature of positive measures that in turn meant that there should be a narrow interpretation of the clauses enabling the introduction of such plans.[94]

Generally speaking, the EU adopts a more liberal approach to equality and is reluctant to adopt a more social reading of the principle, even after the upgrade of positive action through the Treaty of Amsterdam and the entry into force of the Charter of Fundamental Rights. Thus, it still insists upon the fundamental freedoms and the prevailing notion of the free market with certain, albeit not extensive, concessions to the need for social cohesion. At any rate, it seems that in the privileged field of gender, the EU jurisprudence has gone further than the case-law of the US Supreme Court towards a substantive vision of equality. However, albeit of obvious significance with regard to the evaluation of Member States' ability to adopt affirmative action policies, *Kalanke* and *Marschall* did not have a wide spill-over effect as has been the case in other instances of Union case-law and it is strongly doubtful whether this precedent might or will be expanded to race based positive action in Europe (Thomas 1999).

4.2.2 France

Guy Braibant, an emblematic legal figure in France and late vice-president of the French Council of State, suggested that it was his Court which first introduced a solid affirmative action theory worldwide (Braibant 1999: 450–4511). It was not, however, until the 1999 constitutional amendment through the Constitutional Law/Act of 8th July 1999, that a clear mandate was given to the legislature to encourage the equal access of men and women to elective offices and posts as well as to positions of professional and social responsibility, whereas political parties would contribute to the implementation of this principle as provided for by statute.[95] Pursuant to the constitutional amendment, it is provided by statute that (a) in the elections for the National Assembly, the difference between the number of candidates of each sex that a party or group of parties present for a single-member constituency cannot exceed a margin of 2 %[96]; that (b) in the election for the Senate, in electoral districts electing up to two senators, where a two-round majoritarian system applies, the primary and alternate candidate must be of the opposite gender, whereas in electoral districts electing three or more senators, where it is held according to a list under a proportional representation system using party-determined candidate lists, the difference between the number of candidates

[94]See CJEU Judgment of 15th May 1986, Case C-222/84, *Marguerite Johnston v. Chief Constable of the Royal Ulster Constabulary,* Rec. 1986, p. 1651, para. 36; CJEU Judgment of 26th October 1999, Case C-273/97, *Angela Maria Sirdar v. The Army Board and Secretary of State for Defence,* Rec. 1999, p. I-7403, para. 23.

[95]Articles 1 paras. 2 and 4 para. 2 respectively.

[96]Law No. 88-227, Article 9, para. 1.

of each gender cannot be greater than one and there must be an alteration of male and female candidates[97]; and (c) parties must have separate women candidate lists for European Parliament elections and equal participation between men and women in sections of six candidates as well as alternation on candidate lists for regional councils, large municipal councils and specific local government bodies.[98] According to the law, non-compliance with the participation requirements for the National Assembly will result in a correlative diminution of public funding, by a percentage equivalent to three-quarters of the difference between the total numbers of candidates of each sex, out of the total number of candidates. Violations of the Senate or regional quotas might result in an action for annulment brought before the Administrative Court of First Instance.

Unlike other European countries, like Germany, Italy and Greece, where the constitutional entrenchment of affirmative action merely confirmed the position on substantive equality that had pre-existed in the case law, the 1999 constitutional amendment in France was introduced to overcome the obstacles raised by the Constitutional Council, which had ruled that such measures were, in the absence of an explicit constitutional clause to that effect, unconstitutional. The Council, in its decision 98-407, held that the mandatory quota of 25 % participation for both sexes for the municipal election was incompatible with the constitutional right of equality as set out in Art. 3 of the Constitution and Art. 6 of the *Declaration of Rights of Man and Citizen.*[99] This judgment was confirmed by a sequence of decisions of the Constitutional Council concerning quotas for the elections of territorial councils.[100] Eventually, after the 1999 constitutional amendment, the Constitutional Council upheld the constitutionality of legislation introducing indirect positive measures encouraging public participation of women (Sabeg and Sabeg 2004; Blivet 2004).[101]

Outside gender affirmative action programmes, for which explicit constitutional mandate exists, the policy remains a strongly debatable issue. In 2003 there was a political crisis when the then Interior Minister, later President, Nicolas Sarkozy argued in favour of affirmative action measures that would encourage Muslims to occupy public posts, a statement that provoked the reaction of the then First

[97]Article L299 para. 1 and L300 para. 1 of the Electoral Code.

[98]Articles L264 para. 1, L331-2, L346 para. 1 and L370 para. 1 of the Electoral Code.

[99]Conseil Constitutionnel décision n° 82-146 du 18 novembre 1982, *Quotas par sexe,* Rec. 66, (1983) AJDA 128, RJC, p. I-134, Journal officiel du 19 novembre 1982, p. 3475.

[100]Conseil Constitutionnel décision n° 98-407 du 14 janvier 1999, *Loi relative au mode d'élection des conseillers régionaux et des conseillers à l'Assemblée de Corse et au fonctionnement des Conseils régionaux,* Rec. 21, Journal officiel du 20 janvier 1999, p. 1028.

[101]Conseil Constitutionnel décision n° 2000-429 du 30 mai 2000, *Loi tendant à favoriser l'égal accès des femmes et des hommes aux mandats électoraux et fonctions électives,* Rec. 84, Journal officiel du 7 juin 2000, p. 8564 and Conseil Constitutionnel décision n° 2000-430 du 9 juin 2000, *Loi organique tendant à favoriser l'égal accès des femmes et des hommes aux mandats de membre des assemblées de province et du congrès de la Nouvelle-Calédonie, de l'assemblée de la Polynésie française et de l'assemblée territoriale des îles Wallis-et-Futuna,* Rec. 95, Journal officiel du 5 juillet 2000, p. 10128.

Secretary of the French Socialist Party, later President also, François Hollande on the accusation that it was "a particularly liberal Anglo-Saxon theory claiming for representation through religion" (Perreau 2004: 56–59). This perception was allegedly at odds not only with the classical French concept of secular state, but primarily with the traditional view of equality *à la française,* i.e. the formal equality of everyone before the law, a principle enshrined in the French Declaration of Rights of Man and Citizen that had not been challenged for over two centuries. The literature abides by the "French passion for equality" (*passion française de l'égalité*): however, there is not a unanimous actual reflection of this passion; according to Levade (2004: 66), the constitutional principle of equality "à la française" prohibits the legislature from developing a positive discrimination policy and if this appears necessary, the only gateway is a constitutional amendment; according to Costa-Lascoux (2004: 19), the French equality doctrine encompasses, *inter alia,* the policy of compensation for past discriminations and certain measures in favour of the less privileged.

4.2.3 Germany

In Germany, the original wording of Article 3 para. 2 of the Constitution, according to which men and women have equal rights, was amended in 1994 and a new clause was added according to which "the state shall promote the actual implementation of equal rights for men and women and take action to eliminate existing disadvantages". The amendment was proposed by the Joint Commission of Constitutional Reform in order to cure a phenomenon specific in Germany, namely the different treatment of women in former East and West Germany.

Further, even after the constitutional amendment the jurisprudence of the lower courts in Germany is not consistent on the issue either. Whereas some dicta emanating from administrative courts suggest that Article 3 para. 2 cannot provide a legal basis for the introduction of quotas in favour of women,[102] the Federal Labour Court upheld the constitutionality of statutes providing for the preferential treatment of women at work in order to combat their actual disadvantages.[103] Given this jurisprudential fluidity and the fact that the new constitutional provision does not embrace positive measures *eo nomine*, the literature has not as yet firmly established the constitutionally permitted scope of affirmative action policies, especially in the field of employment. Some argue in the affirmative, (Michalowski and Woods 1999: 169) whereas others disagree (Peters 1999: 180; Stock 2006). Nevertheless, in 2012 the Upper House (*Bundesrat*) approved a Bill setting binding

[102]VG Schleswig, 14 *NVwZ* 724 (1995); VG Amsberg, 14 *NVwZ* 725 (1995); OVG Nds., 110 *DVBl.* 1254, 1257 (1995).

[103]Bundesarbeitsgericht judgment of 2 December 1997, 12 *ZTR* 419 (1998); Bundesarbeitsgericht Order of 22 June 1993, 11 *NZA* 77 (1994); Bundesarbeitsgericht Order of 22 June 1993, 11 *NZA* 77, 81 (1994).

quotas for female representation in the boards of the 30 largest publicly listed companies as a proportion of their members of 20 % by 2018 and 40 % by 2023. Although the Bill was rejected by the Lower House (*Bundestag*) as a result of the opposition of the Christian Democratic Union (CDU), the issue was once again raised as one of the Social Democrat Party's (SPD) key conditions for entering into a coalition government after the 2013 German parliamentary elections.

Paradoxically, before the constitutional entrenchment of positive measures in 1994, in light of the general equality clause of the Constitution, the Federal Constitutional Court had taken a quite positive stance towards affirmative action. In a landmark decision in 1987, the Court held that the different treatment of men and women in the field of social security benefits was in conformity with the Basic Law as being legitimately aimed at balancing biological variations and compensating for past discrimination.[104] In fact, the Court did not hesitate to explicitly use the language and rationale of "affirmative action" (Lindecke 1995: 211). Furthermore, in 1992, when examining women's preferential treatment in relation to night work, the Constitutional Court held in *obiter* that the principle of equality suggests that rights should be actually guaranteed equally for men and women in the future and this does not prevent positive measures in favour of the latter to compensate for disadvantages they suffered in the past.[105] Although the Court eventually struck down the employment statute prohibiting women from working between 8 p.m. and 6 a.m. as violating the non-discrimination clause, it essentially declared substantive equality as the prevailing conception of the equality principle and left the door ajar for future gender-related affirmative action (Totten 2003: 42–44).

Unlike federal legislation (which has not yet extensively used this tool), the constitutive part of the federation (*Länder*) has largely introduced positive measures in their respective labour legislation. For example, the labour law of Thuringia[106] *expressis verbis* mandated affirmative action measures in favour of women for public service positions, where they are underrepresented. It is no coincidence that the seminal Court of Justice of the European Union judgments on the matter, *Kalanke* and *Marschall*, arose as a matter of the implementation of affirmative action measures introduced by German Länder (Schiek 1998).

4.2.4 The UK

Britain is a typical paradigm of a legal system which traditionally adheres to formal equality and discourages any deviations from a liberally-oriented view. The first major statutory intervention in the field of positive discrimination measures came through the *Sex Discrimination Act 1975* and the *Race Relations Act 1976*, which

[104]BVerfGE 74, 163 (1987).

[105]BVerfGE 85, 191 (1992).

[106]*Gleichstellungsgesetz* of 11th November 1998, GVBl. Thür. 1998, 309.

provided for the introduction, under certain conditions, of indirect positive measures, such as special education, or the encouragement for national groups when there is underrepresentation of the said groups in employment for more than 12 months, or special measures of social security. More concretely, Article 49 of *Sex Discrimination Act 1975* allows the reservation of seats for women or establishment of additional reserved seats in a professional body the membership of which is wholly or mainly elected. This applies where, in the opinion of the organisation, the provision is in the circumstances needed to secure a reasonable lower limit on the number of members serving on the body. Article 71 para. 1 (b) of *Race Relations Act 1976* also specifies that state authorities shall, in carrying out their functions, have due regard to the need to promote equality of opportunity and good relations between persons of different racial groups.

A further significant step was made through the enactment of the *Equality Act 2010*, which was mostly the synthesis of a variety of already existing non-discrimination instruments[107]; Sections 158 and 159 establish the possibility to launch positive measures. The Act contains provisions which enable service providers, public bodies and other associations to take action to achieve more effective equality outcomes so as to assist people sharing a protected characteristic (i.e. age, disability, gender reassignment, marriage and civil partnership, pregnancy and maternity, race, religion or belief, sex and sexual orientation) and suffering disadvantage or the consequences of past or present discrimination; interestingly, the language of “protected characteristic” in UK legislation seems particularly broad vis-à-vis other jurisdictions. Positive action can involve treating members of a group who share a protected characteristic more favourably than other groups. This will be lawful if disadvantages of a particular group are recognised, if particular needs of the group are met, or if participation of the group is increased. Further, according to the statute, a proposed action is proportionate and will not amount to discrimination under the Act if it enables or encourages persons who share the protected characteristic to overcome or minimise that disadvantage, or meets those needs, or enables or encourages persons who share the protected characteristic to be more actively involved in social and labour life. The Act also sets out examples of positive action, such as providing additional or bespoke services or separate facilities and accelerated access to services or the targeting of resources. The Act provides particularly for voluntary positive action in recruitment and promotions, in specified circumstances, to address the needs or disadvantages shared by members of a protected group in relation to recruitment and promotion, provided that (a) the person in question is “as qualified as” other applicants to be recruited or promoted, (b) the employer does not have a policy of treating persons of the particular underrepresented or disadvantaged group more favourably than persons who do not share the relevant protected characteristic in relation to recruitment or promotion

[107] *Equal Pay Act 1970*; *Sex Discrimination Act 1975*; *Race Relations Act 1976; Disability Discrimination Act 1995; Equality Act 2006; Employment Equality (Religion or Belief) Regulations 2003; Employment Equality (Sexual Orientation) Regulations 2003; Employment Equality (Age) Regulations 2006;* and *Equality Act (Sexual Orientation) Regulations 2007.*

and (c) the more favourable treatment is a proportionate means of achieving the aim of overcoming or minimising the disadvantage, or encouraging participation. Furthermore, the Act also refers to education and training by encouraging employers to direct training at, and promote applications from, members of groups considered to be underrepresented (Wadham et al. 2012: Chap. 11; Hepple 2011; Ashtiany 2011). Finally, Lord Davies' 2011 Report recommended that FTSE 100 listed companies should have female representation of 25 % in companies' Boards of Directors and suggested voluntary soft law quotas to that effect.

Before the enactment of the Equality Act 2010, the most relevant decision of the UK courts is the House of Lords' *James v. Eastleigh Borough Council* judgment.[108] The plaintiff and his wife, who were both aged 61, visited a public swimming pool run by the defendant council, which had adopted a policy of providing free swimming facilities for persons of pensionable age. Since the effect of that policy was that women over 60 were admitted free, while men were not admitted free until they were 65, the plaintiff was charged 75p for admission while his wife was admitted free. He brought an action against the Council, claiming that he had been unlawfully discriminated against, but the judge dismissed the claim and the Court of Appeal affirmed this decision on the grounds that the Council had not intended to discriminate between men and women in the provision of free swimming but had intended to provide free swimming to pensioners, and therefore, it had not been guilty of unlawful discrimination merely because the difference in pensionable age resulted in different treatment. The majority of the House of Lords held that since the statutory pensionable age of 60 for women and 65 for men was itself a gender-based criterion, which directly discriminated between men and women, in that it treated women more favourably than men on the grounds of sex, any other differential treatment which adopted the same criterion likewise involved gender-based discrimination regardless of whether the person doing the discriminatory act used the shorthand expression "pensionable age" or spelt out in full that the act applied to women aged 60 and men aged 65. Thus, the House took a negative view towards positive measures and in a very straightforward way refused to legitimise the aim of protecting certain groups over others, claiming that it was irrelevant whether the motive for the discriminatory act was benign or not, since whether a person was afforded less favourable treatment to another because of his sex was a matter to be determined objectively. In fact, perhaps deliberately, the House refused to use the language of positive measures and strictly adhered to a more formalistic interpretation in order to prevent any confusion as to the real force of this policy.[109]

The legal landscape becomes significantly different in Northern Ireland, within which the hard task of establishing peace between the religious communities has

---

[108](1990) 2 AC 751.

[109]See also *Equal Opportunities Commission v. Birmingham City Council* (1989) 1 All ER 769, (1989) AC 1155 καθώς και *Jenkins v. Kingsgate (Clothing Productions) Ltd* (1981) 1 WLR 1485, *R v. Secretary of State for Education and Science, ex p. Keating* (1985) 84 LGR 469, *Ministry of Defence v. Jeremiah* (1979) 3 All ER 833, (1980) QB 87, *Lambeth London Borough Council v. GRE* (1990) IRLR 231.

resulted in the enactment of diverse quotas for governmental posts. In fact, Council *Directive 2000/78* establishing a general framework for equal treatment in employment and occupation provided for a special geographically located clause for the acknowledgment of positive measures in order to safeguard peace and conciliation among the main local communities, a stipulation particularly akin to Northern Ireland.[110] Accordingly, positive measures were expressly provided in relation to the police service and in education in order to maintain a religious balance of teachers.[111] The basic peace text, i.e. the Good Friday/Belfast Agreement, signed in Belfast on 10 April 1998 by the British and Irish governments, endorsed by most of the political parties in Northern Ireland and by the voters of the region in a referendum on 23 May 1998, set the framework for such quotas. Indeed, Section 45 of *Police (Northern Ireland) Bill 2000* provides that entries to the police will include 50 % Catholics and 50 % non-Catholics, and Articles 55 para. 1 and 58 para. 1 of the *Fair Employment and Treatment [Northern Ireland] Order 1998* use the term '*affirmative action*' (one which is rather uncommon in the EU) to entail reasonable and appropriate measures to secure fair participation in employment (McCrudden 1998).

4.2.5 Italy

The post-war 1948 Italian Constitution established a wide social state with radical protection especially for workers, reading that "Italy is a democratic Republic founded on labour" (Article 1 para. 1). Thus, "it is the duty of the republic to remove all economic and social obstacles that, by limiting the freedom and equality of citizens, prevent full individual development and the participation of all workers in the political, economic, and social organisation of the country" (Article 3 para. 2). Two further provisions complete the relevant constitutional landscape. Apart from the state obligation to ensure that working women are entitled to equal rights and, for comparable work, equal pay as men, the state is mandated to take indirect positive actions in the sense that working conditions must allow women to fulfil their essential role in the family and ensure appropriate protection for the mother and child (Article 37 para. 1), while "regional laws have to remove all obstacles which prevent full equality of men and women in social, cultural, and economic life, and promote equal access of men and women to elective offices" (Article 117 para. 2). Pursuant to this last stipulation, most of the 20 Italian regions have adopted gender quotas in their electoral processes, violation of which mostly results in the imposition of financial penalties.

---

[110]EE L 303 of 2nd December 2000, p. 16. This teleology stems from Recital 34 of the Preamble of Directive 2000/78.

[111]Art 15 para. 1 and 2 respectively of Directive 2000/78.

In light of the above constitutional framework, specific statutory measures which amounted to affirmative action policies were introduced in Italy on the basis of gender since the 1990s. Apart from political representation quotas, Act No. 215/1992 aimed at encouraging female entrepreneurship through financial support, training and supervision and established a Committee for the Promotion and Development of Women's Entrepreneurship (*Commissione per la promozione e lo sviluppo dell'imprenditoria femminile*) (Organisation for Economic Co-operation and Development 2013; Grossman 1993).

The powerful Italian Constitutional Court has given mixed signals as to the constitutionality of affirmative action plans. In the field of labour, when called to interpret the general equality clause, the Court upheld the use of positive measures to establish substantive equality in principle—by holding that "affirmative action constitutes the main tool of the legislator to perform the duty prescribed in Art 3 para. 2".[112] In the field of political representation though, the Court overruled electoral quotas established by law in the 1990s, in light of the original wording of Article 51 of the Constitution establishing equal opportunity of access to public offices and elected positions, the general equality clause and the equal right to vote of Article 48.[113]

As a result of the above constitutional dialogue between the legislature and the judiciary, Article 51 para. 1 of the Constitution was revised by Constitutional Law 1/2003 and a new clause was added to the effect that citizens of one or the other sex are eligible for public office and for elective positions under equal conditions, according to the rules established by law and, to this end, the state adopts specific measures (*appositi provvedimenti*) in order to promote equal chances for men and women. Accordingly, in Italy, the constitutional acknowledgment of affirmative action policies follows as a matter of constitutional construction/interpretation.

Following the 2003 constitutional amendment, Law no. 120/2011, entered into force in 2012, introducing quotas in the field of employment, with an aim to promote wider participation of women in governing bodies of listed companies. Responding to clear evidence of under-representation, the statute requires these companies to reserve one-third of the seats in their board of directors (transitionally before 2015, one-fifth of those seats) to the underrepresented gender (i.e. not expressly referring to women). Although the 2003 constitutional entrenchment of affirmative action has not generated large-scale measures to that effect, there is a wide debate in the country in relation to further enactment of relevant statutes.

4.2.6 Spain

In Spain, equality constitutes one of the foundations of the State according to the 1978 Spanish Constitution: "Spain is hereby established as a social and democratic

---

[112]Const. Court decision no. 215/1987; Const. Court decision no. 109/1993.

[113]Const. Court decision no. 422/1995.

State, subject to the rule of law, which advocates freedom, justice, equality and political pluralism as highest values of its legal system" (Article 1 para. 1). The general equality clause provides that "Spaniards are equal before the law and may not in any way be discriminated against on account of birth, race, sex, religion, opinion or any other personal or social condition or circumstance" (Article 14) and there is also a mandate for the State to promote conditions ensuring that freedom and equality of individuals and of the groups to which they belong are real and effective, to remove the obstacles preventing or hindering their full enjoyment, and to facilitate the participation of all citizens in political, economic, cultural and social life (Article 9 para. 2). Using this foundation, domestic legislation provides for positive actions in the field of labour by authorising reservations and preferences for disadvantaged groups,[114] and in the field of education by authorising compensatory actions aimed at persons, groups and less favoured regions.[115]

Statutory quotas in favour of women in political participation also exist in Spain. In relation to the composition of both Houses of the Spanish parliament and for elected authorities in local government, the electoral law provides that parties' lists of candidates must reflect a balanced proportion of women and men, no less than 40 % per gender, or as close as possible to that quota if the number of eligible posts is less than 5, in which case the list must be to the 40–60 % equilibrium.[116]

On the grounds of non-discrimination, the Constitutional Court annulled a preferential policy in favour of women in relation to a pension scheme,[117] but upheld the constitutionality of positive measures in favour of women with little children on the grounds that favourable treatment is justified to give different treatment to effectively different situations.[118] In the authoritative *Hulleras del Norte* judgment of 1992,[119] the Constitutional Court dealt with a complaint filed for an infringement of the right to non-discrimination on grounds of gender. There, because of the failure of the national company Hulleras del Norte, S.A. (HUNOSA), to acknowledge the claimant's right to occupy a post of assistant miner in conditions which were equal to the male workers, despite her having passed the appropriate admission examinations, due to a statutory exemption of women working in mines based on the grounds of "special working conditions" and danger of accidents, her complaint was ultimately upheld. Both the judgments on the first instance and on appeal upheld the constitutionality and conformity with the international law of the prohibition, but they were reversed by the Constitutional Court. In so doing, the Court, building upon the prior incremental case-law outlined above, held that statutory interpretation implies that in order to achieve effective

[114]Article 17.2 and 17.3 of the Workers' Statute and Articles 30, 35 and 42 of Law 62/2003.

[115]Article 80 of Organic Law on Education (*Ley Orgánica de Educación*) of 2006.

[116]Article 44 paras. 1, 2 and 4 of the Organic Law on general elections regime (*Ley Orgánica del' Régimen Electoral General*) of 1985.

[117]Tribunal Constitucional nº 19/1989, Judgment of 31st January 1989.

[118]Tribunal Constitucional nº 128/1987, Judgment of 16th July 1987.

[119]Tribunal Constitucional nº 229/1992, Judgment of 14th December 1992.

gender equality, it is possible to establish positive rebalancing measures to combat pre-existing discriminatory social situations. Thus, measures favouring women at work are constitutional when designed to remove obstacles which effectively prevent the implementation of equal opportunity. In this respect, the Court held that, although the prohibition on women working in underground mines responded to a historically legitimate purpose, i.e. prevention of exploitation of the female workforce, it could not be justified as a positive action, support or advantage in order to achieve real equality of opportunities, since it restricted the disadvantaged gender from accessing specific jobs. Although the differences in conditions of access to employment and working conditions based on natural biological order were constitutionally legitimate, for this difference to justify the disparity in treatment, the Court ruled that the interests of women employees were relevant. Accordingly, it found that the originally protective legislation, responded to biases and preconceptions by essentially maintaining discrimination, since it conveyed a factual situation of less physical strength and a greater weakness of women compared to men. Irrespective of the soundness of the argument, the Court held that this was the result of stereotyping rather than an appreciation of real, natural or biological differences, and it produced discriminatory labour results. The Court therefore concluded that although this prohibition had been founded upon justified historical grounds, it did not respect the constitutional requirement of equality of rights between men and women.[120]

4.2.7 Portugal

Despite the fact that the Portuguese Constitution is the most extensive in Europe and has been revised 7 times after its original enactment in 1976, it makes no explicit reference to positive measures. The general equality clause reads: "no one is privileged, favoured, injured, deprived of any right, or exempt from any duty because of his ancestry, sex, race, language, territory of origin, religion, political or ideological convictions, education, economic situation, social condition or sexual orientation" (Art 13 para. 2). Thus affirmative action policies could receive constitutional status by merely employing a constitutional construction/interpretation that would require the state to positively remove all obstacles in order to achieve equality and facilitate the participation of everyone in all aspects of human activity.

At the legislative level, Article 27 of the Labour Code Procedure[121] specifies that the discrimination requirements are not met in the case of the enactment of temporary measures benefiting certain disadvantaged groups, indicatively on grounds of gender, reduced working capability, disability or chronic illness, nationality or

---

[120]Tribunal Constitucional nº 229/1992, Judgment of 14th December 1992.

[121]As approved by Decree 480/99 of 09 November 1999 and amended by Decree 323/2001 of 17 December 2001, Decree 38/2003 of 8 March 2003, and Decree 295/2009 of 13 October 2009.

ethnic origin, aiming at correcting situations of factual inequality persisting in social life. The constitutionality of this provision has not yet been challenged before the Constitutional Court, given that no such measure has yet been introduced.

Electoral quotas exist in Portugal in relation to female representation. In the National Assembly and major local government authorities, party lists must be constituted so as to promote a minimum one-third representation of each gender, whereas in multi-member constituencies an alteration between genders must be followed in the sequence of candidates.[122] If a list does not comply with the quota requirement, then the breach is to be publicised and diffused through press releases and a curtailment of electoral public funding also occurs.[123]

4.2.8 Belgium

The 1831 Belgian Constitution, as amended, provides for positive measures to ensure a balanced representation of the ethnic communities clearly facilitated by the federal structure of the state. Thus, according to a constitutional prescription that the Cabinet (composed of a maximum of 15 members) should include an equal number of French and Dutch speaking ministers, except—reasonably—for the position of the Prime Minister, there must be wide representation of the Communities at the Senate (Articles 99 and 67 respectively). In relation to gender equality, it is prescribed that both sexes ought to be represented in the Cabinet and the Governments of the three state communities and the districts; as well as (in principle) in the permanent delegations of the regional councils, the mayoral colleges, the committees and the standing social welfare offices and the administrations of other intra-community organs (Article 11b). All of the above measures are supplemented by the general equality clauses, namely that equality between women and men is guaranteed and that enjoyment of the rights and freedoms recognised for Belgians must be provided without discrimination, while laws and federate laws guarantee the rights and freedoms of ideological and philosophical minorities (amongst others) (Articles 10 and 11 respectively).

At the level of federal legislation, the *Racial Equality Federal Act* and the *Anti-discrimination Federal Act*, both enacted in 2007, allow differences in treatment based on grounds of race, colour, descent, national or ethnic origin, in cases of positive action measures.[124] In order for a positive action measure to be introduced, there must be evidence of manifest inequality, lifting this inequality must constitute a compelling public interest, the measures must be of a temporary nature until the imbalance is effectively overcome and the rights of third parties must not be excessively and adversely affected. If these conditions are met the Federal

[122] Equality Law No. 3/2006 of 21 August 2006, Articles 1 and 2 paras. 1 and 2.

[123] Equality Law No. 3/2006 of 21 August 2006, Article 7.

[124] Art. 10 of both Acts.

Government may authorise the adoption of positive action measures through an Executive Regulation (*Arrêté royal*).[125] In upholding the constitutionality of affirmative action and in interpreting these conditions, the Belgian Constitutional Court (*Cour d'arbitrage*) has categorically stated that admittedly on certain occasions these measures are not incompatible with the non-discrimination principle because they are specifically aimed at remedying an actual inequality (Delpérée 1997: 435–436).[126] In relation to preferential treatment in political representation, the Electoral Law specifies that the difference between the number of candidates and alternates of each gender on electoral lists should not be more than one, and the top two nominations cannot be of the same gender.[127]

At the regional level, the Flemish Parliament adopted the Decree of 8 May 2002 on Equitable Participation in the Employment Market,[128] encouraging the integration of specific target groups (*groupes cibles*) into the labour market by positive action measures, namely the preparation of diversity plans and annual reports on progress made in the field of vocational training, vocational guidance, integration of persons with disabilities in the labour market and education.[129] Furthermore, on 28 June of the same year, another Decree on equal opportunity in education was enacted,[130] guaranteeing equal opportunity to pupils and students by encouraging less favoured groups and by allowing additional financial grants to that effect.

4.2.9 The Netherlands

According to the first Article of the 1815 Dutch Constitution, all persons in the country shall be treated equally in equal circumstances and discrimination on the grounds of religion, belief, political opinion, race, sex or on any other grounds whatsoever is prohibited. On a national legislative level, under the 1994 *General Equal Treatment Act*,[131] different treatment policies are permitted provided that they aim at placing women or individuals belonging to a particular ethnic or cultural minority group or disabled persons in a privileged position in order to eliminate or reduce existing inequalities related to race, sex or disability and the differentiation is in reasonable proportion to this aim. By statute, the conditions on introducing a positive action measure require that it is of a specific nature, it is limited to the

[125] Constitutional Court (*Cour d'Arbitrage*), 27 January 1994, Case no. 9/94, Recital B.6.2.

[126] Cour d'arbitrage, Judgment 9/94 of 27th January 1994.

[127] Electoral Code, Article 117.

[128] *Decreet houdende evenredige participatie op de arbeidsmarkt*, *Moniteur belge*, 26 July 2002, p. 33262.

[129] In contrast to the French-speaking part of Belgium, the Region and Community are merged in the Flemish part.

[130] *Decreet betreffende gelijke onderwijskansen Moniteur belge*, 14 September 2002, p. 40909.

[131] Algemene Wet Gelijke Behandeling, Staatsblad 1994, 230.

beneficiaries exemplified by the Act, it aims at removing or reducing, but not preventing factual inequalities and that it satisfies the proportionality test.

As regards specific positive measures, a well-cited Act, known as *Wet Samen* («*Wet stimulering arbeidsdeelname minderheden*»), was enacted in 1994, aiming at facilitating access to members of underrepresented races. In its original version, the statute obliged employers to introduce work quotas in favour of minority employees through a special archive (later abolished to protect personal data), in which the employees noted the birthplace of their parents and of themselves (Goudappel 1999: 894–895). However, in 2003 the Act and the obligation thereof have been repealed. Further, with a 2009 amendment to the Corporate Governance Code,[132] at the level of soft law, stipulations for company publicity and planning for the composition of the Supervisory Boards (*Raad van Commissarissen*) were introduced to achieve diversity in relation to age, nationality, gender, expertise and societal background. A Monitoring Committee was also launched to hear complaints of non-compliance with the standards set by the Act. Finally, an affirmative action plan favouring, in particular, the participation of women on Boards of Directors was provided by Law on 6 June 2011.[133] Overall, the effort to apply targeted hiring and promotion programmes in favour of women in the public sector has been diluted and eventually undermined through the limitation of scope and the broadening of beneficiaries, including ethnic minorities (Bacchi 1996: 121–139).

4.2.10 Austria

Austria does not have a significant tradition of institutional affirmative action measures. This is despite the constitutional acknowledgment of this policy in the 1920 Austrian Constitution, through an amendment in 1998 entailing that "the Federation, Länder and municipalities subscribe to the actual equality of men and women" and that "measures to promote factual equality of women and men, particularly by eliminating actually existing inequalities, are permissible" (Article 7 para. 2). Incremental measures in favour of the underrepresented gender apply in the field of employment, principally the 1979 federal Equal Treatment for Men and Women Act (*Gleichbehandlungsgesetz*), applying in the private sector, and the 1993 Federal Act on Equal Treatment of Women and Men and on the Advancement of Women in the Civil Service (Federal Equal Treatment Act/*Bundes-Gleichbehandlungsgesetz*) applicable to federal personnel. The former statute, suggests voluntary positive action to achieve equal opportunity, whereas the latter

---

[132]Staatscourant 3-12-2009, 18499.

[133]Law of 6 June 2011, published in the *Staatsblad* 2011, 275. (*Wet van 6 juni 2011 tot wijziging van boek 2 van het Burgerlijk Wetboek in verband met de aanpassing van regels over bestuur en toezicht in naamloze en besloten vennootschappen.*)

entails the implementation of positive measures in all areas of federal administration where women are underrepresented, aiming at a 40 % participation goal (Rasnic 1995; Sauer and Tertinegg 2003).

4.2.11 Ireland

According to the 1937 Irish Constitution, although all citizens shall be held equal before the law, "this shall not be held to mean that the State shall not in its enactments have due regard to differences of capacity, physical and moral, and of social function" (Article 40).

Discrimination in the area of employment is prohibited by the *Employment Equality Acts* 1998 and 2004, covering all aspects of work including recruitment and promotion, the right to equal pay, conditions of employment, training or experience; and the *Equal Status Act* 2000 prohibits any discrimination outside the workplace. The *Employment Equality Act 1998* originally allowed measures to promote equal opportunity for men and women, in particular by removing existing inequalities which affect women's opportunities in the areas of access to employment, vocational training and promotion and working conditions (Section 24). The provision was amended by the *Equality Act 2014*, which permits the maintenance or adoption of measures with a view to ensuring full equality in practice between men and women in their employment and measures providing for specific advantages so as to make it easier for an underrepresented sex to pursue a vocational activity or to prevent or compensate for disadvantages in professional careers (Section 15 para. 1). The *Equal Status Act 2000*, which is the main statutory instrument to secure equality in the country, allows affirmative action policies at the discretion of the authorities by indicating that nothing within the Act shall prohibit preferential treatment or the taking of positive measures, which are *bona fide* intended to promote equality of opportunity for persons who are disadvantaged or who have been or are likely to be unable to avail themselves of the same opportunities as other persons (Section 14 para. 22). Interestingly, the Act makes direct reference to systemic discrimination correlating to group membership, by indicating that discrimination shall be taken to occur where "a person is in a category of persons who share a common characteristic by reason of which discrimination may occur in respect of those persons" (Section 3 para. 1c). Finally, in relation to political representation quotas in Ireland, the *Electoral Act 1997* (Article 17), as amended by the *Electoral (Amendment) (Political Funding) Act 2012*, provides that state payments to political parties are reduced by 50 % unless at least 30 % of the candidates are women and at least 30 % are men (Article 42).

The *Irish Human Rights and Equality Commission Act*, passed by the Parliament in July 2014, and established the Irish Human Rights and Equality Commission, which merged pre-existing equality and human rights entities. Among extensive powers, the Commission may invite a particular undertaking, group of undertakings or the undertakings making up a particular industry or sector thereof to carry out an equality review (relating to equality of opportunity generally or a particular aspect of discrimination), in relation to that undertaking or those undertakings or prepare and implement an equality action plan (Article 32 para. 1). Furthermore, it may itself carry out an equality review or prepare an equality action plan in relation to any undertaking of 50 or more employees or group of such undertakings (Article 32 para. 1).

The most relevant case in the context of the *Employment Equality Act* is *Gillen v. Department of Health and Children* of 2003,[134] where the Equality Tribunal, despite finding that the respondent department had acted illegally by not promoting an officer in well over three years, rejected the complainant's argument that the relevant statutory provisions permitting the enactment of positive measures imposed a strict obligation upon the state authorities. The complainant claimed there had been discrimination on grounds of age in the system of internal promotion to Principal Officer in the civil service, by relying on the provision which permitted positive action to facilitate the integration into employment of persons aged over fifty. The arguments set forth by the Tribunal were that the wording of Section 33 of the *Employment Equality Act* in relation to the launching of positive measures was permissive rather than mandatory, and that this provision as an exception to the 1998 Act ought to be restrictively construed.[135] On the other hand, the most relevant precedent in the context of the *Equal Status Act* is the Clonmel Circuit Court decision *Christian Brothers High School Clonmel v. Stokes* in 2011.[136] The Court allowed an appeal by the high school being blamed for indirect discrimination by refusing to admit an Irish Traveller boy (i.e. a member of the community of Pavee, a traditionally wandering ethnic group of Irish origin). The applicant, albeit meeting the requirements of being a Catholic and of having attended a recognised feeder primary school, was not given priority admission because he could not satisfy the requirement that he would have had a father or brother who attended the school prior to him. This last condition was considered by the Tribunal as indirectly discriminatory against Travellers at the time when the applicant's father was of school-going age. Interestingly, the deciding judge upheld the school's argument that there was a compelling interest in setting out such a condition, but explicitly suggested that the national parliament should look at making positive discrimination mandatory for schools in their admissions policies due to the disproportionate effects produced on Travellers and other minorities with the same characteristics. The High Court ruled that, although admittedly Travellers were indirectly discriminated against by the school's policy, everyone in the same factual situation suffered the same level of discrimination. The case was tried before the Supreme Court and the decision is currently pending.

---

[134]DEC-E2003/035 and Labour Court decision EDA0412.

[135]See also *Glennon v. St. Clare's Comprehensive School*, DEC-E2003/30.

[136]2011 No15 CAT.

4.2.12 Greece

The historical background of affirmative action in Greece is an illustrative example of constitutional mutation in line with social perceptions from absolute negation to fully fledged constitutional entrenchment, now qualifying the country as perhaps the friendliest towards this policy amongst the European states. Until the entry into force of the 1975 Constitution, the jurisprudence of the Council of State (the supreme administrative court), distrusted any deviation from formal equality, thus rejecting affirmative action as a legitimate cause to compensate for past discrimination. Formal equality was constitutionally entrenched in the 1975 Constitution through the standard provisions that "all Greeks are equal before the law" (Article 4 para. 1) and that "Greek men and women have equal rights and equal obligations" (Article 4 para. 2), with exceptions acknowledged only "on serious grounds, in cases where the law specifically provides" (Article 116 para. 2 in the original wording). This constitutional framework was used by the legislature both in a favourable way for women, by acknowledging in exceptional cases special privileges over the male gender, particularly in the field of social security,[137] and in a negative way for women by setting reverse quotas for female entries into the armed forces and the security forces.[138] Generally, however, deviations from formal equality were not easily upheld; for instance, following the American pattern of suspect classifications, domestic case-law invalidated the policy of preferential university admissions for students from border areas, because they had allegedly "suffered the biggest burden from the [*Second World*] War" on grounds of discrimination on the basis of origin.[139]

The institutional environment, in spite of strong criticism by part of the literature (Yotopoulos-Marangopoulos 1998: 21, 71–96), did not know any positive measures. Such measure was first introduced through a statute imposing compulsory participation of at least one female representative at the service councils that were competent according to a specific constitutional clause for decisions on the status of all public servants.[140] The constitutional basis of the provision was recorded in the Explanatory Statement of the statute, indicating that the participation of women in the councils was very low, if not non-existent, resulting in a "flagrant injustice against them". Using this ratio, the Council of State held in plenary for the first time in the late 1990s that affirmative action policies were, in principle, compatible with the constitutional principle of gender equality. It proclaimed that wherever past discrimination due to social prejudice had occurred such that the strict application of the equality principle would result in merely a sham equality which would substantially solidify and perpetuate an existing unequal situation, the legislature

[137]Council of State 274/2004; 135/2002.

[138]Council of State 1000-4/2004, 1850-9/2002, 1893/2002, 2336/2002, 3363-3373/2002, 3714-3735/2002, 3121-2/2002.

[139]Council of State 2216/1975.

[140]Article 29 of Law 2085/19920.

might legitimately take positive temporary measures until real equality is established.[141] On the other hand, in Greece there is a reservation for a number of categories in university admissions, although technically these quotas are on the top of the regular admission numbers and do not affect those entering through the regular procedure. Among the benefiting categories are Greek Muslims of Thrace, children of Greeks living abroad and handicapped persons.[142]

A constitutional amendment in 2001 signified a landmark twofold upgrade for affirmative action: both as a principle of interpretation and as a constitutional mandate (Article 116 para. 2). As a *principle of interpretation*, the Constitution now specifies that "positive measures for promoting equality between men and women do not constitute discrimination on the basis of sex". Accordingly, affirmative action is constitutionally set out in a negative way, in the sense that in principle there is no gender discrimination with the introduction of such measures. With the negative wording of the rule, two questions are left open for interpretation. The first is whether under the constitutional regulation any form of positive measure is permissible. The abstract wording does not provide any meaningful interpretative assistance. What is certain though is that a particular type of positive measure cannot be excluded *in abstracto*. In this respect, all positive measures can, in principle, be implemented through normal legislation, under the expressly formulated constitutional requirement that they are designed to promote equality between men and women. The second question relates to the *scope* of affirmative action plans. It seems *prima facie* permissible to adopt positive measures in every sphere of human activity. As a *constitutional mandate*, the amended provision stipulates that the state shall attend to the elimination of existing inequalities, especially those detrimental to women. The rule seems to supplement the existing framework of the equality principle; in contrast to the above principle of interpretation, it is systematically disconnected from gender equality and can potentially embrace other groups as beneficiaries, albeit "particularly against women". Thus the mandate can generate constitutional legitimacy for affirmative action plans in favour of groups that have suffered discrimination in the past.

The amended constitutional clause does not enjoy direct application. It requires the intervention of the legislature in order to remove existing inequalities, and the tolerance of the judiciary while testing the constitutional limits of affirmative action. Consequently, the corresponding legislation was activated in the fields of employment and political representation. In *employment*, in less than two years, two pieces of legislation were launched implementing EU Directives enabling affirmative action policies in the domains of racial or ethnic origin, religious or other belief, disability, age, sexual orientation[143] and concerning the equal treatment of the sexes.[144] Furthermore, a new statute provided for at least one-third representation of each sex

[141]Council of State 1933/1998.

[142]Laws 2341/1995, 2525/1997 and 2909/2001.

[143]Law 3304/2005 belatedly incorporating EU *Directives 2000/43* and *2000/78.*

[144]Law 3488/2006 afresh incorporating *EU Directives 2002/73* and *76/2007.*

in national institutions and committees engaged in research and technology.[145] In the field of *political representation* three statutes enforcing the participation of women in the electoral processes were introduced requiring that at least one-third of all parties' candidate lists should be composed of members of each sex in local government, national parliament and European Parliament elections.[146]

The Council of State upheld the constitutionality of the political representation quotas.[147] It ruled, by a majority vote, that the state can take appropriate, necessary and temporary positive measures in favour of women when past discrimination is undoubted until genuine gender equality in the respective field has been achieved, where applying formal equality would result in unequal results. The Council accordingly concluded that quotas are constitutionally permissible, provided that the core of other constitutionally entrenched rights is not violated. From this case law, it logically follows that there is a *sui generis* "presumption of constitutionality" of quotas. It seems that substantive equality has replaced equality of opportunities as an imperative public goal, justifying deviations from formal equality. It is further noteworthy that the Council also made an interconnection between affirmative action and the right to one's personality, acknowledged by the Constitution (Article 5 para. 1) as enabling citizens freely to participate in political, social and economic life. Through such a favourable statutory and jurisprudential attitude, affirmative action in Greece is not treated as an exception from equality, but instead mostly as a new version of equality that is to be interpreted rather benevolently.

4.2.13 Nordic Countries

In general, as part of their well-developed social security systems, the Nordic countries feature prominently in the list of the most female-friendly countries (Skjeie et al. 2005).

In Norway, although no reference is made to affirmative action in the 1814 Constitution or its subsequent amendments, satisfactory female participation occurs, particularly through gender quotas which have been employed more extensively than in other Scandinavian countries (Seierstad and Opsahl 2010). Temporary positive measures aiming at substantive equality were envisaged at a general level by a block of statutory provisions introduced in the 2000s: Section 8 of the *Anti-Discrimination Act* (entered into force in 2006), Section 5 of the *Anti-Discrimination and Accessibility Act* (entered into force in 2009) and Sections 13–16 of the *Working Environment Act* (entered into force in 2005). At a specific level, the

[145]Article 57 of Law 3653/2007.

[146]Article 75 para. 1 of Law 2910/2001; Article 3 of Law 3636/2008; and Article 6 para. 5 of Law 4255/2014 respectively.

[147]Council of State 2831-3/2003, 3027-8/2003, 3185-9/2003, 192/2004, 2388/2004 and 3353/2004.

Act of Equal Opportunity 2011 requires all public bodies comprising more than 3 members to be composed of at least 40 % of each gender. Norway's major international contribution in relation to affirmative action is that it provided the prototype for the European Parliament and Council proposal for a Directive on improving the gender balance among non-executive directors of companies listed on stock exchanges and related measures (Burke and Vinnicombe 2009). Indeed, the *Public Limited Companies Act 2003* requires gender balance on the boards of all public limited liability companies and state-owned enterprises where ten or more directors are involved, and entered into force in 2006 with a minimum target of 40 % for each sex within the forthcoming two years and provided for a range of penalties for violations including warnings, fines and in extreme cases company's dissolution (Huse 2007: 91–94). This has resulted in a significant increase of female participation not only in the Boards of Directors but also in crucial managerial positions. Although no overarching judicial pronouncement exists as to the constitutionality of affirmative action plans in Norway, the courts seem to hold a rather favourable stance. In a 2010 judgment, the Oslo Municipal Court of First Instance upheld the government's choice of a female applicant ranked third in the list of candidates for the appointment of the Chief Justice of a Municipal Court on the ground that Section 3a in the 1978 Gender Equality Act, which allows positive action for the underrepresented gender, was valid and applicable since the applicants had similar qualifications, therefore preferential treatment did not discriminate against male candidates with equivalent qualifications.[148] In political representation, although there are no statutory quotas but merely soft-law political commitments, women hold/have held approximately 38 % of the seats in the Parliament and 44 % of Cabinet seats between 2005 and 2009. An interesting point about affirmative action programmes in favour of women in Norway is that they are the outcome of a systematic campaign from the feminist movement, which appealed to a common understanding of the female societal role as nurturers and careers, one which is emphatically rejected by other feminist groups in Europe (Bacchi 1996: 140–158).

In Sweden, the 1974 Instrument of Government (*Regeringsformen*), which along with the 1810 Act of Succession to the Throne, the 1949 Freedom of the Press Act and the 1991 Fundamental Law on Freedom of Expression, constitutes the Swedish constitutional *bloc*, introduced the essence of affirmative action in favour of women by stipulating that "no act of law or other provision may imply the unfavourable treatment of a citizen on grounds of gender, unless the provision forms part of efforts to promote equality between men and women or relates to compulsory military service or other analogous official duties" (Article 16). On the level of ordinary legislation, the 2008 Discrimination Act provides for affirmative action from employers to promote ethnic diversity in working life, and universities are required to promote gender and cultural diversity.[149] However, no large-scale

[148]Oslo Municipal Court of 8 July 2010 (TOSLO-2010-7432).

[149]Chapter 3, Sections 3 and 16 respectively of the *Discrimination Act*.

positive action measures operate in Sweden, although under the leadership of Olof Palme in the 1970s, extensive preferential programmes for vulnerable social groups were introduced. The assertion that the key factor for positive measures in Sweden seems to be class (as opposed to the often applied criteria of race or gender), so as to promote solidarity through corporatist politics, has not operated favourably in relation to targeted underrepresented groups (Bacchi 1996: 101–120).

The relatively recent Finnish Constitution of 1999 prescribes that everyone is equal before the law, that no one shall, without an acceptable reason, be treated differently from other persons on the grounds of sex, age, origin, language, religion, conviction, opinion, health, disability or other reason that concerns his or her person; and that equality of the sexes is to be promoted in social activity and working life, especially in the determination of pay and the other terms of employment, as provided statutorily (Section 6). It further states that public authorities shall provide for the cultural and societal needs of the Finnish and Swedish-speaking populations of the country on an equal basis (Section 17). In light of this last provision, university programmes have launched quotas for individuals proficient in Swedish, a provision that, according to *The New York Times*, renders Swedish speakers in Finland the "world's most pampered minority".[150] On a statutory level the 2004 Non-Discrimination Act provides in Section 7 para. 2, that it does not prevent specific proportionate measures aimed at achieving actual equality in order to prevent or reduce the disadvantages caused by past discrimination, whereas Section 4a of Act 609/1986 on Equality Between Women and Men requires that all public bodies ought to be composed of at least 40 % of each gender. The latter section also entails that public authorities should foster equality, consolidate administrative and operational practices to ensure the fostering of equality in the decision-making process and draft a plan to ensure wide ethnic equality.

Amongst the Nordic countries, Denmark seems to have the most neutral, if not negative, attitude towards positive measures. In the absence of a relevant authorisation by the 1953 Constitution or a constitutional acknowledgment of culture or cultural rights, only incremental statutes make reference to the possibility of launching positive measures. These include the *Equal Status Act 2000* which aims at reinforcing mechanisms to promote equality of opportunities between women and men, and the 1996 *Act on the Prohibition of Discrimination in the Labour Market* indicating (in Section 9 para. 2) that the Act does not prevent measures being taken by the competent minister with a view to improving employment opportunities in the public sector for persons of a specific race, skin colour, religion, political opinion, sexual orientation or national, social or ethnic origin and age. In this respect, incremental positive actions in favour of women have been introduced in male-dominated professional areas (Justesen and Rytter 1999: 661–662).

[150]Issue of 28 December 2005.

4.2.14 Russia

According to the 1993 Russian Constitution, the State guarantees the equality of human and civil rights and freedoms regardless of sex, race, nationality, language, origin, material and official status, place of residence, attitude to religion, convictions, membership of public associations, or of other circumstances, therefore all forms of limitations of human rights on social, racial, national, language or religious grounds are prohibited (Article 19 para. 2). Especially in the field of gender equality, the Constitution stipulates that men and women shall enjoy equal rights and freedoms and equal opportunity to exercise them (Article 19 para. 3). Further, as regards race disparity, the Constitution explicitly declares that the bearer of sovereignty and the sole source of power in the Russian Federation shall be its multinational people (Article 3 para. 1). Accordingly, everyone has the right to determine and declare his/her nationality and the right to use his/her native language and to a free choice of the language of communication, upbringing, education and creative work (Article 26 paras. 1 and 2 respectively). To that purpose, the federation has the power to regulate on the protection of the rights of national minorities but also there is a joint competence of the federation and the constituent entities to protect the rights of national minorities (Articles 71c and 72 para. 1b respectively).

Contrary to what is generally perceived concerning soviet nationalism, in Russia, between 1923 and 1933, Lenin introduced a variety of measures to develop and encourage non-Russian languages, elites, territorial units and cultural forms in order to achieve ethnic diversity, which overall constituted a preferential umbrella for minorities. This policy of indirect positive discrimination qualified Russia at the time, in the words of Terry Martin, as an "affirmative-action empire" (Martin 2001: 1–2). Today, Russia is one of the most ethnically diverse countries of the world with more than 190 separate religious and linguistic ethnic groups and more than 100 spoken languages.[151] Specific statutory and executive measures have been introduced in the country to promote the well-being of the minorities and of the indigenous populations both in education, such as basic general education in their own language, mobile schooling and reservations for admissions to universities and in the employment, such as preferential use of land, special fishing and hunting rights, privileged access to vocational and training, i.e. training of qualified workers for the development of the traditional industries and for industry, construction and other occupations (Tkachenko et al. 1998: 90–95; Ivanovna Nikanorova 2014: 39–53).

The Constitutional Court of the Russian Federation has not as yet dealt with the issue of constitutionality of affirmative action programmes in the national territory. The closest precedent relating to non-discrimination is the *Martin* case decided in

[151]Data retrieved from the Global Population Statistics of GeoHive, http://www.geohive.com/cntry/russia.aspx (last accessed 31.12.2014).

2009,[152] in which a military serviceman was denied parental leave following an explicit statutory stipulation reserving this benefit only to female military personnel. The Court considered the case as constitutionally permitted positive discrimination based on the limited participation of women in military service and the special social role of women associated with motherhood. However, after condemnation by the European Court of Human Rights on the grounds that Articles 8 and 14 of the Convention had been violated,[153] the Constitutional Court, following reference from the local court in Saint Petersburg, in which the proceeding was re-opened, has revisited its precedent in its judgment *Markin (No. 2)*,[154] in the light of the broader issue of the resolution of conflicts between domestic and international law. In doing so the Court refrained from laying down any general principles or from proclaiming its own superiority *vis-a-vis* the European Court and preferred a "pragmatic ambiguity", i.e. an *ad hoc* resolution of conflicts on a case-by-case basis (Vaypan 2014: 131–132). On the merits of the case, it intimated that the cases needed reconsideration, insofar as the complainant still suffered adverse consequences and the compensation granted by the Court of Strasbourg did not provide for the full restoration of violated rights and freedoms.

4.3 Asia

There are quite a few Asian states where affirmative action measures are provided by the constitution, or implemented in practice, especially in South East Asia (Rai et al. 2006). This is particularly the case with countries where there is significant racial division. For example, the 1957 Constitution of Malaysia, following departure from British colonisation, prescribes that equality before the law and equal protection do not invalidate or prohibit provision for the protection, well-being or advancement of the aboriginal peoples of the Malay Peninsula (including the reservation of land) or the reservation to aborigines of a reasonable proportion of suitable positions in the public service (Article 8). Accordingly, Malaysia, basically composed of Malay, Chinese and Indians, has a long tradition on affirmative action (Gomez and Saravanamuttu 2012; Means 1986; Sowell 2004: 55–77).

Other Constitutions, such as the 1978 Sri Lankan Constitution, legitimise affirmative action initiatives in favour of women (Article 12 para. 4). In spite of the very sharp and fierce division between Sinhalese and Tamils in this country, the Constitution merely treats the latter community as a linguistic minority thus providing for equitable use of both languages where appropriate (Articles 19–25), and incremental racial affirmative actions established at the sub constitutional level have produced adverse results with the rise of extremism and nationalism (Sowell 2004:

[152]FCC Ruling of 15 January 2009, 187-O-O.

[153]ECHR Judgment of 22nd March 2012, *Konstantin Markin v. Russia,* 1 (2012) EHRR 141.

[154]FCC Ruling of 6 December 2013.

78–94). A most impressive example of a positive measure in favour of vulnerable social categories is to be found in the 1972 Bangladesh Constitution, declaring the equality of opportunities for all citizens and mandating the State to adopt effective measures to remove social and economic inequalities and to ensure the equitable distribution of wealth among citizens, equality of opportunity and participation of women in all spheres of national life (Article 19). A variety of positive measures has been introduced in the country not merely restricted to female beneficiaries, including very extensive quotas in civil service recruitment (Al Faruque 2012). In all respects, however, research in relation to Asia ought to focus on two states, India and China, due to the size of their population and diversity and because it was the former country that arguably introduced affirmative action programmes—at least in Asia.

4.3.1 India

It is no surprise that India claims to be the first country to have introduced affirmative action plans, through minority quotas following the enactment of the 1949 Constitution. India has the largest number of minorities in the world, with more than 100 spoken languages, and emerged from British colonisation, becoming a sovereign state in 1947. Historically, systematic institutional discrimination occurred for non-Hindus in the country, tantamount to actual segregation. From an institutional point of view, India offers an excellent case study of institutional policy on affirmative action. This is not only because of the extent of the measures which qualify India as the greatest affirmative action laboratory in the world, but also because the Constitution itself sets out a rather analytical framework for the operation of the policy. Indeed the Constitution of India makes the most references to affirmative action policies, not merely by authorising the federal and state legislatures to adopt such measures, but also, on occasions, by setting hard quotas in the first place. Therefore, it provides a very illustrative case as to whether the constitutional upgrade of this mechanism essentially contributes to the maximisation of results. Unsurprisingly, there is a wide body of literature on the legal and political aspects of the policy in India, mostly from a comparative perspective (Tummala 2014; Bajpai 2011a, b; Galanter 1984; Rai 1998; Weisskopf 2004; Sowell 2004: 23–54).

There is a variety of group typologies when it comes to affirmative action beneficiaries. The first broad category is the ancient "*untouchables*", representing specific minority races. This is a historically burdened and politically incorrect term constitutionally replaced by "Scheduled Casts" and "Scheduled Tribes" (often called "Dalits" or "Harijans"). This is why the Constitution explicitly declares that "Untouchability" is abolished and its practice in any form is forbidden, rendering the enforcement of any form of discrimination arising out of it a criminal offence (Article 17). It lies with the President to specify the castes, races or tribes or parts of or groups within castes, races or tribes which are deemed to be Scheduled Castes and Tribes, after consultation with the Governor of the State (if applicable) and by public notification (Articles 341 and 342). Nevertheless, the Parliament may also by statute include in or exclude from the list of Scheduled Castes and Scheduled Tribes any caste, race or tribe or part of a group within any caste, race or tribe. The second broad category of beneficiaries is the socially and educationally "backward classes", which are the groups *de facto* suffering from serious social disadvantages. The all-embracing and mutable latter category today constitutes almost half of the Indian population. Unlike the Scheduled Castes and Scheduled Tribes, which are determined through an institutionally prescribed delineation process, backward classes are not strictly determined but are abstractly inclusive.

According to the Constitution, the State shall not discriminate against any citizen on grounds of religion, race, caste, sex or place of birth; especially in relation to access to shops, public restaurants, hotels and places of public entertainment or the use of wells, tanks, bathing ghats, roads and places of public use maintained wholly or partly out of State funds or dedicated to the use of the general public (Article 15 paras. 1–2). However, it is explicitly provided that the State may take measures for the advancement of any socially and educationally backward classes of citizens or for the Scheduled Castes and the Scheduled Tribes (Article 15 para. 4). This last stipulation was introduced by the 1951 Constitution (First Amendment) Act and came as a response of the Government to the Supreme Court's decision *State of Madras v. Smt. Champakam Dorairanjan* in 1951,[155] where the Court declared that caste-based reservations for Communal Award, i.e. a reservation system granting by British domination in 1932, violated the Constitution which was sacrosanct and not liable to be abridged by any legislative or executive act or order. The Constitution also provides that no citizen shall be denied admission into any educational institution maintained by the State or receiving aid out of State funds on grounds only of religion, race, caste or language (Article 29 para. 2) and that the State shall not, in granting aid to educational institutions, discriminate against any educational institution on the grounds that it is under the management of a minority, whether based on religion or language (Article 30 para. 2).

Broadly speaking, there are three broad areas of implementation of affirmative action policies, especially on a federal level: political representation, public employment and access to education. In the area of *political representation*, race quotas are provided by the Constitution for Scheduled Castes and Scheduled Tribes, whereas the ordinary legislation may introduce affirmative action programmes for other backward classes as well. In relation to Scheduled Castes and Scheduled Tribes, the Constitution establishes a system of hard quotas by reserving elected seats separately in local government authorities of rural areas ("*Panchayat*"), and municipalities (Articles 243D para. 1 and 243T para. 1 respectively). The reservation ratio must be as close as possible to pro rata, and the seats must be allotted by rotation to different constituencies. Pursuant to a constitutional authorisation, secondary pro rata quotas apply for the offices of the Chairpersons allotted by rotation to different Panchayats at each level according to state laws. In relation to

[155] AIR 1951 SC 226.

other backward classes, Articles 243D para. 6 and 243T para. 1 respectively determine that nothing prevents State parliaments from making any provision for the reservation of seats in any Panchayat or offices of Chairpersons in the Panchayats, at any level in favour of the backward class of citizens. A major novelty of the political representation affirmative action system in India is that the temporary nature of the measures is explicitly delineated by the Constitution itself. According to Article 334, the reservation of seats for the Scheduled Castes, the Scheduled Tribes and the Anglo-Indian community in the federal and State Parliaments cease to have effect on the expiration of a period of seventy years from the commencement/entry into force of the Constitution, i.e. in 2019. In spite of the constitutional provisions to safeguard political participation for minorities, there is a significant gap in politics in India because of the lack of internal democratic proceedings in the dominant political parties, resulting in the serious curtailment of the minority groups' power to democratically raise their claims. Obviously, the Hindu majority and the four dominant casts therein, entirely control the political arena.

In the area of *public employment*, the constitutional clause of Article 16 paras. 1 and 2 states that there shall be equality of opportunity for all citizens in matters relating to employment or appointment to any public office and that no citizen shall, on grounds only of religion, race, caste, sex, descent, place of birth or residence or any of them, be ineligible for, or discriminated against. Paras. 4 and 4A allow provisions for the reservation of appointments or posts in favour of any backward class of citizens, the Scheduled Castes or the Scheduled Tribes which, in the opinion of the State, are not adequately represented in the services. In the same constitutional line, Article 335 stipulates that the claims of the members of the Scheduled Castes and the Scheduled Tribes shall be taken into consideration, consistently with the maintenance of efficiency of administration in the making of appointments to services and posts in connection with the competences of the federation and the States. More specifically, the Constitution permits the introduction of programmes in favour of the members of the Scheduled Castes and the Scheduled Tribes to relax the qualifying marks needed in any examination, or to lower the evaluation standards in promotion to any class(es) of service(s) or federal or state posts. For a 10-year transitional period after the enactment of the Constitution, gradually diminishing employment quotas applied for members of the Anglo-Indian community in certain services (railway, customs, postal and telegraph); ever since public authorities may introduce further affirmative action policies in favour of this group provided that the individual beneficiaries are qualified for appointment on merit as compared with the members of other communities.

In the area of *education*, the Constitution mandates the State to promote (with special care) the educational and economic interests of the weaker sections of the people, and in particular, of the Scheduled Castes and the Scheduled Tribes, and requires the State to protect them from social injustice and all forms of exploitation (Article 46). Accordingly, Article 15 para. 5 explicitly enables the state to take measures for the preferential admission to educational institutions of socially and educationally backward classes of citizens, or for the Scheduled Castes or the Scheduled Tribe; this also includes private educational institutions, whether aided or unaided by the State, other than the minority educational institutions based on religion or language, that may be established and administered by these minorities pursuant with Article 30 para. 1 of the Constitution. Furthermore, Article 337 established transitional quotas for a limited period of time with respect to educational grants for the benefit of the Anglo-Indian community, which has not attempted to reverse quotas acting against their interests, i.e. that no educational institution shall be entitled to receive any grant under this article unless at least forty per cent of the annual admissions therein are made available to members of communities other than the Anglo-Indian community.

The Supreme Court of India dealt with the constitutionality of preferences in academic admissions four times in the 2000s. The first two decisions do not provide a clear precedent because of the multiplicity of the opinions rendered by the judges, and the fluidity produced thereof.[156] The authoritative decision came in 2005, in the unanimous Supreme Court decision *P.A. Inamdar and others v. State of Maharashtra and others*. The Court ruled that the State cannot impose a reservation policy upon minority and non-minority private colleges which do not receive public grants, including professional colleges, for granting admission on any criterion outside merit except for providing the qualifications and minimum conditions of eligibility in the interest of academic standards. Further, in *Ashoka Kumar Thakur v. Union of India* (2008), the Court upheld a 27 % quota for other backward castes in centrally-funded educational institutions on four conditions: that the quota scheme should exclude the "creamy layer" (including children of former and present deputies); that the scheme should not be expanded to private universities; that cut-off marks for preferential entries should not be substantially lower than general category candidates; and that a review of the system should take place every five years. Finally, in *Chariman and Managing Director of Central Bank of India v. Central Bank of India Scheduled Castes and the Scheduled Tribes Employees Welfare Association* (2015), the Supreme Court held that the Constitution enables State governments to provide for reservation of Scheduled Castes and the Scheduled Tribes category employees even in promotions, however the courts do not have the competence to issue mandamus to oblige the authorities to introduce such measures.

Although the basic goal of affirmative action policies in India historically relates to racial preferences, positive measures have also been constitutionally acknowledged in favour of women with an aim to secure social and economic inclusion and larger political participation. The former aim is served through a provision that the non-discrimination clause shall not prevent the State from making any special provision for women and children (Article 15 para. 4). The latter aim is served through the constitutional provision that the federal State may introduce special provisions for women, sub-reserving no less than one third of the already reserved seats for Scheduled Castes and Tribes elected in *Panchayats* and Municipalities for

[156] In 2002 in *T.M.A. Pai Foundation and others v. State of Karnataka & others* and in 2003 in *Islamic Academy of Education and another v. State of Karnataka others.*

women representatives of the benefiting categories by rotation to different constituencies (Articles 243D paras. 2–3 and 243T paras. 2–3 respectively). Furthermore, no less than one-third of the total number of offices of Chairpersons in the Panchayats at each level is constitutionally reserved for women (Articles 243D paras. 2–4 and 243T paras. 2–4 respectively). Finally, the Constitution also provides for two-seat reservation in professional associations (Co-operative Societies (Article 243ZI para. 2). In the same line, a number of the States also provides for gender quotas in political representation varying from 33 to 50 %.

In the light of the above constitutional framework, a huge number of affirmative action policies have been introduced at central, state and local government level. However, the desirable social cohesion has not been achieved. This was due either to the reluctance of the potential beneficiaries to take advantage of the preferential schemes, thus on many occasions leaving reserved seats unfilled, or to structural aspects of the architecture suffering from bad design, over or under-inclusiveness (Sowell 2004: 48–54). In the most elaborate assessment of the political representation quota system in relation to minority poverty in India Aimee Chin and Nishith Prakash prove that poverty rates have slightly dropped for Scheduled Tribes, whereas absolutely no difference has been produced for Scheduled Casts from 1960 to 2010 (Chin and Prakash 2010). The same results in effect seem to have been produced in quotas applicable to University admissions. Verónica C. Frisancho Robles and Kala Krishna proved that scheduled caste and scheduled tribe students fall behind their studies and eventually enter the professional arena from a disadvantageous position in relation to their classmates (Frisancho Robles and Kala Krishna 2010).

4.3.2 China

The 1982 Chinese Constitution places particular emphasis on gender equality, cultural preservation and diversity. Accordingly, all citizens are equal before the law (Article 33); women enjoy equal rights with men in all spheres of life: political, economic, cultural and social, and family life; and the state protects the rights and interests of women, applies the principle of equal pay for equal work for men and women alike and trains and selects cadres from among women (Article 48); all nationalities are equal and the state protects the lawful rights and interests of the minority nationalities, upholds and develops the relationship of equality, unity and mutual assistance among all nationalities. Discrimination against and oppression of any nationality and any acts that undermine the unity of the nationalities or instigate their secession are prohibited and the state helps the areas inhabited by minority nationalities to speed up their economic and cultural development in accordance with the peculiarities and needs of the different minority nationalities (Article 4).

The above stipulation reflects the particularities of the most populated country of the world: 9 % of the population belongs to one of the 55 recognised ethnic groups, the most populated of which, the Zhuangs, totals more than 15 million people, while the remaining 82 % belongs to the dominant race Hans constituting the largest ethnic group globally; at the same time though the minority ethnic groups occupy almost half of the Chinese land's territory extending to 9.6 million square kilometers which is rich in resources. Mild positive measures apply in favour of minorities such as disproportionate investment and subsidies, preferential admissions to the academia, lower fees where applicable, tax exemptions, on-going professional training and disproportionately high representation in local councils. Spectacular results have been produced in the field of University admissions in particular, so that the number of minority students has risen significantly, in recent years, which in turn results in a much better positioning in the professional arena and a general group upgrade in collective bargaining with the central government. The overall implementation of preferential treatment programmes in China is, therefore, rated very positively by the literature (Sautman 1998: 86–92, 1999; Zhou and Hill 2009).

China may also reasonably claim the most unusual positive measure, i.e. the exceptional privilege awarded to minority couples to have two children, as opposed to the general limitation of one child, pursuant to a constitutional clause that "the state promotes family planning so that population growth may fit the plan for economic and social development" (Article 25). Although due to the country's population this exemption is not expected to produce significant variations in the ethnic composition of the country, it remains that substantive preferential treatment is reserved for minorities which strengthens its members.

In terms of gender affirmative action, the only known implemented policy is the decision in 2007 of the 10th annual National People's Congress, the legislature that serves China's ruling Communist Party, whereby women representatives in future Congresses must exceed 22 %. However, it was not until the 2013 National People's Congress that this threshold was exceeded by reaching a level of female participation of 23.4 % (Downie 2014: 60–64).[157]

4.4 Africa

According to Antonie Katharina Nord's study conducted in 2012 for the German Institute of Global and Area Studies, 23 out of 49 Sub-Saharan African countries have made use of gender affirmative action measures. In fact, Rwanda and South Africa have been pioneers in the actual participation of women in parliament, the former enjoying an unprecedented female majority at the House (56 and 45 % respectively). According to Nord (2012), the reasons for this wide success lie with the political mobilisation of women in civil society, the strategic allies existing in the state bureaucracy and the proper functioning of political institutions. Apart from

[157]http://www.quotaproject.org/uid/countryview.cfm?CountryCode=CN (last accessed 31.12. 2014).

the self-revealing data, it seems that there are powerful dynamics in favour of gender affirmative action in the continent (Tripp et al. 2006).

For the purpose of the present study, Nigeria and South Africa will be examined. The first constitutes the largest African country, where affirmative actions have been applied widely; the affirmative action system in the latter seems to be the most akin to racial compensatory measures because of the very heavy history of Apartheid.

4.4.1 Nigeria

Nigeria seems to embrace most of the conditions favouring affirmative action plans. It is a federal constitutional republic comprising 36 states and one Federal Capital Territory, composed of more than 450 ethnic groups (70 % from the three largest groups Hausa-Fulani, Yoruba, and Igbo), with 400 native languages currently in use, it is also religiously diverse, with an estimated 50 % Muslim and 40 % Christian population. In light of this diversity, a very extensive and explosive mixture of religions, classes, races, languages and traditions, Nigeria essentially constitutes an artificial state construed for the first time in history at the end of the British colonial era. An analogous situation, albeit one based on different historical incidents, occurred in Europe in post-war Yugoslavia; however, positive measures were rather unknown there due to the imposition of an authoritarian regime.

In Nigeria, affirmative action policies were introduced to serve the task of social cohesion and, in turn, of creating a synthetic national identity as a necessary correlation/condition for the preservation of the federal character of the state. The 1999 Constitution establishes a general non-discrimination clause according to which the State shall direct its policy towards ensuring that all citizens, without discrimination on any group whatsoever, have the opportunity for securing adequate means of livelihood as well as adequate opportunity to secure suitable employment (Article 17 para. 3). The Constitution further introduced the "federal character principle clause" by stipulating that the composition of the government of the federation or any of its agencies and the conduct of its affairs shall be carried out in such a manner as to reflect the federal character of the state and the need to promote national unity, and also to command national loyalty thereby ensuring that there shall be no predominance of persons from a few States or from a few ethnic or other sectional groups in that Government or in any of its agencies (Article 14 para. 3). Accordingly, all aspects of social and financial/economic life were beset by considerations of balancing. Education, procurements and state recruitments were par excellence the areas where this balancing process took place through the introduction of hard or soft quotas (Adele Jinadu 1985, 2002; Nnoli 1996). However, unlike conventional affirmative action, which generally has a temporary character so as to rectify historical discrimination, in the case of Nigeria the award of public preferences was set as permanent not so as to develop a seemingly artificial unity, but in essence presumably to consolidate elite domination by ethnically-based factions of the political class. The constitutional outsourcing of affirmative action supervision to the Federal Character Commission with the competence to enforce compliance with the federal character principle through equitable distribution of employment in the public services and promotion, monitoring and enforcement of compliance with the principles of proportional sharing of all bureaucratic, economic, media and political posts at all levels of government, merely contributed in part to the non-violent resolution of ethnic grievances, whereas effective equality of opportunities was not achieved (Mustapha 2009). Most notably, the most important race-sensitive affirmative action policies, unsurprisingly, have patently failed to produce significant results in developing social cohesion, probably because there was lack of strong political will to effectively implement these policies (Tummala 2014; Adams 1993). Albeit the failure of affirmative action in Nigeria—the main way to identify a citizen remains their ethnicity—still domestic Gross Domestic Product (GDP) Annual Growth Rate is very high, in average 6.12 % from 2005 until 2014.[158]

Finally, in relation to gender affirmative action measures, political parties in parliamentary and local elections obtaining at least 3 seats in a constituency must by law ensure that at least 10 % of their candidates are selected from both genders (Nnoli 1996: 234; Sowell 2004: 95–114).

4.4.2 South Africa

The case of South Africa is rather a unique case study in terms of affirmative action, in the sense that these measures purport to compensate for past discriminations not against minorities, but against the majority race. The apartheid regime systematically excluded non-whites from political and economic participation before the restoration of democracy in 1994 (Hassim 2000; Smith 1995).

For obvious historical reasons relating to the spill-over discriminatory effect of apartheid, the constitutional architecture of the new democracy was built upon the pre-existing claim of social inclusion and non-discrimination. According to the Preamble of the 1996 Constitution: "We, the people of South Africa recognise the injustices of our past, honour those who suffered for justice and freedom in our land…Believe that South Africa belongs to all who live in it, united in our diversity… Lay the foundations for a democratic and open society in which government is based on the will of the people and every citizen is equally protected by law…". The equality principle is quite plethoric and overlapping. Thus, according to constitutional clauses, "everyone is equal before the law and has the right to equal protection and benefit of the law; equality includes the full and equal enjoyment of all rights and freedoms; to promote the achievement of equality, legislative and other measures designed to protect or advance persons or categories of persons disadvantaged by

[158]World Bank data, http://data.worldbank.org/country/nigeria (last accessed 31.12.2014).

unfair discrimination may be taken; the state may not unfairly discriminate directly or indirectly against anyone on any ground; no person may unfairly discriminate directly or indirectly against anyone; national legislation must be enacted to prevent or prohibit unfair discrimination; and, discrimination on any ground is unfair unless it is established that the discrimination is fair" (Article 9).

Affirmative action enjoys a key role in the post-apartheid legal system, especially in the field of employment. The *Employment Equity Act 1998*[159] requires designated employers (those employing more than 50 people, those whose annual income is more than a prescribed amount, municipalities, organs of state, employers ordered to comply by a bargaining council agreement and volunteering employers) to compile and implement an Employment Equity Plan promoting equal opportunity, eliminating unfair discrimination practices and involving affirmative action for designated groups (i.e. black people, women and employees with disabilities) in order to achieve employment equity. The rationale is to redress the disadvantages in employment, to eliminate unfair discrimination, to develop the skills of the disadvantaged groups and to enhance diversity and representation in the workforce in order to ensure equality in all occupational categories and levels in the workplace and to promote equal opportunity in employment (Section 2b). Overall, although the Employment Equity Act does not exclude hard quotas (Section 15 subsection 3), in practice only positive measures of indirect effect have been introduced resulting in indirect preferential treatment in favour of designated groups.

Further, the strategic *Broad-Based Black Economic Empowerment Act 2003*[160] was introduced aiming, according to its Preamble, to promote, *inter alia*, the achievement of the constitutional right to equality, increase broad-based and effective participation of black people in the economy and promote a higher growth rate, increased employment and more equitable income distribution, establish a national policy on broad-based black economic empowerment so as to promote the economic unity of the nation, protect the common market and promote equal opportunity and equal access to government services. The Act does not explicitly refer to the introduction of hard quotas but mandates an overall restructuring of the market so as to establish a balance of the employment personnel. Accordingly, black-owned and/or managed companies are facilitated in terms of financing, mentorships, apprenticeships and internships and in their participation in preferential procurement policies, substantial change in the racial composition of ownership and management structures is envisaged, whereas the Act especially caters for black female entrepreneurship. Outside the field of employment, South African universities and other institutions of higher education more or less employ policies of giving preference to applications from designated races, especially of black candidates, given that the student population is still far from representative of the total South African population (Favish and Hendry 2010).

---

[159] 55/1998.

[160] 53/2003.

In Pretoria High Court's judgment *Christian Roberts v. Minister of Social Development* (2007),[161] it was ruled that different age thresholds between men and women (65 and 60 respectively) established by Section 10 of Social Assistance Act 13/2004 were constitutional. The challenge was brought by Port Elizabeth Justice Centre, on behalf of four Eastern Cape men, who were joined by the Human Rights Commission, the Centre for Applied Legal Studies at the University of Witwatersrand and the Community Law Centre at the University of the Western on grounds of an alleged violation of the constitutional equality clause (Section 9 para. 3) and the right of access to social assistance (Section 27 para. 1c). The Court upheld the argument raised by the Government that the race, class and social discrimination faced by African women during apartheid justified differentiation in favour of women generally and of African women in particular, and allowed the retention of the differentiating scheme at the time the case was heard. Nonetheless, the government then amended the legislation so that the pension age differentiation was eliminated over a three-year period, finally ceasing to exist in 2010.

Authority case law, however, today is *South African Police Service v. Solidarity obo Barnard* of the Constitutional Court in 2014,[162] on the constitutionality of preferential treatment in employment promotions. In this case, the female white Captain for the South African Police Service Barnard applied for the post of superintendent 3 times after 24 years of service. Although in the first two applications she was named most qualified candidate and her appointment was recommended by the interviewing committees on both occasions, the post was not filled and the call was eventually withdrawn by the National Police Commissioner due to equity reasons. Barnard filed a case of unfair racial discrimination, leading to the Johannesburg Labour Court judgment which found in her favour. The respondents appealed to the Labour Appeal Court which reversed the decision on grounds of employment equity requiring proportional representation set by predetermined racial quotas. The organisation Solidarity (a South African trade union that collectively negotiates on behalf of its members with the employers) appealed before the Supreme Court of Appeal, which found in favour of Solidarity and Barnard on the grounds that employment equity cannot be achieved by mechanically applying formulas and numerical targets, thus a flexible and tailor-made approach ought to apply. The Constitutional Court on appeal reversed the decision on the ground that the challenged Employment Equity Plan was a restitutionary measure contemplated in Section 9 para. 2 of the Constitution, which determined how the equality claim was to be evaluated and, therefore, the appellate court misconceived the issue and decided on the wrong principle. A three-justices concurring opinion found that there was a possible infringement of dignity in the implementation of restitutionary measures without adequate reasons and Justice Van Der Westhuizen J ruled that the decision not to appoint the appellant even though she would have suffered past disadvantage did not threaten the long-term constitutional vision of a non-sexist

[161]Judgment 32838/05 of 10th August 2007.

[162]165/2013, (2014) ZACC 23.

society. The decision was characterized by domestic literature as a “missed opportunity”, albeit reaffirming state’s legal and moral commitment to transformation (Premhid 2014).

As for the doctrine, there are plentiful voices suggesting that employment affirmative action has not produced any significant results, while substituting for another form of discrimination (Rossouw 1994: 73), or for the establishment of a permanent racial balance within the employment arena (Horwitz 1998), or the over and under-inclusiveness of the system and the employees’ perception thereof (Thomas 2002). The same is true for academic admissions programmes enhancing preferential treatment policies for non-whites. Concerns vary significantly: establishing post-apartheid meritocracy through racial profiling constitutes a setback, and is argued to be a misuse of race so as to combat racial discrimination which is setting new racial categories (Erasmus 2010); and an immoral setting of racial standards in a country that has suffered from exactly this institutional profiling and constitutes the unacceptable establishment of arbitrary taxonomy of designated racial groups (Benatar 2010).

Overall, in spite of the extremely adverse record on non-discrimination and the constitutional guarantees in favour of positive equality measures, rigid quotas still seem to be widely non-accepted in the country. The same seems to be the case with gender quotas where no such threshold exists in South Africa as to the national parliament; it is only in the elections for local councils where the participating political parties must seek to ensure that 50 % of the candidates on the party list are women and that the candidates are evenly distributed in geographic terms.[163]

4.5 Oceania

Because of the existence of indigenous populations, both Australia and New Zealand are interesting examples of how native races have been treated through positive measures. Māori culture is far more prominent in New Zealand society than Aboriginal cultures are in Australian society; however, both states have introduced relevant positive measures. The two states have also used gender quotas to a lesser extent to reinforce the political participation of women (Krook et al. 2006).

4.5.1 Australia

The Commonwealth of Australia is a federation comprising six self-governed states (New South Wales, Victoria, Tasmania, Queensland, Western Australia and South Australia) and a number of mainland and external territories subject to the authority

[163] Local Government Act, Schedule 1, Section 11(3); Schedule 2, Sections 5(3) and 17(5).

of the federation. The Australian Constitution of 1901 does not include a charter of rights, adhering to the British tradition which gives precedence to the common law, which is unsurprising given that it was enacted as a section of the Westminster *Commonwealth of Australia Constitution Act 1900*. Thus, no equality clause exists within the formal Constitution, save for indirect stipulations, such that the Parliament shall have the power to make special laws deemed necessary with respect to the people of any race (Article 51[26]) and that residents in any State shall not be subject in any other State to any disability or discrimination which would not be equally applicable to them if they were subjects in such other State (Article 117). Pursuant to the latter provision above, the *Racial Discrimination Act 1975* allows "special measures" (Article 8 para. 1) and extends all privileges enjoyed by persons of a particular race, colour or national or ethnic origin to all other respective groups.

Irrespective of the lack of constitutional acknowledgment of affirmative action (or equality in general), Australia may convincingly claim that it has enacted the most elaborate horizontal relevant piece of legislation in the area of employment, the *Affirmative Action (Equal Opportunities for Women) Act 1986*. Irrespective of its actual implementation, taken as a whole it comprises a wide range of novelties on a world-wide level. First, the explicit language of affirmative action, apart from its symbolic importance, raises public awareness on the issue. Second, the statute stipulates the definition of affirmative action (a rather seldom occurrence in relevant statutes) as appropriate action which is taken to eliminate discrimination by the employer against women or promote equal opportunity for women in relation to employment matters. Interestingly, the Act also comprises a definition of "woman", i.e. "a member of the female sex irrespective of age". Third, there is an elaborate indicative list (presumably the most elaborate worldwide) of the modes of affirmative action that a relevant employer (namely a higher education institution or the employer of 100 or more employees) shall provide for (Article 8 para. 1): (a) to issue to the employees by a senior officer concerned with the management a statement to the effect that the employer has commenced the development and implementation of an affirmative action programme; (b) to confer responsibility for the development and implementation of the programme (including a continuous review of the programme) on a person or persons having sufficient authority and status within the management to enable the person or persons to properly develop and implement the programme; (c) to consult with each trade union having members affected by the proposal for the development and implementation of the programme; (d) to consult with employees, particularly employees who are women; (e) to collect and record statistics and related information concerning employment, including the number of employees of either sex and the types of jobs undertaken by, or job classifications of, employees of either sex; (f) to consider policies and examine practices of the relevant employer in relation to employment matters to identify any policies or practices that constitute discrimination against women and any patterns (whether ascertained statistically or otherwise) of a lack of equality of opportunity in respect of women; (g) to set objectives and make future estimates in the programme; and (h) to monitor and evaluate the implementation of the programme and to assess the achievement of those qualitative measures or aims, expressed as a general principle, designed to achieve equality of opportunity for women in employment matters, being a measure or aim that can reasonably be implemented within a specified time ("objectives") and quantitative measures or aims, which may be expressed in numerical terms, designed to achieve equality of opportunity for women in employment matters, being a measure or aim that can reasonably be implemented by the relevant employer within a specified time ("forward estimates"). In order to facilitate the launching and supervision of affirmative action programmes by relevant employers, the Act creates a whole organic architecture. This comprises a Director of Affirmative Action appointed by the Governor-General, advisory committees and external consultants, as well as extensive procedures, such as periodical reports by the Director to the Ministers, public reports by relevant employers, confidential reports by the relevant employers to the Director and requests to the relevant employers for publicity of reports or provision of data.

The jurisprudence of the Australian courts in relation to affirmative action is not extensive and has not produced a solid authority. In relation to the implementation of the *Racial Discrimination Act 1975*, the High Court rendered in 1982 a judgment in *Koowarta v. Bjelke-Petersen*,[164] whereby the members of the Court gave various opinions which left ambiguity on the extent of the competence of the federal legislature to enact "special laws" for underrepresented groups, such as the Aboriginals. Although it was admitted that a certain degree of differentiation is inherent in any special law aiming at curing existing inequalities based on past discrimination, the majority of the Court expressed their opinion that these statutes cannot legitimately produce adverse effects upon individuals or group. A year later, the High Court in *Commonwealth v. Tasmania*,[165] emphasised the distinction between special laws to treat inequalities which are constitutional and genuinely discriminatory legislation which cannot be constitutionally tolerated and on these grounds upheld the special protection of Aboriginal sites under *World Heritage Properties Conservation Act 1983*. In *Gerhardy v. Brown*,[166] mostly a case of discrimination and less an affirmative action case, the High Court took a negative stance towards preferential treatment for a particular Aboriginal race (Pitjantjatjara) and struck down the *Pitjantjatjara Land Rights Act 1981*, which, pursuant to local customs, prohibited non-Pitjantjatjara individuals from entering the designated land. The High Court found that this involved discrimination based on race, contrary to a (literal) interpretation of Article 1 para. 1 of the UN *Convention on the Elimination of All Forms of Racial Discrimination*, which was applicable as superior law in the absence of a constitutional charter for the protection of fundamental rights.

[164](1982) HCA 27; (1982) 153 CLR 168.

[165](1983) 46 ALR 625.

[166](1985) 57 ALR 472.

Affirmative action policies in Australia, especially *Affirmative Action (Equal Opportunities for Women) Act 1986*, have been widely criticised in the domestic literature. One portion of the doctrine argues that the statute is rather theoretical and procedural, and that it lacks any results-oriented force, potentially through the enactment of rigid quotas (Thornton 1990: 230; Poiner and Wills 1991). Others praise the legislation for finding a fine balance between preferential treatment to vulnerable employment categories, while at the same time safeguarding meritocracy by merely establishing large-scale awareness and participatory programmes (Braithwaite and Bush 1998; Bourke and Bourke 2006). Finally, Carol Bacchi considers the Australian paradigm of the politics of incorporation of women through federal affirmative action to be a failure, because targeting women has allowed a diminution of attention to them and has not in any way resulted in an upgrade of their status (1996: 79–100).

4.5.2 New Zealand

New Zealand may also legitimately claim early establishment of affirmative action plans through the preferential treatment reserved for Māoris, especially related to property rights, as early as 1840 with the Treaty of Waitangi, i.e. the founding document of government signed between the British Crown and around 540 Māori chiefs.

Although New Zealand lacks a codified formal constitution, there is a block of instruments which collectively compose its constitutional block. Amongst these statutes, the *New Zealand Bill of Rights Act 1990* and the *Human Rights Act 1993* feature prominently and require a joint reading and interpretation. According to the former statute, everyone has the right to freedom from discrimination, whereas measures taken in good faith for the purpose of assisting or advancing persons or groups of persons disadvantaged because of discrimination that is unlawful do not constitute discrimination (Article 19) and a person who belongs to an ethnic, religious, or linguistic minority shall not be denied the right, in community with other members of that minority, to enjoy the culture, to profess and practise the religion, or to use the language, of that minority (Article 20). The latter statute contains a very analytical/detailed list of prohibited grounds of discrimination, i.e. sex, including pregnancy and childbirth, marital status, religious and ethical belief, colour, race, disability, age, political opinion, employment status, family status and sexual orientation (Article 21). Further, a discriminatory measure does not violate the Act if it is done or omitted in good faith for the purpose of assisting or advancing persons or groups of persons, being in each case persons against whom discrimination is unlawful, and those persons or groups need or may reasonably be supposed to need assistance or advancement in order to achieve an equal place with other members of the community (Article 73 para. 1).

In New Zealand, separate Māori electorates exist by statute, where citizens register at will, and vote for 7 reserved parliamentary seats, whereby the candidates for election are not necessarily Māori-origin nonetheless. The *Māori Land Act 1993* provided for Māori land reservations as a village site, sports ground, catchment area or other source of water supply, place of cultural, historical, or scenic interest and timber reserve. The Ministry for Māori Development, established in 1992, monitors policy and legislation, providing the government with advice on Māori relations (Lashley 2006).

In practice, incremental initiatives awarding preferences to Māoris exist in New Zealand, in both employment and academic admissions. Most prominently, in the field of public employment, the *State Sectors Act 1988* entails that state departments ought to acknowledge the aims and aspirations of the Māori people, the employment requirements relevant to them and the need for greater involvement on their part in the public service. In the field of University admissions, the *Education Act 1989* specifically enables the Universities to give preference to eligible persons who are included in a class of persons that is underrepresented among the students undertaking the class.

There is no judicial authority concerning the above extremely cumbersome statutory environment governing the possibility of introducing affirmative action policies and, especially, its permitted extent. The most relevant case law, albeit low-level, is the decision of the Complaints Review Tribunal in *Amaltal Fishing Company Ltd v. Nelson Polytechnic* (1996).[167] The defendant, while running fishing cadet courses, reserved 4 of the 14 places in the first fishing cadet course and the entire 14 places consequently exclusively for persons of Māori and Pacific Island descent. The applicant's employees applied for and were turned down for the courses because of the reservations. The applicant alleged that the quotas were in breach the *Race Relations Act 1971*, the *Human Rights Commission Act 1977* and the *Human Rights Act 1993*. Given that the applicants' dismissal was evidently based principally on racial grounds, the Tribunal found a breach of all relevant statutes. The key factor in the Tribunal's decision was that action in good faith allowing for the enactment of special measures may be supposed to need, given that an inquiry should be made as to whether the beneficiaries needed or may be supposed to need assistance or advancement to help them achieve equality. On the evidence submitted, the Tribunal was not satisfied.

4.6 International Law

4.6.1 Universal and Regional Conventions

After World War II, the first international law texts intended to safeguard human rights at a global or regional level, mostly written at the United Nations, imposed an unconditional obligation on States to guarantee equality without any reference to its

[167](1996) NZAR 97.

substantive form, regardless of the binding force of each particular document. This is the case, for example, of the 1948 *Universal Declaration of Human Rights* (Recital 4 of the Preamble and Article 2), the 1952 *Convention on the Political Rights of Women* (Article 3), the 1966 *International Covenant on Economic, Social and Cultural Rights* (Article 3) and the 1993 *Vienna Declaration and Programme of Action* (Chapter I, para 18).

The first reference to "special", essentially positive, measures was made in the context of the International Labour Organisation and the *Discrimination (Employment and Occupation) Convention*, adopted in 1958. According to this instrument, the States, after consultation with representative employers' and workers' organisations, may take special measures designed to meet the particular requirements of persons who, for reasons such as sex, age, disability, family responsibilities or social or cultural status, are generally recognised to require special protection or assistance (Article 5 para. 2).

An essential move towards more substantive equality was made by the 1965 *International Convention on the Elimination of All Forms of Racial Discrimination* of the UN.[168] The Convention provides that states parties undertake to adopt immediate and effective measures, particularly in the fields of teaching, education, culture and information, with a view to combating prejudices which lead to racial discrimination and to promoting understanding, tolerance and friendship among nations and racial or ethnical groups. In this frame the Convention makes direct reference to propagating the purposes and principles of the Charter of the United Nations, the Universal Declaration of Human Rights, the United Nations Declaration on the Elimination of All Forms of Racial Discrimination, and this Convention (Article 7). In light of this scope, the States may introduce special measures for the sole purpose of securing the adequate advancement of certain racial or ethnic groups or individuals requiring such protection as may be necessary in order to ensure the equal enjoyment or exercise of human rights and fundamental freedoms, provided that such measures do not lead to the maintenance of separate rights for different racial groups and that they shall not be continued after the objectives for which they were taken have been achieved (Article 1 para. 4).

Furthermore, the *International Covenant on Civil and Political Rights*, signed in 1966 and entered into force 10 years later, provides that the States shall take the necessary steps to adopt such laws, or other measures as may be necessary to give effect to the rights recognised in the Covenant, which include equality before the law and non-discrimination of any kind whether on grounds of race, colour, sex, language, religion, political or other opinion, national or social origin, property, birth or other status (Article 2 para. 2 in conjunction with Articles 26 and 2 para 1). The Covenant also provides for special protection safeguarding gender equality, by stipulating that the parties undertake to ensure the equal rights of men and women

---

[168]The Convention was adopted and opened for signature and ratification by General Assembly resolution 2106 of 21st December 1965 and entered into force 4th January 1969.

to the enjoyment of all civil and political rights set forth therein (Art 3 of the Covenant).

The *Convention on the Elimination of All Forms of Discrimination against Women*, signed in 1979 and entered into force in 1981, provides an explicit and detailed reference to the obligation of UN Member States to take positive measures in favour of women. According to the Convention, the adoption of temporary special measures aimed at accelerating *de facto* equality between men and women is not considered discrimination, albeit that shall in no way entail as a consequence the maintenance of unequal or separate standards and shall be discontinued when the objectives of equality of opportunity and treatment have been achieved (Article 4 para. 1 of the Convention). In fact, the Convention not only elevates positive action to the level of international law, but essentially requires the States to use it in all fields, in particular in the political, social, economic and cultural fields (Article 3).

Also in relation to sex equality, the Committee of Ministers of the Council of Europe adopted on February 5th, 1985, a Recommendation on Legal Protection against Sex Discrimination, which includes a special section entitled "*special temporary measures (positive action)*". This provides that, in order to promote equality of sexes, European States should adopt suitable machinery, such as legislation and advice for public authorities, guidelines and codes of conduct, encouragement for collective bargaining that promotes equality, action to eliminate and avoid sex discrimination in commercial advertisements, conciliation between parties to a dispute and the imposition of sanctions and initiation of legal proceedings where appropriate.[169]

In this respect, the *Framework Convention for the Protection of National Minorities*, signed under the auspices of the Council of Europe in Strasbourg in 1995, is equally worth mentioning. Through this Convention, the parties undertake to adopt, where necessary, adequate measures in order to promote, in all areas of economic, social, political and cultural life, full and effective equality between persons belonging to a national minority and those belonging to the majority by taking due account of the specific conditions of the persons belonging to national minorities (Articles 2 paras. 2 and 3).

A formal version of equality has been adopted by the African Charter on Human and Peoples' Rights widely known as the *Banjul Charter* adopted on June 27th 1981 and entered into force on October 21st 1986. Despite multiple references to equality, inhuman discrimination suffered by black people worldwide and under the apartheid regime survived for decades in the south of the African continent. Different facets of equality are recognised in multiple articles of the Charter: "every individual shall be entitled to the enjoyment of the rights and freedoms recognised and guaranteed in the present Charter without distinction of any kind such as race, ethnic group, colour, sex, language, religion, political or any other opinion, national and social origin, fortune, birth or other status" (Article 2); "every individual shall be equal before the law" (Article 3 para. 1); "every individual shall be entitled to

[169]Recommendation No R (85) 2, Art III.

equal protection of the law" (Article 3 para. 2); "every citizen shall have the right of equal access to the public services of his country" (Article 13 para. 2); "every individual shall have the right of access to public property and services in strict equality of all persons before the law" (Article 13 para. 3); "every individual shall have the right to work under equitable and satisfactory conditions, and shall receive equal pay for equal work" (Article 15); "all peoples shall be equal; they shall enjoy the same respect and shall have the same rights…" (Article 19); and "all peoples shall have the right to their economic, social and cultural development with due regard to their freedom and identity and in the equal enjoyment of the common heritage of mankind" (Article 22 para. 1).

4.6.2 The European Convention on Human Rights

Due to the extensive case-law rendered by the European Court of Human Rights, the European Convention on Human Rights, signed in Rome on November 4th 1950, deserves distinctive analysis. In the same way as other regional human rights treaties, it makes no explicit or implicit reference to positive action as part of the equality principle. Equality is indirectly acknowledged in Article 14 which entails that "the enjoyment of the rights and freedoms set forth in this Convention shall be secured without discrimination on any ground such as sex, race, colour, language, religion, political or other opinion, national or social origin, association with a national minority, property, birth or other status". From its very beginning, the European Court of Human Rights has treated this stipulation in a rather formalistic way and has been particularly reluctant to accept its independent character. Accordingly, Article 14 can only be invoked in an auxiliary way, namely only in cases where another right recognised by the Treaty has allegedly been violated (Melchior 1991).[170] The result of this judicial attitude has been that equality between men and women, or equality between members of different races or religions does not constitute a right protected *per se* in the context of the Convention and the Strasbourg Court does not invoke this ground alone, even though there are incremental judicial dicta to the "principle of equal treatment"[171] and the "equality of sexes".[172] Given the auxiliary nature of Article 14, it is understandable why the Court has been rather reluctant to express an opinion on positive action.[173] Only in *obiter dicta* has the Court implied that when a deviation from formal equality occurs through a positive measure, there must be a legitimate aim and the principle

[170]See the principal judgment of 23rd July 1968, *Belgian Linguistic Case (No. 2),* 1 (1979) EHRR 252.

[171]ECHR Judgment of 23rd July 1968, *Belgian Linguistic Case (No. 2),* 1 (1979) EHRR 252.

[172]ECHR Judgment of 28th May 1985, *Abdulaziz, Cabales and Balkandaliv v. The United Kingdom,* 7 (1985) EHRR 471, para. 78.

[173]ECHR Judgment of 26th March 1985, *X and Y v. Netherlands*, 8 (1986) EHRR 235.

of proportionality ought to be respected.[174] Generally speaking, the Court allows a larger margin of appreciation to the contracting states if the cases are closely linked to the interest of the state and the exercise of political powers by the constitutional organs[175] and becomes more stringent when a state has failed to introduce rules so as to justify different treatment of different factual situations.[176]

On June 26th 2000, the 12th Protocol of the Convention was signed by the Committee of Ministers representing 25 European states. The specific aim of this protocol was to address the inadequate protection provided to the equality principle by upgrading it to the status of a right protected *per se*; new provisions "shall be regarded as additional articles to the Convention and all the provisions of the Convention shall apply accordingly" (Article 3). Thus, "the enjoyment of any right set forth by law shall be secured without discrimination on any ground such as sex, race, colour, language, religion, political or other opinion, national or social origin, association with a national minority, property, birth or other status" and no one shall be discriminated against by any public authority on any ground such as those mentioned above (Article 1 paras. 1 and 2). The Protocol entered into force only 5 years later, after ratification from 10 member states of the Council of Europe, thereby being enforced as of April 1st 2005 (Article 5 para. 1). Until the end of July 2014, the Protocol has been ratified by 18 states, whereas 19 states have signed but not ratified it. In fact, the entry into force of the Protocol is mainly attributed to less influential European states, such as those of Central and Eastern Europe, Finland, the Netherlands, Luxembourg, Cyprus, San Marino and, as of 2008, Spain. Germany, Russia, Italy, Portugal, Ireland and Greece, among other states, have signed the Protocol but have yet to ratify it; whereas the UK, France, Sweden and Switzerland, among other states, have not even signed it. Paradoxically, the UK House of Lords rejected the implementation of the Protocol on the grounds that its text is "*too general and open-ended... it does not make provisions for positive measures...*" (Lester of Herne Hill 2001).[177]

---

[174]ECHR Judgment of 24th September 2002, *Posti and Rahko v. Finland,* 37 (2003) EHRR 6:158 and Commission Decision on Application nr. 11089/84, *DG and DW Lindsay v. UK* (1986) 49 DR 181.

[175]ECHR Judgment of 8th July 2003, *Sommerfeld v. Germany*, 36 (2003) EHRR 33: 565, para. 92; ECHR Judgment of 28th November 1984, *Rasmussen v. Denmark,* 7 (1985) EHRR 371; and ECHR Judgment of 23rd October 1997, *The National and Provincial Building Society et als. v. UK,* 25 (1998) EHRR 127, para. 80.

[176]ECHR Judgment of 6th April 2000, *Thlimmenos v. Greece,* 31 (2001) EHRR 411. The Court has added more unaccepted grounds of discrimination/differential treatment such as sexual orientation through its case-law, ECHR Judgment of 21st December 1999, *Salgueiro da Silva Mouta v. Portugal,* 31 (2001) EHRR 1055, and the legal differentiation between individuals suffering physical as opposed to psychological injuries, ECHR Judgment of 22nd October 1996, *Stubbings et als. v. United Kingdom,* 23 (1997) EHRR 213.

[177]H.L. Deb., Vol 617, col. WA37, October 11, 2000.

The Protocol makes reference to positive measures in its Preamble, according to which the contracting states "*reaffirm*" that "the principle of non-discrimination does not prevent States Parties from taking measures in order to promote full and effective equality, provided that there is an objective and reasonable justification for these measures". It is noteworthy that there is an issue concerning the language of "reaffirmation". In fact, it is not self-evident that the statement refers to any prior statutory or jurisprudential rule. Given that positive measures were treated in the same way as any other deviation from the formal equality principle, reaffirmation can only imply that they are still to be considered as an exception to the non-discrimination clause. This interpretation becomes more convincing if one takes into account the case law prerequisites of a legitimate positive measure. "Objective and reasonable justification" constitutes (along with the principle of proportionality, if conceived as conceptually different from "objective and reasonable justification") the criterion for assessing any deviation from the principle of equality.[178] In that sense, the Preamble to the Protocol reaffirmed that positive action is overall tantamount to an exception from the general principle of equality. According to the Explanatory Report, positive measures are taken in order to promote full and effective equality and are not prohibited insofar as there is an objective and reasonable justification for them. The Report further exemplifies that the fact that there are certain groups or categories of persons who are disadvantaged, or the existence of *de facto* inequalities, may constitute justifications for adopting measures providing for specific advantages in order to promote equality, provided that the proportionality principle is respected.[179]

In any event, the 12th Protocol does not make it *obligatory* for contracting states to take affirmative action measures to curtail factual discriminations. Through an explicit statement the Explanatory Report of the Protocol specifies that "the Protocol does not impose any obligation to adopt such measures", given that "such a programmatic obligation would sit ill with the whole nature of the Convention and its control system which are based on the collective guarantee of individual rights which are formulated in terms sufficiently specific to be justiciable".[180] Accordingly, it constitutes a conscious choice of the Protocol's drafters, who thought that imposing such an obligation upon the states would be as a matter of principle incompatible with the scope of the Convention as fundamentally protecting the traditional liberal rights.

Affirmative action in the domain of equality thus remains in the Convention system at the stage of political declaration and not a clear-cut enforceable right (Arnardóttir 2003: 95–106). Irrespective of this, in marginal cases the Strasbourg Court might assess a state's failure to introduce rules for the prevention of

---

[178]See ECHR Judgment of 26th February 2002, *Fretté v. France,* 38 (2004) EHRR 21: 438, para. 34.

[179]Para. 16 of the Explanatory Report on the 12th Protocol drafted by the Steering Committee for Human Rights and adopted by the Committee of Ministers on June 26, 2000.

[180]*Ibid.,* para. 16.

discrimination, in the sense that clear and serious omission of the state positively to intervene could not be tolerable. Strictly speaking this is not a case of positive measures but merely a legal gap that needs to be covered through interpretation.[181]

4.7 Comparative Syntheses and Antitheses

4.7.1 Structural Variables

The prior analysis showed that, broadly speaking, affirmative action policies are mostly applied in three types of state architecture: high-level social welfare, multicultural, decolonised and federal states.

First, *long standing social states*, such as the Scandinavian ones, tend to employ affirmative action in their broader political agenda of promoting/combining social justice and democracy. On the contrary, states where the social state has traditionally been weak and market economics and politics dominate, such as the UK, are on the low side of the application of these actions. The divergence between "social" and "liberal" states in Europe is reflected in the proceedings before the Court of Justice of the European Union in *Marschall*,[182] in which the question was whether a positive labour measure introduced by a German Land in favour of women was compatible with European Union Law. Finland, Sweden and Norway intervened in favour of upholding the measure, arguing that positive action helps women to gain access to high responsibility posts, previously outside their reach. On the other hand, the governments of France and the UK intervened against the measure on the ground that it resulted in unacceptable discrimination. Interestingly, the interveners—strong social states—have not upgraded affirmative action to a constitutional level; this would presumably be unnecessary, since the general constitutional clause/mandate in favour of the social state arguably provides a more fertile ground for the implementation of such policies, because unlike affirmative action, which is by definition temporary, the social state is a permanent pursuit. A great number of legal systems, especially in Europe, have in the last two decades placed an emphasis on this policy in favour of women and have occasionally upgraded their status to a constitutional level.

Second, *multicultural states*, mainly those composed of a great number of different races in Asia, such as Malaysia, and in Oceania, such as New Zealand, have introduced affirmative action plans in order to minimise the possibility of the dominant race suppressing minorities. This was particularly evident in the case of states, such as the US or South Africa, where racism had/used to have an

---

[181]ECHR Judgment of 26th March 1985, *X and Y v. Netherlands*, 8 (1986) EHRR 235, para. 23 *et seq*.

[182]CJEU Judgment of 11th November 1997, Case C-409/95, *Hellmut Marschall v. Land Nordhein–Westfalen,* Rec. 1997, p. I-6363.

institutional status. A similar situation also occurs in religiously fragmented territories, such as Northern Ireland.

Third, *decolonised states*, such as Nigeria and India, have been historically indicated as fertile venues for the implementation of positive measures, because normally the new states lack social cohesion and suffer from political segregation and social apathy due to a long abstention from the active exercise of political rights. In such a case the goal of affirmative action plans is to raise public awareness in relation to large-scale political participation.

And, fourth, *federal states* aim at easing social differences based on national origin, language or religion. If one tries to probe beneath the shell of state architecture in federal states, it appears that the actual structure of the legislatures in these states is *per se* an indirect form of affirmative action. Given that the vast majority of federal states choose a legislative system composed of two houses, the composition of the upper house is normally an institutional expression of preference in favour of the constituent parts of the state. Unlike the lower house which is normally constituted more or less proportionately in relation to the population of the respective states of a federation, in the upper houses smaller states are overrepresented in relation to their population. The representation of the constituent states of a federation may vary from disproportionately equal representation, like in the US where each state has the same number of senators, i.e. two, irrespectively of their population, to moderate overrepresentation, like in the German federation where the Upper House (*Bundesrat*) is not composed in strict proportion to the population of the Länder, with a view to overrepresentation. Even when there is only a single parliament, normally there is a clause so that a double majority (of votes/population and states) is required; this rationale is also reflected in the EU, when double majority (countries and overall population) is required. Although, strictly speaking, this does not secure an adequate threshold of representation, which is the essence of an affirmative action plan, but rather constitutes an over-representation scheme, it still adheres to the core argument that the state awards benefits that are not naturally akin to the formal concept of equality, either among citizens or among states and intervenes in order to secure social cohesion by institutionally acknowledging and strengthening its diversity.

The above conditions still cannot explain why affirmative action has found such a fertile ground for flourishing in the US. In spite of the historical record of slavery and segregation in the country, the fact that the policy has been in the 20th century by and large an American issue needs further elaboration. Presumably, this is related to the fact that the US was founded upon a concept of pluralism that encourages institutional tools designed to accommodate the ideas of proportional democracy and social geometry that lie beneath affirmative action. Indeed, as Paul Craig, an authority on the issues of pluralism and democracy in the Anglo-Saxon world, eloquently puts it, in the US there has been an original and a contemporary version of pluralism that broadly determine the physiology of democracy in the State. The former version is that envisaged by the founding father of the State, James Madison. The prevailing Hobbesian perception *homo hominis lupus*, inspired by Titus Maccius Plautus' *Asinaria*, broadly defined the original conception of pluralism, resulting in the particularly American ideal of checks and balances and the prevention of fractions acting adversely to the interests of others, rather than and in favour of the aggregate interests of the community.

> Madisonian Democracy stressed balance and the separation of powers, the avoidance of powerful faction, and competition between interests. It would, however, be mistaken to regard Madisonian democracy as a pure blueprint for a pluralist society within which interest groups bargained for their own selfish private interests (Craig 1990: 58).

For, according to Craig (1990: 333), the mandate of the representatives of the nation, according to the republican tradition, would target an objective public good over and above the competing private interests. Hence, the emphasis was placed upon the large republic, as opposed to the small states, and the genuine conflict between diverse groups that would prevent the ascendancy of any particular group for any length of time.

It was exactly on this tradition that modern American pluralists built their contemporary theories. The classic reference is made to the work of Arthur Fischer Bentley in the early 20th century. Bentley's work is of great relevance to the development of the affirmative action doctrine in the sense that he viewed government as the outcome of the interplay between social groups to which individuals belong:

> Still the difficulty in picturing the nation as made up of groups of men, each group cutting across many others, each individual man a component part of many groups, is by no means inconsiderable. But the difficulty disappears as practice shows us how to concentrate attention on the essential features and to strip off incidental points which appear to have extravagant importance because of the prepossessions as to the nature of human individuality with which the task is approached. With increased facility in thus observing society we find we are coming to state more and more adequately the raw material of political life. If a law is in question, we find that our statement of it in terms of the groups of men it affects – the group or set of groups directly insisting on it, those directly opposing it and those more indirectly concerned in it – is much more complete than any statement in terms of self-interest, theories or ideals. If it is a plank in a political platform, again we find we can state its actual value in the social process at a given time in terms of the groups of men for whose sake it is there: a group of politicians and a group of voters holding the prominent places. The whole social life in all its phases can be stated in such groups of active men, indeed must be stated in that way if a useful analysis is to be had. Sometimes the groups, although not territorially distinct, gain a marked separation, so that two opposing parties may face each other with well-closed ranks. Then again all is seemingly confusion, and the crossed lines of different groups seem too tangled to be followed (Bentley 1908: 204).

Bentley's perception of pluralism entails three limbs, which reflect American politics and are relevant to the present analysis. First, governance (legislation, executive and justice) is beset by the existence of social groups; second, public choices constitute the outcome of group interplay and not of any abstract public good; and, third, it is overlap membership which maintains the proper balance in the system of governance and prevents arbitrariness. This orthodox pluralist approach, upon which many varying perceptions of contemporary pluralism have been suggested (Craig 1990: 60–67), seems to explain the American obsession with group politics. It does not, therefore, come as a surprise to see the rise of affirmative action which exactly reflects the idea of group equality.

However, there are two arguments that curtail the reflection of Bentleyan pluralism to affirmative action. *Descriptively*, if a policy choice is necessarily the outcome of a group struggle, most probably affirmative action would never have come into existence. Not only does the policy lack wide acceptance in society, but by definition it favours vulnerable groups, therefore it would be logical to assume that the dominant group would never decide a reduction of the benefits of its own political share. *Normatively*, in the case of affirmative action, a key element of the orthodox pluralist theory is clearly missing—the stabilising effect of overlapping membership. This is so because the unavoidable over- and under-inclusiveness of the policy render multi-membership a constant threat to the firmness of any preferential policy. A white woman in the US is not entitled to any preferential admissions, in the same way that a male belonging to a minority does not enjoy a preference in political participation. Accordingly, it seems that multi-membership endangers rather than stabilises affirmative action.

The above scenery of group politics contrasts with the European libertarian tradition, stemming from the French revolution and the Enlightenment writings, that outside and beyond private interests there is a common good that ought to prevail in governance as a matter of the existence of a social contract. The difference is readily apparent: the European tradition detests group pressure as a political pathology undermining representation, whereas in the US groups' interaction guarantee republicanism. From this viewpoint, the European pattern of limited government seems to operate foremost in a libertarian context of safeguarding rights as opposed to the American pattern suggesting that the state merely organises the rules of the game for the various interests to ensure fair competition amongst them. Unsurprisingly, it was in America that affirmative action made its first steps.

4.7.2 Material Variables

There are three types of material variables concerning the launching and implementation of affirmative action policies in various countries, which reasonably exercise influence upon their determination and scope: the level of formal recognition, the domain of implementation and the beneficiaries. Of course one might conceivably come up with additional variables, especially relating to the historical background of the policy in every region and era, which nevertheless are normally absorbed by the main three variables. Each country varies significantly in terms of its variables, although a common core of argumentation can be traced.

4.7.2.1 Institutional Recognition

Affirmative action might be provided by a variety of legal instruments, i.e. a constitution, statute, executive order, convention, custom, international law or soft law. In relation to this institutional recognition, there are two obviously antithetical poles, the US and Europe. The former embraces affirmative action at a very low formal status (normally executive orders or soft law provisions), as opposed to the latter where affirmative action policies are moving upwards in the hierarchy of norms having reached a constitutional status on many occasions.

In the US, affirmative action lacks constitutional acknowledgment despite now being in its fifth decade of implementation. Interestingly, not only is the possibility of a constitutional upgrade completely outside any political debate at the federal level, but the constitutional initiatives at a state level have occurred in the opposite direction, i.e. to ban such policies. Irrespective of the fact that the amendment procedure to the federal Constitution is cumbersome and very complicated, there is no genuine political convergence in relation to the expediency of such policies, leaving the judge with the task to adjust the Constitution to contemporary calls and needs. It is a common belief that it is primarily for the administration, mostly through executive orders, or other institutions enjoying a wide autonomy in the management of their affairs, such as the universities, to decide on the expediency of such measures, without any legislative or constitutional imperatives. It follows that, within the boundaries of the federal Constitution, affirmative action is mostly a political choice for the state and an option for private entities.

Although in Europe affirmative action is a much more recent institution, there is a tendency towards constitutional upgrade, both at the level of the EU and in the domestic systems. Of course, constitutional upgrade does not necessarily comprise affirmative action as a general policy. Depending on each legal system, constitutional entrenchment is specific and incremental on the basis of the field of application, such as political representation in France, or on the basis of the beneficiaries, such as women in Greece, or joint criteria, such as women in employment in the EU. However, despite this constitutional upgrade, not many affirmative action plans have been launched in Europe—quite the opposite to the situation in the US. This paradox might be explained in light of the fact that affirmative action does not possess historical maturity in Europe so as to become a persistent societal claim and a salient feature on political agendas. Thus, constitutional upgrades have not had the pedagogical effect that one might expect, merely affecting the delimitation of legislative or executive power on the matter.

The evidence following constitutional upgrade of affirmative action confirms that the level of institutional recognition only plays a minor role. This is true both on the level of the measures introduced, but also on the attitude of the judges. Thus, irrespective of the constitutional upgrade, European Courts have, on occasions, treated positive discrimination measures less favourably than their American counterparts. The case of the EU is illustrative. In the aftermath of the Treaty of Amsterdam no significant affirmative action plans have been set in place, whereas the Court of Justice of the European Union did not significantly change its case law. The Court merely adjusted its "prevention or compensation of disadvantages" terminology to align its jurisprudence with Article 157 para. 4 of the TFEU, while remaining faithful to its precedent allowing affirmative action only to the extent that it does not produce automatic end-results. The Court did not embrace the essence of the compensatory rationale of affirmative action, as stipulated by the Treaty of Amsterdam. Indeed, if the constitutional upgrade of affirmative action at EU primary law had had any added value, the Court should have been engaged in a genuine elaboration of the factual surroundings of each case, especially the historical origins of the alleged discrimination, if of course this is not self-evident. Instead, emphasis is merely placed on the aim of removing inequalities in practice, and thus, affirmative actions are allowed only to the extent that they can assist in correcting decision-making processes which lead to discrimination but not in order to compensate for these processes. Thus, affirmative action is considered only a means to achieve actual equal opportunity, without any reference to historical injustices. By the same token, no significant institutional intervention was marked after the upgrade of the Charter of Fundamental Rights through the Lisbon Treaty, which brought the most recent primary law manifestation of affirmative action.

The institutional variable also applies in relation to the federal construction of the State, with the courts being more reserved to exercise thorough control when the impugned regulation derives from the federation. This is evident in the judicial practice in the US, although the composition of the Supreme Court with a majority of conservative or progressive justices is of course of significance. In *Fullilove v. Klutznick*[183] and *Richmond v. Croson*[184] the same legal issue, i.e. the constitutionality of an obligation of the public contractor to partly subcontract to a company of minority ownership was treated differently: the Court in the former case upheld a *federal* affirmative action, whereas in the latter it rejected a respective *state* measure of an equivalent effect. Underlying this distinction was an issue of different legitimacy of the impugned statutes: a federal statute stems directly from the Fourteenth Amendment, thereby setting/enjoying a larger margin of appreciation; it would be unthinkable for the Constitution to set stricter conditions upon the federal government as opposed to the States. Accordingly, the Court applied the intermediate scrutiny when reviewing the federal law, whereas it applied the much more rigid strict scrutiny test for the State law.

In theory, the higher the formal status of recognition, through constitutional, legislative and executive provisions, the more favourable the judicial control of affirmative action will be. This is not, however, reflected in global judicial practice. It seems that the level of institutional acknowledgment of affirmative action has only relative value, their launching remaining at large at the discretion of the political branches of government. Irrespective of the legal foundation of the policy, it is for the judge to have the final say as to whether it has been introduced properly and expediently. It may sound paradoxical but it is apparent that countries without constitutional references to affirmative action, such as the Scandinavian countries or the US, have better scores in implementing such policies. This paradox also occurs when assessing the practical effectiveness of constitutional provisions against soft

[183]448 US 448 (1980).

[184]488 US 469 (1989).

law declarations. In relation to affirmative action, there have been very significant documents of soft law encouraging the application of such policies, such as the above mentioned 1992 Athens Declaration, Recommendations 84/635 and 96/694 of the European Council and political parties' statutes. On occasions, soft law declarations favouring affirmative action may sometimes prove more significant in practice than rules at a constitutional level.

What then, is the added value of a constitutional upgrade of affirmative action, if any? The response cannot be disassociated from the actual wording of the Constitution. If a constitutional mandate to take affirmative action measures is established, the political branches of government enjoy significant leeway in terms of the concrete measures, but nonetheless are required as a matter of principle to encourage the said policies; if, on the other hand, the constitutional language is permissive for affirmative action, i.e. that such measures do not violate the equality and non-discrimination principles, there is ample space for political maneuver, even total abstention. All in all, apart from the symbolic gesture of elevating a policy to the constitutional level, there are both political and legal consequences stemming thereof. From a *political* viewpoint, it follows that state authorities may take affirmative action considerations into account when drafting their policies. Although there is no explicit constitutional penalty attached, the democratic price to pay for failure to implement a policy provided for by the Constitution will potentially be carried over the electoral processes, in the same way as failure to launch or maintain constitutional imperatives of the social state. This of course does not by any means suggest that the constitutional acknowledgment of affirmative action imposes an obligation to set up such measures under any circumstances. By the same token, it does not imply that governments cannot abolish affirmative action measures that have been introduced in the past. Not only is this a political choice that the democratically legitimate political power may make, but by definition there is an endpoint to all affirmative action plans introduced as a matter of historical compensation, i.e. when inequalities cease to exist. Thus, in any case, there is a wide margin of political appreciation when deciding issues of affirmative action policies. From a *legal* viewpoint, in the course of judicial review of constitutionality the courts ought to interpret ordinary legislation or executive orders in a way that allows some space for the enactment of the policy; thus, affirmative action measures become less constitutionally vulnerable, albeit not altogether constitutionally legitimate. Overall, there is some added value in statutory interpretation when it is the constitution itself that facilitates the launching of such policies and determines its scope, domain and beneficiaries.

4.7.2.2 Domains of Implementation

The fields of application of affirmative action are certainly not common in all legal systems. Each country applies such measures mostly where inequalities existed in the past and in areas where there are particular historical sensibilities. Thus, the domain of application constitutes a variable that courts take into account when assessing the constitutionality of an affirmative action measure. Comparative research has revealed four such basic fields: education, public procurement, employment and political participation. Interestingly enough, the order of these four domains is reversed between the two parts of the Atlantic: In the US, education and public procurement are the main fields where this policy has been historically established, whereas in Europe affirmative action in the political representation of women on a national level and employment on the Union level are the usual references. European states have mostly emphasised the field of political participation because of the strong tradition of the representation system, celebrating almost 800 years from the emblematic *Magna Carta Libertatum* upon which political representation was founded in England. Besides, political representation still remains the domain where strict state sovereignty exists and the EU has not as yet entered. In contrast to the US, positive measures in relation to university admissions or public contracting are almost unknown in Europe. Alongside political representation, access to labour is the other privileged area of implementation of positive measures in Europe, especially in the EU.

In relation to *academic admissions*, mostly at the university level, affirmative actions are very widespread in most parts of the world, less so in Europe. This domino effect has occurred not only because academic qualifications constitute a prerequisite for access to profession but also because education normally amounts to a collective upgrade of historically oppressed groups, both in terms of social bargaining as well as in relation to the potential occupation of high administrative or political posts. This is the case in the US where many universities have introduced programmes favouring minorities for admission. These programmes have essentially modified the existing admission policies, so that race, in one or another way, has become an admission criterion. Since *Bakke* in 1978, it is considered that universities may—and indeed they do—use race as an additional factor when assessing applications for admission to ensure the racial diversity of students, but these actions cannot go as far as to introduce rigid quotas or quotas that effectively isolate minority candidates from being assessed against all other applicants. An interesting discussion relating to university affirmative action is currently being held in South Africa, placing emphasis on what education ought to be provided at a higher level, either in the form of the "patriotic" university, i.e. education reflecting South African society and its future aspirations, and the "global" university entailing that there is a universal commitment to provide education to the younger generations (Soudien 2010). Irrespective of the background theory on affirmative action policies in university admissions, the truth is that this field is presumably the most fertile for the implementation of the policy given that it is par excellence in this field where the two major rationales of the policy, namely compensation for past discrimination and diversity, apply conjunctively.

Employment is similarly fertile territory for launching affirmative action plans. This is particularly the case within the EU because of its attributed competences in this domain. Thus, the Court of Justice of the European Union in the authority/seminal *Kalanke* and *Marschall* decisions of 1995–1997,[185] jointly in force today, when examining the compatibility of domestic norms with the secondary EU law, upheld such measures in favour of women, provided that these actions do not automatically confer priority over male employees and the principle of proportionality is respected. In the US, in the late 1970s, the Supreme Court upheld in *United Steelworkers of America v. Weber*[186] privately initiated affirmative action establishing quotas in vocational training, essentially reversing a precedent against such measures in the field of employment. The positive attitude of the Court though mostly reflects private projects and is not directly transferable to executive or statutory affirmative actions.

Public procurement is a rather familiar venue of affirmative action in the US, in particular in relation to the award of public contracts, concessions and licensing. No equivalent measures are widely applied outside the US. Unlike education and employment, for which the state must care as a matter of general social policy, preferential treatment in public procurement is not readily explicable. In the frame of liberal economics, the state is not supposed to structure the bidders in the award of public contracts but need only guarantee participation under equal terms. Furthermore, unlike employment or education, diversity in the distribution of state funds does not lead to an improved result. It seems that the only essential justification of such an action would be compensatory, in the sense that non-preferential groups were essentially excluded from such distribution in the past. However, even this purpose is not immediately convincing, given that it alienates the rudiments upon which the free market is established. This is why substantive reservations have been expressed within the American justice system as to the necessary prerequisite to uphold the constitutionality of such measures, i.e. a compelling public interest, while recent case law seems to reject altogether the remedial purpose of affirmative action. Anyhow, by initiative of federal, state, local authorities and private entities affirmative action programmes have been introduced in the US for public contractors, mostly in favour of racial minorities, in two ways. Either by mandating public contractors to submit along with their bid a statement that they are equal opportunity employers, in the absence of which the administration may, but is not bound to, reject the bidder, or by mandating public sector contractors to subcontract part of the project to companies of minority ownership. This latter requirement gave rise to jurisprudence of the Supreme Court which, after severe fluctuations, resulted in a negative attitude towards such set-asides in *Adarand Constructors Inc. v. Pena* in 1995.[187]

Affirmative action in *political participation* goes far beyond the idea of compensation for past discrimination or diversity; indeed it goes beyond equality itself.

---

[185]CJEU Judgment of 17 October 1995, Case C-450/93, *Eckhard Kalanke v. Freie Hansestadt Bremen*, Rec. 1995, p. I-3051; CJEU Judgment of 11th November 1997, Case C-409/95, *Hellmut Marschall v. Land Nordhein–Westfalen*, Rec. 1997, p. I-6363.

[186]*United Steelworkers of America v. Weber*, 443 US 193 (1979).

[187]*Adarand Constructors v. Pena*, 515 US 200 (1995).

Indeed, the foundation of political equality is not to be traced primarily on the conventional liberal right of equality but mostly on the very essence of popular sovereignty and representative democracy. This variation calls for a different, presumably stricter, constitutional review. This is why the US Supreme Court seems to be very cautious when assessing the constitutionality of political positive measures on the ground that in such a case, there is an intrusion beyond the traditional scope of civil rights, into political rights and representative democracy itself. In the US, affirmative action in political representation, through the reapportionment of electoral districts measures resulting in greater participation for racial minorities through, is not constitutionally tolerable because such plans normally fail to satisfy the strict scrutiny test set by the judiciary. The issue exceeds the idea of racial representation and touches heavily upon politics, since it is commonly known and statistically documented that minorities, in their vast majority, vote in favour of Democrats (93 % of Afro-Americans and 71 % of Hispanics in the 2012 presidential elections),[188] and therefore electoral design might well determine the eventual result of the elections. The negative attitude reserved in the US for affirmative action regarding political participation, in comparison to those applied in education and employment, is certainly interesting with regard to constitutional interpretation. The constitutional foundation of affirmative action in academia and employment, as repeatedly ruled by the Supreme Court, lies with the Fourteenth Amendment, i.e. the Equal Protection Clause. In the field of political participation, the Fifteenth Amendment, stipulating that "the right of persons in the USA to vote cannot be abolished or limited by the federal state or any state based on race, colour or previous slavery status", might be equally applicable. However, no use of the Fifteenth Amendment has so far been made by the Supreme Court in affirmative action cases, presumably because the judiciary feels uncomfortable to enter into a very sensitive legal debate on political rights. Accordingly, whereas in education and employment important steps towards substantive equality have been made, considerations of political participation remain at the level of formal equality. Obviously, access to education and employment, important as they may be, are not equivalent to political rights in terms of the possibilities provided to minorities to elevate their social status.

The European situation is entirely different. In most European countries, positive measures purport to facilitate and encourage the access of women to elected political posts as a means of treating the phenomenon of underrepresentation which, in this view, undermines the substantive legitimacy of any elected body. These measures are mainly in place in the domestic legal systems of the EU, although there are also initiatives on an international level for the reinforcement of women's position in decision-making. Affirmative action in favour of racial minorities is unusual in Europe, but not completely unknown.

[188]Data retrieved from the Roper Center of the University of Connecticut, http://www.ropercenter.uconn.edu/polls/us-elections/how-groups-voted/ (last accessed 31.12.2014), where tables showing presidential vote in elections from 1976-2012 by sex, race, age, income, party, region and other key demographic variables can be found.

In the fields of higher education and employment, affirmative action can be introduced either by the state or by private employers or universities voluntarily. Certainly, the voluntary introduction of affirmative action policies in private relations, which is often allowed by legislation or case-law, creates an intense dilemma. On the one hand, the voluntary introduction of affirmative action may result in legal claims against a private entity by members of the afflicted groups. On the other hand, abstaining from affirmative action practices, if accompanied by statistical evidence of underrepresentation of vulnerable groups, may raise political, ethical or legal claims which would seriously affect the institutions' good standing. Therefore, enhancing affirmative action in the private sector constitutes a challenging exercise of risk management from an entrepreneurial point of view.

Voluntary affirmative action is much more widespread in the US than in Europe. Enterprises and non-profit organisations assume affirmative action plans in employment and education. The standard terminology of affirmative action and affirmative action/equal opportunity employer is very often considered as a plus factor in public bids and has significant appeal to society, particularly amongst members of designated groups. The success of affirmative action in the private economy and their large-scale adoption by colossal companies is an actual novelty/milestone for the US, if one takes into consideration the traditional insecurity governing each employer to assume initiatives that may lead to judicial disputes. Of course, the introduction of affirmative action in the private sector is based on the interpretation of ordinary legislation, particularly title VII of *Civil Right Act*. The US Supreme Court has embraced voluntary affirmative action plans, which is significant given the Court's general reluctance to vest constitutional rights with a third party in private relationships. In any case, the Court has stated that these initiatives are in line with the Constitution insofar as they are voluntarily introduced by the employer; it would be contrary to the law to enforce them upon an employer.

The most striking instance of a regulatory provision containing a disclaimer for private-origin affirmative action in Europe is that of the 12th Protocol of the European Convention on Human Rights. Alongside with Article 1 providing the general prohibition of discrimination, the Explanatory Report states that this prohibition "reflects a balanced approach in relation to possible positive obligations" of the contracting states. According to the Report, although the basic aim is the establishment of states' negative obligations so that they do not discriminate against persons, the establishment of an "indirect horizontal effect", that is, the states' obligation to assume positive measures to prevent discrimination among individuals and to restore cases of discrimination, "cannot be excluded altogether", by reference to "any right set forth by law… [*which*] seeks to define the scope of the guarantee provided for in this paragraph and to limit its possible indirect horizontal effects". The report indicates "so clear-cut and grave" malfunctions to justify the enactment of affirmative action plans in private relations in the public sphere the arbitrary denial of access to work, access to restaurants, or to services which private persons may make available to the public (such as medical care) or utilities (such as water and electricity). The Report explicitly determined that the Protocol does not impose any obligation to adopt such measures: "Such a programmatic obligation would sit ill with the whole nature of the Convention and its control system which are based on the collective guarantee of individual rights which are formulated in terms sufficiently specific to be justiciable".

4.7.2.3 Beneficiaries

By definition, affirmative action does not apply to all individuals. Beneficiaries are members of underrepresented groups or members of groups that have suffered discrimination in the past and, reasonably enough, vary from one legal system to another depending on the social structures and history. Although one might conceivably think of a great number of potential beneficiaries, broadly speaking there are two main categories: racial minorities and women. Racial minorities represent a small part of the population and may or may not exist in a country (with the exception of South-Africa in the Apartheid regime); women constitute at least half of the population.

In relation to beneficiaries, there is an evident differentiation between Europe and the rest of the world. In Europe, the historical claim in this field is gender, whereas in the rest of the world the claim revolves around racial equality. The latter is particularly obvious when one looks at the US prototype of affirmative action. In this country, due to the diverse racial composition, after the 1960s there has been a constant political effort to include minorities in the core social thread. This is due to the long-lasting discrimination against African Americans with slavery existing until after the Civil War, Native Americans and (although less so) Hispanics, which institutionally operated until mid-20th century and arguably is still in practice to some extent. Accordingly, the self-evident remedial rationale could not be directly conveyed to the level of gender equality for which no equivalent historical evidence exists (Browne-Marshall 2013). Therefore, unlike racial minorities, women in the US do not seem to have developed a discrimination conscience that inevitably cultivates the claim for preferential treatment. This is particularly true in the case of political representation. An African-American will rarely vote for a representative outside his/her race; the electoral system in the US which includes large districts, at least for the elections to the Congress, favours in effect the dominant race. Unsurprisingly, the pursuit for equality took an entirely different road for women and races. Although there have been few affirmative action plans in favour of women, especially in public procurement often combined with the criterion of race (i.e. racial minority women), in principle statutory intervention was mostly defensive, for instance trying to tackle existing hindrances against women to achieve true equality of opportunities, such as the abolition of reverse quotas for university admissions, the effects of which were spectacular, with wide reallocation of academic seats from the 1960s onwards. According to Thomas (1999), in Germany (but presumably the same rationale applies across Europe) the legal discussion of positive action has always taken its point of reference from broader political debates about the position of women as a social group. By way of contrast, in the US, although particular policies have been marginally gender-based, the background social vision and cultural meanings that have informed the American affirmative action discourse have revolved almost exclusively around race. In the author's view this renders transatlantic comparisons complicated because it involves a speculation as to what the consistent stance of the US Supreme Court would be on gender based affirmative action measures.

Contrary to what is happening in the US, in Europe affirmative action revolves around gender. The historical evolution of national states after the French Revolution left racial considerations for a long period in the shadow. Unlike in the US, where the civil rights movement was essentially dominated by the claim for racial equality, in Europe the liberal demand for equality has basically inclined to gender in most countries, and arguably less so to race. Of course, the rapid mutation of the racial and cultural, mostly religious, composition in European states, will inevitably cast light upon racial issues in the very near future. Still, at the time, constitutional upgrades in domestic legal systems, where applicable, are generally restricted to measures in favour of women. In the European Union, only gender affirmative action is provided by the Treaty as well as the Charter of Fundamental Rights, whereas it is only secondary law that has provided for such measures on the grounds of national origin, religion or beliefs, disability, age or sexual orientation.

Clearly, the list of potential global beneficiaries of affirmative action, outside gender and race, can be very extensive depending on the actual historical and idiosyncratic particularities of each state. Some of them are quite surprising and somewhat unjustified in the western way of thinking. Such incremental measures, based on motives of political manipulation or mere corruption through nepotism, such as the "Sportsmen" in Pakistan, cannot be generally assessed under the general rubric of affirmative action, since they present a clear ethical problem vis-à-vis equality and justice, but provide an illustration of how positive discrimination may operate as a means to perpetuate the existing social status quo.

4.8 Political Identity: New Left or New Right?

Affirmative action, as part of substantive equality according to the orthodox literature, may fit with most political theories. It might well become part of both a socialist and a liberal agenda. Fredman (2011: 2) argues that affirmative action may similarly serve the purpose of wealth redistribution and easing social divergences, which is in essence, a social-oriented policy; the liberal goal of treating everyone with equal respect; the neo-liberal aim of preserving the free market model or the political goal of participation in the decision-making process.

Indeed, trying to associate affirmative action with political trends and parties is not an easy task. The great disparity in the structure of such measures and their variation through time and jurisdictions make accurate political identification very difficult. Positive measures are mostly linked in Europe with New Leftist constitutionalism, as established and shaped in the 90s by the Tony Blair's New Labour in the UK, by the Social Democrats and the Greens in Germany and by the Socialists of Lionel Jospin in France. This thread targets substantive equality and swings between left-wing rhetoric in economy and right-wing rhetoric in safety and security issues (Maier and Klausen 2001: 3, 13–14; Blair 1998). However, if one tries to go deeper into affirmative action ideology, it will appear that these plans are rather akin to a traditionally liberal approach rather than a conventional left-wing theory. On a *micro-political* level, affirmative action, especially in favour of minorities with a view to multiculturalism, as Banting and Kymlicka (2006: 1) have demonstrated, might on occasion be at odds with long-standing social state institutions, which could raise an identity dilemma for socialist parties. On a *macro-political* level, affirmative action shows implicit tolerance, if not full adherence, to the established capitalist system. Systemically speaking, any political measure aiming at curing a social pathology can be characterised as positive or subversive or, in David Ingram's words (2000: 44–48) *affirmative remedies* or *transformative remedies*. Positive policies, as implied by the terminology itself, do not purport to subvert the existing *status quo* but are merely founded upon the existing systemic architecture in order to produce a more balanced social structure through the enactment of temporary measures *within* this system. Consequently, they are not, strictly speaking, a cure mechanism but rather the conservative management of a social pathology. By way of contrast, subversive policies, in a Marxist way of thinking, purport to dissolve the existing financial framework of the state through the introduction of measures of indefinite duration aimed at healing the *causes*, not the results, of a certain social pathology. In light of the above, it becomes apparent that affirmative action is tantamount to positive social policy, and is, thus, classified as a liberal conservative doctrine far removed from left-wing rhetoric: it is temporary by nature, builds upon existing structures and targets mostly the impacts of a social pathology. Adopting this line of thought it is presumably fair to assume that political parties merely adopt positive action policies in favour of women insofar as they do not jeopardise men's votes (Klausen 2001: 209).

In the US, in the first years of its implementation, affirmative action was characterised as right-wing policy and was rejected by the largest part of the left (Hochscild 1998: 347, 348–349). In reality, Republican President Lyndon Johnson, the strongest affirmative action supporter in US politics in the 60s, adopted positive measures, an unprecedented policy choice for the Republicans, in order to entrap the Democratic Party (Lewis 2004: 17, 36–37). However, this political adoption only lasted for a couple of decades. Republican Presidents Ronald Reagan and George H.W. Bush expressly declared their opposition to affirmative action plans and made sure that the new appointments to the Supreme Court were opposed to them, thus securing an ever fragile judicial majority in adjudicating such issues. During his term in office, President Reagan subverted the liberal orientation of the Supreme Court by appointing three conservative justices. The most crucial substitution was that of liberal Justice Powell, which provoked one of the toughest crises in the process of appointments to the Court in the 20th century. The liberal majority in Congress rejected the conservative nominee Robert Bork and eventually accepted Anthony Kennedy, who himself later joined the conservative wing of the court (Dworkin 1987) and is now considered to be the Court's swing vote after the retirement of Justice O' Connor who had previously assumed that role. The attribution of affirmative action policies to the Democratic Party was essentially consolidated by President Bill Clinton's rhetoric "mend it, but don't end it" as an answer to opposition claiming that the policy had essentially been subject to a negative metamorphosis (Stefanopoulos and Edley 1995). Unsurprisingly, President George W. Bush Jr. had no hesitation to publicly declare his opposition to affirmative action and his reaction culminated in a rather cynical way just before the judicial review of the constitutionality of racial affirmative action measures for admission to the University of Michigan in 2003. The day before submission of evidence, President Bush publicly declared that affirmative action's effect on university entries was to unjustifiably award benefits and to condemn future students merely on grounds of race (Stohr 2004: 241–247).

In Europe, political treatment of positive measures in favour of equality has been rather diverse. In France, right-wing President Jacques Chirac merely suggested an indirect constitutional upgrade through an amendment of rather procedural nature that would grant Parliament the competence to legislate on issues of equality of access to administrative positions, whereas socialist Prime Minister Lionel Jospin advocated an amendment of the first Article of the French Constitution to the effect of encouraging the equal access of men and women to administrative and labour positions (Giraud and Jenson 2001: 69, 81–84). As a result of this political struggle and the prevailing view of Jospin, the general principle of equality was rephrased in order to embrace the possibility of positive measures of the underrepresented sex.

By the same token, a strong statement for the constitutional acknowledgment of affirmative action as a means of compensation for past discrimination was proposed in Germany by the Social Democrats, whereas the Christian Democrats were rather skeptical, fearing that quotas would be introduced in all aspects of politics and the economy. A moderate compromise was the eventual outcome, according to which there is no explicit obligation of the state to introduce positive measures but, on the other hand, a principle of interpretation was introduced in order to prevent the eventual judicial annulment of such initiatives (Limbach 2001: 177, 179). Political disparity is still in motion after the constitutional amendment, since the Christian Democrats claim that positive action does not fall within the ambit of the new provision, whereas Social Democrats claim the opposite is true (Totten 2003: 27, 40–41).

Finally, in Greece, the agreement of the two major political parties in the constitutional amendment of 2001, socialist PASOK and right-wing New Democracy, with the only opposition, interestingly, coming from the Communist Party, resulted in a constitutional provision that may be deemed as the most favourable in Europe. The new provision, approved by 275 members of parliament out of 280, states that adoption of positive measures for promoting equality between men and women does not constitute discrimination on the basis of sex and that the State shall attend to the elimination of inequalities currently existing, especially to the detriment of women.

The reasons why political parties often introduce internal quotas in favour of women may be *ideological*, if this relates to the party's political agenda; *political*, if the background thought is that more women's votes will be attracted, thus it is rational from a political competition point of view to maximise their influence; *administrative,* if it is thought that gender diversity will enrich and rationalise internal decision-making; *personal,* when female preference stems as a matter of solidarity when there is one or more women in leadership positions; and *strategic*, when the aim is to achieve better balance of powers within the party and to reinforce or weaken the party leader.

Affirmative action on a party level aimed at enhancing the participation of women may take two different forms: obligatory quotas set by the party's statute, on a certain fixed level, or supportive measures encouraging women's participation, according to their percentage in the total number of party members and political declarations. There are two variables concerning the extent of the implementation of internal quotas by political parties in each legal system: the political variable, i.e. the political orientation of the party, and the constitutional variable, i.e. the historical and political structure of each state. In relation to the *political* variable, obligatory quotas are provided today by most socialist and left-wing parties in Europe, as well as by small parties from the ideological centre leaning towards the left. On the contrary, right-wing parties are much less prone to configuring rules of obligatory participation for women and usually prefer milder means of encouraging this participation in a less concrete manner. In relation to the *constitutional* variable, where there is an established historical tradition of permanent party structures, such as in Europe, quotas emerge more easily. By contrast, in countries where parties do not constitute fixed mechanisms bridging state and society outside the election period, such as in the US, party quotas are not used extensively.

In particular, due to the fact that positive measures in favour of women are more widespread in Europe than any other part of the world, a great number of European political parties, certainly/mostly socialist, centre and centre-left have introduced in their statutes relevant mandatory quotas applicable to lists of candidates and the composition of party organs. Overall, such quotas appear in 23 European countries. The data cited hereinafter are drawn from field research, relevant databases (International Institute for Democracy and Electoral Assistance 2003a, b, 2004, 2005, 2007; Socialist International Women 2014) and academic literature (Ballington and Karam 2005; Dahlerup 2006; Wettig-Danielmeier 1997; Deller 1995; Lépinard and Bereni 2004; Bergqvist 1999)

Amongst the European socialist and social-democratic parties: the Social Democratic Party of Austria (*Sozialdemokratische Partei Österreichs, SPÖ*) has a 40 % quota for women on party lists as of 1985; in Croatia the Social Democratic Party (*Socijaldemokratska Partija Hrvatske, SDP*) has adopted a formal mandatory 40 % quota for men and women on candidates lists as of 2000; in Cyprus the Movement of Social Democrats (*Kinima Sosialdimokraton, KISOS*) has a 30 % quota for women; in the Czech Republic the party of Social Democrats (*Česká strana sociálně demokratická, ČSSD*) has a 25 % quota for women; in France the Socialist Party (*Parti Socialiste, PS*) has a 50 % quota for candidates lists as of 1990; in Germany the Social Democratic Party of Germany (*Sozialdemokratische Partei Deutschlands, SPD*) requires a quota of at least 40 % of each gender in boards and lists; in Greece the Pan-Hellenic Socialist Movement (*Panellenio Sosialistiko Kinima, PASOK*) has a 40 % minimum quota for women on party lists; in Hungary the Hungarian Socialist Party (*Magyar Szocialista Párt, MSzP*) has a 20 % quota for women; in Iceland in the Social Democratic Alliance (*Samfylkingin, S*) each sex should be represented with no less than 40 % in all elected bodies within the party; in Italy the Democratic party (*Partito Democratico, PD*) has a 50 % quota for women, placed with strict alternation on candidates lists; in Lithuania the Social Democratic Party (*Lietuvos socialdemokratų partija, LSDP*) has a quota of at least one-third of either sex; the Luxembourg Socialist Workers' Party (*Lëtzebuerger Sozialistesch Arbechterpartei, LSAP*) has adopted a one-third quota for internal positions; in Malta the Labour Party (*Partit Laburista, MLP*) has a 20 % quota for women on party lists; in the Netherlands the Labour Party (*Partij van de Arbeid, PvdA*) has a policy of alternating between men and women in national lists along with other criteria such as age and ethnicity; in Norway the Norwegian Labour Party (*Det Norske Arbeiderparti, DNA*) has as of 1983 a 50 % quota for both sexes and both sexes are to be represented in the first two positions; the Social Democratic Party of Romania (*Partidul Social Democrat Romania, PSDR*) had a 25 % quota for women on party lists, but since 2001 the party is a member of the Social Democratic Party (*Partidul Social Democrat, PSD*), with the latter having adopted a 30 % gender quota as of 2004; in Slovakia the Party of the Democratic Left (*Strana Demokratickej Lavice, SDL*) had a 20 % quota for women on party lists, before merging with the social democratic SMER which has no such quota; in Slovenia the Social Democrats (*Socialni Demokrati, SD*) currently has a 40 % target; in Spain the Spanish Socialist Workers' Party (*Partido Socialista Obrero Espanol, PSOE*) has a 40 % quota for either sex as of 1997; in Sweden the Social Democratic Party (*Socialdemokraterna, S*) has introduced gender quotas as of 1978, supplemented with a gender alternating system as of 1993; the Social Democratic Party of Switzerland (*Sozialdemokratische Partei der Schweiz, SPS/PSS*) has a 40 % quota for women on party lists; in the United Kingdom the Labour Party has a commitment that 50 % of all winnable parliamentary seats will be filled from all-women shortlists.

Amongst the European right and centre-right-wing parties: the Austrian People's Party (*Österreichische Volkspartei, ÖVP*) has a one-third quota for women on party lists as of 1995; the Democratic Rally of Cyprus (*Dimokratikos Synagermos, DISY*) has a 30 % gender quota in its candidates for the parliament, municipal and European elections, as well as for the party's internal structures; in Germany the Christian Democratic Union (*Christlich-Demokratische Union, CDU*) has a one-third quota for women in candidates lists and party officials; in Luxembourg the Christian Social People's Party (*Chrëschtlech Sozial Vollekspartei, CSV*) has a one-third quota for women on their party lists; in Norway both the Christian People's Party (*Kristelig Folkeparti, KrF*) and the Centre Party (*Senterpartiet, SP*) have a 40 % quota for both sexes since 1993 and 1989 respectively; in Romania the Democratic Party (*Partidul Democrat, PD*) has adopted a 30 % quota; in Sweden the Moderate Party (*Moderaterna, M*) requires that members of each gender should be placed on the top four positions on the party list for the elections to the European

Parliament; in Turkey, the Republican People's Party (*Cumuriyet Halk Partisi, CHP*) and the Peace and Democracy Party (*Barış ve Demokrasi Partisi, BDP*) have a one-third and a 40 % quota for women in candidates lists respectively.

Amongst the European left or leftist parties: in Germany the Left Party (*Die Linkspartei*) requires that on nomination lists, the first two and then every other place are reserved for women; in Luxembourg the Left (*Déi Lénk*) has a 50 % quota for party organs and for candidates lists; in Norway the Socialist Left Party (*Sosialistisk Venstreparti, SV*) has been the first in Europe to introduce a 40 % quota for both sexes on candidates lists as of 1975; the Communist Party of Slovakia (*Komunistická strana Slovenska, KSS*) has one woman among the eight first candidates; in Spain the United Left (*Izquierda Unida, IU*) has a 40 % quota for either sex as of 1997; in Sweden the Left Party (*Vänsterpartiet, V*) has a 50 % minimum quota for women on party lists as of 1993 for the party organs as of 1978.

Amongst the European Green parties, the Austrian Greens-Green Alternative (*Die Grünen-Die Grünen Alternativen, GA*) has a 50 % quota for women on party lists as of 1993; in Germany the Alliance 90/The Greens (*Bündnis 90/Die Grünen*) have a 50 % quota for women on party lists as of 1986; in Hungary the Politics Can be Different (*Lehet Mas a Politika, LMP*) can compose its candidates lists with a maximum of two consecutive candidates of the same gender; in Iceland the Left-Green Movement (*Vinstrihreyfingin-grœnt framboð, VG*) caters for gender equilibrium in party organs; in Luxembourg the Green Party (*Déi Gréng/Les Verts*) caters for gender equilibrium both in candidates lists and in party organs; in the Netherlands the Green Left (*GroenLinks, GL*) has introduced 40 % quota for women; in Sweden the Green Party (*Miljöpartiet de Gröna, MP*) has a 50 % gender quota on party lists and party organs as of 1997 and 1981 respectively.

Amongst the liberal and social-liberal parties: in Iceland the Progressive Party (Centre Party) (*Framsóknarflokkur*) has a 40 % quota for candidates lists and party organs; in Slovakia the Alliance of the New Citizen (*Aliancia Nového Obcana, ANO*) has a policy of one-third quota for women in party structures; in Slovenia the Liberal Democracy Party (*Liberalna Demokracija Slovenije, LDS*) has set a target of 40 % representation of each gender in party structures; in the United Kingdom the Liberal Democrats have on occasions placed 40 %women in winnable seats.

Further, all regional political parties in Spain provide for a 40 % quota for either sex: the Republican Left of Catalonia (*Esquerra Republicana de Catalunya, ERC*) as of 2004, the Socialist Party of Catalonia (*Partit dels Socialistes de Catalunya, PSC*) as of 2000, the Nationalist Galician Block (*Bloque Nacionalista Galego, BNG*) as of 2002, the Initiative for Catalonia—Greens (*Iniciativa per Catalunya-Verds, ICV*) as of 2002 and the Canarian Coalition (*Coalición Canaria, CC*) as of 2000. Finally, in Europe there was one all-women party with significant political presence, i.e. the Women's Party in Iceland (*Kvennalistinn*), before merging with the Social Democratic Alliance in 1998.

In America, quotas in favour of women in party lists and organs appear in 11 countries. Amongst the American socialist and social-democratic parties: in Bolivia the National Unity Front (*Unidad Nacional, UN*) has a 50 % quota for women both for candidates lists and party organs; in Canada the New Democratic Party NDP adopted a target of 50 % women among its candidates as of 1985; in Chile the Party for Democracy (*Partido por la Democracia, PPD*) has a 60 % gender ceiling in candidates lists for either gender; the Socialist Party of Chile (*Partido Socialista de Chile, PS*) has a 60 and 70 % gender ceiling in candidates lists and parliamentary seats respectively for either gender; in Costa Rica the National Liberation Party (*Partido Liberación Nacional, PLN*) has a 40 % quota for candidates lists for each gender together with an alternate gender system; in Guatemala the National Unity for Hope Party (*Unidad Nacional de Esperanza, UNE*) has a 40 % quota for women on candidates lists as of 2007; in Mexico the Institutional Revolutionary Party (*Partido Revolucionario Instituional, PRI*) has a 50 % quota for women; in Nicaragua the Sandinista Front for National Liberation (*Frente Sandinista de Liberación Nacional, FSLN*) has a 30 % quota for women; the Socialist Party of Uruguay (*Partido Socialista del Uruguay, PS*) has a pro-rata membership quota for women for party structures.

Amongst the American right and centre-right wing parties, the Argentinian Justice Party (*Partido Justicialista, PJ*) has 30–50 % quotas for both candidates lists and party organs; in Chile the Christian Democratic Party (*Partido Demócrata Cristiano PDC*) has a 20 % quota for women on candidates lists as of 1996; in Costa Rica the Christian-Social Unity Party (*Partido Unidad Socialcristiana, PUSC*) has in principle a 60 % ceiling for representation to party organs by either gender; in Paraguay the National Republic Association (*Asociación Nacional Republicana/Partido Colorado, ANR*) has a 30 % quota for women on candidates lists.

Amongst the American left-wing or leftist parties, in Costa Rica the Citizen Action Party (*Partido Accion Ciudadana, PAC*) has a 50 % quota for women candidates placed at every second place (zipper system) on candidates lists; in El Salvador the National Liberation Front Farabundo Martí (*Frente Farabundo Martí para. la Liberación Nacional, FMLN*) has a 35 % quota for women; in Guatemala, Guatemalan Revolutionary Unity (*Unidad Revolucionaria Nacional Guatemalteca, URNG*) has a 30 % quota for each sex on candidates lists; in Nicaragua the Sandinista Renovation Movement (*Alianza del Movimiento Renovador Sandinista, MRS*) has a 40 % quota for each gender on candidate lists; in Paraguay the Party for a Country of Solidarity (*Partido País Solidario, PPS*) has a 30 % quota for women and an alternate system on candidates lists, whereas the National Union of Ethical Citizens (*Partido Unión Nacional de Ciudadanos Éticos, UNACE*) has a 30 % gender quota on candidates lists.

Amongst the American liberal and social-liberal parties, the Liberal Party of Canada LPC set a target to elect 25 % women as of 1993; in Costa Rica the Libertarian Movement Party (*Partido Movimiento Libertario, PML*) has a 40 % quota for women for the seats to be allocated in a possible government of the party; in Nicaragua the Liberal and Constitutionalist Party (*Partido Liberal Constitutcionalista, PLC*) has a combined 40 % quota for women and youth on candidates lists; in Paraguay the Authentic Radical Liberal Party (*Partido Liberal Radical Auténtico, PLRA*) has a one-third quota for women on candidates lists.

In Africa, quotas in favour of women in party lists and organs appear in 11 countries. Amongst the socialist and social-democratic parties: the Botswana

Congress Party (*BCP*) and the Botswana National Front (*BNF*) have a 30 % quota for women on candidates lists as of 1999; in Cameroon the Social Democratic Front (*Front Social Démocrate, SDF*) has adopted a 25 % quota; in Côte d'Ivoire the Ivorian Popular Front (*Front Populaire Ivoirien, FPI*) has a 30 % quota both for candidates lists and party organs as of 2001; the Alliance for Democracy in Mali (*Alliance pour la Démocratie au Mali/Parti Africain pour la Solidarité et la Justice, ADEMA–PASJ*) has a gender quota of 30 %; the Front for the Liberation of Mozambique (*Frente de Libertação de Moçambique, FRELIMO*) has a 40 % gender quota for candidates lists; in Namibia the South West Africa People's Organisation (*SWAPO*) has a 50 % quota along with a gender alternation system for candidates lists; in South Africa the African National Congress *ANC* adopted a 50 % gender quota in local elections as of 2006; in Zimbabwe the Movement for Democratic Change—Tsvangirai *MDC-T* adopted a policy of 50 % women's representation in candidates lists as of 2011. Amongst the right and centre-right wing parties: the Cameroon People's Democratic Movement (*Rassemblement démocratique du Peuple Camerounais, RDPC*) has a 25–30 % quota for women on candidates lists as of 1996; in Kenya the Democratic Party, *DP* has a one-third gender quota in party structures; in Niger the National Movement for a Society in Development (*Mouvement National pour la Société de Développement, MNSD-NASSARA*) has a 10 % quota for women on candidates lists as of 1999; in Zimbabwe, the Zimbabwe African National Union Patriotic Front (*ZANU-PF*) has a one-third quota for women on candidates lists. Amongst the left-wing or leftist parties: In Malawi, the Malawi Congress Party (*MCP*) has a 33 % target quota for women in party structures. Among the liberal and social-liberal parties: in Kenya, both the SAFINA Party (*SAFINA*) and the National Rainbow Coalition (*NARC*) have a one-third gender quota for candidates lists; in Malawi the United Democratic Front (*UDF*) has set a 25 % quota target for women in its parliamentary seats.

In Asia, quotas in favour of women in party lists and organs appear in 4 countries. Amongst the socialist and social-democratic parties: in Israel the Labour Party (*Ha'avoda ILP*) has a 20 % quota for women in blocs of ten and the *Meretz-Yachad* has a 40 % gender quota on its candidates' list in blocs of five; the Philippines Democratic Socialist Party (*Partido Demokratiko-Sosyalista ng Pilipinas, PDSP*) has a 25 % quota for women. Amongst the right and centre-right-wing parties: in Israel both the Likud and the Jewish Home (*Haba'it Ha'ye'hudi*) have set quotas in favour of women; in the Republic of Korea the Grand National Party (*Hannara Dang GNP*) has set a 30 % quota for women in candidates lists. Among the liberal and social-liberal parties: in Israel the National Democratic Assembly (*Balad*) has a one-third quota for women in candidates' lists in blocks of three. Finally, there is one Asian all-women party, i.e. the General Assembly Binding Women for Reforms, Integrity, Equality, Leadership, and Action (GABRIELA) in the Philippines.

Finally, in Oceania, quotas in favour of women in party lists and organs appear only in Australia, where the democratic socialist Australian Labour Party (*ALP*) introduced a 35 % quota both for candidates' lists and party organs in 1994, rising to 40 % in 2002.

Although the above overview indicates a tendency for more gender sensitive party politics, in most cases, there is no institutional means to judicially enforce these party regulations. Where the participation of women is provided by political party statutes or merely through political declarations, external judicial control is not, in principle, applicable. Usually, the level of compliance with the relevant rules, as with all rules of intra-party organisation, rests with the leader and the party's collective bodies, where any member alleging violation of the statutes adversely affecting him/her may appeal before the party organs. The most interesting judicial decision on the issue is that of the British Industrial Tribunal in the case of *Jepson v. The Labour Party.*[189] The Tribunal was called upon to decide on an application filed by members of the Labour Party claiming that the party decision to hold primaries solely for women was against the law. In particular, the party rule provided that at least 50 % of 'strong challenger seats' (i.e. in electoral constituencies where the Labour candidate had a strong possibility of winning, in order to prevent only formal participation) and of 'inheritor seats' (i.e. where a labour seat had become vacant), should be attributed to women after primaries in which only women might participate. The Tribunal held that it had jurisdiction to adjudicate on the issue, given that the party selection process facilitated access to labour, and found that the party rule for the participation of women was illegal on the grounds of legislative prohibition of sex discrimination. The judgment was reaffirmed in *Sawyer v. Ahsan,*[190] which acknowledged the right to compensation for a party member who had been exempted from the candidates' list due to the implementation of a quota system. *Jepson* has left a memorable passage on judicial self-restraint towards affirmative action, later cited in the context of the Court of Justice of the European Union by Advocate General Jacobs:

> It may well be that many would regard [*redressing the imbalance between the sexes in the House of Commons*] as a laudable motive but it is of no relevance to the issue of whether the arrangement as applied to the facts before us results in direct unlawful sex discrimination against the two male applicants.[191]

References

Adams, C. (1993). *Affirmative Action in a Democratic Africa.* Kenwyn, Cape Town: Juta Academic.

Adele Jinadu, L. (1985). Federalism, the consociational state and ethnic conflict in Nigeria. *Publius,* 15(2), 71-100.

Adele Jinadu, L. (2002). Ethnic Conflict and Federalism in Nigeria. Discussion Papers on Development Policy nr. 49. *Zentrum für Entwicklungsforschung.*

---

[189](1996) IRLR 116 (IT).

[190](1999) IRLR 609 (EAT).

[191]Opinion of Advocate General Jacobs of 15 May 1997 in Case C-409/95, *Hellmut Marschall v. Land Nordhein–Westfalen,* Rec. 1997, p. I-6363, para. 46.

Al Faruque, A. (2012), The law and policies of Affirmative Action: Rhetoric and reality. *Bangladesh Journal of Law,* 12(1-2), 1-28.

Anderson, T.H. (2004). *Pursuit of fairness: A history of affirmative action.* Oxford-New York: Oxford University Press.

Araujo, C., and Garcia, I. (2006). Latin America: the experience and the impact of quotas in Latin America. In D. Dahlerup (Ed.), *Women, Quotas and Politics* (pp. 83-111). Oxford-New York: Routledge.

Arnardóttir, O.M. (2003). *Equality and Non-Discrimination under the European Convention on Human Rights.* Boston: Martinus Nijhoff Publishers.

Ashtiany, S. (2011). The Equality Act 2010: Main Concepts. *International Journal of Discrimination and the Law,* 11(1-2), 29-42. doi:10.1177/135822911101100204.

Bacchi C.L. (1996), *The Politics of Affirmative Action: 'Women', Equality and Category Politics.* London: Sage Publications.

Bajpai, R. (2011a). *Debating Difference: Group Rights and Liberal Democracy in India.* New Delhi: Oxford University Press.

Bajpai, R. (2011b). Beyond Identity? UPA rhetoric on social justice and affirmative action. In: L. Saez, and S. Gurharpal (Eds.), *New Dimensions of Politics in India: The United Progressive Alliance in Power* (pp. 79-96). London: Routledge, Routledge Advances in South Asian Studies, 21.

Ballington, J., and Karam A. (Eds.) (2005). *Women in Parliament: Beyond Numbers.* 2nd revised ed., Stockholm: International Institute for Democracy and Electoral Assistance.

Banting, K., and Kymlicka, W. (2006). Multiculturalism and the welfare state: Setting the context. In K. Banting, and W. Kymlicka (Eds.). *Multiculturalism and the welfare state. Recognition and redistribution in contemporary democracies* (1-48). Oxford–New York: Oxford University Press.

Barnard, C. and Hervey, T. (1998). Softening the approach to quotas: Positive action after *Marschall. Journal of Social Welfare and Family Law.* 20, 333-352.

Benatar, D. (2010). Just admissions: South African universities and the question of racial preference. *South African Journal of Higher Education* 24(2), 258-267.

Bentley, A.F. (1908). *The process of Government. A study of social pressures.* Chicago: The University of Chicago Press.

Bergqvist, C. (Ed.), (1999). *Equal Democracies? Gender and Politics in the Nordic Countries.* Oslo: Scandinavian Universities and the Nordic Council of Ministers.

Bickel, A.M. (1962). *The Least Dangerous Branch. The Supreme Court at the Bar of Politics.* New York: Bobbs-Merrill Company Inc.

Blair, T. (1998). *The third way: New politics for the new century.* London: Fabian Society.

Blivet, L. (2004). *Ni quotas, ni indifférence: l'entreprise et l'égalité positive.* Paris: Institut Montaigne.

Bourke, E., and Bourke, C. (2006). Indigenous Australian university. In Myers S.L.Jr., and Corrie B.P. (Eds.), *Racial and Ethnic Economic Inequality. An International Perspective* (ch. 9). American University Studies Volume 10, New York, Bern, Berlin, Bruxelles, Frankfurt am Main, Oxford, Wien: Peter Lang.

Braibant, G. (1999). Réflexions sur le principe d'égalité. *European Review of Public Law,* 11(2), 443-454.

Braibant, G. (2001). *La Charte des droits fondamentaux de l'union européenne. Témoignages et commentaires.* Paris: Collection Essais, Editions du Seuil.

Braithwaite, V., and Bush, J. (1998). Affirmative Action in Australia: A Consensus-Based Dialogic Approach. *National Women's Studies Association,* 10(3), 115-134.

Browne-Marshall, G.J. (2013). *Race, Law and American Society: 1607 - Present.* New York-London: Routledge.

Bribosia, E. (Ed.), (1999). *L'Union européenne et nationalités. Le principe de non-discrimination et ses limites.* Bruxelles: Bruylant.

Burke, R. J., and Vinnicombe, S. (2009). Women on corporate boards of directors: international issues and opportunities. In S. Vinnicombe, V. Singh, R.J. Burke, D. Bilimoriam, and M. Huse

(Eds.), *Women on corporate boards of directors* (pp. 257-268). Cheltenham: Edward Elgar Publishing Ltd.

Busby, N. (2006). Affirmative Action in Women's Employment: Lessons from Canada. *Journal of Law and Society,* 33(1), 42-58.

Cabral, P. (1998). A step closer to substantive equality. *European Law Review.* 23, 481-487.

Carlier, J.-Y. and Schutter O. de (Eds.), (2002), *La Charte des droits fondamentaux de l'Union européenne. Son apport à la protection des droits de l'homme en Europe.* Bruxelles: Bruyant.

Carson, C., Shepard, K., and Young, A. (2002). *A Call to Conscience: The Landmark Speeches of Dr. Martin Luther King, Jr.* Clayton: Warner Books.

Chin, A., and Prakash N. (2010). *The Redistributive Effects of Political Reservation for Minorities: Evidence from India.* Cambridge MA: National Bureau of Economic Research, Working Paper No. 16509.

Clancy, S. (2004). Affirmative action as a way to overcome disadvantage: Inspiration from Canadian law. In S.L. Newman (Ed.), *Constitutional Politics in Canada and the United States* (pp. 175-197). New York: State University of New York Press.

Costa-Lascoux J. (2004). Les échecs de l'intégration, un accroc au contrat social. *Pouvoirs – Revue Française d'Études Constitutionnelles et Politiques (Discrimination Positive)*, 111, 19-27.

Craig, P.P. (1990). *Public law and democracy in the United Kingdom and the United States of America.* Oxford: Clarendon Press.

Da Silva Martins, S., Alberto Medeiros C., and Larkin Nascimento, E. (2004). Paving Paradise: The road from 'Racial Democracy' to Affirmative Action in Brazil. *Journal of Black Studies,* 34, 787-816.

Dahlerup, D. (2006). *Women, Quotas and Politics.* London–New York: Routledge Research in Comparative Politics.

Dale, C.V. (1995). *Congressional research service report to Robert Dole: Compilation and overview of federal laws and regulations establishing affirmative action goals or other preferences based on race, gender, and ethnicity.* Washington DC: Library of Congress, Congressional Research Service.

Deller C. (1995). *Die Zulässigkeit von satzungsrechtlichen und gesetzlichen Quotenregelungen zugunsten von Frauen in politischen Parteien.* Aachen: Shaker, Berichte aus der Rechtswissenschaft.

Delpérée, F. (1997). L'égalité en droit public belge. In Conseil d'Etat, Rapport public 1996 sur le principe d'égalité. In *Etudes et documents du Conseil d'Etat n° 48*, pp. 435-436. Paris: La Documentation française.

Downie, E. (2014). Continuity and change: Women's representation in reform-era Chinese politics. *Columbia University Journal of Politics and Society,* 25(1), 53-66

Dworkin R. (1987). What is equality? Part 4: Political equality. *University of San Francisco Law Review,* 23(1), 1. Reprinted in R. Dworkin (2002), *Sovereign virtue: The theory and practice of equality* (pp.184-210). Cambridge MA: Harvard University Press.

Eastland, T. (1996), *Ending affirmative action.* New York: Basic Books.

Eeckhout, P. (2002). The EU Charter of Fundamental Rights and the federal question. *Common Market Law Review,* 39, 945-994. doi: 10.1023/A:1020832600674.

Ely, J.H. (1980). *Democracy and Distrust: A Theory of Judicial Review.* Cambridge MA: Harvard University Press.

Erasmus, Z. (2010). Confronting the categories: equitable admissions without apartheid race classification. *South African Journal of Higher Education,* 24(2), 244-257.

Favish, J., and Hendry J., (2010). UCT's admissions policies: is the playing field level? *South African Journal of Higher Education,* 24(2), 268-297.

Francis, A.M., and Tannuri-Pianto, M. (2013). Endogenous Race in Brazil: Affirmative Action and the Construction of Racial Identity among Young Adults. *Economic Development and Cultural Change,* 61(4), 731-753.

Fredman, S. (1996). Reversing discrimination. *Law Quarterly Review,* 113, 575-600.

Fredman, S. (2011). *Discrimination law.* 2nd ed., Oxford-New York: Clarendon Law Series Oxford University Press.

Fredrickson, G.M. (1998). A liberal defense of affirmative action. In R. Post and M. Rogin (Eds.), *Race and representation: Affirmative action* (339-340). New York: Zone Books.

Frisancho Robles, V.C., and Kala Krishna, K. (2010). Affirmative Action in Higher Education in India: targeting, catch up, and mismatch. Cambridge MA: National Bureau of Economic Research, Working Paper No. 17727.

Galanter, M. (1984). *Competing Equalities: Law & the Backward Classes in India.* Berkeley: University of California Press.

Giraud, I., and Jenson, J. (2001). Constitutionalizing equal access: High hopes, dashed hopes? In J. Klausen and C.S. Maier (Eds.), *Has liberalism failed women? Assuring equal representation in Europe and the United States* (pp. 69-88). New York: Palgrave.

Gomez, E.T., and Saravanamuttu, J. (Eds), (2012). *The New Economic Policy in Malaysia: Affirmative Action, Ethnic Inequalities and Social Justice.* Singapore: National University of Singapore Press.

Goudappel, F. (1999). Race equality: The Netherlands. *European Review of Public Law,* 11(2), 881-900.

Grossman, D.A. (1993), Voluntary affirmative action plans in Italy and the United States: differing notions of gender equality. *Comparative Labor Law Journal,* 14, 185-225.

Hassim, A. (2000). Affirmative action policies in the United States and South Africa: A comparative study. *Saint Louis – Warsaw Transatlantic Law Journal,* 119-129.

Hepple, B.A. (2011). *Equality: The New Legal Framework.* London: Hart Publishing.

Hochscild, J. (1998). Affirmative action as culture war. In R. Post and M. Rogin (Eds.), *Race and representation: Affirmative action* (pp. 347-352). New York: Zone Books.

Hollinger, D.A. (1996). Group preferences, cultural diversity and social democracy: notes towards a theory of affirmative action. *Representations,* (55), 31-40. Re-pubilshed in R. Post, and M. Rogin (Eds.), (1998). *Race and representation: Affirmative action* (97-111). New York: Zone Books.

Horwitz, P.M. (1998). The Employment Equity Bill: A Critique. *South African Bulletin,* 22(3), 80-83.

Hubert, A. (2001). From equal pay to parity democracy: The rocky ride of women's policy in the European Union. In C.S. Maier and J. Klausen (Eds.). *Has liberalism failed women? Assuring equal representation in Europe and the United States* (143-163). New York: Palgrave.

Huse, M. (2007). *Boards, Governance and Value Creation. The Human Side of Corporate Governance.* Cambridge: Cambridge University Press.

Ingram, D. (2000). *Group rights: reconciling equality and difference.* Lawrence: University Press of Kansas.

International Institute for Democracy and Electoral Assistance (2007). *The Arab Quota Report: Selected Case Studies. Resource document.* http://www.quotaproject.org/quotas.cfm. Accessed 31 Dec 2014.

International Institute for Democracy and Electoral Assistance (2004). *The Implementation of Quotas: African Experiences. Resource document.* http://www.quotaproject.org/quotas.cfm. Accessed 31 Dec 2014.

International Institute for Democracy and Electoral Assistance (2003a). *The Implementation of Quotas: Asian Experiences. Resource document.* http://www.quotaproject.org/quotas.cfm. Accessed 31 Dec 2014.

International Institute for Democracy and Electoral Assistance (2003b). *The Implementation of Quotas: Latin American Experiences. Resource document.* http://www.quotaproject.org/quotas.cfm. Accessed 31 Dec 2014.

International Institute for Democracy and Electoral Assistance (2005). *The Implementation of Quotas: European Experiences.* Resource document. http://www.quotaproject.org/quotas.cfm. Accessed 31 Dec 2014.

Ivanovna Nikanorova L. (2014). *The role of affirmative action in higher education for indigenous people: the case of Yakutsk (Russia) and Tromsø (Norway).* M.Phil. Thesis. Faculty of

Humanities, Social Sciences and Education. http://munin.uit.no/bitstream/handle/10037/6478/thesis.pdf?sequence=2&isAllowed=y. Accessed 31 Dec 2014.Tromsø: The Arctic University of Norway.

Joint Statement (1989). Constitutional Scholars' statement on affirmative action after City of Richmond v. J. A. Croson Co. Yale Law Journal, 98, 1711-1716.

Justesen, P., and Rytter J.E. (1999). Race equality: Denmark. *European Review of Public Law,* 11(2), 649-672.

Klausen, J. (2001). When women voted for the right: Lessons for today for the conservative gender gap. In J. Klausen and C.S. Maier (Eds.), *Has liberalism failed women? Assuring equal representation in Europe and the United States* (pp. 209-228). New York: Palgrave.

Klinck, E. (1997). Limiting affirmative action legislation: The European Court of Justice in Eckhard Kalanke v. Freie Hansestadt Bremen. *South African Journal of Human Rights,* 13, 638-651.

Krook, M.L., Lovendurski, J., and Squires, J. (2006). Western Europe, North America, Australia and New Zealand: gender quotas in the context of citizenship models. In D. Dahlerup (Ed.), *Women, Quotas and Politics* (pp. 194-221). Oxford-New York: Routledge.

Kushman, B. (1998), *Rethinking the New Deal Court. The structure of a constitutional revolution.* Oxford: Oxford University Press.

Lashley, M.E., (2006). Remedying Racial and Ethnic Inequality In S.L. Myers Jr., and B.P. Corrie (Eds.), *Racial and Ethnic Economic Inequality. An International Perspective* (ch. 13). American University Studies Volume 10, New York, Bern, Berlin, Bruxelles, Frankfurt am Main, Oxford, Wien: Peter Lang.

Lépinard, É. and Bereni (2004), L., La parité ou le mythe d'une exception française. *Pouvoirs – Revue Française d'Études Constitutionnelles et Politiques (Discrimination Positive),* 111, 73-85.

Lester of Herne Hill, Lord Anthony (2001). Equality and United Kingdom Law: Past, present and future. *Public Law,* 77-96.

Levade, A. (2004). Discrimination positive et principe d'égalité en droit français. *Pouvoirs – Revue Française d'Études Constitutionnelles et Politiques (Discrimination Positive),* 111, 55-71.

Lewis, E. (2004), Why history remains a factor in the search for racial equality. In P. Gurin, J.S. Lehman, and E. Lewis (Eds.), *Defending diversity: Affirmative action at the University of Michigan* (pp. 17-60). Ann Arbor: University of Michigan Press.

Limbach, J. (2001), Constitutional reform and gender mandates. In J. Klausen and C.S. Maier (Eds.), *Has liberalism failed women? Assuring equal representation in Europe and the United States* (pp. 177-181). New York: Palgrave.

Lindecke, C. (1995). *Frauen und andere Minderheiten: Zur Entstehung und Konkretisierung der US-Amerikanischen Gleichstellungsregelungen zugunsten von Frauen und zur Frage eines möglichen Transfers auf die Bunderepublik Deutschland.* Munich-Merign: Hampp.

Lipset, S.M. (1996), *American exceptionalism: A double-edged sword.* New York W.W. Norton.

Maier, C.S., and Klausen, J. (2001). Introduction. In C.S. Maier and J. Klausen (Eds.). *Has liberalism failed women? Assuring equal representation in Europe and the United States* (3-17). New York: Palgrave.

Martin, D. (2006). *Égalité et non-discrimination dans la jurisprudence communautaire. Étude critique à la lumière d'une approche comparatiste.* Bruxelles: Bruylant.

Martin, T. (2001). *The Affirmative Action Empire: Nations and Nationalism in the Soviet Union, 1923-1939.* The Wilder House Series in Politics, History and Culture. New York: Cornell University Press.

McCrudden, C. (1998). Mainstreaming equality in the governance of the Northern Ireland. *Fordham International Law Journal,* 22(4), 1696-1775.

Means, G.P. (1986). Ethnic preference policies in Malaysia. In N. Nevitte and C.H. Kennedy (Eds.), *Ethnic preference and public policy in developing states* (105). Boulder CO: Lynne Reinner Publishers.

Melchior, M. (1991). Le principe de non-discrimination dans la Convention européenne des droits de l'homme. In A. Allen and P. Lemmens (Eds.), *Egalité et non-discrimination*, pp. 3-32. Anvers : Kluwer.

Michalowski, S., and Woods L. (1999), *German Constitutional Law: The protection of civil liberties.* Aldershot: Ashgate-Dartmouth.

Moore, S. (1996). Nothing positive from the Court of Justice. *European Law Review,* 21, 156-161.

Mustapha, A.R. (2009). Institutionalising ethnic representation: How effective is affirmative action in Nigeria? *Journal of International Development, Special Issue: Diversity and Discord: Ethnicity, Horizontal Inequalities and Conflict in Ghana and Nigeria*, 21(4), 561-576. doi: 10.1002/jid.1573.

Nnoli, O. (1996). Ethnic and regional balancing in Nigerian Federalism. In J. Isawa Elaigwu and R.A. Akindele, (Eds.), *Foundations of Nigerian Federalism: 1960-1995.* Foundation of Nigerian Federalism Series 3. Abuja: Institute of Governance and Social Research.

Nord, A.K. (2012). Mehr Geschlechtergerechtigkeit? Zur Frauenquote in Afrika. *German Institute of Global and Area Studies, Institut fur Afrika-Studien,* 5.

Organisation for Economic Co-operation and Development (OECD), (2013). Italy: Affirmative Action for Female Entrepreneurship (Act No. 215/1992). In OECD and The European Commission (Eds.), *The Missing Entrepreneurs: Policies for Inclusive Entrepreneurship in Europe*. Paris: OECD Publishing.

Pager, S. (2003). Strictness and subsidiarity: Institutional perspective on affirmative action at the European Court of Justice. *Boston College International and Comparative Law Review,* 26, 35-76.

Perreau, B. (2004). L'invention républicaine. Éléments d'une herméneutique minoritaire. *Pouvoirs – Revue Française d'Études Constitutionnelles et Politiques (Discrimination Positive),* 111, 41-53.

Peters, A. (1996). The Many Meanings of Equality and Positive Action in Favour of Women under European Community Law - A Conceptual Analysis. *European Law Journal,* 2(2), 177-196.

Peters, A. (1999). *Women, quotas and constitutions. A comparative study of affirmative action for women under American, German and European Community and international law.* London: Kluwer Law International.

Poiner, G., and Wills, S. (1991). *The Gifthorse: a critical look at Equal Employment Opportunity in Australia.* North Sydney: Allen and Unwi.

Premhid, K. (2014). *Barnard Case - a Missed Opportunity.* Helen Suzman Foundation. Resource document. http://hsf.org.za/resource-centre/hsf-briefs/barnard-case-a-missed-opportunity. Accessed 31 Dec 2014.

Rai, S. (1998). Cass, caste and gender-Women in Parliament in India. In A. Karam (Ed), *Women in Parliament: Beyond numbers.* Stockholm: International Institute for Democracy and Electoral Assistance.

Rai, S.M., Bari, F., Mahtab, N., and Mohanty, B. (2006). South Asia: gender quotas and the politics of empowerment – a comparative study. In D. Dahlerup (Ed.), *Women, Quotas and Politics* (pp. 222-245). Oxford-New York: Routledge.

Rasnic, C.D. (1995). Austria's affirmative action for women workers versus protective legislation for the "weaker sex": Incongruous concepts? *Labor Law Journal,* 46(12), 749-762.

Rossouw, D. (1994). *Business Ethics: A Southern African Perspective.* Johannesburg: Southern Book Publishers.

Rubery, J., Smith, M., and Fagan, C. (1999). *Women's employment in Europe. Trends and Prospects.* London Routledge.

Rubio, Ph.F. (2001). *A History of Affirmative Action, 1619-2000.* Jackson: University Press of Mississippi.

Sabeg, Y., and Sabeg, Y. (2004). *Discrimination positive: Pourquoi la France ne peut y échapper.* Paris: Calmann-Lévy.

Sauer, B., and Tertinegg, K. (2003). *Policy frames and implementation problems: the case of gender mainstreaming state of the art and mapping of competences in Austria.* Vienna: Institute for Human Sciences.

Sautman, B. (1998). Affirmative action, ethnic minorities and China's Universities. *Pacific Rim Law and Policy Journal,* 7(1), 77-116.

Sautman, B. (1999), Ethnic law and minority rights in China: Progress and constraints. *Law and Policy,* 21(3), 283-314.

Scalia, A. (1989), The rule of law is a law of rules. *University of Chicago Law Review,* 56, 1175-1188.

Schiek, D. (1998). Sex equality law after Kalanke and Marschall. *European Law Journal,* 4, 148-166. doi: 10.1111/1468-0386.00047.

Schiek, D. and Chege V. (Eds.), (2009). *European Union Non-Discrimination Law: Comparative Perspectives on Multidimensional Equality Law.* Oxford-New York, Routledge-Cavendish.

Seierstad, C., and Opsahl, T. (2010). For the few not the many? The effect of affirmative action on presence, prominence, and social capital of women directors in Norway. *Scandinavian Journal of Management* 27/1, 44-54. doi: 10.1016/j.scaman.2010.10.002.

Selanec, G. and Senden, L., (2011-2012). *Positive Action Measures to Ensure Full Equality in Practice between Men and Women, including on Company Boards.* Brussels: European Commission Directorate-General for Justice, Unit JUST/D1, Equal Treatment Legislation, European Network of Legal Experts in the field of Gender Equality.

Skidmore, Th. E. (2003). Racial Mixture and Affirmative Action: The Cases of Brazil and the United States. *The American Historical Review,* 108(5), 1391-1396.

Skjeie H., Freidenvall L. and Dahlerup D. (2006). The Nordic Countries: an Incremental Model. In D. Dahlerup (Ed.), *Women, Quotas and Politics* (pp. 55-82). Oxford-New York: Routledge.

Skrentny, J.D. (1996), *The ironies of affirmative action: Politics, culture and justice in America.* Chicago: University of Chicago Press.

Smith, N. (1995). Affirmative action under the new Constitution. *South African Journal of Human Rights,* 11, 84-101.

Socialist International Women (2014). The Quota System. Resource document. http://www.socintwomen.org.uk/en/quota.html. Accessed 31 Dec 2014.

Soudien, C. (2010). Some issues in affirmative action in higher education in South Africa. *South African Journal of Higher Education*, 24(2), 224-237.

Sowell, T. (2004). *Affirmative action around the world. An empirical study.* New Heaven-London: Yale University Press.

Stefanopoulos, G., and Edley Ch. Jr. (1995). *Affirmative action review: Report to the President.* Washington DC Government Printing Office.

Sterba, J.P (2003). Defending Affirmative Action. Defending preferences. In C. Cohen and J. P. Sterba. *Affirmative action and racial preference. A debate* (pp. 258-275). Oxford-New York: Oxford University Press.

Stock, A.J. (2006). Affirmative action: A German perspective on the promotion of women's rights with regard to employment. *Journal of Law and Society,* 33(1), 59-73.

Stohr, G. (2004). *A black and white case: How affirmative action survived its greatest legal challenge.* Princeton: Bloomberg Press.

Sugrue, Th. (2001). Breaking through: the troubled origins of Affirmative Action in the workplace. In J. Skrentny (Ed.). *Color Lines: Affirmative Action, Immigration, and Civil Rights Options for America* (31-52). Chicago: University of Chicago Press.

Sullivan, K.M. (1993). The Supreme Court 1991 Term. Foreword: The Justices of rules and standards. *Harvard Law Review,* 106, 22-123.

Swain, M. (2001). Affirmative action: Legislative history, judicial interpretations, public consensus. In N.J. Smelser, W.J. Wilson, and F. Mitchell, (Eds.), *America becoming: Racial trends and their consequences* (p. 318-347). Washington DC: National Academy Press.

Szyszczak, E. (1996). Positive action after Kalanke. *Modern Law Review,* 59(6), 876-883. doi:10.1111/j.1468-2230.1996.tb02699.x.

Telles, E., and Paixao, M. (2013). Affirmative action in Brazil. *LasaForum,* XLIV(2), 10-12.

Telles, E.E. (2004), *Race in Another America: the significance of skin color in Brazil.* Princeton: Princeton University Press.

Thomas, A. (2002). Employment equity in South Africa: lessons from the global school. *International Journal of Manpower*, 23(3), 237-255.

Thomas, K. (1999). The political economy recognition: Affirmative action discourse and constitutional equality in Germany and the USA. *The Columbia Journal of European Law*, 5, 329-364.

Thornton, M. (1990). *The liberal promise: Anti-discrimination legislation in Australia.* Melbourne: Oxford University Press.

Tkachenko, A.A., Koryukhina, A.V., and Matveeva, T.V. (1998). The Russian Federation. In J. Hodges-Aeberhard and C. Raskin (Eds.), *Affrimative action in the employment of ethich minorities and people with disabilities* (pp. 85-96). Geneva: International Labour Office.

Tong, D., and Pue, W.W. (1999). The best and the brightest?: Canadian Law School admissions. *Osgoode Hall Law Journal,* 37(4), 843-876.

Totten, C.D. (2003), Constitutional precommitments to gender affirmative action in the European Union, Germany, Canada and the United States: A comparative approach. *Berkeley Journal of International Law,* 21(1), 27-61.

Tripp, A., Konate, D., and Lowe-Morna, C. (2006). Sub-Saharan Africa: on the fast track to women's political representation. In D. Dahlerup (Ed.), *Women, Quotas and Politics* (pp. 112-137). Oxford-New York: Routledge.

Tummala, K.K. (2014). *Politics of Preference: India, United States, and South Africa.* Boca Raton: Public Administration and Public Policy Series, CRC Press Taylor and Francis Group.

Vaypan. G. (2014), Acquiescence affirmed, its limits left undefined: the Markin judgment and the pragmatism of the Russian Constitutional Court vis-à-vis the European Court of Human Rights. *Russian Law Journal*, 3(II), 130-140.

Wadham, J., Ruebain, D., Robinson, A., and Uppal S. (Eds.), (2012), *Blackstone's Guide to the Equality Act 2010.* 2nd ed. Oxford: Oxford University Press.

Weisskopf, T.E. (2004). *Affirmative action in the United States and India. A comparative perspective.* London: Routledge.

Wettig-Danielmeier, I. (Ed.), (1997). *Greift die Quote?.* Köln: Stadtwege-Verlag.

White, C.E. (2000). *The Constitution and the New Deal.* Cambridge MA: Harvard University Press.

Yotopoulos-Marangopoulos, A. (1998). *Affirmative Action. Towards effective gender equality.* Athens–Brussels: Ant. N. Sakkoulas Publishers - Établissements Émile Bruylant.

Zhou, M. and Hill, A.M. (Eds.), (2009). *Affirmative Action in China and the US. A dialogue on inequality and minority education.* New York: Palgrave MacMillan, International and Development Education Book Series.

Chapter 5
The Legal Question: Method and Intensity of Judicial Review

5.1 Methodology of Judicial Review

There are three issues relating to the methodology of judicial review of affirmative action policies: setting the standard of review; identifying and assessing the goal pursued; and applying the proportionality test. Although these three topics are distinctive and connote different theoretical and practical questions, the case law of international and domestic courts does not always treat them with unique clarity.

5.1.1 Setting the Standard of Review

5.1.1.1 Principal Position (a): State Discretion or Obligation?

Irrespective of the wording of the enabling provision, either constitutional or statutory, it seems that at present there is no legal system which altogether legitimises all forms of affirmative action policies. The case of the US is the most indicative: according to the Supreme Court, the applicable Equal Protection Clause enshrined in the Fourteenth Amendment neither altogether prevents affirmative action measures, nor *in globo* embraces them. From this viewpoint, two further judicial statements reasonably follow: state authorities enjoy an ample power when deciding whether or not to introduce concrete measures; they may decide either to launch specific measures or entirely ban them; the same is also true for "employers' voluntary compliance efforts, which are essential to the statutory scheme and to Congress' efforts to eradicate workplace discrimination".[1] In the light of these two premises it is perfectly conceivable for a constituent State to include a provision in its Constitution (or ordinary legislation) prohibiting affirmative action altogether,

[1]*Ricci v. DeStefano*, 557 US 557 (2009).

G. Gerapetritis, *Affirmative Action Policies and Judicial Review Worldwide*,
Ius Gentium: Comparative Perspectives on Law and Justice 47,
DOI 10.1007/978-3-319-22395-7_5

without suffering a declaration of violation of the federal Constitution. On the other hand, it might be held unconstitutional to establish a general obligation to launch such measures on all levels, given their exceptional character and the requirement that they ought to be narrowly tailored. Accordingly, in the 2014 decision *Schuette v. Coalition to Defend Affirmative Action,*[2] the US Supreme Court held that the First and Fourteenth Amendments allow the States to introduce racial or gender preferences but they do not mandate them; thus, a State may well prohibit the enactment of affirmative action programmes altogether.

5.1.1.2 Principal Position (b): Policy or Enforceable Right

Further, a critical juridical question is whether affirmative action constitutes an individual right, in which case potential beneficiaries may legitimately claim its enforceability before a court of law, or is merely policy guidance, in which case it is addressed primarily to state organs and cannot be directly invoked by the potential beneficiaries. The above question becomes relevant only insofar affirmative action is a state obligation; on the contrary, if the Constitution merely and to some extent allows affirmative action, no enforceable right can be extracted. In either case, it appears that there is no legal system, even those with a constitutional recognition of affirmative action, which allows potential beneficiaries to seek damages on the ground of the state's omission to remove actual inequalities through the enactment of affirmative action measures. This lack of enforceability is justified by the peculiar nature of the policy as well as collateral technical issues of evidence. Affirmative action is not tantamount to a civil right, which is institutionally strengthened with a justiciable claim in order to ensure its defensive operation. Furthermore, claiming damages for a failure to implement affirmative action would cause serious juridical issues, especially in legal systems which do not uphold class action. This is because the beneficiaries of affirmative action are not usually designated in an obvious and easily distinguishable way. With the exception of the gender criterion, more often than not criteria may comprise a penumbra of hard cases and a wide number of sub-groups, such as the criterion of race or religion, or even more generic criteria such as members of underrepresented groups.

The most indicative example of the limited scope of explicit constitutional upgrade of affirmative action is provided by its incorporation in the policies of the EU through the Treaty of Amsterdam as well as, more recently, the Charter of Fundamental Rights. Also in the frame of the European Convention on Human Rights, a cautious stance towards affirmative action is noticed. Although the 12th Protocol institutionally acknowledged the ability to assume affirmative action, the Explanatory Report accompanying it explicitly provided that the Protocol does not impose any obligation upon contracting states to take on such measures, since this would be contrary to the nature of the Convention. This emphatic refusal reflects an

[2]572 US, Case No. 12-682 (2014).

intimate fear of the judicialisation of a policy that is mostly addressed to powerful political interests, does not have a direct effect on citizens and which, of course, has costs. This fear is also obvious in the US, where the very extensive debate on the expediency and constitutionality of affirmative action is held on a permissive rhetoric instead of a compelling language. The Supreme Court has in many cases emphasised its "voluntary" character, carefully abstaining from any *obiter dictum* that might, even remotely, trigger a claim on the part of underrepresented beneficiaries to claim damages or file an application of mandamus against a federal or state authority.

5.1.1.3 Equality of Results or Opportunities?

There is virtually no legal system, with the potential exception of India, which has in all respects accepted equality of results as the prevailing doctrine of equality, thus reserving a much more prominent institutional status for affirmative action. Thus, in the case-law of the US Supreme Court equality of opportunities seems to be the boundary for the enactment of affirmative action programmes. Also in Europe, where in spite of the short institutional history of the policy, gender affirmative action is becoming more and more instrumental and socially acceptable, the prevailing notion is that of equality of opportunities, according to the original wording of Article 2 par. 4 of Directive 76/207. Accordingly, the Court of Justice of the European Union allowed measures that were necessary in order to remove barriers or inequalities preventing women from achieving, in equal terms, the same outcomes with men, without nonetheless ensuring equal end-results. In *Kalanke*, the Court held that national rules which guarantee women absolute and unconditional priority for appointment or promotion "go beyond promoting equal opportunities"; such a system essentially substitutes for equality of opportunity the result which is, nonetheless, only to be arrived at by providing such equality of opportunity.[3] Advocate General Tesauro in his Opinion in the same case went further in drawing the prevailing concept of equality in the EU law, by categorically stating that giving equal opportunity can only mean putting people in a position to attain equal results and hence restoring conditions of equality as between members of the two sexes merely as regards starting points.[4] The wording of equal opportunity has also been embraced by domestic constitutions, such as the 1993 Russian Constitution (Article 19 para. 3) and the 1999 Swiss Constitution (Article 2 para. 3). Even in the absence of a formal constitutional provision as to the institutional position of affirmative action towards equality, normally it is the jurisprudence of the constitutional and higher courts which assumes this responsibility.

[3]Judgment of the CJEU of 17 October 1995, Case C-450/93, *Eckhard Kalanke v. Freie Hansestadt Bremen*, ECR 1995 I-03051, paras. 22–23.

[4]Opinion of Advocate General Tesauro of 6 April 1995, para. 13.

5.1.1.4 Restrictive or Benevolent Interpretation?

As discussed in chapter two,[5] affirmative action can be seen either as an intrinsic dimension of equality or as an exception from it. The former version calls for a rather benevolent statutory interpretation of said policies, whereas the latter for a restrictive one by setting rigid conditions and a high standard of review.

In the US, constitutional review of affirmative action policies falls within the general typology of judicial review depending on the subject-matter. Thus, "strict scrutiny" is the peak in terms of intensity of judicial control, over the "intermediate scrutiny" and "rational basis test" consisting only of the investigation of whether the contested measure is unreasonable. Strict scrutiny leads the judicial reasoning to a level of substantive evaluation and, respectively, produces such a high burden of proof that the chances for annulment of the impugned measure rapidly increase. The selection of the type of control essentially predisposes the final result of the judgment. It is also not very far from the judicial reality, the often-repeated saying, first used by Gunther (1972), that strict scrutiny is "strict in theory, fatal in fact", although Winkler (2006) tried through judicial statistics to soften the fatal judicial choice of strict scrutiny, by proving that the impugned regulations survived in an average of 30 % of the cases where strict scrutiny applied (27 % in suspect classification cases, including racial discrimination, 22 % in cases of freedom of expression, 33 % in cases of freedom of association and 59 % in cases of freedom of religion). The Supreme Court itself in *Adarand Constructors v. Pena*[6] explicitly dispelled the notion that strict scrutiny is "strict in theory but fatal in fact", thus confirming this disconnection between standard of review and ultimate result, an idea confirmed by sequel decisions upholding affirmative action despite applying strict scrutiny, such as in the *Grutter v. Bollinger.*[7]

The US Supreme Court varies the level of its review on the basis of whether the impugned affirmative action is gender or race based. It sets the threshold for upholding racial measures higher than gender measures, even when statistical discrepancies may occur against minorities, treating such affirmative actions as suspect classifications, and thus essentially discouraging the legislature and the executive from introducing such measures. On the contrary, the intensity of constitutional review over gender affirmative action is milder.

In cases of racial discrimination, which are deemed as suspect classifications, the Supreme Court has applied strict scrutiny standards as early as 1886 in *Yick Wo v. Hopkins*,[8] later confirmed in war-time cases *Hirabayashi v. United States*[9] and *Korematsu v. United States.*[10] In the field of affirmative action, the Supreme Court

---

[5] *Supra* 2.1.

[6] 515 US 200 (1995).

[7] *Grutter v. Bollinger*, 539 US 306 (2003).

[8] 118 US 356 (1886).

[9] 320 US 81 (1943).

[10] 323 US 214 (1944).

initially differentiated the level of review depending on the criterion of differentiation. In racial affirmative action for a long period of time, even after *Bakke* in 1978,[11] the Court did not seem to assume a clear approach. The main concern of the Court was whether affirmative action should be dealt with as though it was any other case of deviation from the equality amounting to a suspect classification, or whether it should enjoy a special (softer) judicial treatment. The first sign of the establishment of strict scrutiny was provided in 1986 *Wygant v. Jackson Board of Education,* where the Court ruled that any preference based on racial criteria should be subject to "*a most searching examination*".[12] With significant delay, the Court expressly declared that affirmative action in favour of minorities should be considered as a common deviation from equality, thus subject to strict scrutiny. As illustratively indicated by Justice O'Connor in the majority opinion in *Richmond v. Croson,* since the plan denied certain citizens the opportunity to compete for a fixed percentage of public contracts based solely on their race, strict scrutiny standard of review must be applied, which required a firm evidentiary basis for concluding that the underrepresentation of minorities is a product of past discrimination. In this context, Justice O'Connor inquired whether the city is pursuing a remedial goal important enough to warrant use of a highly suspect tool and whether the means chosen fitted this compelling goal so closely that there is little or no possibility that the motive for the classification was illegitimate racial prejudice or stereotype.[13] The significance of the selection of this measure for the survival of such affirmative actions is obvious from the fact that the judges adopted a rather defensive attitude, by declaring that strict scrutiny does not *automatically* entail invalidation of the impugned measure. In other cases, such as in the 1990 licensing case *Metro Broadcasting Inc. v. Federal Communications Commission,*[14] it was suggested that strict scrutiny in the context of affirmative action does not have its regular in-depth characteristics. Although the Court essentially applied intermediate scrutiny, the precedent still suggests that strict scrutiny fully applies.

In relation to *gender* discrimination, the Supreme Court initially limited itself by exercising the rational basis control when in the 1948 case *Goesaert v. Clear*[15] it upheld the constitutionality of a State law prohibiting selling alcohol to women in bars, unless they were wives or daughters of the owner. The rational basis control essentially established a presumption that any act using gender as a criterion for differentiation was indeed compatible with the Constitution. As decided in *McGowan v. Maryland* (1961), the States' wide scope of discretion in enacting laws which affect some groups of citizens differently than others is offended only if the classification rests on grounds wholly irrelevant to the achievement of the State's objective; accordingly, State legislatures are presumed to have acted within their

[11] *Regents of the University of California v. Bakke*, 438 US 265 (1978).

[12] 476 US 267 (1986), 273–274.

[13] *Richmond v. Croson*, 488 US 469, 493 (1989).

[14] 497 US 547 (1990).

[15] 335 US 464 (1948).

constitutional power despite the fact that, in practice, their laws result in some inequality.[16] The Court later elevated its level of review by finally reaching intermediate scrutiny. The first application of this control, albeit where the Court refused to accept that it had moved the level of its control, was in 1971 in *Reed v. Reed*,[17] where the Supreme Court held that a mandatory provision of the Idaho probate code that gave preference to men over women when persons of the same entitlement class apply for appointment as the administrator of a descendant's estate is based solely on a discrimination prohibited by and violating the Equal Protection Clause. Consequent judgments applied equivalent standards of intermediate scrutiny,[18] but its consolidation came in *Craig v. Boren* (1976), where the Court held in a 7-2 decision that the impugned Oklahoma law prohibiting the sale of 3.2 % beer to males under the age of 21 and to females under the age of 18 made unconstitutional gender classifications.[19] Thus, while for the justification of deviations from racial equality a compelling public interest must be proven, for deviations based on gender, including affirmative action policies, it is sufficient to prove, according to Justice Brenann in *Craig v. Boren* that they serve "important governmental objectives" and "are substantially related to achievement of those objectives".[20] Interestingly, in *Craig v. Boren,* Justice (later Chief Justice) Rehnquist suggested that the Court should adhere by the rational basis test; had this opinion been accepted, obviously most of the statutory differentiations against women would have prevailed (for the same reason also positive measures in favour of women) due to the very low standard of judicial review this implied. Two small case-law exceptions exist in relation to the judicial review of gender affirmative action. First, the Court has hampered the discretion to introduce gender affirmative actions by restricting the ambit of their application merely in employment, as a result of the landmark *Johnson v. Transportation Agency* decision (1987).[21] Second, on one occasion in 1973, already outdated now, in *Frontiero v. Richardson*,[22] the Court incrementally applied the strict scrutiny test in statutory gender differentiations as suspect classifications.

In summary, in the US, race-based treatments are subject to strict scrutiny, whereas gender-based treatments are subject to intermediate scrutiny, irrespective of whether the treatment in question burdens or benefits members of the historically disfavoured groups. The same standard also applies for judicial review of affirmative action policies. The different attitude in the US towards affirmative action in

[16]366 US 420, 425–426 (1961).

[17]404 US 71 (1971).

[18]*Stanley v. Illinois*, 405 US 645 (1972); *Cleveland Board of Education v. LaFleur,* 414 US 632 (1974); *Schlesinger v. Ballard,* 419 US 498 (1975); *Stanton v. Stanton*, 421 US 7 (1975); *Weinberger v. Wiesenfeld,* 420 US 636 (1975).

[19]429 US 190 (1976).

[20]404 US 71 (1971).

[21]480 US 616 (1987).

[22]411 US 677, 688 (1973).

favour of racial minorities as opposed to women is also reflected in the jurisprudence of the Supreme Court. There are two main differences, regarding the intensity of judicial review and the extent of permitted measures. Due to the history of slavery and segregation in the US, and the fact that gender affirmative action does not seem to split the American society, the judiciary is much more inclined to strictly control the use of race as a criterion of differentiation as opposed to the use of gender. Of course, technically speaking, the criteria for upholding gender classifications, as opposed to racial classifications, are indeed easier to be met, since in gender relations there is only *one* group oppressing and only *one* group historically suffering discrimination. In Europe, the judiciary seems comparatively more prepared to annul gender discriminations and require evidence relating to the causal link between the gender differentiation and the goal pursued in order exceptionally to uphold such measures,[23] although statistical underrepresentation in a professional field seems to set up a *prima facie case* for upholding positive measures.[24]

5.1.1.5 Evidence and Burden of Proof

Setting the threshold of required evidence and the collateral burden of proof practically follows judicial choice/determination as to the level of intensity of judicial review and the goals of the impugned measures as identified by the competent court. Accordingly, there is a largely different evidentiary process according to whether the purpose is remedial or cultural. This difference signals the significance of the preliminary jurisprudential stage of determining the goal pursued by the impugned affirmative action plan and calls for the researcher to compare the respective case-law requirements. In fact, wherever the courts accept diversity as a compelling interest, evidence is limited to the verification of actual inequalities. In this case statistical underrepresentation suffices without requiring proof that this has been caused because of previous discrimination. Given that diversity tends nowadays, mostly in the US, to be the prevailing public interest against which an affirmative action policy is measured, the relatively easy evidentiary process which this requires shifts the emphasis of judicial review to the proportionality of the impugned measure, i.e. whether the particular scheme is suitable and necessary to serve the aim pursued.

On the other hand, if the action's purpose is remedial, prior discrimination must be proven. This is not, however, as simple as it may seemingly appear. The first issue is what benchmark is to be used, against which inequality is measured. The second issue relates to the body that has discriminated and its relevant field, i.e. whether evidence of general "social" inequality suffices or discrimination *in situ* ought to be proven. The third question concerns the proof that inequality is due to

[23]ECHR Judgment of 18th July 1994, *Schmidt v. Germany*, 18 (1994) EHRR 513.

[24]CJEU Judgment of 11th November 1997, Case C-409/95, *Hellmut Marschall v. Land Nordhein–Westfalen*, Rec. 1997, p. I-6363.

past discriminatory practices. The fourth question, if the answers to the previous questions are in the affirmative, is who carries the burden of proof and what the suggested standard of this burden is.

The first judicial task is the *determination of the inequality benchmark.* Actual inequality may emerge in different ways, and accordingly, there is a wide range of benchmarks that can be used to assess potential discrimination. In employment for example, gender inequality may concern: (a) all women employees in comparison to all active populations of working men; (b) the number of women employees in the public or private sector; (c) the number of women employees in a sector of productive activity, e.g. the provision of services; (d) the number of women employees in a particular professional environment, e.g. a particular enterprise; (e) the number of women employees in a department of a professional environment, e.g. commercial department of an enterprise; and, (f) the number of women employees in high-ranking positions. Unlike the practice of the Court of Justice of the European Union, the question of the discrimination field has been extensively elaborated by the jurisprudence of the US Supreme Court, which probes into the particularities of any given statistical imbalance within the working environment in question. Firstly, the Court examines the level of the employment positions filled. In low-level jobs, where no particular expertise is required (e.g. truck drivers), the initial benchmark is the ratio of underrepresented groups against the totality of the employees in broadly analogous jobs. In high-level jobs, where special qualifications are necessary (e.g. teachers), the initial benchmark is the ratio of employees of the disadvantaged groups against the total number of the same groups who have the necessary skills for the job. Respectively, in the field of public procurement, the benchmark is the ratio of companies owned by underrepresented groups in the relative market which are qualified to take on subcontracts, and not the ratio of these companies against all companies operating in the same field.

The second judicial task is the identification of *the field and body of discrimination.* Obviously, from a technical point of view, it is much easier to prove the existence of general social inequality, e.g. the overall institutional discrimination of African Americans in the US or women in Europe, as opposed to past inequality in a particular venue. Here again, the case-law of the US Supreme Court has extensively dealt with the issue and has established that general social discrimination is not sufficient but must be proved in the particular field where affirmative action applies, for instance discrimination against women in particular electoral districts for the enactment of gender quotas or against African Americans in particular education environments for university admission positive measures. This premise comes as reasonable collateral to the jurisprudential principle that affirmative action constitutes an exception to the general principle of equality and must satisfy the tough strict scrutiny test. In US Supreme Court judgment *Wygant v. Jackson Board of Education,*[25] in order to uphold the constitutionality of an affirmative action plan providing preferential treatment of African American teachers by the Board of

[25] 476 US 267 (1986).

Education on grounds of compensation for past discrimination, the Court sought proof that the Board itself had proceeded in the past in actions constituting discrimination against members of this community. The Court, by a marginal majority, was unconvinced that previous discrimination regarded this particular entity and rejected the allegation that the action was justified due to the small ratio of African American teachers in relation to their same-gender students. By the same token, when an action is locally-based, the case-law of the Supreme Court requires a geographically detected inequality in the critical area of application, without examining issues of wider geographic inequalities, thus excluding overall discrepancies in the country. A typical paradigm is *Richmond v. Croson*[26] in 1989 regarding the constitutionality of obligatory subcontracting to minority owned companies in public procurements. The Court, by a 6-3 majority, discarded the justification provided for the action, that a racial discrimination was found in the field of public works on a national level, essentially suggesting that each geographic market faces differentiated issues of inequalities. The case-law rejecting previous country-wise and requiring local discriminatory practices received extensive criticism from Ronald Dworkin on the ground that it constituted a "perverse decision", both on the level of justification of the political aims pursued as well as on a level of moral or constitutional rights, in that it perpetuated injustice by guaranteeing an economic hierarchy in which few blacks operate as entrepreneurs (Dworkin 1997: 158). In fact, the evidence of focused discrimination is much more difficult in cases of voluntary affirmative actions, which is very often the case in the US, unlike Europe. This is because institutional discrimination, such as apartheid or segregation is historically self-explanatory and connotes no significant further side-effects. On the contrary, in private affirmative action initiatives there is a major paradox that the Supreme Court, in order to uphold their constitutionality, essentially requires a confession that the initiating body has performed discrimination in the past. This is, however, a huge discouragement for any institution wishing to introduce such measures because this might trigger issues of civil liability or even, in extreme cases, criminal offences. In this way, there is a clear difference on the basis of the initiator of affirmative action policies: the state is cleared and legitimate, whereas individual and private companies are stigmatised and potentially held liable.

The third judicial task is the *proof of genuine past discrimination practices*. The aim of compensation for past discrimination, unlike diversity, requires a more complex evidentiary process because it entails proof of discrimination. The reasonable start of the discussion is a basic premise: not every form of actual/statistical underrepresentation is necessarily due to discrimination. One could suggest that limited participation of underrepresented groups is mainly due to personal choices related to professional disposition and/or priorities or a conscious choice not to merge with the dominant race/gender/religion. In such a case, the past discrimination requirement does not apply/is not met. In the fields where the rationale of compensation for past discrimination still prevails, such as employment, public

[26] 488 US 469 (1989).

procurement and political representation, even though there is a history of institutional discrimination, the US Supreme Court demands proof that discrimination was not sporadic or temporary. By way of contrast, domestic and international European courts do not seem to elaborate widely on the actual causes of inequalities in practice. The mere fact of statistical imbalance seems to justify the enactment of positive measures, without any further requirements as to whether this imbalance is causally linked to past discrimination practices.

The fourth judicial task is the setting of the *burden and standard of proof*. Clearly, in the case of constitutional assessment of affirmative action policies compensating for past discrimination, the contextual evidence acquire an unusually high significance for the standards of mainstream constitutional review, which is in most cases rather abstract in nature. Historical, sociological, anthropological, political, financial and other relevant variables can be used to suggest and prove past discrimination. Because of the inherent complexity of this multi-tasking experiment, the allocation of the burden of proof and the required threshold to satisfy this burden become all more important. This is particularly true when discrimination does not have a direct and, thus, visible character, but is indirect; in which case the judge will have to assess the effects or even the motives of those performing the said practice, an assessment which happens nowadays in the vast majority of discrimination cases.

In the US, the methodological prevalence of strict scrutiny in cases of suspect classifications, including racial affirmative action plans, entails that the authority or individual/private company arguing in favour of upholding its constitutionality must prove beyond reasonable doubt—a very high methodological/evidentiary threshold indeed—that past discrimination had existed; overall, rules of evidence seem to operate in principle against the constitutionality of affirmative action. The suspect classification rule in the adversarial process suggests that the mere use of a generally unaccepted criterion, such as race, triggers the competence of the court to probe deeply into the facts of the case, which in effect constitutes a significant hindrance. Thus there is a two-stage evidentiary process: first evidence that there is statistical imbalance and, second, that this imbalance is causally linked to past discrimination practices.

The first stage broadly requires the submission of statistical data. In affirmative action cases in the US, an immense volume of documentation is normally provided by the parties and the Supreme Court has expressly found that the use of such data is lawful and necessary, insofar as they are accurate and specific, but not abstract and generic. However, the Court is not bound by statistical evidence and may not only assess their accuracy but also depart from the basic findings stemming thereof by using tools which are not always strictly legal, such as the stereotyping and stigma factors. The causal link between inequality and discrimination practices must be proved by the defendant. This is normally a difficult task since discriminatory policies are normally covered under a disguise of objective equality. In the US Supreme Court judgment *Griggs v. Duke Power CO*, a discrimination case focusing on disparate treatment rather than discriminatory intent, the applicant filed a class action on behalf of African-American employees against the respondent company's inside transfer policy requiring from employees who wanted to work in the company's higher positions a high school degree plus a minimum score on two separate aptitude tests. The Supreme Court unanimously reversed the Court of Appeals judgment and held the company's policy indirectly discriminatory, thus violating Title VII of the *Civil Rights Act* of 1964, on the grounds that neither requirements were directed or intended to measure an employee's ability to learn or perform a particular job or category of jobs within the company but merely purported to give preference to white employees: According to the Court, the evidence showed that employees who had not completed high school or taken the tests continued to perform satisfactorily and made progress in departments for which the high school and test criteria used. Although it found that there was no discriminatory intent on the part of the Company, it held that the Congress had directed the thrust of the Civil Rights Act to the consequences of employment practices, not simply the motivation and that it had placed on the employer the burden of showing that any given requirement must have a manifest relationship to the employment in question.[27]

High level of proof was required by the Court in the cases relating to mandatory subcontracting to minority owned enterprises. In *Richmond v. Croson* (1989), the Court actually rejected very extensive and wide data in relation to the actual disadvantage suffered by such enterprises in the local market alleging that it was "highly conclusory and of little probative value". It further rejected reliance on the disparity between the number of prime contracts awarded to minority businesses and the city's minority population, claiming that the proper statistical evaluation would compare the percentage of Minority Business Enterprises in the relevant market that were qualified to undertake city subcontracting work with the percentage of total city construction dollars that were at the time awarded to minority subcontractors, neither of which was known to the city. Finally, the Court rejected the Congress' finding in connection with the set-aside approved that there had been nationwide discrimination in the construction industry on the ground that by including a waiver procedure in the national programme, the Congress had explicitly recognised that the scope of the problem would vary from market area to market area.[28]

The Supreme Court showed the same strictness in assessing evidence in cases of gender discrimination. In discrimination case *Craig v. Boren* (1976), the Court rendered the statistics relied on by the state of Oklahoma in order to differentiate drinking ages between genders insufficient to show a substantial relationship between the law and the maintenance of traffic safety. It, thus, asserted that protection clauses were not to be rendered inapplicable "by statistically measured but loose-fitting generalities concerning the drinking tendencies of aggregate groups".[29]

By way of contrast, in cases challenging the constitutionality of the reapportionment of electoral districts favouring representation of African Americans,

[27]Justice Burger, *Griggs v. Duke Power CO*, 401 US 424 (1971), pp. 432–433.

[28]488 US 469, 471 (1989).

[29]429 US 190, 209 (1976).

the Supreme Court substantially differentiated its methodological approach.[30] Firstly, it accepted a presumption of unconstitutionality where there was a prima facie irregularity, by stating that a district's shape is relevant for the equal protection clause in the field of electoral districting not because bizarreness was a necessary element of the constitutional wrong or a threshold requirement of proof, but because it might be persuasive circumstantial evidence that race for its own sake, and not other districting principles, was a legislature's dominant and controlling rationale in drawing district lines. Given this lower evidentiary threshold, the Court admitted that, in some exceptional cases, a reapportionment plan might be so highly irregular that, on its face, it rationally could not be understood as anything other than an effort to segregate voters based on race, essentially generating in this case even an irrefutable presumption, although admitting that redistricting usually implicates a political calculus in which various interests compete for recognition, it does not follow that individuals of the same race share a single political interest (Rush 1995). Secondly, the Court did not require direct evidence, i.e. evidence without the aid of presumptions, and essentially downgraded the threshold of proof by accepting circumstantial evidence, i.e. facts not directly related to those in challenge but by reason and experience able to be inferred, such as demographic and anthropological assumptions. In that respect it merged to some extent the legislative intent with the actual implications of a districting plan, by admitting that sometimes a clear pattern, unexplainable on grounds other than race, emerges from the effect of the state action even when the governing legislation appears neutral on its face and, therefore, the impact of the official action may provide an important evidentiary starting point also for the legislative intent.[31] The restrictive case law in electoral engineering, notwithstanding its coherence as to the applied standard of review, entails a paradox, which renders state activity unsettled. Although by statute (*Voting Rights Act 1965*), race might be used for electoral purposes, the Supreme Court has substantially curtailed this discretion on constitutional grounds by setting the standard of review very high. This reflects the reservation of the Court when the political power departs from the formal standpoint and is positively involved in resetting every group's political position.

In Europe, on the other hand, where domestic and international courts seem to extract a very strong presumption of past discrimination wherever statistical imbalance obviously occurs, rules of evidence seem to operate in principle in favour of the constitutionality of affirmative action. This shift in the burden of proof has acquired a statutory basis in the context of EU law. Indeed, Council Directive 97/80 of 15 December 1997 on the burden of proof in cases of discrimination based on sex, stipulates that Member States must ensure that, when persons consider themselves as having been discriminated and there is an adequate factual background of discrimination, it shall be for the respondent to prove that there has been

[30]*Supra*, 4.1.1.

[31]*Arlington Heights v. Metropolitan Housing Development Corp.*, 429 US 252, 266 (1977).

no relevant breach (Article 4).[32] The same rule also applies pursuant to Council Directives 2000/43 (Article 8), 2000/78 (Article 10) and 2004/113 (Article 9).[33]

According to the above Directives, a shift of the burden of proof occurs when statistical imbalances operate, thus substantially facilitating anyone claiming discrimination and arguing in favour of positive measures, especially in cases of measures which are not *prima facie* discriminatory but produce an equivalent result in effect. In order to substantiate the argument of actual inequality, the Court of Justice of the European Union requests the litigants to submit specific evidence concerning the grounds of gender imbalance and not mere assumptions relating to the housework, children etc. This evidentiary requirement was obvious in the *Oumar Dabo Abdoulaye and others v. Régie Nationale des Usines Renault SA* case,[34] issued on reference for a preliminary ruling from the Industrial Tribunal of France. The case regarded the compatibility with then Article 119 of the EC Treaty (currently Article 157 TFEU) prohibiting discrimination between men and women, of the Company's policy to provide a payment to pregnant women commencing maternity leave. In assessing the company's claim that the policy constituted a legitimate discrimination aiming at restoring equality by offsetting the disadvantage suffered by women in their career advancement because of their temporary absence due to pregnancy, the Court requested that the company shows how women employees dealt with such professional drawbacks. Furnishing wide data, the company convinced the court on the causal link between inequality and disadvantage on the following grounds: a woman could not be put forward for promotion during maternity leave and upon her return there was a *pro rata* reduction in the experience record; a pregnant woman could not claim salary increases linked with personal performance; a working woman could not participate in training activities; and finally, the adjustment of women returning from maternity leave to rapidly evolving new technologies was particularly difficult.

Apart from the EU legal order, domestic systems also favour the evidentiary process in relation to the proof of discrimination, especially within professional environments. The most illustrative case comes from the *UK Equality Act 2010*, which provides a very analytical legal definition of indirect discrimination and specifies that it can only be justified if it can be shown that the policy or practice is a proportionate means of achieving a legitimate aim. The Act also specifies the grounds of indirect discrimination, i.e. age, race, religion or belief, sex, sexual orientation and marriage, civil partnership, disability and gender re-assignment; it does not apply to pregnancy or maternity. In this way the burden of proof becomes more lenient in cases of actual inequalities which have not been produced as a consequence of directly discriminatory practices. This shift ought to be seen in conjunction with a significant change of the statutory standard imposed in the UK upon the state in relation to safeguarding equality. Indeed, equality laws currently

---

[32]OJ L 014, 20/01/1998, p. 6.

[33]*Supra*, 4.2.1.

[34]CJEU Judgment of 16 September 1999 in Case C-218/98 of 24 April 1998, (1999) ECR I-5723.

require the decision-makers to "have due regard" to equality, rather than "taking action" to achieve such objectives. This shift has resulted after a change of the attitude of the courts, which assume a more interventionist role so as to probe into the real causes of inequality within society (Fredman 2012).

5.1.1.6 Judicial Predilection

Irrespective of the above, setting the standard of judicial review is not (and cannot be) an issue of strict legal methodology. This is particularly true in the case of the US legal thought in light of the overwhelming importance of legal realism, as opposed to the still prevailing doctrine of deductive judicial reasoning in Europe. Judicial predilection also plays a significant role in determining the level of control exercised by the courts. This is particularly true when the cases to be decided reflect issues of acute social or political significance. Indeed, affirmative action is a hardcore social policy (as intimated by "affirmative"), essentially aiming at the redistribution of social benefits. From this viewpoint, everyone has a personal attitude towards this policy, basically originated as a matter of political or moral ideology or determined by utilitarian considerations. Personal predilection becomes even more important when it comes to the judges who are called to decide on the constitutionality of such measures. With the risk of becoming over-simplistic, one might reasonably argue that conservative, as opposed to liberal, judges are more reluctant towards affirmative action and are more susceptible to annulment when technical interpretation so allows. As Dworkin (1992: 72–74) rightly observed, in affirmative action cases there is a tendency of the judges with a strong predilection on the matter, especially the conservative opponents of affirmative action to try to convert liberal proponents of the policy, with somewhat strong wording on occasions. Two variables might facilitate intrusion in the contents of judgments of judicial predilection on politically and/or socially sensitive cases: the personal/collegiate style of each court (the functional variable) as well as the number and origin of the deciding judges (the organic variable).

The *functional* variable suggests that the more individualistic the court is, the more susceptible it becomes to departures from precedent because it allows ample space for judicial predilection to enter into the rationale of each judge. This is why, more often than not, the courts which are based on the personalities of the judges as opposed to an *esprit de corps*, tend to be more pragmatic in their approach, less formalistic and their decisions are far more extensive, normally attaching at the end the dissenting opinions of each judge instead of including them within the text of the decision. The common law courts (as well as in principle the European Court of Human Rights) have this long tradition of individualistic operation emphatically focusing on precedent, at least verbally, whereas the continental European courts (including the Court of Justice of the European Union) are more collegiate and their decisions are more formalistic and dense. In his well-substantiated work with reference to the US Supreme Court, Devins (2013: 101–106) suggests that there is a distinction between 'coherent' supreme courts (i.e. those with a majority of justices agreeing on major issues) and 'incoherent' supreme courts (i.e. those without a majority of justices committed to some vision of legal policymaking). He argues that the former type of court tends to aggressively advance its legal policymaking agenda by making doctrinal innovations intended to bind it and subsequent courts, whereas the latter type of court is more inclined to undermine or overrule precedent. The idiosyncratic characteristics of each court are particularly evident when it comes to affirmative action cases, where judicial predilection is more evident and argumentation tends to be quite heated among the judges. Unlike European courts, within which majority and minority justices are very technical in their approaches, in the US Supreme Court this equilibrium is beset by an intense, sometime furious, exchange of arguments with the justices often trying to convert rival judges to their own opinion. For instance, Justice Rehnquist's in his dissenting opinion in 1979 *United Steelworkers of America v. Weber*[35] fiercely criticised the majority ruling on the ground that it abandoned literal construction in favour of a "newly discovered legislative history". In a rather non-orthodox statement, he claimed that the majority decision could more appropriately have been handed down five years from then, in 1984, because of the year coinciding with the title of a book from which he speculated the Court's opinion subconsciously borrowed the idea. He thought that in the same way as Orwell described in his book a governmental official of Oceania, one of the three great world powers, denouncing the current enemy, Eurasia, to an assembled crowd, thus being impossible to listen to him without being first convinced and then maddened, "the Court behaves much like the Orwellian speaker earlier described, as if it had been handed a note indicating that Title VII would lead to a result unacceptable to the Court if interpreted here as it was in our prior decisions".

The *organic* variable suggests that, first, the smaller the number of the judges, the more fragile case law becomes; and second, that the more political the judicial appointment process, the more manipulative and predictable the relevant judgments. Combining the above two premises, supreme or constitutional courts with a small composition and judges appointed by the executive and/or the legislature may easily shift the case-law in a direction opposite to precedent and in conformity with the prevailing political beliefs. This is particularly the case with the US Supreme Court, where 9 justices always decide in plenary and are appointed by the President with the consent of the Senate. In this Court, the appointment of one new justice might conceivably reverse established case-law, especially when the precedent involved a sharp division of the judiciary. A typical example is that of the case law on affirmative action. In the authority Michigan Cases of 2003 the actual delimitation of constitutionally permissible measures was essentially placed by a single justice, i.e. Sandra Day O' Connor (Byrne 1998). Until 2001, Justice O'Connor was a solid part of the conservative group of the Court, also composed of Chief Judge

[35] 443 US 193 (1979).

Rehnquist and Judges Scalia, Kennedy and Thomas.[36] In *Bush v. Vera*, in 1996, upholding that the strict scrutiny test applies in case of race as a predominant factor, rather than merely a motivation, Justice O'Connor categorically stated that race should not constitute "a motivation for the drawing of a majority-minority district". In 2001 *Easley v. Cromartie*,[37] with exactly the same constitutional dispute over reshaping electoral districts for the reinforcement of minority political rights, she joined the liberal group of Justices Stevens, Souter, Ginsburg and Breyer, ruling that this policy was constitutionally tolerable. Her complete turn was justified on the basis of a rather formalistic reiteration of her ruling on *Easley v. Cromartie* that race can be "a *motivation*" but not "the *predominant* factor". Two years later, in *Gratz*[38] she took the side of the conservative group, stipulating that a positive discrimination quota was unconstitutional, whereas in *Grutter*[39] she joined the liberal group, thus upholding the constitutionality of the soft affirmative action providing minorities with a plus factor over the assessment for university entries. Given that the two decisions were issued simultaneously by a reverse 5-4 majority, the swing vote of Justice O' Connor was absolutely critical.

By the same token, the sharp division of the Court rendered the Michigan University case-law from 2003 extremely fragile. The appointments of new Chief Justice John Glover Roberts Jr. on September 29th 2005 (replacing the deceased William Rehnquist) and Justice Samuel Alito on January 31st 2006 (replacing Sandra Day O'Connor who resigned) created a new landscape in the composition of the Court. Both new members were selected by President Bush Jr. with the rationale that the Court's "conservative" profile ought to be reinforced. Although the placement of the new Chief Justice has not caused until now significant changes in the judicial balance within the Court, since he replaced a member traditionally aligned with the group of conservatives, the selection of Justice Alito, former judge at the US Court of Appeals for the Third Circuit and member of the Solicitor General's Office under Ronald Reagan's presidency, was expected to cause significant turbulence in the Court's case law on affirmative action, due to the fact that he replaced O'Connor. In his former capacity, Justice Alito had only participated in one case in which he joined the majority in discarding an affirmative action policy of firing white teachers from schools in order to promote racial diversity in education.[40] In his latter capacity, he had taken part in the submission of *amicus curiae* in 3 pending cases before the

---

[36] *Wygant v. Jackson Board of Education*, 476 US 267 (1986); *Richmond v. Croson*, 488 US 469 (1989); *Adarand Constructors v. Pena*, 515 US 200 (1995).

[37] 532 US 234 (2001), decided with *Smallwood* et al. *v. Cromartie* et al.

[38] *Gratz v. Bollinger*, 539 US 244 (2003).

[39] *Grutter v. Bollinger*, 539 US 306 (2003).

[40] *Taxman v. Board of Education of the Township of Piscataway*, 91 F.3d 1547 (3d Cir. 1996).

Supreme Court, alleging unconstitutionality of affirmative action policies.[41] Interestingly, in 1985, when he had applied for the position at the Solicitor General's Office, he claimed to have been "particularly proud" of his critical stance towards affirmative action policies. However, in light of his prospective appointment he retracted some of his extreme/previous legal views,[42] there was intense criticism of his selection and his placement was not politically easy. Furthermore, the two appointments within one year (August 8, 2009 to August 7, 2010) of Justices Sonia Sotomayor and Elena Kagan, both appointed by Barack Obama, replacing David Souter and John Paul Stevens respectively have brought into the Court a very interesting mixture of people; i.e. for the first time there are three women sitting in the Court (two new entries along with Justice Ruth Joan Bader Ginsburg) and for the first time there is also a Hispanic Justice (Sonia Sotomayor). Still, Obama appointments were not in a position to alter the Court's balance, given that they replaced justices of the liberal wing.

It seems that the structure and composition of a court largely determine its activist or self-restrained character. This is particularly true when there is a policy issue involved, such as affirmative action, where legal and political considerations cannot easily be distinguished. In the US Supreme Court *United Steelworkers of America v. Weber* decision the legal question was whether a formalistic or more historical interpretation of para. 703(d) of *Civil Rights Act* of 1964 should be taken to prohibiting discrimination in employment based on race, colour, religion, gender or national origins. The majority took an affirmative action-friendly interpretation by departing from statutory letter. Chief Justice Judge Burger argued to the contrary with reference to the idea of the separation of powers and judicial self-restraint. He claimed that the majority "under the guise of statutory construction", effectively rewrote and amended the statute to do precisely what both its sponsors and its opponents agreed the statute was not intended to do, given its "extraordinary clarity":

> The judge, even when he is free, is still not wholly free. He is not to innovate at pleasure. He is not a knight-errant, roaming at will in pursuit of his own ideal of beauty or of goodness. He is to draw his inspiration from consecrated principles. He is not to yield to spasmodic sentiment, to vague and unregulated benevolence. He is to exercise a discretion informed by tradition, methodized by analogy, disciplined by system, and subordinated to "the primordial necessity of order in the social life". Wide enough in all conscience is the field of discretion that remains....[43]

Still, when it comes to affirmative action, the US Supreme Court demonstrates a rather activist attitude, the most typical example being its decision in *Sheet Metal Workers' International Association v. Equal Employment Opportunity Commission*

---

[41]*Wygant v. Jackson Board of Education*, 476 US 267 (1986); *Local 28 of the Sheet Metal Workers' International Association v. Equal Employment Opportunity Commission (EEOC)*, 478 US 421 (1986); *Firefighters v. Cleveland*, 478 US 501 (1986).

[42]Washington Post 3rd December 2005, p. A1.

[43]443 US 193 (1979).

(1996).[44] A federal court of first instance had found a local labour syndicate guilty of racial discrimination, but instead of proceeding to enforce any penalty or trying to open participation for minority employees, thus preventing discrimination in the future, it imposed on the syndicate a goal of 29 % minority participation. When the Court found that the aim was not achieved, the syndicate applied to the Supreme Court pleading an excess of judicial power. The Supreme Court decided that the legislation did not prohibit courts from providing an "affirmative race-conscious relief" as restoration of "egregious" discrimination, or where the affirmative action was considered necessary so as "to dissipate the lingering effects of pervasive discrimination". The Court held that the traditional remedy of *injunction* would be ineffective to achieve the public interest envisaged by Civil Rights Act of 1964. Interestingly enough, while the Supreme Court hinders public or private initiatives to introduce positive discrimination quotas, the judiciary does not face such constitutional obstacles. The situation becomes even more paradoxical if one considers that in the particular case there was no statute even remotely mandating quotas.

In this context, unsurprisingly, it is the Supreme Court in the US that primarily raises social awareness on affirmative action issues. Its relevant judgments receive extensive social publicity, as well as legal and political commentary, contrary to what happens in Europe with relatively fewer decisions of domestic and international courts. In the US, it is essentially the Supreme Court which takes on the task of adjusting institutions at present. Given that the Court only hears approximately 1 % of the applications submitted,[45] revisit timing lies entirely with the Court. Thus, by act or even by omission, when the Court refuses leave, for which no reasons are required, the Court becomes the key actor in institutional advancement. This judicial activism or self-restraint is particularly evident in the case of affirmative action. Prior to the Michigan Cases in 2003, the Supreme Court had refused to decide on merits in racial university admission cases which had been decided by state courts of appeal. It is noteworthy that in this way the Supreme Court effectively retained in force rulings from lower federal and state courts, thus provoking serious variances in terms of precedent since the 1978 *Bakke*[46] case-law was not itself deprived of ambiguities. This long Supreme Court inertia was ceased in a rather unorthodox way. The Court of Appeal based in the city of Cincinnati, which decided/ruled on the Michigan University admission policy in 2001, did not follow the ordinary three-member composition, but decided due to the major significance of the cases to hear them in a broader composition. For the *Grutter* case, the Court of Appeal upheld with a 5-4 majority that the admission policy served a compelling public interest and was, therefore, constitutional and lawful. For the *Gratz* case, paradoxically, an appeal decision was never issued. The case was essentially

[44]478 US 421 (1986).

[45]In break down figures, around 4 % for paid petitions and 0.1 % for *in forma pauperis petitions*; data retrieved for 2011–12 from the official data of the Supreme Court, http://www.supremecourt.gov/orders/journal/jnl11.pdf (last accessed 31.12.2014).

[46]*Regents of the University of California v. Bakke*, 438 US 265 (1978).

assumed by the Supreme Court, which heard it jointly with *Grutter* by using a procedural vehicle rarely used in the past. The 9 justices of the Supreme Court seem to have consciously considered that it was a good time to reconsider the issue and set firm case-law for the future. Good timing was perhaps accompanied by procedural considerations, given that the two different cases could serve the task of delimiting permitted affirmative action in academia, or even considerations of judicial policy since the members of the Court were at the time quite aged and new appointments seemed very probable at the time.

Judicial politics in Europe are not so evident or striking; they exist but in a rather eloquent manner. An equivalent (but different in style) to Chief Justice Burger's statement of self-restraint was furnished by Advocate General Jacobs in *Marschall*, who made an initial point that unequal gender representation in employment is due to a variety of factors and that, possibly, preferential treatment for women might be a way to treat this phenomenon. However, he forcefully rejected the idea that an assessment on the expediency of the policy should be made by the Court on the ground that the Court was not asked and could not have been asked to rule on the desirability of affirmative action generally, which would be a matter for the legislature: "Any temptation for the Court to tailor the result to policy, however attractive it may be seen, should be resisted".[47] By the same token, in his 2004 Opinion in *Serge Briheche v. Ministre de l'Intérieur* et al., Advocate General Maduro categorically stated that it was not for the Court to assess the merits of a debatable policy, such as affirmative action programmes, but only whether, and to what extent, they can be regarded as compatible with the principle of equal treatment.[48] In Europe, thus, generally judicial decisions operate much more as acceleration for constitutional or statutory initiatives, which essentially confirm judicial precedent. This is not the situation in the US where in most cases new precedent is set following a Court's ruling, and there is no need to amend the law respectively, since case law constitutes part of the official and bounding hierarchy of norms.

5.1.2 Identifying and Assessing the Goal Pursued

5.1.2.1 Legitimacy of Goals in the Judicial Reasoning

In order for a proper constitutional scrutiny, a necessary opening question is against which goal should each particular scheme be measured? A preliminary question in relation to the constitutionality of affirmative action policies is the

[47]Opinion of Advocate General Jacobs of 15 May 1997 in Case C-409/95, *Hellmut Marschall v. Land Nordhein–Westfalen*, Rec. 1997, p. I-6363, paras. 11, 46.

[48]Opinion of Advocate General Poiares Maduro of 29 June 2004 in Case C-319/03, *Serge Briheche v. Ministre de l'Intérieur, Ministre de l'Éducation nationale and Ministre de la Justice*, Rec. 2004, p. I-8807, para. 49, fn. 3.

identification and assessment of its goals. This test constitutes a negative presupposition for the proportionality test that follows. If the goals pursued are not deemed legitimate by the judiciary, then there is no room for the proportionality test and the measure should be discarded without any further assessment. Especially in the case of the US, the Supreme Court will assess the goal pursued as important in the case of intermediate scrutiny (applying in gender-based classifications) or of compelling public interest in the case of strict scrutiny (applying in race-based classifications). If the impugned measure is considered by the court as serving a legitimate (or important/compelling depending on the case) goal, judicial review will develop to the next step of proportionality. From this viewpoint, identification and assessment of the goals pursued constitute a *conditio sine qua non* so that the suitability and necessity of the measure can be examined (Gerapetritis 1997: 126 *et seq.*).

Goal *identification* is a judicial process broadly based on historical evidence relating to the actual motives of the act in question and of the authority introducing the impugned affirmative action plan. Motives may stem from the actual text of the statute, the parliamentary debates, contextual conditions surrounding the enactment of the act, regulations of the enacting authority and other direct or circumstantial evidence. In the absence of these elements, given that the court cannot legitimately abstain from rendering a decision due to a lack of relevant evidence, the judicial task may turn to a psychological experiment of reproducing the mental approach of the legislator and of the enacting authority. Once the goals are identified, their legal *assessment* becomes a juridical task based primarily on the interpretation of the values deriving from the text and the spirit of the constitution and of the common law, an exercise which is not devoid of elements of political and ethical ideology.

This legal endeavor operates in two stages. On an *abstract* level, the judge must first shape the particular characteristics that must be satisfied for a purpose to be characterised as constitutionally permissible. In the US, as collateral of the strict scrutiny test and the conception of affirmative action as an exception rather than a feature of equality, quantitative criteria mostly apply in the sense that a permissible goal must serve a "compelling interest" or relate to "the most compelling reasons". In Europe, where positive discrimination seems much more to be genuinely rooted in the essence of equality, judges apply qualitative criteria and look for the constitutional standing of the corresponding goal, without any further restraints as to quantative criteria. On a *specific* level, judicial control further subjects each goal invoked by the defendant or extracted by the norm to the standards set out in the abstract. Obviously, when quantitative criteria mostly apply the judge has a wider discretion in assessing the goal: diversity of compensation may or may not according to one's personal view be a "compelling" state interest. Conversely, if quantitative criteria apply, the judge is more restrained to orthodox constitutional interpretation which forms the basis of the relevant reasoning: in order for diversity or compensation to constitute a legitimate interest, the judge ought to have recourse to the historical or contemporary reading of the constitution. In this thread, it becomes apparent that when evaluating the goals of the challenged measure, the American judge is more pragmatic and policy-oriented. Although qualitative criteria in terms of the legitimacy of the goal broadly apply in Europe and the US alike, in the latter case additional qualitative criteria are required for a state interest to qualify as compelling.

5.1.2.2 Goals Upheld in the Context of Affirmative Action

In most systems, the identification of the ratio of affirmative action fluctuates in relation to the beneficiaries and the area of application of the measure, mostly between compensation for past discrimination and diversity. Positive measures in favour of racial or religious groups are particularly akin to the goal of diversity, whereas measures in favour of women mostly tend to compensate for past discriminations. In the US racial affirmative action, although originally and typically fulfilled a remedial purpose, as of the *Bakke* a repositioning was triggered in terms of focusing on diversity as a more suitable goal to withstand constitutional scrutiny. On the other hand, in the field of education or broadcasting, diversity plays a dominant role because obviously an enriching academic environment can have particularly benevolent side-effects in the same way that broadcasting diversity secures the expression of a wide range of voices, whereas in the fields of labour or public procurement the remedial character of affirmative action is more apparent since there is not an equal need to address cultural issues. At any rate, one should not overlook the assumption that remedial and cultural purposes, in spite of their variations in a legal environment, may on occasions overlap. The need and claim for further participation in educational or political environments of underrepresented groups derives from the history of past discrimination, which in one way or another, prohibited wider participation.

Europe and America employ a fundamentally different approach when it comes to the interests served by affirmative action. In Europe, particularly in the EU legal system, the basic ratio for taking positive action lies with the idea of compensation for past discrimination with a view to restoring full equality, conceived primarily as equality of opportunities. Thus, purely remedial purposes are considered as legitimate, whereas the argument of diversity has been disregarded. Despite the fact that in this way the emphasis is given to the restoration of the statistical imbalance, what lies beneath is the constitutional choice to restore the unfair results of past discrimination against women. The most illustrative extract in this respect has been furnished by Attorney General Tesauro in his Opinion on *Kalanke,* explicitly admitting that the rationale for the preferential treatment given to women lies in the general situation of disadvantage caused by past discrimination and, also, in the existing difficulties connected with playing a dual role. In his mind, the existence of a different historical social and cultural condition (for instance, the disparity in education and vocational training) continued to marginalise women on the employment markets. Accordingly, may not be regarded, even less employed, as a means of remedying, through discriminatory quota measures, which are even irrelevant to that end, a situation of impaired inequality in the past.[49]

By way of contrast, the US case-law has fluctuated between the goals of diversity and compensation for a long time. Originally, it was the remedial purpose that prevailed in the Supreme Court's rationale. In *United Steelworkers of America v. Weber* (1979),[50] the Court invoked the history of the enactment of the *Civil Rights Act* 1964 and equity as well as the "broad remedial purposes" of the measure and upheld the constitutionality of voluntary labour affirmative action in favour of minorities without any reference to diversity; whereas in *Richmond v. Croson* (1989), a 6-justice majority ruled that affirmative action measures were reserved strictly "for remedial settings".[51] However, diversity seems today to have become the prevailing compelling public interest in the context of affirmative action. In fact, the Supreme Court in *Regents of the University of California v. Bakke*[52] rejected the argument of compensation on the grounds that collective damage cannot be established and that concrete damage can only be asserted if based on judicial, legislative or administrative findings of constitutional violations. According to Justice Powell's critical vote, only the legislature and the executive and no other institutions, such as the universities, can identify such findings in order to justify the introduction of affirmative action plans on the ground of diversity as a compelling public interest.

The *Bakke* case law was reaffirmed in the Michigan University admission policy decisions, especially in *Grutter v. Bollinger.*[53] The Court not only confirmed diversity as a compelling public interest, but categorically rejected the remedial purposes of affirmative action, essentially prompting the University to withdraw the argument that its admission policy aimed at compensating for past discrimination and to retreat from certain extracts of its Regulations to that effect. In fact, remedial purposes were invoked through a writ of certiorari by intervening universities but this was rejected by the Supreme Court without extensive reasoning, merely by stating that there was no sufficient evidence that the grounds for the enactment of the measure were discrimination or its side effects. By exclusively upholding the diversity rationale, the Court emphasised that a "critical mass" of minority students was necessary for their uninhibited progress in academia through the creation of a "diverse student body" that improves educational experience. The Court did not set

[49]Opinion of Advocate General Tesauro of 6 April 1995 in Case C-450/93, *Eckhard Kalanke v. Freie Hansestadt Bremen*, Rec. 1995, p. I-3051, paras. 18–19.

[50]*United Steelworkers of America v. Weber* 443 US 193 (1979).

[51]*Richmond v. Croson*, 488 US 469, 493 (1989). Also see the characteristic Court of Appeal cases *Contractors Association of Eastern Pennsylvania v. Secretary of Labor*, 442 F.2d 159 (3rd Cir. 1971) and *Podberesky v. Kirwan,* 956 F.2d 52, 57 (4th Cir. 1992).

[52]438 US 265 (1978).

[53]539 US 306 (2003).

out a fixed number of minority students that would satisfy the critical mass requirement, but merely demanded that some minority students are admitted so that they did not feel isolated.[54] At any rate, the Court left a wide margin of appreciation to the university to numerically define the necessary critical mass, a discretion which is nevertheless judicially controllable.

The argument of diversity was not, however, unanimously embraced by the members of the Court. Obviously, the critical mass criterion is particularly fluid and essentially conveys that the diversity requirement forms the level of objective ratios in group representation to a level where psychological security is reached in order for the diversity to achieve its goals; as Justice Scalia rightly put it in his dissenting opinion in *Grutter v. Bollinger* the critical mass is so "mystical" that it "challenges even the most gullible mind". In his dissent in the same case, Justice Thomas further used a very technical line of argumentation in order to methodologically combat diversity and, in turn, affirmative action in general. In his view, in order for a goal to be assessed as a public interest and most importantly as "compelling" it must be acknowledged as such unanimously from the federal state and states: although it is not sufficient *ipso facto* that certain states adopt this policy, if some states reject it then it cannot by definition be a compelling public interest. In consequence, given that certain US states institutionally overrule the policy, diversity cannot qualify as a public interest.[55] In the same line of reasoning, the US Court of Appeals had previously held in *Hopwood v. Texas*[56] that diversity of the student body was not a justification; indeed, the court said, pursuit of racial diversity is irrational, like pursuit of diverse blood types.

The dominance of diversity over compensation was reaffirmed in *Parents Involved*[57] concerning primary and secondary education, where Chief Justice Roberts, writing for the Court, further exemplified the diversity argument by requiring a compact plan to achieve this measure and not merely incremental measures. In terms of compensation for the past, he mentioned that schools could not plead this compelling interest, because they operated in a non-segregated or desegregated environment and the harm being remedied by mandatory desegregation plans is the harm that is traceable to segregation, while the Constitution is not violated by racial imbalances in the schools without further evidence of discrimination. In terms of diversity, the Court held that this interest can only be accepted if race is part of a broader effort to achieve exposure to widely diverse people, cultures, ideas, and viewpoints whereas in the facts of the case, the plans employed only a limited notion of diversity, viewing race exclusively in terms of white/nonwhite or black/other.

[54]135 F. Supp. 2d 790, 795 (ED Mich. 2001).

[55]*Grutter v. Bollinger*, 539 US 306, 357–8 (2003).

[56]*Hopwood v. Texas*, 78 F.3d 932, 945 (5th Cir. 1996).

[57]551 US 701 (2007).

The diversity goal is also prevalent in the field of broadcast licensing. In *Metro Broadcasting Inc. v. Federal Communications Commission,* where the Supreme Court with a 5-4 majority rested on an intermediate scrutiny and upheld the Federal Communications Commission's policy to award an enhancement for minority ownership in comparative proceedings for new licenses and to permit a limited category of existing radio and television broadcast stations to be transferred only to minority-controlled firms ("distress sale" programme). The majority held that minority ownership policies were substantially related to the goal of promoting broadcast diversity, in order to compensate for a dearth of minority broadcasting experience; thus, it effectively addressed both the problem of inadequate access to capital by lowering the sale price of existing stations and the problem of lack of information regarding license availability. The Court also examined the adverse effect upon other competitors for the same licenses and concluded that there is no violation of any legitimate expectations (since no one had First Amendment right to a license); that in granting licenses considerations of public interest factors are required; and, that this policy did not produce disproportionate effects, since it might be invoked only with respect to a small fraction of broadcast licenses, only when the licensee chooses to sell out at a low price rather than risk a hearing and only when no competing application has been filed. Given that the impugned measure did not constitute a quota or fixed quantity set-aside and that non-minorities were free to compete for the vast remainder of other available license opportunities, the majority upheld the legality and constitutionality of the plan.[58]

Occasionally, other public interests, more or less relative to the idea of diversity, have been invoked by justices of the US Supreme Court to justify affirmative action. These include social cohesion and inclusion (mainly the prevention of stigma and social bias against minority groups),[59] the improvement in service provision given the tendency of minority members to professionally address members of the same group,[60] the need to have members of minorities in significant posts to operate as role models[61] and the need to treat cases of social emergency.[62] It seems that after the *Michigan cases*, diversity has become the prevailing ground for the justification of affirmative action in the US. However, serious doubts have been expressed according to which the adoption of diversity is merely an opportunistic approach, in the sense that it transfers the focus of discussion of the intensely heated issue of past discrimination (for which a sense of social guilt is not to be excluded) to the objective and neutral issue of racial balance (Schuck 2002: 34; Rubenfeld 1997).

[58]497 US 547 (1990).

[59]*Brown v. Board of Education*, 347 US 483, 494 (1954).

[60]*DeFunis v. Odegaard*, 416 US 312 (1974).

[61]*Wygant v. Jackson Board of Education*, 476 US 267 (1986).

[62]Justice Scalia in the cases *Hirabayashi v. United States*, 320 US 81 (1943) and *Korematsu v. United States*, 323 US 214 (1944).

5.1.3 Applying the Proportionality Test

Examining the constitutionality of an affirmative action is performed in all legal systems, in one way or another, through the proportionality test. In the US, as well as in Europe, the judiciary has refused to provide altogether *ipso jure* constitutional cover to affirmative action but upholds them only in an *ad hoc* manner, provided that certain conditions of proportionality are met.

The typical proportionality test is very well-known in European legal systems, unlike the common law tradition focusing on a basic level on a more pragmatic approach of the evaluation of the reasonableness/rational basis test. In the particular US legal context, strict scrutiny (and, less so, intermediate control), seems to resemble more to a stringent proportionality test. In any case, the outcomes of judicial control are very similar in most legal orders, irrespective of the judicial vehicles of review applied (Gerapetritis 1997: 136 *et seq.*). Inflexible quotas are intolerable because, according to US jurisprudence, they cannot conceivably be narrowly tailored since they could generically apply in any case of statistical inequality. From this viewpoint they are not combating the roots of discrimination that have caused this social pathology and, at any rate, there can be milder means to achieve this purpose, i.e. measures that are not so detrimental to the rights of non-benefiting individuals. So, if the early retirement scheme for female workers was challenged before the US Supreme Court, the outcome would most probably be annulment on the ground that it was not narrowly tailored to serve the admittedly important interest of supporting motherhood. The scenery remains the same even in legal systems where domestic constitutions have explicitly recognised and upgraded affirmative action. Thus, the judiciary is bound to apply the standards of constitutional review on each particular measure and assess the compatibility of the measure against the fundamental equality principle. In this way, it seems that in terms of constitutional review, it makes no significant difference if affirmative action has been constitutionally acknowledged, such as in many EU Member States and the EU itself, or if it stems as a matter of interpretation from the constitutional principle of equality. Constitutional recognition is not—and cannot be—open-ended.

The proportionality test comprises 3 sub-tests: suitability, necessity and *stricto sensu* proportionality. Suitability and necessity are present in all judicial methodologies in one way or another. *Stricto sensu* proportionality, i.e. the direct weighting of competing rights, generally does not appear with technical clarity. This is predominantly because this form of review is very intense and might well lead to the substitution of the view of the court for that of the legislature or the executive. Given that affirmative action is par excellence a policy with intense political and social ramifications, the judiciary exercises a significant level of self-restraint and regularly abstains from a direct weighting of competing interests. Accordingly, suitability and necessity remain the main methodological tools when assessing the constitutionality of positive measures departing from formal equality.

5.1.3.1 Suitability

Suitability constitutes the first parameter of proportionality, inquiring as to whether the impugned measure may produce results that serve the goal pursued. This sub-test, which entails a yes/no response, is a prerequisite before proceeding to the following two aspects of the proportionality test. Thus, if the answer to the question is in the negative, the measure has already failed to meet the requirements of proportionality. It is noteworthy, because it is often an issue of academic misapprehension, that the suitability control does not entail a comparative evaluation amongst the possible alternative measures to achieve a legitimate aim. Once two affirmative action measures satisfy the suitability threshold, thus deemed capable of producing the desirable goals, there is no question as to which measure is more "suitable" or "drastic", but the control is transferred to the level of their necessity, which entails a cross-examination.

In spite of the clear-cut question, finding the answer is not always straightforward. In the context of judicial review of affirmative action measures, the suitability sub-test is two-fold: appropriateness and fit test. This latter test is more akin to the American jurisprudence.

Appropriateness

Although the appropriateness test is commonplace in European courts, this review does not go in-depth so as to usurp legislative or executive powers. Also, the Court of Justice of the European Union, when applying the suitability control, seems to be cautious in not shrinking the leeway of Member-States to introduce measures in their respective field of competence.

In the *Griesmar* judgment (2001), the plaintiff, a French *magistrat* and father of three children, claimed sex discrimination on the ground that he received a retirement pension calculated on the basis of the years of service that he had actually completed, in accordance with the legislation in force at the time, without any calculation which took account of his children, unlike what would have happened had he been a female employee. The Court reaffirmed that the equality of pay principle established by then Article 119 of the EEC Treaty (currently Article 157 TFEU) should also apply in retirement pensions for civil servants, who constitute a particular category of workers, and that this did indeed constitute pay since it was directly linked to the post previously occupied. The Court held that the credit granted to civil servants who were mothers could not be authorised as being a measure designed to help women in their career since, being granted at the date of their retirement, it did not provide a remedy for the problems which they might encounter in the course of their professional career. Although in principle the appropriateness control is done on an *ex ante* basis and it not equivalent to a subsequent effectiveness control of the measure, the Court made extensive use of data which proved that, although the national provision began in 1924, problems in the careers of female employees had not been resolved in the time leading up to the

Griesmar decision. In so doing, the Court essentially discarded the measures as failing to satisfy the suitability test. This ruling was based on a two-fold test. First, the Court made a diagnosis as to the actual disadvantage that the impugned measure purported to treat, namely if the credit was designed to offset the occupational disadvantages arising for female workers as a result of being absent from work during the period following childbirth (in which case the situation of a male worker is not comparable to that of a female worker), or whether it was designed essentially to offset the occupational disadvantages which arose for female workers as a result of having brought up children (in which case it would be necessary to examine the question whether the situations of a male civil servant and a female civil servant were comparable). Once determined that both goals are legitimate, the Court held that the measure in question was limited to granting female civil servants who were mothers a service credit at the date of their retirement, without providing a remedy for the problems which they may encounter in the course of their professional career, thus being in reality unsuitable to serve the desired purpose.[63]

Interestingly, in *Griesmar* the Court abstained from the Opinion of Advocate General Alber who had concluded that the contested provision was suitable to compensate for motherhood disadvantages and was, therefore, compatible with the principle of equal treatment. His reasoning started with the statement that the biological mother enjoys a special position in terms of her employment at the time before, during and after giving birth, which has an impact on her working life: before birth, during pregnancy, an expectant mother was already covered by special protective provisions which would have a restrictive effect on her occupational activity and which prevent certain duties being assigned to a pregnant woman; after birth, there is a prohibition on employment, a minimum period of maternity leave, an option of extended maternity leave and breast-feeding period restrictions. As a matter of these special conditions akin to women (pregnancy, childbirth and breast-feeding), Advocate General held that there were objective grounds justifying compensatory measures in favour of one sex. All the above, taking into account that there are secondary effects stemming from motherhood, such as delay in training, thereby postponing the opportunity of entering the civil service or possible secondment, during which the institution of secondment would also have to apply the maternity protection provisions together with the restrictions thereby entailed. The conclusion of this syllogism was that the granting of a service credit for biological motherhood in calculating pension entitlements appeared objectively justified.[64] The disagreement between the Court and the Advocate General on the suitability test was essentially on the time that the compensation ought to be granted to the

[63]CJEU Judgment of 29 November 2001, Case C-366/99, *Joseph Griesmar and Ministre de l'Économie, des Finances et de l'Industrie, Ministre de la Fonction publique, de la Réforme de l'État et de la Décentralisation*, Rec. 2001, p I-9413, paras. 46, 65–66.

[64]Opinion of Advocate General Albert in CJEU Judgment of 29 November 2001, Case C-366/99, *Joseph Griesmar and Ministre de l'Économie, des Finances et de l'Industrie, Ministre de la Fonction publique, de la Réforme de l'État et de la Décentralisation*, Rec. 2001, p I-9413, paras. 70–71, 92.

disadvantaged groups: the former presumed that it has to be on time of employment, whereas the latter that it might occur even at a later stage.

Another typical example of appropriateness control is provided in the 2009 *Commission v. Greece* judgment,[65] where the Court of Justice of the European Union examined the provision of the Greek Civil and Military Pensions Code according to which women had a lesser retirement age and minimum length of service in order to address the disadvantages faced by them as a result of their social roles, and the fact that they have generally fewer years of paid employment. The Court, after having affirmed that the pension scheme in question was based on an employment record and was not a social security scheme, considered the benefits attributed to women as pay so that no differentiation could be tolerable. Although the Court explicitly acknowledged that Member States could introduce positive action measures to treat labour disadvantages, different retirement ages could not by their nature serve the legitimate remedial purposes, since the multiple roles of women in society, especially that related to motherhood, were not by any means eased if women workers retired earlier.

Fit

The suitability control in the jurisprudence of the US Supreme Court is much stricter in cases of deviations from the Equal Protection Clause based on suspect classifications such as race, adding a further requirement to the suitability control. Accordingly, the measure must be "*narrowly tailored*" to serve the goal pursued in the particular field of its implementation. This premise is peculiar to the US jurisprudence and constitutes the most substantial hurdle that needs to be crossed in order for a measure to be held constitutional. It has a negative aspect, i.e. that a measure should not be of such a generic character that it might reasonably apply in all cases, and a positive aspect, i.e. that the measure ought to be designed taking into consideration the contextual background and the needs of each particular field and case. The first premise seems to exclude altogether and automatically rigid quotas, which by definition might apply in all cases, whereas the second premise requires a more elaborate analysis of the case and a wide submission of evidence against or in the light of which the measure ought to be assessed.

Two sets of Supreme Court cases regarding academic admissions and public procurement, with ultimately opposite results, prove the significance of the "narrowly tailored" requirement. In academic admissions relating to Michigan University in 2003, in *Gratz* the Court invalidated the policy according to which every applicant from an underrepresented racial or ethnic minority group was automatically awarded 20 points of the 100 needed to guarantee admission because it was not narrowly tailored to achieve the respondents' asserted interest in diversity, thus violating the Equal Protection Clause. As Chief Justice Rehnquist put it,

[65]CJEU Judgment of 26th March 2009, Case C-559/07, *Commission v. Greece,* (2009) ECR I-47.

the University's policy which automatically distributed 20 points or one-fifth of the points needed to guarantee admission, to every single "underrepresented minority" applicant solely because of race, was not narrowly tailored to achieve the interest in educational diversity. He further gave concrete examples of how the lack of a cumulative individualised selection process and a comparative cross-assessment of candidates might result in altogether unfair results, i.e. if a student was an extraordinary artistic talent that "rivaled that of Monet or Picasso", the applicant would receive, at most, five points whereas every single underrepresented minority applicant would automatically receive 20 points for merely submitting an application, thus hampering the eventual compelling interest of diversity because a student that would greatly contribute both academically and culturally would be left out because of his/her race. On the other hand, Justice Souter, in dissenting, claimed that there was no issue of suitability or unnecessary generality of the admissions' scheme, but admitted a "deliberate obfuscation" in that the "percentage plans", guaranteeing space to students at the top of each high school class in the state, were just as race conscious as the point scheme, but they got their racially diverse results without saying directly what they were doing or why they were doing it. In contrast, he claimed that Michigan frankly stated its purpose directly, for which it ought to be credited.[66]

On the other hand, in *Grutter* the Supreme Court upheld Michigan's Law School admissions policy that admittedly used race as a "plus factor" in admissions on the ground that the narrowly tailored use of race to further a compelling interest in obtaining the educational benefits that flow from a diverse student body was permissible, given that because there was a highly individualised review of each applicant, there was not an automatic admission or denial of a candidate but a joint assessment of all relevant factors, including race. In this judgment the Court broke down and codified the criteria that need to be met in order for an affirmative action plan to be properly characterised as narrowly tailored. Accordingly, a University programme *cannot* insulate each category of applicants with certain desired qualifications from competition with all other applicants: universities cannot establish quotas for members of certain racial or ethnic groups or put them on separate admissions tracks. On the contrary, a University programme *can* consider race or ethnicity only as a "plus" in a particular applicant's file, in a way that it is flexible enough to consider all pertinent elements of diversity in light of the particular qualifications of each applicant and to place them on the same footing for consideration, although not necessarily according them the same weight. The Court was satisfied that, in the context of the individualised consideration of the possible diversity contributions of each applicant, the race-conscious admissions programme did not unduly harm nonminority applicants. In both cases cited above, the Supreme Court explicitly rejected an argument raised by the petitioners that diversity as a basis for employing racial preferences is simply too open-ended, ill-defined and indefinite to constitute a compelling interest capable of supporting narrowly-tailored means.

[66]*Gratz v. Bollinger*, 539 US 244 (2003).

If the argument was to be accepted, evidently the acknowledgment that diversity constitutes a compelling governmental interest would have no practical effect.

The second set of cases concerns public procurement. In *Fullilove v. Klutznick* (1979),[67] the minority business enterprise provision of the Public Works Employment Act of 1977 which required that (in principle) at least 10 % of federal funds granted for local public works projects must be used by the state or local grantee to procure services or supplies from businesses owned by minority group members was upheld by the Supreme Court. The argument set out was that the programme was not constitutionally defective just because it might disappoint the expectations of access to a portion of government contracting opportunities of nonminority firms who may themselves be innocent of any prior discriminatory actions since "when effectuating a limited and properly tailored remedy to cure the effects of prior discrimination, such "a sharing of the burden" by innocent parties is not impermissible". Key factors for the decision of the Court were the existence of waivers when there were insufficient numbers of minority businesses capable of doing the work at non-exorbitant prices located in the relevant contracting area and the provision for an administrative mechanism to ensure that only *bona fide* Minority Business Enterprises were encompassed by the programme, thus preventing unjust participation by minority firms whose access to public contracting opportunities had not been impaired by the effects of prior discrimination. In the Court's view, when a programme narrowly tailored by Congress to achieve its objectives came under judicial review, it should be upheld if the courts were satisfied that the legislative objectives and projected administration of the programme gave reasonable assurance that the programme would function within constitutional limitations. In this way, the Court in *Fullilove* refrained from applying strict scrutiny (part of which is the "narrowly tailored" prong of the test.

On the other hand, in *Richmond v. Croson* (1983),[68] Richmond's regulations requiring companies awarded city construction contracts to subcontract 30 % of their business to minority business enterprises was challenged before the Supreme Court. Delivering the opinion of the Court, Justice O'Connor concluded that the Plan was not narrowly tailored to remedy the effects of prior discrimination, since it entitled a black, Hispanic, or Oriental entrepreneur from anywhere in the country to an absolute preference over other citizens based solely on their race. In the Court's view, the Plan's waiver system, unlike in *Fullilove,* focused upon the availability of Minority Business Enterprises and did not inquire whether the particular enterprise seeking a racial preference had suffered from the effects of past discrimination by the city or prime contractors. It thus concluded that, given that the city ought to consider bids and waivers on a case-by-case basis, the city's only interest in maintaining a quota system, rather than investigating the need for remedial action in particular cases, would have been simply administrative convenience, which, standing alone, could not justify/withstand strict scrutiny review.

---

[67] 448 US 448 (1979).

[68] 488 US 469, 507–508 (1989).

The narrowly tailored requirement is not found as such in the case-law of European Courts. However, the European equivalent to this standard is the requirement that any measure carries an adequate degree of individualised justice enabling enough flexibility to treat cases which present variations from the general rule. Thus, in *Kalanke*,[69] the Court of Justice of the European Union rejected a system of direct preference for females against male candidates with the same qualifications, regarding access to work; whereas in *Marschall*,[70] it upheld a relevant measure, essentially because it provided an escape clause. In both cases, the Court based its rationale on the fact that evaluation should be made based on objective criteria, which shall take into consideration all relative skills and abilities of candidates and shall ignore elements unrelated to the very nature and logic of the work to be performed. The point that the Court made was that the evaluation process in *Marschall* was adequately individualised, although part of theory/the literature thought this flexible admission policy as merely a rhetoric device. The *Kalanke-Marschall* joint reading was codified in the subsequent *Badeck* judgement (2000), where the Court expressly set out the criteria that ought to be met so that a deviation from gender equality at work might be permissible. Thus, a measure which was intended to give priority in promotion to women in sectors of the public service where they are underrepresented must be regarded as compatible with Community law, if it did not automatically and unconditionally give priority to women when women and men are equally qualified, *and* the candidatures have been the subject of an objective assessment taking account of the specific personal situations of all candidates.[71] Assessment as to whether these conditions exist lies with the national courts on the basis of an examination of the scope of the provision at issue. Advocate General Tesauro in his opinion in *Kalanke* expressly discarded the logic of rigid quotas as unsuitable in the sense that they would not remove the obstacles raised by inequality.

In the above *Kalanke, Marschall* and *Badeck* decisions, the Court dealt with challenges relating to domestic legislation where affirmative action regarded the selection of a female candidate over male candidates with equal formal qualifications. For the first time in the *Abrahamsson* judgment (2000),[72] the Court was faced with an intriguing legal situation whereby a female candidate's qualifications were fewer than the respective qualifications of male candidates. In particular, although accepting that priority for women where their qualifications are equal as a way of restoring balance was not contrary to Community law provided that an objective assessment of each candidature is guaranteed, the Court found that the impugned

---

[69]CJEU Judgment of 17 October 1995, Case C-450/93, *Eckhard Kalanke v. Freie Hansestadt Bremen*, Rec. 1995, p I-3051.

[70]Case C-409/95 *Marschall v. Land Nordrhein-Westfalen* [1997] ECR I-6363.

[71]CJEU Judgment of 28 March 2000, Case C-158/97, *Georg Badeck et als*, Rec. 2000, p I-1875, para. 23.

[72]CJEU Judgment of 6 July 2000, Case C-407/98, *Katarina Abrahamsson and Leif Anderson v. Elisabet Fogelqvist*, Rec. 2000, p I-5539.

Swedish legislation, which favoured access for women to public posts even where their qualifications were not equal to those of the male candidates, was not permissible. In the facts of the case, the University of Göteborg announced a vacancy for the chair of Professor of Hydrospheric Sciences. There was an express indication that the appointment should contribute to promotion of equality of the sexes in professional life and that positive discrimination might be applied in accordance with the Swedish legislation, which provided that appointments to posts of professor/such academic posts are to take account of the need to accord priority to the underrepresented sex where it proves necessary to do so in order for the candidate belonging to that sex to be appointed and provided that the difference between the candidates' qualifications is not so great as to give rise to a breach of the requirement of objectivity in the making of appointments. The selection board responsible for nominating a candidate to the Rector of the University ranked the candidates, taking into account both of the candidates' scientific merits and the above gender statutory criteria. Eventually, the female candidate, albeit with less qualifications was preferred over a male candidate. The Court observed that the assessment of the candidates' qualifications in the selection procedure at issue was not based on clear and certain criteria (for example, seniority, age, date of last promotion, family status or income of the partner), therefore there was a high risk of arbitrary assessment of candidates' qualifications. The Court concluded that the selection method under the Swedish legislation did not conform to Community law: the selection was ultimately based on the fact of belonging to the underrepresented sex and candidatures were not subjected to an objective assessment taking account of the specific personal situations of all the candidates, thus the selection method was disproportionate having regard to the aim pursued. In the above case Advocate General Saggio reached a different conclusion to the one he took in *Badeck*. In his view, a positive measure could only be permissible if the shortlisted candidates were equal in terms of qualifications and merits, otherwise the system would accord absolute and unconditional priority, thus reserving posts for women (as a quota by effect). He found no difference in the light of the escape clause of the impugned regulation that the right to an appointment might arise only if there is no significant difference between the candidate who is selected and the one who was rejected, since the process was distorted from the beginning.[73]

5.1.3.2 Necessity

In the context of judicial review of affirmative action, the necessity of an affirmative action measure sub-test is two-fold: a qualitative control for the existence of less restrictive alternatives for the afflicted rights and a time control for the duration of the measure.

---

[73]CJEU Judgment of 28 March 2000, Case C-158/97, *Georg Badeck et als*, Rec. 2000, p I-1875, para. 28.

Less Restrictive Alternatives

Arguably, the most significant part of the proportionality test is the investigation as to whether there could be in each particular case alternative measures that could equally serve the legitimate aim pursued but would produce less adverse effects for individual rights involved. This test, unlike suitability, is much stricter in the case law of the European Courts.

In *Grutter* (2003), the US Supreme Court explicitly rejected the argument that the Michigan Law School should have used other race-neutral means to obtain the educational benefits of student body diversity "e.g., a lottery system or decreasing the emphasis on GPA and LSAT scores" on the ground that narrow tailoring does not require the exhaustion of every conceivable race-neutral alternative or mandate that a university choose between maintaining a reputation for excellence or fulfilling a commitment to provide educational opportunities to members of all racial groups.[74] Accordingly, the Court stated that it was satisfied that the Law School adequately considered the available alternatives. Before this, in *Fullilove* the majority found that Congress had carefully examined and rejected race-neutral alternatives before enacting the medium business enterprise set-aside.[75] In contrast, in *Richmond v. Croson* (1983),[76] Justice O'Connor, delivering the opinion of the Court, concluded that although many of the barriers to minority participation in the construction industry relied upon by the city to justify the Plan appeared to be race-neutral, there was no evidence that the city had considered using alternative, race-neutral means to increase minority participation in city contracting and, therefore, the Court struck down the plan; in *Palmore v. Sidoti* (1984), the Court merely held that racial classifications must be necessary to the accomplishment' of their legitimate purpose[77]; similarly, in *Wygant v. Jackson Bd. of Ed.* (1986), the Court held that narrow tailoring requires the consideration of lawful alternatives, which must serve the acknowledged compelling interest[78]; in *United States v. Paradise* (1987),[79] the Court reiterated that in determining whether race-conscious remedies were appropriate, attention should be addressed to several factors, "including the efficacy of alternative remedies"; and in *United States v. Lopez* (1995), a case of general discrimination, Justice Kennedy held in his concurring opinion that "the States may perform their role as laboratories for experimentation to devise various solutions where the best solution is far from clear".[80]

---

[74] *Grutter v. Bollinger*, 539 US 306, 309 342–343 (2003).

[75] 448 US, at 463–467.

[76] 488 US 469, 507–508 (1989).

[77] 466 US 429, 432 (1984).

[78] 476 US 267, 280.

[79] 480 US 149, 171 (1987).

[80] 514 US 549, 581 (1995).

In the EU legal system, in the 2009 *Commission v. Greece* judgment,[81] once established by the Court of Justice that early retirement is not appropriate to ease the multiple roles of women in society, it was held that what would have satisfied the proportionality test, i.e. the less restrictive alternative test, would be the timely establishment of motivation for mothers of young children, such as flexible working conditions, full child care services, modes of distant working etc., so as to be able in fact to conduct their professional life on an equal footing with men. Given that admittedly there were these alternatives, which were milder from the point of view of those affected by the measures, namely male workers who were unequally obliged to support the social security system for the early retirees, the measure was found patently disproportionate.

Duration

To the extent that affirmative action is restorative, its application cannot be extended further than the point at which the compensating logic of the action has been exhausted, i.e. until the establishment of actual equality. However, this end-point cannot be accurately defined. The most evident benchmark could be the statistical balance produced as a matter of the implementation of the affirmative action measure. In any case, the requirement for a merely temporary application of such measures should apply when the goal pursued is compensation for past discrimination, because when diversity is the primary target, its pursuit becomes a steady feature in the allocation of state or social benefits. Accordingly, in Europe where the goal is almost exclusively compensatory, the time requirement applies in all cases, whereas in the US diversity tends to dominate over the compensatory purpose, meaning that the time requirement should in principle apply in a more limited number of cases. However, this is not the case. In all countries where affirmative action measures have been introduced, the courts when controlling their constitutionality, strictly and explicitly require that the impugned measures are launched for a limited period of time until at least a statistical balance is roughly established.

The most vibrant time-limitation phrasing is to be found in the United Nation's Convention on the Elimination of All Forms of Discrimination against Women. In a rather plethoric and overlapping manner, it provides that temporary special measures aiming at accelerating *de facto* equality between men and women shall not be considered discrimination provided that they are "temporary" and "shall be discontinued when the objectives of equality of opportunity and treatment have been achieved" (Article 4 para. 1). In the jurisprudence of the Court of Justice of the European Union, the transitional character of positive action measures is crucial for upholding the impugned act.

Interestingly, although no relevant statute or regulation provides for a particular time-limit, the case law of the US Supreme Court does on occasions set such

[81]CJEU Judgment of 26th March 2009, Case C-559/07, *Commission v. Greece*, (2009) ECR I-47.

standards. In *Grutter* (2003), the Court, treated affirmative action policies as any other policy introducing a suspect race classification and declared that race-conscious admissions policies must be limited in time. In the Court's view, the requirement that race-conscious admissions policies must be limited in time reflected that racial classifications, however compelling their goals, were potentially so dangerous that they might be employed no more broadly than the interest demands; otherwise the equal protection principle would be offended. It further illustrated that, in the context of higher education, the durational requirement could be met by sunset provisions in race-conscious admissions policies and periodic reviews to determine whether racial preferences were still necessary to achieve student body diversity. In the light of the above, the Court took the Law School at its word that it would "like nothing better than to find a race-neutral admissions formula" and would terminate its race-conscious admissions programme as soon as practicable; the Court also declared the expectation that "25 years from now, the use of racial preferences will no longer be necessary to further the interest approved today".[82] Irrespective of the rather optimistic statement of the Court that de facto equality in University admissions will have been reached by 2028, it is extraordinary (especially in the eyes of a continental European Lawyer), that the court navigated to such clearly extra-judicial speculation. This is why Justice Thomas made a rather strong statement in his dissent in *Grutter* that the Law School's use of race violated at the time the Equal Protection Clause and that the Constitution meant the same thing then as it would be in 300 months. He concluded in a rather ironic tone: "Now we must wait another 25 years to see this principle of equality vindicated".[83]

Prior to *Grutter*, in *Richmond v. Croson*, the Court held that the requirement that race-conscious programmes (set-asides) giving preference to minority business enterprises in public contracting have a termination point assures all citizens that the deviation from the norm of equal treatment of all racial and ethnic groups is a temporary matter, a measure taken in the service of the goal of equality itself.[84] The most empathic and repeatedly cited expression was however made by Justice Blackmun in his separate opinion in *Regents of the University of California v. Bakke* (1978), while not setting a concrete time limit: "At some time, however, beyond any period of what some would claim is only transitional inequality, the United States must and will reach a stage of maturity where action along this line is no longer necessary. Then persons will be regarded as persons, and discrimination of the type we address today will be an ugly feature of history that is instructive, but that is behind us".[85]

[82]*Grutter v. Bollinger,* 539 US 306, 342–343 (2003).

[83]*Ibid.* at 351, 378.

[84]488 US 469, 510 (1989).

[85]438 US 265, 403 (1978).

The temporary nature of affirmative action is probably the only worldwide common thread when judicially assessing the constitutionality of affirmative action. In the landmark Australian case *Gerhardy v. Brown* in 1985 relating to a challenge to measures aiming at preserving and protecting the culture of the Pitjantjatjara peoples,[86] Justice Mason, who delivered the opinion, although admitting that "the legislative regime has about it an air of permanence" in that "it may need to continue indefinitely", he went on to say that the fact that it may prove necessary to continue the regime indefinitely does not involve an infringement of the non-discrimination principle since "there remains a continuing avenue for judicial review of special measures if, in the light of changed circumstances, they no longer meet the requirements". The interest of the judgment lies with the acknowledgment that even in the absence of a specific sunset clause, the measure is by its nature deemed to be of a limited duration and the judge may at any time over the years of the implementation assess whether in the light of the contemporary circumstances it is appropriate to render the same judgment as to the validity of the impugned act. Thus, the expiration clause is implicitly incorporated into any relevant measure (Sadurski 1986).

By the same token, the Belgian *Cour d'arbitrage* dealt with a preferential social security scheme in favour of widows in 1993.[87] The Court respectively held that the legislator, when introducing such a measure as a result of economic and social evolution, is only justified to the extent that discrimination still exists. And, although setting the termination date for the positive discrimination measure lies within the discretion/leeway of the legislature, since it is also related to the state's budgetary needs, this time limit should not be manifestly unreasonable (*manifestement déraisonnable*).

5.2 The Importance of Affirmative Action for the Human Rights Theory

The question of whether the affirmative action doctrine, both constitutional and statutory recognition as well as judicial reception, brings significant alterations to human rights theory is of acute importance. Irrespective of the legal quality of affirmative action, either as a feature or as an exception of equality, its mere existence in legal systems is not devoid of consequences. The two basic consequences are related to the qualification of the policy as a social right and its quality as a group right.

[86](1985) 57 ALR 472.

[87]Judgment 53/93 of 1st July 1993.

5.2.1 A "New" Social Right in a Broadly Declining Context

The reasons for the rise of the social state clearly overcome the ambitions of this book. For the purposes of the present analysis, it is sufficient to say that this evolution was largely the outcome of two factors: the failure of liberalism as a unique model of human co-existence, and the globalisation of the protection of human rights.

There is not a single milestone indicating the failure of liberalism in time. Enlightenment and the great revolutions of the late 18th century and of 1848 saw liberalism set forth as the prevailing social claim and dominating constitutional–political thought. However, liberalism in the context of representative democracy has failed to fully fulfil its potential. This was due to major social upheavals, the crisis of the industrial state, the rapid development of labour syndicates which acquired a political form and assumed authority, the international financial crisis in the first decades of the 20th century, the great wars and the crisis of the constitutional state with the emergence of authoritarian regimes. The alternative proposal set out by the October Revolution, in a chain reaction against the inherent limits of liberalism and related to widespread popular discontent at the time, led to the construction of a strict social state, which was degenerated by authoritarianism and the absolute negligence of fundamental freedoms. Still the ascent of socialism seriously curtailed the idea of liberalism as the sole viable system determining the relations between people and the state. Although the great constitutional texts of the world, such as the Bill of Rights, the American and the French revolutionary constitutions, the Declaration of the Rights of Man and Citizen, or even before that, the *Magna Carta Libertatum*, focused on political and civil rights, the 20th century, first through the Constitution of Weimar, and particularly after World War II with domestic and international law texts, marked a significant turn towards the recognition of the social state.

The acknowledgment of the value and necessity of social state could not avoid exercising pressure on traditional civil rights such as equality, as perceived in the original thought of Mill (1869). This is because liberalism can only tolerate a certain level of social concessions, especially in relation to rights associated with the economy; thus, for example the social economy cannot impair the core of property rights. Property as a civil right may in fact perpetuate social inequalities, when at the same time the social welfare state struggles to produce a balanced society by redistributing benefits in favour of the weaker social actors. The traditional distinction between public and private space, which dogmatically backed the idea of liberalism, could not resist the self-evident premise that the state was not the only source of imposition; social interaction produces many domains where equilibrium is unknown, with employment first and foremost. Civil liberalism accompanied by free market domination and the monetary obsession require social defenses. In this context, Shapiro (1999) abandons the dipole liberty/equality distinction; he emphasises on the issue of participation in decision-making relevant to market regulation, and on a minimum of social solidarity as a guarantee for the effectiveness of the system. It is, therefore, reasonable that when moving from a liberal to a social state, the traditional values of the liberal state (predominantly equality) are subject to institutional adaptation. The transformation towards this sort of enriched equality is not necessarily composite or conscious and does not exactly reflect the structural transformation from the traditional liberal state to a social state; rather a more proactive role for the state is sought without disdaining the essential features upon which the state of law was built.

Globalisation of human rights protection has been the result of the cultural domination of the west and arose in the aftermath of the two world wars. The recognition of the ecumenical character of basic human rights signified the transfer of an important portion of institutional protection, from the domestic to the international legal systems. The Society of Nations after World War I and the United Nations after World War II were designed to guarantee peace at an international level since the atrocities of the wars revealed the structural inability to preserve rights at the level of the states. Post-war Europe, which had been the main venue of the wars, was built on two pillars to prevent future conflicts: democracy and the rule of law; the former was thought to be better preserved through the establishment of a common market and common rules on basic industrial materials, i.e. the European Communities, whereas the latter was thought better protected through a regional European Convention on Human Rights. The equilibrium, however, between the two was uneven. The European Communities had a rapid institutional development with a fully-fledged system of organs developing, which brought them close to the standpoint of a traditional sovereign state; whereas the European Convention on Human Rights was based almost exclusively on the competence of the European Court of Human Rights, which nevertheless did not enjoy an appropriate mechanism of enforcement. Furthermore, unlike the European Communities with its constant legislative procedure adjusting and producing new regulations, the Convention remained a broadly immutable legal text whose adjustment generally remained at the Court's good will through evolutive interpretation techniques taking into account changing circumstances, considering the Convention as a living instrument. In parallel to the Convention, the dogma of a "European social model" was developed, mainly through the launching of regional social charters and conventions, particularly in the field of employment, as well as other documents of varying binding force. Accordingly, a dynamic pan-European matrix of guarantees tends to be established which is based on a composite reading of domestic and regional European law. This trend redefines the equilibrium between liberty and equality, with a relative shift in favour of the latter in the form of *equal* freedom and dignity. This triangular relationship between liberty, dignity and equality was exemplified in Case C-13/94 *P v. S and Cornwall County Council*, where the Court of Justice of the European Union held that to tolerate discriminations based on sex (in particular gender reassignment cases) "would be tantamount, as regards such a person, to a failure to respect the dignity and freedom to which he or she is entitled, and which the Court has a duty to safeguard".[88]

[88]CJEU Judgment of 30 April 1996 in Case C-13/94, *P v. S and Cornwall County Council*, ECR 1996, p. I-2143, para. 22.

The term "European social model" was used by the European Commission's 1994 White Paper as containing democracy and individual rights, free collective bargaining, the market economy, equal opportunity for all, social protection and solidarity.[89] Through a series of legislative instruments,[90] as Hatzopoulos (2005: 1634) points out, essentially aspire to cover the social deficit within the EU through a convergence of classical economic liberties with the non-discrimination principle. According to Däubler (1995: 313), this results in a social state which departs from the idea of policies and resembles state architecture.

In the same vein, human rights, including providing for the social protection of citizens, followed the pattern of globalisation. The *American Convention on Human Rights* (the Pact of San José) signed in 1969 in the context of the Organization of American States covers 35 American states, and belatedly came into force in 1978; the *African Charter on Human and Peoples' Rights* signed in 1981, embracing 53 states of the African Union (the Banjul Charter), whose effective implementation is entrusted to the African Commission on Human and Peoples' Rights set up in 1987, and the *Asian Human Rights Charter*, declared in Kwangju, South Korea in 1998, along with the 10 country Association of Southeast Asian Nations, which established the Intergovernmental Commission on Human Rights in 2009–10 all provide the international scenery on human rights protection.

In fact, the general principle of equality always faced problems in relation to Jellinek's (1892) classic three-fold classification of rights, i.e. civil, political and social. This is predominantly because non-discrimination essentially constitutes a prerequisite for the effective implementation of all three types of rights (Abendroth 1976: 77). In a sense, as Alice Yotopoulos-Marangopoulos (1998: 30) points out,

---

[89]EC Commission White Paper, European social policy—A way forward for the Union, COM (1994) 333 final.

[90]The *European Social Charter*, signed under the auspices of the Council of Europe in 1961 and revised in 1996, which enshrined most of the traditional social and economic rights, is a milestone for Europe not only because it established a social state umbrella, but also because it has been widely cited by European Courts when interpreting interferences with social rights (CJEU Judgment of 2nd February 1988, Case 24/86, *Vincent Blaizot κατά University of Liège*, 1988 ECR 379. Furthermore, *Regulation 883/2004* of the European Parliament and of the Council of the 29th of April 2004 on the coordination of social security systems (OJ L 166 of 30th April 2004, p. 1), *Regulation 631/2004* of the European Parliament and of the Council of the 31st of March 2004 on the application of social security schemes to employed persons, to self-employed persons and to members of their families moving within the Community and on the alignment of rights and the simplification of procedures (OJ L 100 of 6th April 2004, p. 1), *Regulation 859/2003* of the 14th of May 2003 extending social security provisions to nationals of third countries who are not already covered by those provisions solely on the ground of their nationality (OJ L 124 of 20th May 2003, p. 1), *Directive 2004/38* of the European Parliament and the Council of 29th of April 2004 on the right of citizens of the Union and their family members to move and reside freely within the territory of the Member State (OJ L 158 of 30th April 2004, p. 77), *Directive 2002/73* of the European Parliament and Council of 23rd of September 2002 amending Council *Directive* 76/207 on the implementation of the principle of equal treatment for men and women as regards access to employment, vocational training and promotion, and working conditions (OJ L 269 of 5th October 2002, p. 15), as well as the Community *Charter of Fundamental Social Rights for Workers* adopted in 1989 by the European Commission (COM 89/471).

social rights render effective the equal enjoyment of human rights on a general social level, whereas positive action accomplishes and effectuates equality for certain social categories and groups. Therefore, one might convincingly argue, as Fredman (2011: 176–177) does, that equality constitutes a class of its own, a "fourth generation" right, which crosses all other constitutional rights. The truth of this premise should be tested against each of the concrete aspects of equality. Although no one would challenge the validity of the statement that equality involves elements of both civil and political rights, its social rights dimension is not equally evident. The basic restorative ratio of affirmative action, which obviously connotes elements of a social character, might not be sufficient to uphold the claim that the policy is tantamount to a social right since the classification criteria of a right cannot be the rationale, which eventually tends to satisfy a just social co-existence.

Overall though, it seems that affirmative action fits well with any contemporary notion of *social* equality. It features in the idea of liberal welfare state, as opposed to a social-democratic welfare state or a post-industrial conservative-corporatist welfare state, in the classical distinction used by the famous Danish sociologist Esping-Andersen (1990). It also features well in the definition set out by Ewing (1999: 105–106), distinguishing between substantive or material rights, and procedural/non material rights; the former serving two related goals of social justice and equality of opportunity, "including those designed to eliminate irrational discrimination in terms of access to or participation in civil society, whether in the public or the private sphere". Relevantly, in describing what he perceives as "principle of autonomy" in contemporary democracy, David Held suggests that persons should enjoy equal rights and, accordingly, equal obligations in the specification of the political framework which generates and limits the opportunities available to them, so long as they do not deploy this framework to negate the rights of others (Held 2006: 264). In fact, the social dimension of affirmative action seems to be well-accommodated not only in America, Asia or Oceania, where there is a long history of such measures, but also in Europe, as part of the common European culture, which, according to Häberle (1997: 33), takes on apart from the general concept of the rule of law, also tolerance and minority protection.

There are four aspects of affirmative action which resemble a social right. First, if it is taken for granted that there is an inherent scarcity in the benefits to be attributed to people, which Luhmann (1988: 180 *et seq.*) has contested on the basis of looking afresh at property, affirmative action policies essentially constitute a mode of redistribution of wealth through a benevolent award to disadvantaged individuals in a much more radical way than conventional social rights. Second, they do not constitute a mere defense against the state but require its positive intervention in order for the preferential treatment to be effectuated. Third, in principle, violation of the deemed preferential treatment owned to disadvantaged groups does not in principle raise a claim for damages; this claim can only be triggered once legislation is enacted to that effect, insofar as it stays within the boundaries set out by the Constitution. Fourth, like the implementation of any other social rights, affirmative action policies entail serious costs. The costs are born both by the state or the authority, which might lose effectiveness because of partial withdrawal of formal meritocracy; or more often by individuals, who might be treated unfavourably for admissions, appointments, participation or promotions due to their gender or race.

In a sense, one might argue that affirmative action goes beyond social rights. Public schools and hospitals, materialising the social rights of education and health respectively, are funded by proportionate income taxation and contribute indirectly to the redistribution of wealth, in the sense that these services will predominantly be used by lower income individuals who cannot otherwise have access to private medical treatment or education. Thus, social services are in principle addressed to *everyone* and the burden of implementing them is borne by *everyone* in proportion to their relevant wealth. On the contrary, beneficiaries of affirmative action are *limited* (i.e. the members of the designated groups) and those bearing the cost of the policies are also *limited* (i.e. members of the traditionally dominant groups finding themselves in a formally disadvantaged position in competitive struggles). This might be the reason why, in spite of its above quality, affirmative action has not been raised to the level of a constitutional social right, since this acknowledgement might raise issues of liability on the part of a range of individuals, such as those bearing the cost of the policy (a person disqualified because of his/her gender or race) or those unjustifiably left out of the preferential treatment as a matter of under-inclusiveness. One of course cannot underestimate the actual cost for the design and implementation of affirmative action measures. Mfume estimated this cost in the domain of the mandatory sub-contracting of public works to minority-owned enterprises in the US as 20 million dollars per annum (1996).

Although affirmative action has been initiated by the political powers, legislatures and executives, its institutional upgrade more often than not lies with the judge. This upgrade does not result in its elevation to a constitutional status but mostly reflects a new quality in the principle of equality, namely its move from a purely formal and libertarian model to a more substantive and social version. This judicial policy is not unknown to the judicial culture in Europe and America and is akin to countries and organisations whose constitutions and treaties go back in time or whose amendment is not easy or usual in practice. Especially in the US though, although this is the country where the most ancient constitution still in force exists, this institutional transformation of conventional liberties to social rights has not been a commonplace. The absence of wide political, financial and demographic consequences for the US after World War II did not raise the need for an immediate social rights re-orientation in the same way as in Europe which was the main venue of the war. After September 11th 2001, the equilibrium between civil rights, as collectively expressed through a claim for public security, and social rights was further consolidated in the US in favour of the former. That might reasonably explain the not particularly favourable affirmative action case law of the US Supreme Court, as established by the Michigan University admission policies cases in 2003. Albeit the ever-expanding debate on the implementation of affirmative action policies, as a result of the heavy heritage of slavery and segregation, the US still seems to be very far away from according affirmative action the status of social right with a constitutional status, outside the mere equality of opportunities. In Europe, although affirmative action does not result in a justiciable claim against the state, it seems that there is a tendency towards a constitutional upgrade that links the policy with the catalogue of protected human rights.

In any case, no one can deny the essential contribution of affirmative action in the osmosis between liberal and social states through the dominance of equality of opportunities. This is effectuated in essence, pursuant to the German dogma of fundamental rights, through a simultaneous implementation of equality in a substantive sense both as a subjective right and as an objective rule applying horizontally within the legal system (Hesse 1984). Affirmative action, which is the major institutional vehicle to achieve equality of opportunities through the award of temporary benefits to underprivileged groups, features prominently in the current discussion of equality on a global basis. The idea is, as expressed by Stasse (2004: 128) that equality of opportunities through positive discrimination will lead to an overall upgrade of the level of freedom of everyone, in the sense that it aspires to set a state of substantive freedom and autonomy of people through actual equality.

5.2.2 Not Individual, not Collective but "Group" Rights

The idea of group rights constitutes the opposite edge to group interests as formed in the pluralist theories in the US. If, as Bentley and his successors suggest, government is merely the outcome of rival group interests competing among each other, then it is reasonable and desirable that group rights are recognised. This is because in the same way those collective claims are legitimised in the decision-making process (which according to the pluralist theory ought to be determined so as to guarantee equal procedural footing) group rights also need to be established, mostly in a procedural sense:

> But now, even after the ruler… has been, so to speak, split up in time and split up in space in these ways, there still remain the technical methods for direct group control of him just as he stands at any given moment… As the group process continues, we find developed by it in the government all the different forms of the differentiated suffrage, of party organization both inside and outside the government, as the expression goes, of parliamentary technique, and of the referendum. All of these are direct functions of the group process, resting on the mass of the society, on facilities for contact and communication, and on the varieties and intensities of the interest oppositions (Bentley 1908: 309).

Affirmative action seems to place more emphasis on the group than the individual as human rights beneficiaries. As Calvè (2004: 30–34) shrewdly puts it, historically rights refer to persons (natural and later, legal) and ignore "groups". Insofar as positive measures are addressed to a certain social sub-category, the group seems to take precedence over the person. This conversion obviously causes a series of doctrinal and practical problems that need to be treated, such as the question of (self-) determination of one's identity or issues of social inclusion. In this context, the traditional tools of interpretation used by the judiciary as a means of delineating constitutional rights seem out of date, if not methodologically inadequate. The conventional liberal approach of rights vested in individuals is being conceded as rights attributed to groups seem to receive more constitutional accommodation. History, which is rather marginal when it comes to constitutional interpretation, becomes a necessary component when reading the requirement for positive measures or assessing their compatibility with the Constitution when the estimated goal of affirmative action is compensation for *past* discrimination. Therefore, a Constitution transcends time and at the same time history becomes a contemporary actor that brings a large portion of past factual situations into legal reasoning.

Of course, the rise of group rights has upset the absolute truth of rights merely being conferred to individuals in two ways. On the one hand, certain social subgroups have emerged, which were acknowledged by the political powers and, eventually, by law as requiring special care. On the other hand, in addition to the human-oriented liberal approach to rights, the general public also became a subject to be protected by law. The latter phenomenon was originally formed in economic terms by demanding that vital services should be granted to the public at large in good quality and under tolerable conditions. After the expansion of terrorism and asymmetrical threats, the claim was transformed towards the protection of the society as a whole through a right to security.

Still, national constitutions providing for positive measures to compensate for past discrimination generally abstain from explicitly referring to "group rights"; exceptions to this rule are to be found in the 1978 Spanish Constitution establishing the responsibility of the public authorities to promote conditions ensuring that freedom and equality of "individuals and groups" to which they belong are real and effective (Article 9 para. 2) and in the Canadian Charter of Rights and Freedoms, entrenched in the Constitution Act 1982, allowing for programmes or activities aiming at the amelioration of conditions of disadvantaged "individuals or groups" (Article 15 para. 2). The same reluctance to uphold group rights is evidenced by the relevant case-law of national courts in cases of alleged violations of human rights. In the US, most judgments refer to the landmark 1948 Supreme Court case *Shelley v. Kraemer*. The case concerned a white couple who owned a residence in a Missouri neighbourhood governed by a private agreement preventing blacks from owning property. In deciding that State courts could not constitutionally prevent by injunction the sale of real property to blacks when that property is covered by a racially restrictive covenant the Court held that the rights created by the first section of the Fourteenth Amendment are "by its terms guaranteed to the individual" and "are personal rights".[91] By the same token, the French Conseil Constitutionnel discarded a Corsican local government statute referring to "Corsican people composed of French" (*peuple corse, composante du peuple français*) as violating the

[91]334 US 1, 22 (1948). Also se prior case law *McCabe v. Atchison, Topeka Santa Fe R. Co.*, 235 US 151, 161–162 (1914); *Missouri ex rel. Gaines v. Canada*, 305 US 337 (1938); *Oyama v. California*, 332 US 633 (1948).

Declaration of Rights of Man and Citizen and the Preambles of both 1946 and 1958 Constitutions, which categorically state that the French people is "a category not subject to any subdivision" (*catégorie insusceptible de toute subdivision*).[92] By way of contrast, international Courts are readier, albeit not consistently, to uphold the existence of group rights; evidently, this is basically due to the lack of any nationally oriented risks incurred by international courts when interpreting international covenants and regulations. In the domain of EU case law, it is mostly the opinions of the Advocate Generals which seem to be keen on proceeding to a group-oriented interpretation of the rights of European citizens. Advocate General Tesauro in his 1995 opinion in *Kalanke* stated that "in taking the group as such into consideration, positive action moreover marks a transition from the individual vision to the collective vision of equality".[93] In contrast, Advocate General Maduro in his 2004 opinion in *Briheche* was rather skeptical in categorically upholding group rights. In his mind, in order for a positive measure to be compatible with the principle of equality there must be no automatic preference for women and the measure must be proportionate in balancing the benefits of positive action in promoting equality for women against the costs imposed on other individuals. "These requirements appear necessary to prevent equality between individuals from being overridden by concerns of substantive equality between groups".[94]

In favour of the ontological upholding of group rights, Ingram (2000: 242–257) argues that political rights, the right to assembly and cultural rights are "group specific rights". Even classical liberal rights, such as the right to one's personality, are also connected to social groups to the extent that their exercise presupposes their participation in a political community which recognises and protects them, through, for instance, police or other regulations determining social interaction. The truth is that, in practice, law very often makes group differentiations, against which people at large are rather accustomed to. Examples of *generic* grouping are persons with disabilities and large families. Examples of *field* grouping include: senior citizens/adults/students/children in public transportation/entrance to museums/admission to events; low income/high income and individuals/companies in taxation; local residents/commuters in city parking; nationals/foreigners in university admissions. No one in a rational society would object to allowing certain privileges to some of the above (vulnerable) groups against others. As Braibant (1999: 448) put it, "there are inequalities which are permissible, even desirable". However, the fact that civil or political rights are exercised in a social context is not sufficient to properly characterise them as group rights; otherwise all rights would essentially be group

---

[92]Conseil Constitutionnel décision n° 91–290 du 9 mai 1991, *Statut de la Corse,* Rec. 50; RJC, p. I-438, Journal officiel du 14 mai 1991, p. 6350.

[93]Opinion of Advocate General Tesauro of 6 April 1995 in Case C-450/93, *Eckhard Kalanke v. Freie Hansestadt Bremen,* Rec. 1995, p. I-3051, para. 8.

[94]Opinion of Advocate General Poiares Maduro of 29 June 2004 in Case C-319/03, *Serge Briheche v. Ministre de l'Intérieur, Ministre de l'Éducation nationale and Ministre de la Justice,* Rec. 2004, p. I-8807, para. 41.

rights. Even when human rights are exercised collectively, such as the right to assembly or religious worship, the right remains with the person.

In the above context, affirmative action constitutes a crack in the coherence of individual rights doctrine. By applying a strategy of "depersonalisation", it discerns social categories which are granted preferential treatment. Therefore, a person falling into the affirmative action beneficiaries is granted a right not as an individual but as member of a respective category prescribed by law. Thus, the policy inexorably connotes an institutional acknowledgment of the "group", which consequently becomes a subject in law per se. There are three characteristics of affirmative action that are akin to group rights. First, designation of a vulnerable group does not presuppose the identification of the actual victims or the actual number of victims of past discrimination but follows common sense or statistical evidence. Second, individual beneficiaries do not have to prove past discrimination but mere membership of the group that has collectively suffered discrimination in the past, which is essentially tantamount in Feher's (1998: 175) words to "identity politics". Preference stems as an automatic consequence of the inclusion in a designated group; in a sense there is a *de lege* irrefutable presumption that mere membership in a group suggests that a person has suffered from past discrimination. Posner (1974) uses the presumption language on this occasion by stating that racial characteristics are used to establish a presumption that this person also carries other social characteristics. Third, the subjection of an individual to the designated group is a mandatory requirement in order to take on the benefit of the affirmative action plan.

A series of conceptual problems are raised as a result of the above shift in the human rights dogma towards group rights. Firstly, the mere recognition of "groups" suggests a fragmented society. On a deontological level the statement is erroneous, if not dangerous. This is equally true when the "group" is composed of a minority, as well as when it constitutes a large portion of society, in fact the majority, such as in the case of women. It is semantically interesting that the feminist movement in the 19th century was beset by claims of the "rights of woman", whereas in the 20th century it evolved to the "rights of women", which exactly indicates the promotion of the grouping idea (Smith 2001: 188).

Secondly, it is questionable whether groups can maintain moral entitlements, since this would misunderstand the relationship between damage and treatment (Cohen 2003: 185). A man who has individually suffered discrimination in the past, might not be entitled to institutional group compensation; on the contrary a woman who has not suffered any discrimination in the past is entitled to institutional compensation just because she is woman, i.e. in a class of people who has in their vast majority suffered in the past. In fact there is not, to my knowledge, a constitutional clause, outside classical civil liability, which provides for compensation to *individuals* who have been discriminated in the past. This false mechanics constitutes an aberration from individualism as a focal point of the rights dogma. Judicial dicta suggest skepticism on this point. Justice O'Connor in her dissent in *Metro Broadcasting Inc. v. Federal Communications Commission,* stated that social scientists might debate how peoples' thoughts and behaviour reflected their background, but the Constitution provided that the Government must not allocate benefits and burdens among individuals based on the assumption that race or ethnicity determines how they act or think. In the context of the case, i.e. upholding of mandatory sub-contracting quotas in public works, she found that the Court departed from those fundamental principles and from the traditional requirement that racial classifications were permissible only if narrowly tailored to achieve a compelling interest: "This departure marks a renewed toleration of racial classifications and a repudiation of our recent affirmation that the Constitution's equal protection guarantees extend equally to all citizens".[95] By the same token, Circuit Judge Jerry Smith wrote in *Hopwood v. State of Texas*: "Diversity fosters, rather than minimizes, the use of race. It treats minorities as a group, rather than as individuals. It may further remedial purposes but, just as likely, may promote improper racial stereotypes, thus fueling racial hostility".[96] The natural reservation against accepting the idea of group rights as a counter-value to liberalism is opposed by Sterba (2009: 31–35), one of the greatest proponents of affirmative action, by arguing that even if groups cannot enjoy entitlements or rights, they can still be the recipients of preferences which are introduced for a legitimate cause, such as diversity and compensation, through democratic procedures.

Thirdly, and most importantly, group rights essentially operate so as to establish social hierarchy. By moving from the individual to the group, the risk of arbitrary institutional awards becomes all more dangerous since it could conceivably result either in racial/religious/national balancing or in the formation of class layers. John Caldwell Calhoun, 7th Vice-President of the US, was arguably the first to suggest positive measures in the first half of the 19th century in favour of slaves' proprietors, provided that there was a powerful majority for this scheme (Maier and Klausen 2001: 5–6). By way of contrast, Hochscild (1998: 348–349) and Hollinger (1996: 103), in separate writings, seem to agree that racial affirmative action in the 1970s greatly contributed to the constitution of a large Afro-American middle class. The fear for social balancing is also reflected in judicial dicta in US Supreme Court judgments. According to Justice O'Connor in 1989 *Richmond v. Croson,* there is an inherent danger in accepting the claim that past societal discrimination alone can serve as the basis for rigid racial preferences. This would allegedly open the door to competing claims for "remedial relief" for every disadvantaged group so that "the dream of a Nation of equal citizens in a society where race is irrelevant to personal opportunity and achievement would be lost in a mosaic of shifting preferences based on inherently unmeasurable claims of past wrongs". In turn, she considers that courts would be asked to evaluate the extent of the prejudice and consequent harm suffered by various minority groups in a way that those whose societal injury is thought to exceed some arbitrary level of tolerability then would be entitled to preferential classifications.[97] In such a case, not only constitutional liberalism but also free market economics, based on the value of individual (mostly economic)

[95]497 US 547, 602 (1990).

[96]84 F.3d 720 (5th Cir 1996).

[97]488 US 469, 505–506 (1989).

rights could be seriously jeopardised (Haquet 2001; Prechal 2004). According to Ingram (2000: 24 *et seq.*), the presumption that the liberal version of equal rights derives from the faith in mankind; this is why civil liberties cannot be subject to the interest of groups in a way that these groups eventually exercise coercion upon their members. According to Maier and Klausen (2001: 10–11), however, there is nothing contradictory between liberalism and affirmative action, the latter merely constituting an answer to the failure of the former to achieve equality through neutral constitutional provisions. Given that equality clauses operate within the generally commodious context of liberal democracy which has at times operated so as to overcome entrenched inequalities in various social fields, such as education, medical treatment and opportunities in general, the claim of parity does not constitute a wide change in the existing structures of liberalism. In a similar vein, the most convincing theory of group rights has been provided by Kymlicka (1995: 34–74). He suggests "group-differentiated rights" that recognise and accommodate group differences with a view to cultural and religious diversity (multiculturalism). Such rights include religious exemptions or language accommodations for linguistic minorities aiming at increasing equality by allowing minorities' full participation in society. Such state regulation is fully compatible with the classical notion of liberalism on the ground that it advances autonomy and equality through the recognition of cultural membership as a distinctive human feature, thus allowing an adequate range of options to redress unchosen and inherent social inequalities and cultivating individual self-respect which constitutes a key element in self-determination.

On the opposite side, Klor de Alva (1998: 151), a specialist on American history and anthropology, argues that if affirmative action is truly against the mainstays of liberalism, as a matter of historical and theological accuracy then it should be tantamount to a Christian heresy. Based on the premise that liberalism was essentially conceived and legitimised by Christianity, the scholar considers that the use of random human characteristics comes at odds to the Christian mainstays. This is caused due to the expansion of protestant ideas in the 20th century amongst the Afro-American community and its/their inclusion as the conceptual backing in the civil rights movement; indeed, according to Klor de Alva, a liberating heresy inserted into contemporary currents may restore the adverse effects caused by a prior oppressing heresy. In the light of the above sharp division of the doctrine on the harmonic coexistence of liberalism and group rights, some writers have tried to provide alternative foundations to ease the conceptual problems stemming thereof. South African professor Gouws' (2010) reconceptualisation of race as a seriality seems the most intriguing in this respect. Building on Jean Paul Sartre's notion of seriality, the scholar discerns series as a social collective, whose members are passively and sporadically gathered by the aims beset by their activities, from groups whose members categorically acknowledge themselves and others as ultimately pursuing the same goal. Affirmative action is conceptually based on the former category, which by its nature does not result in identity politics.

Liberalism, as Sandel notices (1998: 1), referring to the Kantian doctrine reflecting "deontological liberalism", essentially constitutes a theory of justice, according to which justice prevails over moral and political ideals through the formal establishment of rights. In this sense, liberalism is not necessarily confined to an idea of individual right, but mostly reflects disassociation of the prevailing interests from any particular perception of good. Accordingly, affirmative action is not as such against liberalism, since by definition it reflects a common good over the expected and established rights of the dominant class in society. Thus, it seems that the dilemma "individual or group rights" in the context of affirmative action is misleading. Race, gender, religion etc. are not mere criteria of inclusion of an individual to a group. They are mostly criteria of self-determination within society and against the state, thus essentially standards of differentiation. Normatively, these criteria should be used cautiously; as Fredman suggests (2011: 10–11), they should not be used descriptively only for reasons of institutional convenience to award preference to individuals and not as a genuine guarantee of the equality of opportunities.

References

Abendroth, W. (1976). Zum Begriff des demokratischen und sozialen Rechtsstaates im Grundgesetz der Bundesrepublik Deutschland. In Kempen O. (Hrsg.), *Sozialstaatsprinzip und Wirtschaftsordnung* (pp. 70-96). Frankfurt-New York: Campus.

Bentley, A.F. (1908). *The process of Government. A study of social pressures.* Chicago: The University of Chicago Press.

Braibant, G. (1999). Réflexions sur le principe d'égalité. *European Review of Public Law,* 11(2), 443-454.

Byrne, J.R. (1998). Toward a colorblind Constitution: Justice O'Connor's narrowing of affirmative action. *Saint Louis University Law Journal,* 42, 619-675.

Calvè, G. (2004). Les politiques françaises de discrimination positive: Trois spécificités. *Pouvoirs – Revue Française d'Études Constitutionnelles et Politiques (Discrimination Positive),* 111, 29-40.

Cohen, C. (2003). Why race preference is wrong and bad. In C. Cohen and J.P. Sterba. Affirmative action and racial preference. A debate (1-188). Oxford-New York: Oxford University Press.

Däubler, W. (1995). Les droits sociaux dans l'Union européenne: de la symbolique à la pratique politique? In M. Telò (Ed.), *Démocratie et construction européenne* (pp. 313-326). Bruxelles: Editions de l'Université de Bruxelles.

Devins N. (2013), Group formation and precedent. In J.C. Peters, (Ed.), *Precedent in the United States Supreme Court* (pp. 101-119). Heidelberg-New York, Dordrecht, London: Springer, Series: Ius Gentium: Comparative Perspectives on Law and Justice, Vol. 33.

Dworkin, R. (1992). Unenumerated rights: Whether and how *Roe* should be overruled. *University of Chicago Law Review,* 59, 381-432. Reprinted: What the Constitution says. In R. Dworkin (1997), *Freedom's Law. The moral reading of the American Constitution* (pp. 72-116). Oxford: Oxford University Press.

Esping-Andersen, G. (1990). *The Three Worlds of Welfare Capitalism.* Princeton: Princeton University Press.

Ewing, K.D. (1999). Social rights and constitutional law. *Public Law,* 104-123.

Feher, M. (1998). Empowerment Hazards: Affirmative action, recovery psychology and identity politics. In R. Post and M. Rogin (Eds.). *Race and representation: Affirmative action* (175-184). New York: Zone Books.

Fredman, S. (2011). *Discrimination law.* 2nd ed., Oxford-New York: Clarendon Law Series Oxford University Press.
Fredman, S. (2012). Breaking the Mold: Equality as a Proactive Duty. American Journal of Comparative Law, 60(1), 265-289.
Gerapetritis, G. (1997). Proportionality in Administrative Law: Judicial Review in France, Greece, England and in the European Community. Athens: Ant. Sakkoulas ed.
Gouws, A. (2010). Race as seriality: a response to David Benatar and Zimitri Erasmus. *South African Journal of Higher Education*, 24(2), 313-317.
Gunther, G. (1972). Foreword: In Search of evolving doctrine on a changing court: A model for a newer Equal Protection. *Harvard Law Review,* 86, 1-48.
Häberle, P. (1997). *Europäische Rechtskultur.* Frankfurt: Suhrkamp.
Haquet, A. (2001). L'action positive, instrument de l'égalité des chances entre hommes et femmes. *Revue trimestrielle de droit Européen,* 37(2), 305-333.
Hatzopoulos, V. (2005). A (more) social Europe: A political crossroad or a legal one-way? Dialogues between Luxembourg and Lisbon. *Common Market Law Review,* 42, 1599-1635.
Held, D. (2006). *Models of Democracy.* 3rd ed. Stanford: Stanford University Press.
Hesse, K. (1984). *Grundzüge des Verfassungsrechts der Bundesrepublik Deutschland.* Karlsruhe: Muller.
Hochschild, J. (1998). Affirmative action as culture war. In R. Post and M. Rogin (Eds.), *Race and representation: Affirmative action* (pp. 347-352). New York: Zone Books.
Hollinger, D.A. (1996). Group preferences, cultural diversity and social democracy: notes towards a theory of affirmative action. *Representations*, (55), 31-40. Re-pubilshed in R. Post, and M. Rogin (Eds.), (1998). *Race and representation: Affirmative action* (97-111). New York: Zone Books.
Ingram, D. (2000), *Group rights: reconciling equality and difference.* Lawrence: University Press of Kansas.
Jellinek, G. (1892). *System der subjektiven öffentlichen Rechte.* Nachdruck Darmstadt: Wissenschaftliche Buchgesellschaft, 1963.
Klor de Alva, J.J. (1998). Is affirmative action a Christian heresy?. In R. Post and M. Rogin (Eds.). *Race and representation: Affirmative action* (135-154). New York: Zone Books.
Kymlicka, W. (1995). *Multicultural citizenship. A liberal theory of minority rights.* Oxford: Oxford Clarendon Press.
Luhmann, N. (1988). *Die Wirtschaft der Gesellschaft.* Frankfurt: Suhrkamp
Maier, C.S., and Klausen, J. (2001). Introduction. In C.S. Maier and J. Klausen (Eds.), *Has liberalism failed women? Assuring equal representation in Europe and the United States* (3-17). New York: Palgrave.
Mfume, K. (1996). Why America needs set-aside programs. In G.E. Curry, *The Affirmative Action debate* (pp. 121-129). Cambridge MA: Perseus.
Mill, J.S. (1869). *The subjection of women.* New York: Appleton.
Posner, R.A. (1974). The DeFunis Case and the Constitutionality of Preferential Treatment of Racial Minorities. *The Supreme Court Review,* The University of Chicago Press, 12, 1-32.
Prechal, S. (2004). Equality of treatment, non-discrimination and social policy: Achievements in three themes. *Common Market Law Review,* 41, 533-551.]
Rubenfeld, J. (1997). Affirmative action. *Yale Law Journal,* 107, 427-472.
Rush, M.E. (1995), From Shaw v. Reno to Miller v. Johnson: Minority Representation and State Compliance with the Voting Rights Act. *Publius: The Journal of Federalism,* 25(3), 155-172.
Sadurski, W. (1986). Gerhardy v. Brown v. the concept of discrimination: Reflections on the landmark case that wasn't. *Sydney Law Review,* 11, 5-43.
Sandel, M.J. (1998). *Liberalism and the limits of Justice.* 2nd ed. Cambridge: Cambridge University Press.
Schuck, P.H. (2002). Affirmative action: past, present and future. *Yale Law and Policy Review,* 20, 1-97.
Shapiro. M. (1999). Equality and diversity. *European Review of Public Law,* 11(2), 371-416.

Smith, R.M. (2001). The distinctive barriers to gender equality. In J. Klausen and C.S. Maier (Eds.), *Has liberalism failed women? Assuring equal representation in Europe and the United States* (pp. 185-199). New York: Palgrave.
Stasse, F. (2004). Pour les discriminations positives. *Pouvoirs – Revue Française d'Études Constitutionnelles et Politiques (Discrimination Positive),* 111, 119-132.
Sterba, J.P. (2009). *Affirmative Action for the Future.* New York: Cornell University Press.
Winkler, A. (2006). Fatal in Theory and Strict in Fact: An Empirical Analysis of Strict Scrutiny in the Federal Courts. *Vanderbilt Law Review,* 59(3), 793-871.
Yotopoulos-Marangopoulos, A. (1998). *Affirmative Action. Towards effective gender equality.* Athens-Brussels: Ant. N. Sakkoulas Publishers - Établissements Émile Bruylant.

Chapter 6
Conclusion

Affirmative action constitutes one of the most heated discussions in the field of human rights today: necessary treatment for some, anathema for others. The economic crisis, which has increased the gap of existing inequalities, casts even more light upon this debate and has enriched it with more relevant considerations. A wide range of individuals are involved in this debate: decision-makers, lawyers, academics and judges. The political and judicial dicta cited here demonstrate the intensity of the arguments both in favour and against the policy. In the context of affirmative action judicial review, Justice Wilson of the Australian High Court, wrote in the decision *Koowarta v. Bjelke-Petersen* that there is a touch of irony in the fact that the state seeks to support the validity of an Act to give effect to the principle of equality by relying on a power to enact discriminatory laws, whether for good or ill, for the people of any race: "[It] is basic to an understanding of the scope of the power to recognise that even when it is used for wholly benevolent and laudable purposes it remains a power to discriminate with respect to such people".[1] More aggressively U.S. Senator Orrin Hatch declared that "affirmative action is an assault upon America conceived in lies and fostered with irresponsibility so extreme as to verge in the malign" and that "if the government officials and politicians who presided over its genesis had injected heroin into the bloodstream of the nation, they could not have done more potential damage to our children and our children's children" (quoted in Kirp et al. 1986: 159). On the other hand, affirmative action proponents consider the policy as a condition for the prosperity of the community; in James Sterba's words enhancement of affirmative action does not require a move from "is" to "ought" but merely derives one's "oughts" from other "oughts" (Sterba 2003: 307). Two sets of conclusion will be presented hereinafter, based on conceptual and pragmatic levels.

On a *conceptual* level, three premises are drawn. First, affirmative action faces significant problems when set alongside the traditional values of the constitutional state; second, the remedial rationale of affirmative action poses both doctrinal and evidentiary difficulties, therefore it seems to concede in favour of the rationale for diversity; and, third, affirmative action seeks vital space within orthodox human rights theory both as a social or post-social right and as a group right.

[1](1982) HCA 27; (1982) 153 CLR 168.

G. Gerapetritis, *Affirmative Action Policies and Judicial Review Worldwide*,
Ius Gentium: Comparative Perspectives on Law and Justice 47,
DOI 10.1007/978-3-319-22395-7_6

In relation to the first premise, affirmative action seemingly aspires to find a way through equality of opportunities towards substantive equality. Although one might conceivably argue that affirmative action is merely a feature of proportional equality, suggesting that equals should be treated alike, by embracing criteria of treatment (such as race and gender) as legitimate markers of similarity or difference because of past discriminatory use, the move from the individual restoration of damage to collective (group) compensation as a result of affirmative action policies seems to depart from the rudiments of equality. If this is so, then by embracing criteria that would otherwise be unacceptable, affirmative action ought to be treated as an *exception* from equality like any other deviation from it. Consequently, affirmative action policies must be interpreted restrictively and the correlating judicial review must be intense. This is indeed the case, depending on the criterion of differentiation, the level of formal recognition of the policy and the field of application, in most of the relevant legal systems. Intense judicial review occurs through strict scrutiny mechanisms and the principle of proportionality, which requires that the measure is suitable to serve the aim pursued and narrowly tailored and that it is necessary to achieve such aims, i.e. that there are no other less restrictive alternatives and that the impugned measure is of a temporary nature. Restrictive interpretation of affirmative action policies is also compatible with other central notions of the constitutional state, such as justice, democracy and meritocracy. Even in the forms akin to positive measures, i.e. distributive justice, proportional democracy and structural meritocracy, affirmative action produces significant adverse effects which also call for a strict assessment on the basis of a cost-benefit analysis. The danger of setting a form of proportional democracy, which would formally reflect the ratio of people but will not represent the will of the electorate, and a "social geometry" that goes contrary to the idea of non-contextual merit and justifies heavy paternalism, calls for a very cautious tailoring of affirmative action policies. This is particularly true when rigid quotas or quotas by effect are set in place, which by definition intrude more acutely upon protected rights, and less so when positive measures merely award indirect preference to the designated groups. The difficult accommodation of affirmative action within the fundamental values of human interaction is probably the reason why this policy has not succeeded in enhancing a political identity: although in theory they are more comfortably affiliated to a social democratic/centre left agenda, the fact that it essentially presupposes and perpetuates the existing political status quo, without any subversive effects, keeps the policy in political shadows.

In relation to the second premise, a variety of public interests have historically been put forth in order to substantiate the claim for launching positive measures: the remedial purpose entailing compensation for past discrimination, the cultural purpose promoting diversity, the societal purpose aiming at social homogeneity, the pedagogical purpose envisaging role model functions and the economy purpose targeting balanced growth. Regulation and case-law from across the world seem to emphasise the first two of the above purposes: compensation for past discrimination and diversity. The former purpose has been the first to be elaborately developed and extensively used. It suggests that members of groups that have suffered compensation in the past need to be temporarily assisted in order to regain their positioning in the social arena and acquire true equal opportunity against other social competitors until a fair starting point balance has been established. There are two sets of counter-arguments against the compensatory purpose of affirmative action: the doctrinal and the utilitarian. The *doctrinal* argument is that the policy is not neutral but essentially aspires to reset the social balance by imposing burdens not upon those who have actually benefited from the preferential treatment of the dominant groups in the past but upon their descendants, who have in principle nothing to do with the historical harm caused to the underrepresented groups and might well be in a practically inferior position. This historical reflection of group compensation imposed on individuals, from the point of view of political economy, constitutes a form of privatisation of the state's social policy, which unlike traditional social policies, is not burdened by society collectively, but rather by particular individuals based on specific characteristics they carry. The *utilitarian* argument suggests that affirmative action policies cannot be practically drafted in a way which effectively serves its remedial purpose, and therefore is bound to fail in relation to its aspired results. Even if one overcomes the hindrance of the untimely burdens upon social actors, it is practically impossible to come up with a system of preferential treatment that will serve those in true need amongst the vulnerable social groups. Logic and evidence suggest that those who are in a better position to take advantage of the preferential treatment introduced by affirmative action are in fact those who already have the means effectively to compete with the dominant race or gender, and are therefore by definition, not in genuine need of being assisted.

The diversity purpose of affirmative action, although appearing as collateral to the original compensatory purpose, tends more and more to overshadow the latter and is becoming the dominant purpose in some countries, certainly in the US. It is rooted in the theory of multiculturalism, which enhances and encourages tolerance vis-à-vis difference. There are some significant dogmatic and practical differences between the goals of diversity and compensation. First, unlike the temporary nature of the compensatory affirmative action, diversity is a moral quality that, if accepted, transcends time; therefore positive measures based on diversity must in principle operate for an unlimited period of time. Second, the areas of implementation may significantly differ depending on the purpose sought. If the compensatory purpose is preferred, positive measures might be enacted in those areas where past discrimination has placed members of the designated groups in an inferior position, for example public procurement contracts or licensing. If the diversity purpose is preferred, such measures ought to be enacted in domains with intense social interaction, where diversity may enrich processes, such as universities, or deliberative organs, such as parliaments or juries. However, the theory of diversity seems to approach the issue of participation with a particular dogmatism. This is because the policy seems to accept that any member of a designated group carries the same idiosyncrasies as any other member of the same group which they shall convey to their respective environment. This premise is not only dangerous but patently false. Evidence demonstrates that affirmative action beneficiaries in critical positions have not always operated in order to assist members of their respective groups or the groups as such, or at least not wholeheartedly. This is probably due to the unavoidable over-inclusiveness of any affirmative action plan but surely curtails the practical effect of the policies: affirmative action policies neither guarantee that there will be better outcomes for the preferential group altogether, nor cultural enrichment for the group they participate in.

In relation to the third premise, due to its peculiarities, affirmative action employs an amalgam of characteristics that are akin to social and group rights. Indeed, affirmative action trespasses the boundaries of traditional civil liberties, which place the individual at the heart of constitutional protection and merges liberal and social state. Affirmative action might, also, end up in identity politics, which is vulnerable to a series of objections relating to the indirect fragmentation of society, the improper award of moral entitlements and the establishment of social hierarchy as a potential result of arbitrary institutional awards, i.e. a social geometry. This geometry would be established on a perception of each group as opposed to any other groups; in Bentley's (1908: 217) classical saying "no group has meaning except in its relations to other groups". Furthermore, the risk of ethnic/racial/gender balancing or, even worse, favouritism because of the "depersonalisation" due to affirmative action needs to be treated both in terms of policy-drafting as well as in judicial review in the course of the identification and assessment of the goal pursued and the application of the proportionality test. From a dogmatic point of view, it is expedient and safe to adhere to the existing typology of fundamental rights, thus considering affirmative action as a mechanism to achieve equality of opportunities and not a right per se, which would presumably produce doctrinal and practical hindrances.

On a *pragmatic* level, three premises are drawn: First, the task of designing a proper affirmative action plan is exceptionally difficult, if not impossible; second, significant counter-effects are, or might be, caused following the enactment of affirmative action policies; and, third, affirmative action has not, at least not always, produced the desirable results in relation to the increase of participation of members of designated groups.

In relation to the first premise, the main characteristics that any such plan must at least contain is the designated group of beneficiaries, the duration of the measure, the nature of the preference and the procedure of its award. Beyond any doubt, the most challenging experiment is that of delineating the beneficiaries. Indeed, this is the province where most policy failures have occurred. When the goal pursued is compensation for past discrimination, the task is to determine who (individuals or groups) has actually been the victim. In such a case, any policy cannot be devoid of a degree of over and under-inclusiveness. Over-inclusiveness arises when members who suffered no prior direct or indirect discrimination and could not have suffered on grounds of their social status (or otherwise) exploit the mechanism of preferential treatment. Under-inclusiveness arises when the particular measure arbitrarily excludes individuals or groups/sub-groups that have indeed suffered discrimination in the past. Accordingly, a plan might be either very narrow, thus disproportionately favouring some of those who have suffered discrimination in the past, or very broad so as to eventually embrace the majority of the population in one way or another. In either case, the plan is bound to fail due to flawed architecture, or at least it will not fully materialise its aspired purposes, and an improper social balancing might emerge. When the goal pursued is diversity, there is no need to identify who suffered discrimination in the past; delineation of the beneficiaries, thus becoming almost exclusively a policy choice regarding the applied criteria. In this case, since there is no descriptive benchmark like in the remedial purpose, the question is why certain categories are altogether excluded. If one tries to press the argument to the edge, an algorithm to embrace members reflecting all human characteristics to participate in a collective body is not inconceivable.

In relation to the second premise, one cannot underestimate the direct or collateral damage that might be caused by affirmative action policies. For non-beneficiaries, the damage is evident in the sense that they are treated unfavourably in admissions, elections, appointments or promotions. Indirect results will inevitably arise for the harmed individuals since there is always a social sequence in the benefits gained. Thus, if not admitted by a University, an individual will not be able to gain vocational qualifications to exercise a profession, where applicable; if not appointed in a job, there is no experience gained that is necessary for professional upgrading in general. Additionally, there might be overall disappointment that prevents them from fully developing their skills. For beneficiaries, indirect side-effects can comprise the stigma of failing to succeed on one's own merits that might be attributed to them. The psychological argument, crudely put, is that the implementation of the policy causes serious adverse secondary effects against the beneficiaries. The most evident effect of this kind is the stigma caused as a result of the use of an instrumental tool that is not based on pure merit but mostly on non-relevant considerations. In this way a perception of collective group weakness is maintained and potentially reinforced, which obviously produces the opposite results from those anticipated. The extent of this form of stereotyping may vary depending on the nature of the measure in question. The imposition of rigid quotas might be very harmful, not only because they constitute a direct, if not oppressive, intervention in social competition, but also because they are not adjusted to the peculiarities of each case and the causes of discrimination. For society as a whole, there is the risk of social anxiety due to varying standards for granting benefits and of less productivity because of the discard of merited individuals and the non-achievement of full potential by both beneficiaries and non-beneficiaries.

In relation to the third premise, the effectiveness of affirmative action policies cannot be fully assessed. The results stemming from the above surveys are of course mixed. The clear result is that countries which extensively apply quotas, like India, Malaysia and Nigeria, do not always manage to achieve either better representation for underrepresented groups or adequate levels of social inclusion. It seems that a better record in substantive gender and race equality is managed by countries which do not use affirmative action at large, nor do they provide in their respective constitutions for such measures, but enjoy a very high level of social welfare overall, like the Scandinavian countries. This result makes absolute sense. Affirmative action is merely a tool to achieve better results in formal representation; it does not guarantee substantive improvement of the position of disadvantaged groups, nor does it operate effectively unless the broader context is favourable for the implementation of social policies. From this viewpoint, rigid quotas might be proved to be causally ineffective, in that they aspire to moderate the statistical imbalance, whereas they do not operate on the actual causes that have provoked the pathology. It is not therefore a systemic surgery but merely a conservative treatment providing temporary comfort, unlike measures of indirect effect that might be less drastic but provide substantive long-term results by structurally improving and upgrading vulnerable groups and liberating the potential of their members. This is why, from a political point of view, the policy has not been as fully endorsed as one might reasonably expect by social democratic/centre left parties around the world; and this is also probably why in most legal systems there is a general distrust of quotas or quotas by effect, including both the US where the Supreme Court has set a red line in relation to measures awarding direct preference and the Court of Justice of the European Union.

Generally speaking, extremity dominates when it comes to the assessment of affirmative action. Those in favour tend to attribute to the policy gigantic, almost mystical, capacities in treating social malfunctions. Those against the policy, employ a language of overall aphorism and fail to see any merit in it. The truth of the matter is that affirmative action cannot stand alone to combat discrimination which has survived for centuries and is incumbent in the genes of a great number of people, but might produce positive results when applied in the context of a strong social welfare state. Experimentation is needed to find the fine tuning that will allow the policy to achieve its highly ambitious goals. An over-reliance on the policy might produce the exact opposite results. Asklipios, the ancient Greek God of medicine, had six daughters: Aglaia [radiance of health], Akeso, [healing], Hygeia [good health], Iaso [remedy], Meditrina [restoration] and Panacea. This last deity was thought to be all-healing; and although the most ambitious, she has been the least appreciated because she never fulfils her potential.

References

Bentley, A.F. (1908). *The process of Government. A study of social pressures.* Chicago: The University of Chicago Press.

Kirp, D., Yudof, M, and Franks, M.S. (1986). *Gender Justice.* Chicago: The University of Chicago Press.

Sterba, J.P. (2003). Reply to Carl Cohen. In C. Cohen and J.P. Sterba (Eds.). *Affirmative action and racial preference. A debate* (pp. 305–349). Oxford-New York: Oxford University Press.

Index (Country)

G. Gerapetritis, *Affirmative Action Policies and Judicial Review Worldwide*,
Ius Gentium: Comparative Perspectives on Law and Justice 47,
DOI 10.1007/978-3-319-22395-7

Index (Subject)

G. Gerapetritis, *Affirmative Action Policies and Judicial Review Worldwide*,
Ius Gentium: Comparative Perspectives on Law and Justice 47,
DOI 10.1007/978-3-319-22395-7

MIX
Papier aus verantwortungsvollen Quellen
Paper from responsible sources
FSC® C105338

If you have any concerns about our products,
you can contact us on
ProductSafety@springernature.com

In case Publisher is established outside the EU,
the EU authorized representative is:
Springer Nature Customer Service Center GmbH
Europaplatz 3, 69115 Heidelberg, Germany

Printed by Libri Plureos GmbH
in Hamburg, Germany